LAND SYSTEM AND RURAL SOCIETY IN EARLY INDIA

READINGS IN
EARLY INDIAN HISTORY

General Editor
B.D. Chattopadhyaya

Land System and Rural Society in Early India

Edited by

BHAIRABI PRASAD SAHU

MANOHAR
2026

First published 1997
Reprinted 2026

ISBN 978-81-7304-295-9

Published by
Ajay Kumar Jain *for*
Manohar Publishers & Distributors
4753/23 Ansari Road, Daryaganj
New Delhi 110 002

Printed and bound in India

Contents

GENERAL EDITOR'S PREFACE ix

ACKNOWLEDGEMENTS xi

ABBREVIATIONS xiii

Introduction
Bhairabi Prasad Sahu 1

Section I
RURAL SETTLEMENTS

1. Land-System as Reflected in Kauṭilya's *Arthaśāstra*
Sibesh Bhattacharya 61
2. Village Life and Settlements in the Light of Vākāṭaka Inscriptions
R.N. Mishra 74
3. Settlement Pattern in Lalgudi Taluk, Tiruchirapalli District, Tamil Nadu
K.V. Raman and *P. Shanmugam* 81

Section II
THE CONCEPT OF VILLAGE COMMUNITY AND GENERAL PROBLEM OF OWNERSHIP OF LAND

4. Ownership of Agricultural Land in Ancient India
Lallanji Gopal 95

5. Assignment to Officers and Royal Kinsmen in Early Medieval India *c.* AD 700-1200
Krishna Kanti Gopal 118
6. Merchants and Landed Aristocracy in the Feudal Economy of Northern India: Eighth to Twelfth Century
B.P. Mazumdar 142
7. Property Rights in Medieval Tamil Nadu as seen from the Saledeeds in Chola Inscriptions
Y. Subbarayalu 151
8. Landownership and Succession in Medieval Karnataka
G.R. Kuppuswamy 163
9. Village Communities in South India
T.V. Mahalingam 178
10. Indian Village Community according to the *Kṛṣiparāśara* and some other Contemporary Literary Sources
Guyla Wojtilla 193

Section III
AGRARIAN CHANGE, STRUCTURE OF RURAL SOCIETY AND RURAL UNREST

11. The Peasant in Indian History
Irfan Habib 205
12. The Role of Peasants in the Early History of Tamiḻakam in South India
M.G.S. Narayanan 237
13. From the Ancient Labour Tax to the Feudal Corvee: A Marxist Approach to the Study of *Viṣṭi*
Marlene Njammasch 261
14. Landholding and Peasantry in the Brahmaputra Valley *c.* Fifth-Thirteenth Centuries AD
Nayanjot Lahiri 279
15. The Socio-Economic Milieu of the Kerala Temple: A Functional Analysis *c.* AD 800-1200
Rajan Gurukkal 290
16. Agriculture under the Kākatīyas of Warangal
Y. Gopal Reddy 306

17. Landed Magnates as State Agents:
The Gāvuḍas under the Hoyśāḷas in Karnātaka
Kesavan Veluthat 322
18. Immobility and Subjection of Indian Peasantry
in Early Medieval Complex
B.N.S. Yadava 329
19. Problems of Peasant Protest in Early Medieval India
R.S. Sharma 343

BIBLIOGRAPHY 361

CONTRIBUTORS 379

General Editor's Preface

Land System and Rural Society in Early India, edited by Dr B.P. Sahu, is the first in the series: Readings in Early Indian History. The series is designed to make available to students, researchers, teachers and interested general readers significant contributions, in the form of select published essays or parts of monographs, relating to what may be considered important themes in early Indian history. Not all contributions are recent; their selection is guided principally by the criterion of how each has contributed meaningfully, through the wealth of empirical evidence and the quality of analysis, to our understanding of an area of history and of its relation to other areas. Historiography is an important perspective expected to be present throughout the series, to an extent as a reminder that whatever is new is not necessarily final. The anthology of selected readings, the Editor's 'Introduction' and the 'Bibliography', which is intended to be a guide to further and more intensive readings on the theme, are all expected to reflect this perspective.

In editing the present volume Dr Sahu has been careful to draw his material from a wide range of publications, representing varieties of source material and approach. The broad area of agrarian history includes various sub-themes, and although historical writings so far available are very much unevenly distributed between the themes, Dr Sahu has tried to ensure widest coverage for the volume. His 'Introduction' too has attempted to be comprehensive both with reference to different aspects of the theme of the volume and to the significant debates which researchers on early Indian agrarian history have been generating.

Land System and Rural Society in Early India is the first fruit of a new venture. The other volumes in the series relate to trade, traders and networks of trade, urbanization, religion, technology and society, and women and the state in early India. It is hoped that readers will find this first volume savoury and wholesome.

Centre for Historical Studies
School of Social Sciences
Jawaharlal Nehru University

B.D. CHATTOPADHYAYA

Acknowledgements

The editor and the publishers thank the following for granting permission to reprint the articles included in this volume: *The Indian Economic and Social History Review* for Sibesh Bhattacharya, 'Land System as Reflected in Kauṭilya's *Arthaśāstra*'. Agam Kala Prakashan, Delhi, for R.N. Mishra, 'Village Life and Settlements in the Light of Vākāṭaka Inscriptions', in B.M. Pande and B.D. Chattopadhyaya (eds.), *Archaeology and History*, Vol. II. Institute for the Study of Languages and Cultures of Asia and Africa, Tokyo University of Foreign Studies, Tokyo, for K.V. Raman and P. Shanmugam, 'Settlement Pattern in Lalgudi Taluk', in N. Karashima (ed.), *Socio-Cultural Change in Villages in Tiruchirapalli District, Tamilnadu, India. Journal of the Economic and Social History of the Orient* for Lallanji Gopal, 'Ownership of Agricultural Land in Ancient India' and Nayanjot Lahiri, 'Landholding and Peasantry in the Brahmaputra Valley *c.* 5th-13th Centuries AD'. *University of Allahabad Studies* for K.K. Gopal, 'Assignment to Officers and Royal Kinsmen in Early Medieval India (*c.* 700-1200 AD)'. Calcutta University, Calcutta for B.P. Mazumdar, 'Merchants and Landed Aristocracy in the Feudal Economy of Northern India (8th to 12th Century AD)', in D.C. Sircar (ed.), *Land System and Feudalism in Ancient India.* Y. Subbarayalu for 'Property Rights in Medieval Tamil Nadu as seen from the Saledeeds in Chola Inscriptions'. *The Journal of Karnatak University—Social Sciences* for G.R. Kuppuswamy, 'Landownership and Succession in Medieval Karnataka'. *Transactions of the Archaeological Society of South India* for T.V. Mahalingam, 'Village Communities in South India'. *Recueils De La Société Jean Bodin Pour L' Historie Comparative des Institutions* for Guyla Wojtilla, 'Indian

Village Community According to the *Kṛṣiparāśara* and some other Contemporary Literary Sources', in *Les Communautes Rurales. Proceedings of the Indian History Congress* for Irfan Habib, 'The Peasant in Indian History' and Kesavan Veluthat, 'Landed Magnates as State Agents: The Gāvuḍas under the Hoyśāḷas in Karnataka.' *Social Scientist* for M.G.S. Narayanan, 'The Role of the Peasants in the Early History of Tamilakam in South India' and R.S. Sharma, 'Problems of Peasant Protest in Early Medieval India'. *Social Science Probings* for Marlene Njammasch, 'From the Ancient Labour Tax to the Feudal Corvee: A Marxist Approach to the Study of *Viṣṭi*'. *Studies in History* for Rajan Gurukkal, 'The Socio-Economic Milieu of the Kerala Temple: A Functional Analysis *c.* AD 800-1200'. *Itihas* for Y. Gopal Reddy, 'Agriculture under the Kākatīyas of Warangal'. *The Indian Historical Review* for B.N.S. Yadava, 'Immobility and Subjection of Indian Peasantry in Early Medieval Complex'. Texts have been mostly reproduced in their entirety; however for the sake of uniformity some copy-editing changes have been made.

I am more than grateful to my wife Gayatri and dear Devavrata whose cooperation has made this work possible. Thanks are also due to Shri Ajay Kumar Jain and Mr. B.N. Varma of Manohar for the care they have taken in bringing out this volume.

BHAIRABI PRASAD SAHU

Abbreviations

ABORI	-	*Annals of the Bhandarkar Oriental Research Institute*
AR/ARE	-	*Annual Report of South Indian Epigraphy*
AT	-	*Antik Tanulma + Yok.*/Classical Studies, Budapest
BSOAS	-	*Bulletin of the School of Oriental and African Studies*
CII	-	*Corpus Inscriptionum Indicarum*
CSSH	-	*Comparative Studies in Society and History*
DHNI	-	*Dynastic History of Northern India,* by H.C. Ray
Disalkar	-	D.B. Disalkar, 'Some Unpublished Copper-Plates of the Rulers of Valabhi', *JBBRAS,* New Series, 1, 1925.
EAZ	-	*Ethnologisch-archaeologische Zeitung, Berlin*
EC	-	*Epigraphia Carnatica*
EHD	-	*The Early History of the Deccan, Ed. by G. Yazdani*
EI	-	*Epigraphia Indica*
Gaut.	-	*Gautama Dharmaśāstra*
HAS	-	P. Sreenivasachari, *A Corpus of Inscriptions in Telengana Districts of Andhra Pradesh, Hyderabad Archaeological Series,* No. 13, Hyderabad, 1942-56
HCIP	-	*History and Culture of the Indian People,* Ed. by R.C. Majumdar and A.D. Pusalkar
HDS	-	*History of Dharmaśāstras,* by P.V. Kane
IA	-	*Indian Antiquary*
IAA	-	*Inscriptions of Ancient Assam,* Ed. by M.M. Sharma
IESHR	-	*The Indian Economic and Social History Review*
IHQ	-	*The Indian Historical Quarterly*
IHR	-	*The Indian Historical Review*
JAHC	-	*Journal of Andhra History and Culture,* Guntur

JAHRS - *Journal of the Andhra Historical Research Society*
JASB - *Journal of the Asiatic Society of Bengal*
JBBRAS - *Journal of the Bombay Branch of the Royal Asiatic Society*
JBORS - *The Journal of the Bihar and Orissa Research Society*
JESHO - *Journal of the Economic and Social History of the Orient*
JESI - *The Journal of the Epigraphical Society of India*
JIH - *Journal of Indian History*
JPS - *Journal of Peasant Studies*
JRAS - *Journal of the Royal Asiatic Society*
JUPHS - *Journal of U.P. Historical Society*
Ka - Kauṭilya's *Arthaśāstra*
KI - *Karnataka Inscriptions*
NDI - A. Butterworth and V.V. Chetty, *A Collection of Inscriptions on Copper Plates and Stones in the Nellore District*, Madras, 1905
PIHC - *Proceedings of the Indian History Congress*
SII - *South Indian Inscriptions*
VDI - *Vestnik Drevney Istorii, Moskva*

Introduction

Bhairabi Prasad Sahu

In the past thirty years there has been a vast outpouring of literature on landownership, revenue system and such aspects of rural society as the lords, peasants and their world, with the agrarian history of early India being the central concern of the scholarly research community. History is, as it has been said, 'the record of what one age finds worthy in another'. Thus, the changing concerns and the shifts in methods and approaches since the later part of the 1950s explains scholarly interest in the rural way of life, the tiller of the soil and village society.[1] The most celebrated works of historians on early India can be situated in this context. Among the many fascinating studies on agrarian history one may mention D.D. Kosambi's perceptive studies and R.S. Sharma's wide-ranging examination of aspects of land and rural society, for these are pioneering efforts and set the agenda for writing alternative histories.[2] As for studies of earlier historians the works of N.C. Bandyopadhyaya, K.M. Gupta, Pran Nath, U.N. Ghoshal and A.N. Bose, among others, may be mentioned.[3] These scholars essentially compiled the incidental material in the corpus of early Indian literature, sporadically supplementing it with inscriptional evidence, with varying degrees of success.

Modern writings on a wide spectrum of India's past began with the early Orientalist, particularly British, enterprises. The nineteenth century British writings on interrelated aspects of

*Acknowledgements: This essay has benefited from discussions with Professor B.D. Chattopadhyaya and from the comments of Professors R.L. Shukla and T.K. Venkatasubramanian and Dr. R.K. Chattopadhyay.

landownership, caste and village community went on to make a series of hegemonic assertions which easily acquired the character of totalising constructs.[4] These have a relevance in the present context in so far as they have had a bearing on such concepts as Oriental Despotism and the Asiatic Mode of Production, which have influenced and curiously continue to cloud historical constructions of early India. It needs no emphasis that imperialist perspectives on India were motivated and were tools for British hegemony and colonialism.[5] They were largely intended to provide justification for the British Indian enterprise, drill in their categorical cultural superiority, administer silence and flowing from it ensure the subservience of the 'natives'.[6] The overt emphasis on the 'unchanging East', as against the dynamic West, unabashedly differentiating between the two civilizations, more than reinforces this impression.

Indian historians, both within and outside the nationalist historiography, questioned some of the basic premises of colonial writings in the early decades of the twentieth century. Aspects such as landownership, agriculture and the revenue system attracted the notice of N.C. Bandyopadhyaya, Pran Nath and U.N. Ghoshal.[7] They generally argued for private ownership of land, absence of oppressive taxation, the happy condition of the people and took a favourable view of the economic conditions in early India on the basis of brahmanical literature. Through a combined use of the Jātakas, Smṛtis and epigraphic and numismatic evidence A.N. Bose provided an excellent description of north Indian rural economy.[8] Thematically he covered almost the same ground as that of the earlier historians, but he seems to have been influenced by Marxism. In his work there is an awareness of the exploitative social relations in early historical India. Almost during the same period K.M. Gupta, K.A.N. Sastri and A. Appadorai laid the foundations for the study of land system and society in south India.[9] While Gupta produced more of a traditional treatise, Sastri's work on the Cholas marked a definite advance in the study of the economic history of south India. Largely on the basis of inscriptional evidence he provided a detailed discussion of agriculture, land and taxation as well as the socio-economic role of the south Indian temple. Drawing on the chronicles of travellers and epigraphic material Appadorai presented a useful narrative of aspects of rural life, including the village community, in the first half of the second millennium AD. In these works early medieval society in south India has largely been viewed as harmonious, undifferentiated and devoid of contradictions.

Much of the literature in this traditional genre of writing were a compilation of factual details from different sources, at times even belonging to different periods. The evolution of institutions and structures and the specificity of historical experience during a particular period were lost in the maze of descriptive details cutting across time segments. The analysis and explanation of agrarian life within incorporative concepts was unknown and the peasant was, more often than not, missing in the discussions. Thus, much of the narratives were devoid of their social context.

The significance of these works perhaps lies primarily in their description of the sources.[10] Contemporary research is no more confined to mere collection of data on land types, varieties of land measures, crops, revenue terms or the theoretical position of the *varṇas*, but has extended to seeing developments in the round. Social stratification, social mobility and their changing forms in relation to land rights and the state are the kind of issues that have occupied the centre stage in historical reconstructions since the later part of the 1950s. There has been a shift from the presentation of the theoretical position as enunciated in the normative texts to efforts at understanding rural life as it was actually lived.

Colonial historiography set the trend for macro generalizations about India as a single undifferentiated entity. Indian nationalist writings in all its efforts at rebutting the imperialist perceptions on land and society never really recognized the problem. Interestingly, they reinforced it and helped in the making of a stereotype. In recent times despite an entirely different characterization of the history of early India the assumption of Indian reality to have been homogeneous remains largely unchallenged. Generalizations from the perspective of Gangetic northern India tend to ignore both the specificity and dynamics of regional experiences[11] and consequently have a bearing on our understanding of the evolution and consolidation of the agrarian foundations of Indian society.

It is perhaps necessary at this point to define the term early history in the context of its contemporary historiographical usage. Early India, in the scheme of periodization in Indian history, has usually been used as a synonym for ancient India and its upper limit extends up to the end of the twelfth century. Within this time-frame it accommodates the terms early historical and early medieval, the first extends up to and includes the Gupta period and the latter corresponds to the post-Gupta phase. This broad two-fold division does not exhaust the possibility of delineating further stages within them,[12] nor, as the following discussion would point out, does it warrant the assumption of homogeneous patterns for the whole of India as a geographical entity at any given stage in her history. The extrapolation of stages in early India challenges the earlier notion of the absence of change in Indian society.

Briefly stated, contemporary historical writings have contrasted the broadly two phases of early Indian history at the level of the structure of agrarian economy and rural society, trade, commerce and urbanization, and administrative organization. The early historical period is envisaged as marked by wide-ranging exchange networks, horizontal spread of urban centres, monetization of the economy and comparatively less unequal distribution of land, if not produce. Although society was stratified, it was relatively open and less exploitative compared to the later times. The vaiśyas were the principal tax payers and the śūdras constituted the basic source of labour. The post-Gupta period which is visualized in terms of a feudal social formation, it is stressed, was socially and politically hierarchic and economically ruralized. It is postulated that the decline of inter-regional and trans-oceanic trade, decay of urban centres and paucity of metallic money inevitably led to a closed, self-sufficient, predominantly agrarian economy in a situation of the localization of arts, crafts and exchange activities. The transformation was reflected in the domain of culture as well.[13] The earlier vibrant economy is thus juxtaposed to the closed, natural economy of early medieval times.

Notwithstanding this summarized picture of the dominant historiography, which characterizes the early medieval in opposition to early historical society, it is imperative to note that there are differences within the Indian feudalism school at the level of analysis and explanation of historical processes and that all of them do not subscribe to identical views. The variations in the perceptions can perhaps be made clear by citing the authors' position on the transition from antiquity to the Middle Ages and their treatment of the last two centuries of the early medieval phase. Sharma in his initial formulation characterized the eleventh-twelfth centuries as a categorically distinct phase,[14] whereas R.N. Nandi discerns potentialities of growth in rural economy within the early feudal context[15] which then shaped the said period. Similarly, the explanation of the transition to the early medieval phase has over the years shifted from the decline of long-distance inter-regional and maritime trade and commerce to urban decay and even Kali Age crisis,[16] symbolizing a systemic failure, despite a radically different characterization of historical processes of change in early India in more recent times.[17]

Historians of the Indian feudalism school while locating the passage from the early historical to the early medieval times in a crisis, even a breakdown of the early historical civilizational universe, have interestingly remained, as one author puts it, 'judiciously agnostic' as to its categorization in terms of conventional social formation.[18] Slavery as an analytical category has floundered on the touchstone of empirical validity.[19] The phase continues to be envisaged variously as early historical, pre-feudal and even as vaiśya-śūdra society. The 'vaiśya-śūdra mode', though not rigorously pursued by Sharma, is supposed to have crystallized in pre-Mauryan and Mauryan times. The nomenclature derives from the *varṇas* engaged in production, but there are difficulties in assuming the brahmanical, conventional, normative social order to have been the actual operational reality, more so in the context of the different perspective provided in Buddhist literature.[20] The landgrants have been visualized as a response to the ubiquitous crisis by the state, which has been assigned the role of a prime-mover in the entire gamut of socio-political change, including even the curious decision to preside over its own demise, by unleashing the processes of political fragmentation and parcellization of sovereignty. This perspective tends to play down the phased, uneven evolution of historical society in the cultural regions.

The dominant historiography has come to be perceived as being essentially Eurocentric and inadequate on various counts, especially at the level of providing a long-term explanation of change. Admittedly, the two broad phases in early Indian history are not questioned. The dissimilarity between the two phases is admitted, but their characterization in mutual opposition is contested. It is the explanation of the change from the early historical to the early medieval period and the causation which have been the ground of contestation, providing us in the process an alternative mode for understanding the dynamics of change.[21]

The tendency to equate and identify a political system characterized by extensive territoriality, especially the Mauryan polity, with a socio-economic pattern or uniform social formation has perhaps unwittingly led to the construction of undifferentiated, homogeneous stages in early India, despite the recognition of the co-existence of a series of parallel forms and several modes in Indian history quite early within the dominant historiography.[22] It is the uneven nature of historical and cultural developments in early India and the 'complex synthesis of different societies and cultures at different stages of development' at any given point in history that is beginning to receive the necessary attention of historians. Tribal organizations, pastoralists, peasant societies, chiefdoms and larger state systems existed in a situation of interaction and change, as so often today, and not necessarily in isolation.[23]

It is these interactional processes and the consequent change from within that constitute the focus of more recent writings. As against the current framework of catastrophic break and the decline and relapse to subsistence economy of agriculture in the post-Gupta phase, agrarian expansion leading to the emergence of regional agrarian structures, the horizontal spread of state societies through the process of local state formation, peasantization of the tribes and the positioning of their segments differentially in the caste hierarchy, within the scheme of *varṇa* ideology and such other related processes have been identified by B.D. Chattopadhyaya as markers of the change.[24] The transition is perceived as deriving from an acceleration and expansion of early historical/societal processes of change. In this alternative mode of analysis landgrants and the religious beneficiaries have been perceived as instruments of state formation, as against their earlier characterization as agents of dismemberment and vivisection, facilitating the extension and consolidation of state power through the integration of rural economy and society.[25] Historical transformation is thus viewed in terms of the multiple and simultaneous processes of change. The perspective from the regions acquire the necessary centrality and this construction of the past while accommodating the regional variations also recognizes the wider network of linkages.

We must here treat the early historical and early medieval continuously, as, of course, they were continuous. The early medieval centuries were dynamic in so far as they heralded a series of developments leading to the evolution and crystallization of historical regions in India. It started to a great extent with widening the orbit of peasant activity and state society; and behind them they had the driving force of brahmanical ideology, structures and institutions in centres of early historical growth. In so far as early medieval society reached a higher level of elaboration and complexity than the early historical period it was largely due to the formation of agrarian regions. There was a natural fusion between elements beyond the Gangetic heartland and early north Indian elements through a process of interaction, the beginnings of which date back to the time of the enormous spatial spread of the Mauryan state.[26] The movement towards complex society in peninsular India, as in other regions, has been located in these processes of interaction and change.

It is clear that perspectives on early Indian agrarian history have gone through changes and dimensions which had not been discussed before are being added on. New sets of questions are being asked and there has been a shift from the narration of factual details to efforts at understanding structures and processes.[27] It is being realized that studies on agrarian order, society and polity have a bearing on each other and need to be studied in their interrelatedness. The role of institutions such as *brahmadēyas* and temples in the development of the agrarian order, consolidation of state power and the organization of social differentiation have been delineated. There is change both in the historiographical concerns as well as methods of study. There have been some efforts, though occasional, towards the use of statistical methods and quantification in analysing archaeological material bearing on settlement history, among other things, and inscriptional sources from south India.[28] The growing concern with historical experiences, structures and processes brings out the limitations of a certain kind of sources, their optative and normative character. Anyone familiar with the *Arthaśāstra* and *Manusmṛti* will understand the difficulties involved in reconstructing the dimensions of historical evolution from such sources.[29] Our intention is not to question the validity of these sources or the uses to which they have been put, but to highlight the inherent problems. Their usefulness in reconstructing past perceptions, ideology and such other related aspects needs no emphasis. A balanced assessment comes through quite lucidly in the following observation of G.M. Bongard-Levin: 'The śāstras' value resides in that they provide a generalized picture of ancient India without regard to the infinite varieties of time and space.'[30]

The above quote is also intended to demonstrate why there has been a visible shift among the practitioners of the craft in their preference for epigraphical and archaeological evidence.

The influence of the changing perspectives, understandably, has not been uniform across the country. There has been very little change in the approaches to agrarian history in certain regions like the Deccan, Andhra, Orissa and large parts of Central India; while studies on Tamil Nadu, Kerala and Karnataka have registered noteworthy advances by shifting the focus to changes in agrarian organizations and society in their wider context. The range of variation in regional studies is further enhanced by the few insightful analyses on Bengal and Rajasthan.

Our objective is to present a brief account of the trends and possibilities of research on land system and rural society. The Harappan context is left outside the ambit of discussion largely owing to the canons of conventional historiographic usage and the fact that it has become an altogether separate area of specialization. One is not sure how competently this can be done because of both the widely varying perspectives on the related problems and the sheer spectrum of issues in the field. Although historians have particularly debated the overall nature of economy and society, certain themes have received greater attention than others. Aspects such as landownership, revenue system, village community, social relations and the structure of society have been objects of alternative interpretations. We would like to dwell on some of these general, but important problems.

I

Geographical boundaries and rural landscapes in early India were neither static nor undifferentiated. There was continuous fragmentation of habitats with settlements encroaching into and separating woodlands and forests. The ongoing formation of new rural settlements led to the extension of agrarian space in erstwhile tribal frontiers and virgin territories. In some cases earlier tribal hamlets could be transformed into peasant villages. It also implied increase in the density of settlements in already settled areas. Thus, a space segment is not an immutable, uniform historico-geographic unit. It has always been a conglomeration of smaller segments, encompassing different types of settlements and levels of socio-political organization. *Vana/araṇya* and *janapada/kṣetra* have been juxtaposed in north Indian literature. While the former represent forest or jungle, the latter are identified with well-settled, inhabited space with plough agriculture. The same contrast in Tamil literature may be seen in the distinction between *vanpulam* (jungle tracts/pasture lands) and *menpulam* (paddy land).[31] It has been postulated that 'this dichotomy of *vana* and *kṣetra* is not mutually exclusive, but is rather complementary or a continuum similarly as the continuum from tribe to caste'.[32] The continued manifestation of *janapadas* since their first emergence in the Doab in the later vedic period and the appearance of new ones like Kāmarūpa, Gauḍa and Dakṣiṇa Kośala, among numerous others, in the first millennium AD, suggesting the emergence of regions, derived form such processes of continuous spatio-historical transformation.

An understanding of the hierarchy of regions—nuclear regions, areas of relative isolation and areas of isolation—explains partly, if not entirely, their chronologically phased formation. It is generally recognized that the distinction between these categories was not unalterably fixed and the nuclearity or otherwise of a region is linked to how historical factors converge on it. It would be interesting to study the pattern of the evolution of agrarian regions in India and the history of rural settlements in relation to it. In the absence of adequate detailed studies on rural settlements in the early historical period, and this being largely true for the early medieval situation as well, the two aspects may be studied interminglingly so as to lend the discernible patterns amenable to wider correlations.

The emergence of peasant farming, artisanal production, settlements and state societies in the mid-first millennium BC have been explained in terms of long-term dynamics of change starting with Ṛg vedic pastoralism through the inchoate stage of development in the later vedic period. In such analyses the evidence in vedic literature and early Pāli sources have been normally used, admittedly though for the later vedic context and beyond the available archaeological data have been compared and correlated to present a more comprehensive picture. The perspective provided by archaeological cultures, especially those succeeding the Harappan civilization, some of them overlapping with the Late Harappan and others having an independent origin, assume importance in the context of the shift from the primacy of vedic literature to a greater reliance on archaeological evidence to understand the long-term history of the evolution of regions, settlements and peasant units of production. The plurality of archaeological cultures between the later part of the second millennium BC and the middle of the first millennium BC; manifested in the BRW, OCP, Copper-Hoards, PGW and Black slipped ware,[33] suggests the possibility of contacts and interactions between different cultures and mutual adaptations and adjustments as well. The non-Sanskritic terms associated with agricultural activities in vedic texts support this presentation.[34] Similarly, interactions between the Upper and Middle Gangetic plains, it is said, produced not only the deluxe NBPW but also gave rise to such languages as Pāli and Prakrit.[35] Such analyses transfer the focus from invasion, physical movement and 'colonization', involving ethnic groups, to the interactional process as the agent of change.

The spread of iron technology with considerable chronological variance into culture regions is important as a marker of the transition to full-fledged sedentary agriculture. This seems to have happened at various points of the first millennium BC in the varied zones. However, the origins of agriculture, emergence of first farming communities and settlements predate the use of iron in these regions. To say this, however, does not mean that there was a continuity in the evolution and spread of cultures and settlements across the disparate regions. While some kind of continuity is noticed in the Upper and Middle Gangetic plains there are discernible breaks or disjunctures in the history of settlements in the Deccan and western and central India.[36] The chalcolithic sites suffered desertion and decay at various stages in time and the same areas were not reoccupied until the fifth-third centuries BC.

In the Upper and Middle Ganga plains pre-Iron settlements are known and their role in the emergence of Iron Age sites is beginning to be grasped.[37] A study of settlement patterns in Kanpur district,[38] in the Upper plains, shows a steady increase in the number of sites from the chalcolithic to the NBPW/early historic period. There is a marked enlargement in the size of settlements and geographic extent of the occupied area over time. In the NBPW period land which was well drained but away from the rivers as well as lakes was also occupied. In the later part of the NBPW period even less hospitable tracts were colonized, pointing to increased population pressure. It has been pointed out that during this entire period the Yamuna between Agra and Allahabad was largely uninhabited owing, it seems, to the unattractiveness of the soil in terms of agriculture. One may add that the Mathura area remained pastoral for centuries and that may perhaps explain the absence of stable sites. In a recent analysis of the emergence of complex society in the Middle Gangetic plains,[39] which takes cognizance of the pre-Iron Age cultures in a long-term perspective, it is posited that unlike in the Doab (Kanpur and Allahabad districts) there were no settlement clusters or nucleated villages in the region prior to 500 BC. The density of settlements, their relationship to one another over an area and the study of change through time help us to generalize about cultural processes, but such studies are far and few between. Notwithstanding the limitations of analytical archaeological[40] studies and the problem involved in the correlation of archaeological and literary evidence, it is generally agreed that agriculture and pastoralism co-existed in the Ṛgvedic and later vedic societies. While the former was primarily pastoral but familiar with agriculture, in the latter the relative importance of these forms of subsistence was reversed.

R.S. Sharma and Romila Thapar, despite their differences in the overall reconstruction of the developments leading up to and including the pre-Mauryan period, show how through the convergence of a variety of historical factors the process of *janapada* formation acquired a greater socio-political visibility during the sixth-fifth centuries,[41] especially in the Middle Ganga plains. It was a period characterized by agrarian expansion, introduction of iron tools for maximizing production, proliferation in the number and variety of settlements, invention of metallic money and the extension of communication and trade networks. The period also marked the beginnings of stratified society. The opening of trade routes seems to have helped the greater use of iron as the metal was not always available locally. The spread of plough cultivation, paddy transplantation and knowledge of varieties of rice (*śāli* being a generic term), wheat, barley, sesamum, mustard, lentils, plantation and mangoes indicate the crystallization and consolidation of sedentary peasant farming. Wet paddy cultivation and the attendant increase in yield led to the proliferation of settlements. The spread of rural economy and spurt in agrarian settlements is indicated both by early Pāli texts and the distribution of NBPW sites in Bihar and eastern Uttar Pradesh. On the basis of the explored and excavated data an increase in the size and number of NBPW settlements has been postulated, though all the sites may not be as early as 500 BC. Pāṇini's work and Pāli literature refer to various types of settlements, including *grāma, nigama nagara* and craft settlements of potters and carpenters. The classification and preparation of fields, and demarcation of village space into *kṣetra, vathu, gocara,* etc., suggest the increasing preoccupation with land and cultivation. The mode has been characterized as peasant mode insofar as free peasants dominated production. Slavery was known, but it was incidental and largely confined to the domestic sector.

Land clearance was not only a consequence of the transition from tribalism to peasant economy but was also related to population rise. Demographic change led to fissioning of communities. A part of the social unit or a younger generation would break away and form a new nucleus in another cultivable wasteland. Although the establishment of new settlements in the process is known as early as the PGW culture in the Doab,[42] it seems to have gained momentum during the Age of the Buddha. Historical examples of the process are attested in early Buddhist sources.[43] The role of iron in this transformation has been a much debated issue. In the face of the fact that iron was known in the Ganga valley centuries before the spread of settlements and that no discernible changes are marked in the crop patterns between the BRW-chalcolithic and NBPW and related phases one group of scholars argue against positing any causal link between iron technology and the spread of agriculture and settlements, and flowing from it the rise of complex state societies.[44] The other group of historians led by Sharma point to the shift in the method of cultivation, rising yields and the unprecedented proliferation of settlements, crafts and artefacts with the introduction of iron for productive purposes.[45] The point of inference, however, is that while it is difficult to deny the transformative potentiality of iron technology, it may not be very useful to reduce the explanation of societal processes of change to a factor, in this case technological determinism, howsoever important. Developments may be situated in the wider context of environment, patterns of land use and the interrelationship between the gamut of other variables.

The processes under discussion came into their own and blossomed fully in the Ganga valley during the Mauryan period. By the third century BC we see a certain homogeneity in the material culture of Gangetic northern India and the fringes of central India. Over the last decade there has been a departure in the characterization of Mauryan state and society from the earlier view which assumed a certain measure of material and cultural uniformity for the subcontinent,[46] deriving largely from the paradigm of centralized pan-Indian empire. It is steadily being recognized that an empire by its very nature accommodates a variety of social formations and the transition to the early historical phase in the region south of the Vindhyas acquired momentum during and after the Mauryas.[47]

In spite of the difficulties in accepting the *Arthaśāstra* as being reflective of the realities of the Mauryan period much of the reconstruction of the contemporary agrarian economy is based on it. The *Arthaśāstra* recognized that the basis of the state's wealth and power lay in agricultural production, hence every effort had to be made to increase it. The concern is evident in the details dealing with the founding of new rural settlements (*janapadaniveśa*). Details with regard to reclamation of wasteland, preference for śūdra cultivators in newly settled areas, employment of sharecroppers, crops, agricultural taxes and village administration suggest a thriving rural economy.[48] Discussions on types of land, organization of production, including the provision allowing the state to ask the peasants to produce extra crops in situations of emergency, reflect on aspects of agriculture as well as settlements.[49] The possibility of the use of prisoners of war, besides slaves and hired labourers, in extending the orbit of peasant activity has been conceded. The increase in the number of settlements and quality of material culture during the period is demonstrated in the archaeological record of the later phase of the NBPW culture.

It is becoming increasingly evident from recent writings that the post-Mauryan period extending up to the Guptas was seminal in various ways for the Deccan and south India. It marks the transition from pre-state to state societies bringing in its wake other concomitant changes. However, for long the period was characterized as a 'Dark Age', largely owing to the absence of imperial formations, in what appears to be empire-centred discourses. Even in the current historiography the agrarian dimensions of the epoch have not received the attention they deserve.[50] Agrarian history tends to be subsumed under discussions on towns, inter-regional trade and maritime commerce, which then is assumed to explain the broad contours of the period. The fact that even in a very recent publication, intended to be a survey of research on early India, the post-Mauryan space is occupied by a chapter on trade is suggestive of the problem.[51] Crafts, trade and urban centres need to be located in the context of their rural hinterland and agrarian foundations. The dearth of focus on the agrarian history of this period, marked by enormous extension of the peasant frontier beyond the north Indian plains, reinforces the impression of a break between the early historical and early medieval periods. Deriving from this gap in our understanding the two phases located at the opposite ends of the post-Mauryan period appear to be sharply dissimilar and the concentration on non-agricultural activities during *c.* 200 BC–AD 300 has helped to enhance the perceived contrast.

In fact, the post-Mauryan period was the formative period for most of the Deccan and south India. The archaeological data from early historical settlements, bearing on stratigraphy, in these regions support this line of thinking. Continued manifestation of 'locality'/*janapada* formation is discernible in the disparate data from the various regions.[52] Together with the archaeological evidence, the epigraphic material and locality circumscribed coins of various individual chiefs and those of the Mahāmeghavāhanas, Mahāraṭhis, Mahātalavāras, Kuras, Ānandas, Sadās, etc., suggest the emergence of a ruling stratum in various areas in the Deccan, Andhra and Orissa.[53] An almost analogous picture of the gradual evolution of plough agriculture and peasant society has been obtained for ancient Tamiḷakam through a judicious mix or archaeology and Saṅgam literature.[54] Parts of the Deccan and the eastern coast emerged into historical limelight. Kaliṅga, the Godavari-Krishna deltaic zone and the Tamil coast acquired a visible political profile. The shifts in the power centres on the coast, however, indicate the complex interplay of historical forces and caution against notions of unilinear development.

The trajectory of internal transformation across regions was not uniform. The differences may be understood in terms of the processes that went into shaping them. In Vidarbha, Andhra and Karnataka the megalithic cultures appear crucial to any long-term explanation of the unfolding of historical society. These cultures exploited local mineral and agricultural resources and also yield evidence for craft production, exchange networks and internal differentiation, which subsequently got elaborated in historical times. Many of the megalithic communities began with a preference for mineral rich areas but gradually expanded into the riverine and flood plains, indicating the diversification of the resource base and a greater reliance on agriculture.[55] At this stage of development they experienced the Mauryan interaction, which is seen as a quickening impulse. The transition in the varied regions thus, derived from the horizontal spread of the Mauryan state and the consequent interaction. The autochthonous chiefs were accommodated in a relationship of subordination to the 'metropolitan state' for the manipulation of labour and transfer of resources. If interaction constituted the mechanism of change, it was propelled by the Mauryan concern for revenue maximization. However, the structure of Mauryan state and economy necessitated differential levels of interaction with the periphery.[56] The regional resource potential and the stage of historical development being the determining factors in the nature and intensity of interactions, the end results were understandably varied.

The western Deccan shows evidence for settlements from the Mauryan period onwards. Developments in much of Andhra and Karnataka seem to have been different. Settlements spread in these regions during the second-first centuries BC and more particularly by the late first-early second centuries AD.[57] Even the agriculturally unattractive south Konkan experienced occupation by late first century BC. The westerly trade from Bharuch and Sopara opened the northern Deccan to communication from Andhra and Karnataka. The overland route connecting the lower Krishna and

Bharuch and Ujjain was dotted by a number of settlements. The northern Deccan ecologically and culturally seems to be different from Andhra and Karnataka. While the latter provide evidence for megalithic settlements the former had none of it. There seems to have been an earlier and heavier concentration of settlements in the northern Deccan. The scanty evidence from Orissa seem to be largely within the post-Mauryan tradition on the east coast.[58] Pāli texts of this period mention three types of settlements, one of which stood on the periphery of the countryside or forest frontier. Such areas were potential zones for rural expansion. All sites yielding early historic artefacts may not have been urban centres after all, as is normally assumed. Some may well have been overgrown, prosperous rural settlements. The lead provided by H. Sarkar and Chattopadhyaya perhaps needs to be pursued.[59] It is ultimately the cultural ensemble that defines a site. The problem is compounded, as is widely recognized, by the urban bias of early historical archaeology. Rural studies have received no attention and we usually end up with general statements on the town and country relationships. A study of Kathiawar reveals the occupation of many new areas through the Mauryan and post-Mauryan centuries. Agriculturally productive areas, it is said, show density of settlements.[60] The spatio-temporal pattern of settlements suggests that farming was more successful in the region in the early historic period, especially since the first century BC.

The proliferation of settlements, monasteries and rock-cutting activities in the Deccan presupposes surpluses from contemporary trade and agriculture. Iron ploughshare and irrigation-based agriculture seems to have been induced by north Indian contacts. Areas of concentration of agrarian settlements can be seen in the river valleys and the Krishna-Tungabhadra Doab.[61] The lower Krishna valley and the coast were areas of attraction and therefore more densely settled. *Āhāra* as a territorial unit finds mention in the Sātavāhana inscriptions from various areas. *Āhāra* means food and the term in a territorial sense possibly tried to differentiate the food-producing eco-zones from other kinds of terrains. Such units of production were dispersed and spread over parts of Gujarat, Maharashtra and Karnataka.[62] Excavation reports indicate the cultivation of a variety of crops, including rice, millet and lentils. Dhanyakataka, an important place-name in Andhra, alludes to rice cultivation. The *Gāthā-Saptaśatī* records rice and mango cultivation and betel-leaf plantations.[63] Two major cash crops, coconut grown in northern Konkan and pepper in Malabar, are reported during this period. The *Gāthā-Saptaśatī* and a Nasik inscription refer to some hydraulic contrivances.[64] Similarly the Sudarśana lake in Gujarat, the canal at Nagarjunakonda in Andhra, Khāravela's restoration of a water channel in Kaliṅga and Chola Karikaḷa's embankment enterprise in the Kaveri delta bear testimony to contemporary concern for water resources. However, in Mauryan and post-Mauryan times state initiative in irrigation seems to have been marginal and small-scale irrigational works based on local initiative seem to have been the normal prevailing condition.[65]

The *gahapatis* emerge as a powerful category patronizing religious establishments. Amaravati and Sanchi provide evidence for such rural donors. Some of the inscriptions at Sanchi even record donations by villages.[66] Rural settlements are mentioned in the context of land donation to ascetics and monasteries.[67] The monasteries in the Deccan emerged as important centres of integration, providing cohesion to society.[68] The phenomenon of landgrants, with all its implications for ownership rights in land and/or control over produce, made its first appearance during this period.

The epicentre seems to have shifted from the Gangetic plains to areas peripheral to it in the post-Mauryan phase. These regions exhibited early patterns of socio-economic transformation. Notwithstanding the pulsating trade and urbanization, agriculture continued to be the dominant economic pursuit and rural society perhaps, the hub of social reproduction all through.

Historico-geographic transformation of space continued unabated and manifested itself in the protracted rise of secondary states. The Aśokan edicts refer to the troublesome forest (*aṭavi*) people of central India. The Allahabad *praśasti* of Samudragupta mentions the emergence of forest kingdoms (*āṭavika-rājyas*) in the same region. The appearance of *rājyas* in a forest tract shows the distance it had travelled in socio-political terms since the Mauryan times. Expressions such as *Pulindarāja rāṣṭra* in an inscription from Bundelkhand, belonging to the Gupta period, shed light on local state formation and are important for mapping such transition. Again the perpetuation and survival of the *Gaṇa-saṅgha* polities in Punjab till about the fourth century suggests the co-existence of varied cultural milieux. However, as elsewhere, here too the internal transformation and final dissolution of the *gaṇa-saṅgha* tradition have been located in the long history of network of linkages and interactions with the Gangetic plains and Taxila and beyond.[69] Post-Gupta Punjab experienced the process of state formation in the hills, within the framework of brahmanical ideology. Continued manifestation of the process is noticed in the landgrant charters. Between *c.* AD 400 and 650 about fifty kingdoms surfaced in Maharashtra, eastern Madhya Pradesh, Andhra, Orissa and Bengal.[70] It is a continuous but largely forested terrain. The emergence of state societies in pre-state tracts are markers of transition in the rural landscape and socio-political organization. The state does integrate, though it also splits up communities. The expanding frontiers of state society and the corresponding rise in the landgrants and temple building activities during Gupta and post-Gupta times bring out their obvious interrelatedness.[71] The transition came from within society and was neither just a matter of colonization nor had it anything to do with fragmentation from an epicentre. The early medieval centuries are replete with examples of ruling lineages emerging from autochthonous foundations as a consequence of such processes of change.[72] Internal transformation of tribal societies continued into medieval centuries in central and north-eastern India.[73]

During the two hundred years of Vākāṭaka rule pockets in central India and the northern Deccan experienced the spread of rural settlements. Out of the 131 settlements listed in their inscriptions many are believed to have come up during this period.[74] The Vidarbha region, constituting the eastern half of the Vākāṭaka dominions, opened up. The dissemination of Sanskritic culture and attendant acculturation are discernible in the records.[75] Similar processes of socio-economic and political change in the region around Narmada can be delineated from the copper-plates of the chiefs of Valkha (identified with Bagh).[76] These inscriptional sources illuminate the drive towards the establishment of new rural settlements in central India, almost simultaneously with the opening up of Vidarbha. The absence of detailed boundary delineations of gift lands in the records is quite instructive.

The rapid expansion in the agrarian base doubtless came courtesy the complex web of interactions, introduction of plough agriculture, spread of iron technology, etc., but growth in turn bred tensions and occasional setbacks. The *Harṣacarita* not only beautifully encapsulates the contrast between Srikantha *janapada* (parts of modern Haryana) and the Vindhya forest region, but also provides evidence to show that unprecedented growth was not entirely frictionless. Early forms of resistance come through in the 'zealous foresters violently seizing the axes of trespassing woodcutters'.[77] The 'Kaḷabhra interlude' seems to have provided non-brāhmaṇas in south India the opportunity to appropriate the *ekabhoga-brahmadēyas.* Indirect evidence for it is registered in the records of the Pallavas and Chāḷukyas. Positive proof for non-brāhmaṇa resistance to the expansion of *brahmadēyas* comes from the Dalavaypuram plates of the early Pāṇḍyas.[78] The juxtaposing of the negative injunctions against misappropriation of *brahmadēyas* and the extolling of the merits of protection in the imprecatory verses in landgrant charters concede the possibility of such eventualities. The precedence accorded to *Rājaśāsanas* over other sources of law in early medieval India, it is said, was aimed at preventing and resolving such situations.[79] Even later the efforts of peasants and/or the local dominant castes to extend agriculture was resisted by neighbouring tribals. The Bhil revolts in the history of Mewar point to the complexities in the socio-cultural integration of a region.[80]

The formation of agrarian bases at the locality and sub-regional levels was an ongoing process and it introduced a new kind of comparable socio-political structure throughout. The spread of vedic-śāstric-purāṇic ideas, as gleaned from epigraphic records and sculptural art in Tamil Nadu, Orissa and other regions[81] from the sixth-seventh centuries onwards strengthened the authority of the ruling lineages while simultaneously legitimising the social order and facilitating cultural integration over wider areas. The spread of *tīrtha* clusters across regions and their recognition and eulogization in the purāṇas demonstrate the integrative process. The induction of tribal deities into the purāṇic pantheon allowed for their integration into the *tīrtha* tradition. Consequently, through the connectivity that pilgrimage provides it ensured their elaboration and universalization.[82]

The post-Gupta centuries were characterized by the formation of sub-regional agrarian bases, best manifested in the rise of a plethora of ruling lineages across the country; leading to the emergence of regional agrarian and state structures from the ninth/tenth century onwards. Bengal under the Pālas and Senas, Orissa under the Somavaṁśis and Later Gaṅgas, Western Gaṅga and Hoysāḷa Karnataka and Tamil Nadu during the Pallava, Pāṇḍya and Chola times amply exhibit these developments within the regions. Usually the post-Gupta period has been treated as a different phase, which then admits of two sub-phases, with the tenth century constituting some kind of a dividing line. The fourth-seventh centuries mark the transition to the early medieval stage in so far as they anticipate many of the later developments. It is, however, not our intention to argue for a rigid schema of uniform validity all over the country. Historical evolution in Assam, Kerala and Rajasthan, for example, show dissimilar spatio-temporal trajectories. Nevertheless, on the basis of the available regional trends some broad patterns are discernible and it may be surmised that from the seventh century onwards the varied regions experienced the operation of almost similar historical processes.[83] These processes seem to have further accelerated around the tenth century.

The study of regional agrarian histories have been varied and disparities can be noticed both in terms of the quality and quantity of historical output. While in the case of Tamil Nadu, Kerala, Karnataka, Bengal and Assam aspects of agrarian economy have been worked out at some length and in Andhra, Orissa and Rajasthan some beginnings have been made, we are less fortunate about other regions insofar as the details are concerned.

Tamil Nadu may be taken as a case study because of the availability of a number of imaginative, rigorous analytical works on the region. The agrarian map of the Tamil country began to change from the time of the Pallavas. The rise and spread of settlements unequivocally show the spread of agriculture. The patronage extended to tank building activities is yet another marker of agrarian expansion. There seems to have been a correspondence between the increase in irrigational works and the rise in the number of *nāḍus* between the seventh and tenth centuries. Reclamation of land affected by floods and breaches in the embankment of the Kaveri began under Parāntaka I and continued well into the times of Kullōtuṅga.[84] Fallow lands were similarly brought under cultivation. A micro study of a taluk too suggests that the Pallava period constituted a turning point in the history of the proliferation of settlements.[85] The phased growth may be seen in the gradual spread of settlements from the wet to the dry zone under the Cholas. A recent study reveals the pattern of agrarian expansion in the region and suggests that the southern Kaveri delta witnessed hectic activity in the post-tenth century.[86] The Pāṇḍyan territory (Vaigai-Tamraparni valleys) opened up during the seventh-ninth centuries and more particularly from the ninth century onwards. The intensive colonization of the upper reaches of the Tamraparni, it is said, reflects conscious state policy towards an area for strengthening its own economic foundations.[87] The emergence and proliferation of *nāḍus* through the Pallava-Chola periods were inextricably linked to expanding agrarian pursuits. In contrast to the smaller *nāḍus* in the river valleys, the less fertile tracts were characterized by larger *nāḍus* with lesser density of settlements. Some kind of a peak was attained in different areas in course of the eleventh-twelfth centuries[88] and beyond it there was a slowing down of the process.

The picture obtained for some other regions, though not synonymous, is very close to the pattern of development in Tamil Nadu. The intra-regional variations and the phased development of sub-regions is discernible in the context of early medieval Orissa and Kāmarūpa.[89] In the Orissa setting the deliberate royal choice of certain sub-regions for development as agrarian resource bases during the ninth-eleventh centuries, as in Tamil Nadu, attracts attention.[90] There is a perceptible rise in the number of settlements in the Brahmaputra valley in the post-tenth century. The fact that about fifty settlements are reported for this period as against thirteen for the earlier phase is very instructive.[91] Andhra in the post-Ikṣvāku phase exhibits the phenomenon of landgrants, but interestingly all these early dynasties and their grants were confined to coastal Andhra.[92] It is a pattern that is largely corroborated in the developments in pre-eighth century Orissa. Not that the areas of Telengana and Rayalasema were economically barren, but evidently they opened up to agriculture on a large scale in subsequent times. The history of agriculture and irrigation, especially the care bestowed on the construction of tanks and reservoirs, in Warangal under the Kākātiyas[93] and the attendant visible profile of the Reddis points to the step-wise agrarian integration of the region.

The trends available for Assam, Bengal, Karnataka and Rajasthan endorse the picture of burgeoning rural economy during the period under discussion. While a study on irrigation in Rajasthan alludes to a general growth in agricultural production through royal initiative in irrigation works,[94] another contribution confined particularly to the Abu-Sirohi belt in south-western Rajasthan shows the growth of rural settlements[95] and the growing complexity of rural society over time. The reclamation of waste lands, inducements such as the initial exemption from taxes in newly settled areas, geographical spread of rural settlements and the concern for man-made water resources characterized the countryside in Karnataka.[96] The formation of agricultural guilds, non-brāhmaṇa corporate bodies and the rise of substantial non-brāhmaṇa peasants as exemplified in such terms as *Ūrār, Uḍaiyān, Oḍeya, Eḷame, Nāṭṭār, Gāvuṇḍa*, etc.,[97] in south India indicate the process of agrarian change in the later half of the first and early centuries of the second millennium. Evidence for land improvement programmes and large-scale irrigational works in Kerala during the same period is not forthcoming, though small-scale reclamations by tenants are attested. Developments in Kerala charted a different course, with temples emerging as the nucleus of extensive agrarian corporations.[98] Regional variations in course of transformation can be seen in the adoption of different modes. While in Bengal, for example, large groups of brāhmaṇas, were settled to colonize a tribal pocket,[99] in Assam settlements stood largely isolated and seem to have experienced a gradual expansion in their agrarian space.[100] Although there were broad patterns of agreement, there were features of a specific nature as well; showing the individual path of development in the regions.

Rural settlement patterns, as so often today, were not the same all over. There were distinctions even between geographically proximous regions. For Bengal the possibility of a unity of homestead (*vāstu*) and farm land (*kṣetra*) has been negated,[101] whereas in the case of Assam a diametrically opposite picture has been worked out. In other words while the rural folk lived in compact groups in Bengal, in Assam the habitations were widely scattered.[102] Again, as against the clusters of villages in Bengal in the Gupta period, we have the picture of dispersed settlements in Assam at least up to the ninth-tenth centuries. Variations across regions can also be seen by comparing changes over time. Whereas Assam in the early centuries of the second millennium appears to be a loosely structured primarily agrarian society, Rajasthan during the same period, characterized as it was by hierarchies in rural settlements and pulsating mercantile activities, presents a very different picture.[103]

The increasing density of settlements and the greater utilization of agrarian space finds reflection in the increasingly complicated and detailed boundary delineations of donated land, especially from the ninth-tenth centuries onwards. It is borne out by epigraphic evidence from regions such as Tamil Nadu, Andhra, Orissa and Assam.[104] There is evidently a shift in the boundary marks from trees, stones, ant-hills and the conventional unspecified *catuḥsīmā* to adjoining settlements and plots owned by others.[105] Landmarks such as rivers, tanks, wells, orchards, marshy land, cattle track, cremation ground, temples and *maṭhas*[106] not only provide insights into rural settlement geography but also give us an idea about the constituent elements of the villages. It may be of some interest to note that early medieval villages mostly derived their names from local flora, mineral resources or even occupational associations.[107] Villages having Prakrit names and named after trees, autochthons and so on are generally considered to have had a greater antiquity and correspondingly those with Sanskritized names and having a migrant population, including brāhmaṇas, were supposedly later settlements.

Notwithstanding the continued extension of the peasant frontier, there were spaces outside the orbit of plough agriculture and organized state intrusion. Certain Pāṇḍya records, especially those from the dry zone mention pastoral groups and pastoral headmen who were entrusted with the security of the local villages.[108] The *vīragals*, a type of herostone, belonging to the Rāṣṭrakūṭa period, were situated on the periphery of their dominion and are mostly concerned with cattle raids. Such areas were inhospitable for agriculture and best suited to pastoral activities.[109] Instances such as these, suggesting the co-existence of pastoralism side by side with agriculture show the uneven nature of development within regions. The normally invisible pastoral sector cannot be discounted and it poses a challenge to historians. Subsistence activities need not be viewed in terms of cultivation alone. The 'autonomous spaces' as in the case of the Pāṇḍya territory or that of the Rāṣṭrakūṭas exhibit the continued importance of pastoralism. Large-scale lamp endowments and gift of cattle for their upkeep in Tamil Nadu and Andhra reveal that these livestock were maintained by shepherds and cowherds in the service of the temple.[110] All through Indian history pastoralists and cultivators have lived in a relationship of symbiosis. Similarly, tribals and forests too played an important role in the life of the peasants. The mention of forest route (*vanamārga*) in one of the inscriptions of the Guhilas of Kiṣkindha is an interesting piece of information revealing the possible tribal-non-tribal linkages.[111] The interaction between people of the valley and hills in Kāmārūpa for the exploitation of forest products in the form of wood, cane, bamboo, cotton, etc., has been pointed out.[112] And such cases can be multiplied.

The frequent references to different types of water resources in the context of land donations and burgeoning rural settlements drive home their importance for irrigational purposes and the role they played in transforming the countryside. In some cases administrative divisions were named after rivers.[113] In other regions the riverine character of settlements attracts attention. That the pattern of the geographical distribution of settlements was related to water resources and the agrarian potentiality of the landscape has been persuasively argued in a comparative study of the Sabarmati and Godavari basins during the Rāṣṭrakūṭa period.[114] Evidently there was a correspondence between the increase in man-made water resources and the spread of settlements. South India during the Pallava-Chola periods, Telengana under the Kākātiyas and the northern Deccan during the Rāṣṭrakūṭa times illustrate the point. In the Tamil country the villages had water management committees (*ēri-vāriyams*) to look after the construction and maintenance of tanks, reservoirs and canals. By the turn of the first millennium *araghaṭṭas* were in vogue in parts of Rajasthan. The *Harṣacarita,* in an earlier context, mentions irrigational devices such as the *Udghaṭaghaṭi* and *ghaṭiyantra,* which were perhaps in operation in the region around western Uttar Pradesh. A recent work shows how the significant landmarks in rural Bengal were rivers and ponds, in south-eastern Marwar were wells and in southern Karnataka were tanks.[115] These contrasts are then emphasized to bring out the distinctions among rural settlements of the varied regions. Irrigation was not the only area of concern. Early medieval texts like the *Kṛṣiparāśara* and *Kāśyapīyakṛṣisūkti,* among others, deal with the entire range of issues related to agriculture.

The early medieval centuries were characterized by immense

dynamism in terms of the proliferation of crops and cereals, improvement in agricultural techniques, awareness of plant preservation methods and expansion of irrigational facilities.[116] Rising agricultural productivity provided the basis for the emergence of *hāṭṭas*, local fairs and nodal points, which in turn lubricated the mobilization, exchange and distribution of resources. The turn of the millennium coincided with the emergence of supra-local polities. The economic and political changes appear to have been simultaneous, interrelated developments.

Rural settlements in early medieval India were the hub of all activity. Ironically however, rural settlement studies are in their infancy. This somewhat curious lapse may have much to do with the fact that the study of early medieval rural settlements so far was subsumed under general studies on economy and society. The importance of the study of rural settlement geography in the wider context of contemporary society and polity is beginning to be recognized. This, however, is not to suggest the total absence of earlier works in the area. A.S. Altekar's study[117] of the origin and growth of villages in western India is a pioneering work in the field, but is understandably circumscribed by the intellectual climate of his times. A.K. Choudhary's work on villages in north-eastern India is an important contribution[118] insofar as it for the first time focused on constituents of villages and the typology of rural settlements. *Grāma* was the usual term for villages. However, all rural settlements were not of the same kind and we come across a variety of terms such as *Pallī, Pāṭaka, Padra, Ghoṣa,* etc., denoting typological distinctions between rural settlements.[119] While *Pallī* normally meant a tribal village, *Pāṭaka* stood for a part of a village or a hamlet adjoining a larger village. Settlements of herdsmen were called *ghoṣas.* Works of a similar, though not identical, genre are available for the northern Deccan and central India under the Vākāṭakas.[120] Linguistic analyses of place-names and suffixes mentioned in the charters have led to interesting derivations in terms of hierarchy of settlements, size variations and their functional associations. Such analyses are indubitably useful, but it is good to remember that inferences based on place-names are tricky exercises and accepting them on their face value has its pitfalls.[121]

Place-names normally outlive the historical context of their origin. Owing to the convergence of several factors, settlements could change and assume different dimensions. Sarkara-*padraka* of the Sarabhapurīya records came to be known as Sarkara-*pāṭaka* by the time of the Pāṇḍuvaṁśis. Similarly, again in Dakṣiṇa Kośala we come across the transformation of Khala-*padraka* into Khala-*vaṭika* between the sixth-seventh and fifteenth centuries.[122] However the persistence of old names, despite changes in the character of settlements, in many cases tends to complicate matters. Settlements were not static and the typological distinctions between categories were not unchangeable. The history of Kalikaṭṭi, a village in south Karnataka during the Hoyśāḷa period, over a hundred years beautifully sums up the inherent possibilities of change in rural settlements in the early medieval set-up.[123] Although it was initially administered by a series of *sāmantas*, at a certain stage it came to be associated with groups linked to the royal court and finally it was converted into an *agrahāra.*

We are told that in Lalgudi taluk, in Tamil Nadu, shifts in the site of settlement broadly within the same geographical area have been noticed. For example, many Pallava settlements stood at a distance from early historic sites. Such exercises point to the changes in landscape profile and suggest the usefulness of the study of settlement complexes[124] as against individual sites in an area, for wider correlations. The formation of *taniyūrs*[125] with major *brahmadēya* and temple settlements as its nucleus and the acquisition of several hamlets (*Piḍāgais*) or revenue villages under its jurisdiction or the coming together of numerous hamlets to form a big village in the Chola period suggest the existence of settlement clusters rather than dispersed habitations. They also illustrate the alterations in agrarian space and the introduction of a hierarchy among settlements. There are instances of separation of hamlets from villages as well as their addition to new ones, indicating the emergence of new realignments. During Rājarāja II's time nine hamlets were brought together to constitute a big village.[126] Without getting into details it may be surmised that both the processes of fusion and bifurcation of rural landscape were in operation.

Rural settlement studies relate to the relationship of the habitation area to other spatial features of a settlement and the changing profile of segments of space over time. Such aspects have received detailed treatment in the work of Chattopadhyaya, which marks a departure from the current historiography on many counts.[127] The perception of rural society as isolates has been questioned and it has been situated in the context of the contemporary processes of change. The evolution and the making of hierarchies in rural settlements with some of them emerging as nodal points owing to political intervention from the top or compulsions of mobilization and circulation of resources have been revealed.[128] The strategic geographical location or favourable socio-economic make-up of settlements too may have contributed to the formation of hierarchies. Changes such as these had a bearing on the relations between settlements.

Generally a distinction is made between brahmanic and non-brahmanic villages and it is posited that they differed from each other both at the level of administration and social organization. While *sabhā* represented the brahmanic settlement, the *ūr* was the corporate body of an ordinary village in south India.[129] These distinctions have their own merit and are helpful insofar as they exhibit differentiation between rural settlements, but as some recent studies show one has to go beyond it and look for the social composition in the habitations so as to have an idea of the growing complexity of social organization in the villages and their immense variety.[130] Brāhmaṇas may have been the dominant category in some whereas in others a section of non-brāhmaṇas may have been important and yet in some other instances a wide social cross-section, including brāhmaṇas, may have constituted the substantial landowning group. The stage and scale of the introduction of brāhmaṇas in a settlement would have had much to do with its social organization. The donation of a few plots in a settled village would have made no substantial difference to its organizational structure except for extending the network of linkages of the village.[131] Brahmanic settlements and temple land in most regions formed only a part of the totality, but the ratio between such donated areas and tax-paying ordinary villages remains to be worked out for the different regions. A study on south-western Rajasthan shows that only one out of the ten villages discussed was an *agrahāra* with full exemptions.[132] Similarly, it is tentatively suggested that three-fourths of the settlements in the Chola country were non-brahmanic villages.[133] The brahmanic settlements have been the focus of investigations for a long time now[134] and the non-brahmanic rural settlements and their spatial and chronological distribution have to be part of any future agenda on early medieval agrarian history.

II

The question of landownership, especially ownership of agricultural land, has engaged the attention of scholars since the early part of the nineteenth century. The complexity of evidence on land rights in literature and inscriptions, not to speak of variations in time and space, have contributed to the lack of clear perception. The problem was compounded earlier by the British administrative compulsions[135] and subsequently by ideological considerations. In the search for overall neat patterns the evidence and the complexity of the problem have been somewhat eclipsed. There are broadly three positions depending on their point of emphasis. The first vests ownership in the peasant proprietors,[136] the second perceives that no private individual could hold land as a matter of absolute right or exclusive ownership because the state/sovereign was the ultimate owner with superior rights[137] and the third focuses on common or joint ownership,[138] which seemingly preserved the corporate atmosphere in the villages. Instead of getting bogged down with questions like whether community or individual ownership was the basic element in early India, it may be useful to see how it functioned.

A few points of clarification are required to be made here. Notwithstanding the above mentioned general positions that emerge from modern writings, it needs to be mentioned that early Indian literature such as the *Arthaśāstra* and Dharmaśāstras as well as inscriptions furnish evidence for the simultaneous prevalence of multiple forms of ownership. However, discussions on land ownership usually revolve around royal ownership and peasant proprietary rights. Many crucial areas such as the problem of communal ownership rights and property rights in non-landgrant areas remain hazy. On the basis of the evidence of landgrant charters and the exemptions and privileges granted to the donees through these records a multiplicity of hierarchically graded rights over land has been posited for the early medieval centuries.[139] Substantive landgrants are said to have cut into and destroyed community rights.[140] In other words they transformed communal property into feudal property. It had a bearing on the means and process of production, leading to the subjection of the peasantry. This standard explanation of early medieval land relations largely subsumes other possibilities. However, the search for these possibilities or the coexistence of multiple complex forms of proprietary rights has just begun.

Not before the emergence of peasant society in the middle Ganga plains in the mid-first millennium BC do we have any indication of private ownership over land.[141] Rights of occupation over generations may have developed into ownership rights to demarcated space, leading to the emergence of family/individual holdings. The *gahapati* in the Buddhist texts emerges as a well-to-do owner of cultivable land as distinguished from the *kassaka,* who was a cultivator.[142] The *gahapatis,* however, were an inclusive, even internally differentiated, category and we come across brāhmaṇa *gahapatis* too who owned and supervised cultivation of their substantial holdings. They constituted the dominant peasantry in the monarchical states, as against the subsistence farmers, and used the labour of hired workers and slaves. In the *gaṇasaṅghas,* on the other hand, land was held individually and collectively by the kṣatriyas.[143] The social distribution of landed property was fairly widespread and not merely concentrated in the hands of the brāhmaṇa landlords as some earlier historians believed.[144] The picture of landholdings that emerges from the *Arthaśāstra* broadly confirms the pre-Mauryan situation.[145] Apart from the king's personal lands and the state farms there were private lands held by big landholders (*gṛhapati* or *gahapati*) and owner cultivators (*kuṭumbins*). Sharecroppers, tenants, wage-earners and slaves worked on state farms and private holdings. Restrictions on the sale of private lands point to the right of preferential purchase by family members, relatives and members of the community as well as the fact that proprietary rights in land were tied to membership in the village community.[146]

The post-Mauryan period was marked by the rise and spread of big landholders, medium farmers and owner-cultivators even outside the orbit of the Ganga valley. The *Gāthā-saptaśatī* mentions *gahāvai,* the Prakrit form of *gṛhapati,* in numerous verses[147] and in one instance he is also referred to as *halika* (ploughman). The earlier trends continued into the early centuries of the Christian era in north India. A passage in the *Milinda-pañha*[148] amply illustrates the agrarian relationships while bringing out the distinction between the men of substance on the one hand and the ordinary villagers, hired workers, servants and slaves on the other in the village set-up. The growth of a class of landed aristocrats is best manifested in the high profile village headmen during this period.[149]

Rural society had already acquired a measure of complexity in terms of the composition of the landholders in the Gupta period. In Bengal the *kuṭumbins* and *mahattaras* along with the brāhmaṇas could be distinguished from other villagers as significant propertied categories. In course of time other well-off non-brāhmaṇa dominant sections such as the *mahāmahattara* and *mahāpradhāna* emerged, making the structure of rural society quite complex. The picture to some extent is repeated in Kathiawar during the sixth-seventh centuries. *Mahattaras* and *kuṭumbins* as independent well-to-do peasants co-existed with *brahmadēya* owners in many villages.[150] Some of the small brāhmaṇa donees, in the absence of tenants, were themselves peasant cultivators.[151] Such categories then economically would have had much in common with the *kuṭumbins* than the *mahattaras*. However, there are instances of larger donations involving the transfer of the earlier inhabitants of the granted land as well. We do not know how and to what extent such privileged islands in the villages would have affected the structure of the peasant communities. Nevertheless, it is discernible that though the brāhmaṇas were a part of the rural gentry they were not a homogeneous category enjoying similar rights.

The non-brāhmaṇa peasantry evolved with the passage of time, especially in the post-tenth century. N. Karashima has significantly suggested that in the peasant villages (*ūr*), in Tamil Nadu, in the early centuries of the second millennium communal property gave way to private holdings.[152] His findings have been reinforced by Y. Subbarayalu's contributions.[153] The rise of men of substance in non-*brahmadēya* settlements is gleaned from the use of titles such as *kilān* or *uḍaiyān*, connoting a sense of ownership. A big landholder owned about ten *vēli* or 65 acres of land while a small owner held about two *vēli* or thirteen acres.[154] It may be of interest to note that 'an average brāhmaṇa donee was assigned a share of one or two *vēli* of land only'.[155] The rise of the *veḷḷāḷas* in Tamil Nadu has its parallel in the emergence of the *gāvuṇḍas* and *eḷame* in Karnataka.[156] Owing to their ownership of land, high caste position and other privileges as members of the non-brāhmaṇa corporate body they acquired the status of notables in society. Such landed magnates were identified and incorporated into the state apparatus.[157] Categories such as these came to enjoy both class and state powers. The history of the evolution of the non-brāhmaṇa dominant peasantry in non-landgrant areas adds new dimensions to our understanding of landownership as well as the structure of rural society in early medieval times. However, it needs to be recognized that these groups were a part of a larger hierarchically structured society. These developments point to the composite character of the landed aristocracy and take us away from the notion of total brahmanic dominance of the agrarian system.

Epigraphic evidence for the sale and purchase of land date to the time of Śaka Usavadata (second century AD), who for purposes of donation bought a field from a brāhmaṇa who had inherited it from his father.[158] There are some Gupta and post-Gupta land sale transactions as well from north India, but they are not too many. The sale of land many a time was wrapped in formalities and euphemistically presented as a gift.[159] This among other factors such as the pressure on land and the willingness or ability to alienate it may account for the scarcity of such records in north India. In the south Chola inscriptions, however, provide evidence for 276 sale transactions relating to agricultural land and in a few cases to house-sites as well.[160] Such material unambiguously demonstrate private property rights in land. Brāhmaṇas, non-brāhmaṇas, merchants[161] and even royalty was involved in these transactions. The queens and in one instance the king himself purchased land but they do not appear as sellers. Brāhmaṇa villages were stratified and characterized by private ownership, but the emergence of rich *Veḷḷāḷa* peasants and the beginnings of stratification in the non-brāhmaṇa settlements perhaps had much to do with these developments in the twelfth and thirteenth centuries. The rights of 'use, mortgage, resale and gift' were acquired with the land and the buyer could do whatever he pleased with such property.[162] In many cases temples were the ultimate beneficiaries of such transactions and they emerged as landed magnates.[163] Given the nature of the sources where the purpose was to record charities it is not surprising that the instances of secular transactions are not many.

Evidently the rise of feudal property and the extraction of labour rent (*viṣṭi*) were interrelated phenomena. Epigraphic evidence for forced labour (*viṣṭi*) comes from western, central and south India[164] in the second half of the first millennium. What is striking, however, is that after about AD1000 the practice seems to have waned and fallen into disuse. Inscriptions of the Paramāras, Chāḷukyas, Chāhamānas, Gāhaḍavālas and Chandellas, though they mention myriad revenue terms, do not refer to forced labour.[165] An almost analogous picture has been obtained for south India under the Cholas. In the post-tenth century the incidence of labour rent (*veṭṭi*) went on decreasing while the produce rent (*kaḍamai*) kept on increasing.[166] Rising productivity, formation of agrarian regions, evolution of the non-brāhmaṇa peasantry and a more complex stratified society were perhaps not entirely unrelated to rising taxes and the gradual demise of forced labour. The consolidation of caste society was inextricably related to the emergence of a permanent stock of landless agricultural labour, usually within the fold of the untouchables.[167]

Land tenures varied across regions. In Assam private holdings and communal property coexisted. The brāhmaṇas were the dominant landholding categories but the diverse peasantry also held land.[168] The temple owned the land in Kerala and a bulk of it was leased out to the Nayars, who occupied the middle position in the land-power pyramid as tenants of the temple.[169] In addition there were service tenures to servants of the temple who received occupation rights. In Rajasthan land was distributed as assignments among royal kinsmen in the clan monarchies which arose with the decline of the Gurjara-Pratīhāra kingdom.[170] Such distribution was perhaps crucial to the process of the evolution of Rajput polities. Chattopadhyaya has, however, recently argued that these need not be seen as hereditary assignments because epigraphic evidence from Rajasthan and south Karnataka reveal how frequently they changed hands.[171] The range of possibilities have been elaborated in a different way by G.R. Kuppuswamy's study of the Hoyśāḷa and other records.[172] He not only shows the continued persistence of common ownership but also delineates three subtypes within it. The consent of family members and relatives was necessary in matters of sale. References to coparcenary rights and the rights of women and female children, even female servants, in matters of succession and inheritance add to our understanding of property rights.

Many ruling lineages, as would be clear from the preceding discussion, emerged from a local base during the Gupta and post-Gupta periods. It is obvious that in such cases their rights evolved with the passage of time, in course of the transition from pre-state to state societies in the relevant localities/sub-regions, and did not necessarily devolve from an epicentre. Thus the phased evolution of proprietary rights in undeveloped areas together with gradual agrarian expansion and the coming of peasant society cannot be overlooked. The overt correlation between landgrants and local state formation comes out clearly in the peripheral areas.[173] Again, unvarying land systems cannot be presupposed within landgrant areas. Backward tracts naturally distinguished themselves from settled areas and in the case of the former, as H. Kulke[174] aptly posits, it needs to be demonstrated that the donor had been exercising the rights which he transferred to the donee. It is quite likely that much of the phraseology in such grants was conventional and repetitive whereas actually the royal donor may have been asserting his rights for the first time over an area through the very act of donation. Peasants of a certain village owning land in other settlements[175] either through donation, inheritance or purchase further complicate the scenario. Instances of scattered grants[176] allude to similar problems of land relations. In such cases the owner-cultivator in one village happened to be a lord, howsoever modest, vis a vis his tenant in another.

Admittedly landgrants generated differential access to power as well as resources and complex relations of domination and subordination in donated areas by affecting the socio-economic competence of the various strata of local inhabitants. However, their impact in terms of immediate consequences certainly varied over areas depending on whether the donation was in a settled area with a long history of agriculture or in a virgin tract or tribal frontier. Land relations were more nuanced than is generally assumed and it is not entirely unproblematic to reduce them to a standard argument. The manifestation of feudal property in early medieval times did not exhaust other possibilities.[177] The whole question of landownership, its immense varieties, changing forms and related issues have significant implications for the socio-political dimensions of 'Indian feudalism' as well as the notion of the 'village community'.

III

The concept of the 'Indian village community' with its well known postulates of common ownership of land, political autonomy, self-sufficiency, both in terms of economy as well as community structure; and flowing from these social homogeneity and an unchanging character of the rural society was born in colonial administrative literature, which tried to simplify the Indian reality to serve its own ends.[178] Marx's often quoted writings on the Indian village within the paradigm of the Asiatic Mode of Production strengthened the suggestion that the village was autarkic, isolated and stagnant. However, it cannot be overlooked that Marx mostly used the British writings and earlier travellers' accounts[179] which were flawed on account of their neglect of crucial aspects like differentiation and domination within the villages and the complex web of conflictual as well as complementary external linkages. The notion of the 'village community', an imaginative construct, since its inception has been used in a variety of senses, depending on the compulsions of its users.[180] Nationalist historians in their enthusiasm for equality and democracy and opposition to colonial rule projected these ideas back into the past, inventing democratic government in the 'village republics' in the process.[181] Such constructions focusing on the political dimension of the community perhaps unwittingly reinforced the image of idyllic, isolatory rural India. Within this framework the writings on south India in particular emphasized the *sabhā*, the corporate body of the brāhmaṇas, largely to the exclusion of non-brahmanic settlements and corporate bodies such as the *ūr* and *nāḍu*.[182] Not surprisingly therefore the envisaged reality, with its focus on co-operation and harmony, corresponded to the brahmanical perception of it and failed to accommodate conflict and change.

The distortions associated with the facile notion of village community have been recognized and addressed by historians within and outside the dominant historiography. Marxist historians have extrapolated significant changes through the stages in early Indian history, including the village and rural life, and exposed the inadequacies of the Asiatic Mode of Production. Interestingly, however, closed, self-sufficient rural units have been resurrected in the context of the early medieval situation.[183] Instead of debating the validity of the formulation at this juncture it may be pointed out that it distinguishes itself from earlier writings at least on two counts: first by suggesting that such entities emerged at a certain stage owing to a specific configuration of historical forces and secondly by taking cognizance of differentiation and exploitative power relations in rural society.

The persistence of certain stereotypes about villages in antiquity may be ostensibly related to the dearth of village studies. The study of rural settlements, their social composition and structure, independent of wider generalized studies on agrarian history, are in their nascency. Bongard-Levin's contribution on the changing structure of village communities and their spatial and political linkages in the second half of the first millennium BC and early centuries of the Christian era is perhaps just about all we have in this genre of writing[184] for the early historical period. The early medieval scene is slightly better illuminated. Notwithstanding the paucity of such works, the available literature presents a different image of village society and community life in early India.

The communal ownership of land as the principal form of landholding has been consistently disproved, following Baden-Powell, by many historians. Our knowledge of the inner structure of communities is not sufficient, but as recent researches show they were far from being undifferentiated. We have already noticed the emergence of dominant groups in rural society at different stages.[185] Without going into details it may be pointed out that landownership and caste status formed an organic whole, with the lower castes being the landless; ranging from tenants to agricultural labourers.[186] Even early medieval literary sources attest the growing stratification,[187] with the village elders/landholders constituting the dominant group and servants and hired workers (*bhṛtyah, dāsa*) the servile category. The *gṛhapati* and *kuṭumbin* gradually suffered degradation and eclipse. Landlessness as a structural element can be noticed in rural India from the middle of the first millennium BC onwards. What emerges is the different levels of interaction between social groups with differential access to resources. Social mobility and stratification bring out the limitations of the 'village community' in the sense of a static, cohesive community structure.

Villagers may have continued to share a common experience in terms of their homogeneous approach to agriculture and participation in communal customs and festivals centring around the annual agricultural cycle,[188] but that is, as they say, another story.

Within the dominant historiography rural society in the post-Gupta period, it is envisaged, was largely self-sufficient, localised and closed. We do not know how self-sufficiency worked in early medieval times in north India. Nevertheless on the basis of inscriptional evidence it has been shown by Karashima that every village in the far south did not have all the necessary caste/ occupational groups to ensure self-sufficiency and that social interdependence functioned beyond the boundaries of a settlement, encompassing wider areas during the Chola period.[189] Cremation grounds and temples were not common to all settlements and it is posited that inter-village cooperation imposed itself not only for fulfilling everyday requirements but also for funeral, ritual and festive observances.

Notions of village self-sufficiency and egalitarianism get further ruptured when examined on the touchstone of caste. Marriages were territorially exogamous and thus they helped to establish a wider network of linkages. Burton Stein while demonstrating that self-sufficiency of the village was a myth in historical terms has gone on to substitute it by another kind of autarky related to the *nāḍu*.[190] The isolability of the *nāḍu* in south India has been refuted on such considerations as marriages across *nāḍus*, among others.[191] Intra-caste relations, it is said, are inter-village relations, while intra-village relations are inter-caste relations.[192]

Villages by no means were uniform. They varied from region to region and time to time as also in terms of their size, land relations, social composition, placement in the geographical profile and the hierarchy of settlements. It is time the focus shifted from the 'village community' to its plural form, i.e. 'Indian villages' or 'village communities' so as to accommodate the immense varieties. Internal changes in villages, socially and spatially, have been continuous historical processes. *Pallīs* (hamlets) with the passage of time could become *grāmas*. Place-names such as Kuraṭapallikāgrāma and Cūṭapallikāgrāma in the Bangarh record of Mahīpāla (eleventh century) help us to map such transformation.[193] The rise of *hāṭṭas* and formation of nodes in the rural landscape, especially from about the tenth century while suggesting similar changes also point to inter-village networks.[194] It is beginning to be realized that the situation in the villages in terms of their internal differentiation and external linkages was far more complex and dynamic than has been generally recognized. The interactional orbit of the villages went beyond their individual boundaries and in the process they became a part of larger entities, existing through a network of socio-cultural, economic and political linkages[195] that held early medieval society together.

IV

Within the orientalist and nationalist discourses early Indian society was studied not on its own terms but as a part of larger designs, i.e. to provide justification for social reforms, a make-believe utopia to momentarily get away from the emotionally destabilising aftermath of the industrial revolution or to prove the great historico-cultural heritage of India by creating an ideal type, bereft of disharmony and asymmetrical relations, so as to inspire pride in one's civilization and buttress the cause of the national movement.[196] Caste, like the 'village community', was identified as a significant constitutive element of the Indian civilization and naturally received considerable attention in the early British writings. However, the racist ideas and idealist conceptions resulted in ahistorical constructions.[197] The failure of the early writings to take cognizance of elements of change and continuity through stages and their refusal to address the seamy and unpleasant aspects such as the problem of the lower orders, among other limitations,[198] largely led to the creation of elite centred narratives sans their historical moorings. These approaches were circumscribed by their inability or refusal to discuss society at a given point of time in terms of its organization as a whole and to relate it to wider historical processes.

The study of society, especially rural society, in all its interrelatedness began with the writings of D.D. Kosambi and R.S. Sharma from about the mid-50s, though the beginnings of Marxist historiography in the area can be dated to the early 40s.[199] Rural society has come to be perceived in terms of a bipolar constellation. The early historical social formation was by and large characterized by the exploitation of the Vaiśyas and Śūdras by the Brāhmaṇas and Kṣatriyas, who were the recipients of gifts and taxes.[200] The process was accentuated in the early medieval period 'marked by the formation of two major classes related to the prevailing mode of production: the landed intermediaries, including a hierarchy of ruling landed aristocracy, and a large body of peasantry which was mostly dependent and impoverished'.[201] The iniquitous distribution of the produce or land, caste stratifications and customary and ritual practices, it is said, constituted the cosmos within which most peasants lived, producing wealth for landowners and subsistence for themselves. Such images of iniquity of rural society, manifested in the steady growth of landed intermediaries and the increasing subjection and immobility of the peasantry,[202] in fact, represent the misery and drudgery of the substantial majority. These structural arrangements within the agrarian system, the inherent contradictions and resultant peasant protests have attracted the historians' notice in recent times.[203] The overall structural contours and exploitative character of the social formations being the central concerns in this perception, stratification and differentiation within the dominant and subject strata have remained largely peripheral; if not entirely untouched.

The problem of internal differentiation within the peasantry and the emergence of well-to-do categories, placed differentially in the hierarchical social structure are beginning to get the necessary attention. Chattopadhyaya vividly portrays differentiation in rural society in early medieval Bengal, Rajasthan and south Karnataka.[204] In Orissa, as in Bengal, we do come across well-to-do peasant groups such as the *mahattaras, pradhānas* and *mahāmahattaras* in the post-Gupta period.[205] The *Vel̤l̤āl̤as* and *gāvuṇḍas* in south India were not undifferentiated categories and included both the rich and medium peasants.[206] References to *prabhu-gāvuṇḍas* and *prajā-gāvuṇḍas* in inscriptional records amply bear it out. The presence of the *okkalu*, well-off tenant-cultivators,[207] in Karnataka further adds to the complexity of rural society. The stratification of rural society in north India, particularly in the post-tenth century, including the evolution of an intensely differentiated peasantry and hierarchised menial categories, with the sharecroppers and village artisans in between, is alluded to in the lexiconised Sanskrit terms for peasants and the agricultural workforce.[208] Even in the context of early historical society the composition of the peasantry was much more varied than has normally been assumed.[209] Not only were the wealthy and the very poor juxtaposed in Buddhist literature but it also provides evidence for the *gahapatis*, who were an inclusive category in terms of their *varṇa* affiliation. However, they were internally differentiated as there were some who worked the land themselves and there were others who employed extra-familial labour.[210] Similarly, Saṅgam literature makes a distinction between those who were ploughmen and others who engaged cultivators in early Tamil̤akaṁ.[211] Among the *karṣakas* there were owner-cultivators and landless hired labourers. The history of the *kuṭumbin* or *kuṭumbika* elaborates the story of differentiation within the peasantry. 'During the period from the fourth to the sixth centuries AD, the *kuṭumbin* emerged as a rural landed interest-group which could not raise itself above the stage of middle peasant (who mainly uses family labour).'[212]

The contempt for manual work, gender differentiation and patriarchal domination made their appearance in the early historic period itself.[213] They were further refined in the context of the specific configuration of historical forces in the early medieval centuries. The expansion of agrarian society and consolidation of caste differences were closely connected with women's subordination, for the purity of caste and lineage was contingent on the control of women's sexuality.[214]

The emergence of the śūdras from diverse foundations and their hierarchical placement in the caste structure exemplifies an important aspect of the making of early Indian society. Peasantization of the tribes has been a continuous process. The assimilation of autochthonous communities at various levels of socio-cultural attainment allowed scope for their hierarchical assignment with reference to the dominant social structure.[215] The rise of the Jats from an ostracized community to peasant castes within the Śūdra fold[216] illustrates the process of change. The origin of the Rajputs and other ruling lineages in the general context of regional agrarian transformation represents the same historical processes.[217] Similarly, the emergence of the kāyasthas, including those associated with the countryside as village functionaries,[218] alludes to the growing stratification within and between social groups. Rural society encompassed diverse groups ranging from the rulers through the grades of *sāmantas* to numerous region-specific peasant castes,[219] including the untouchables.

It is difficult to perceive rural society in terms of the conventional Dharmaśāstra orders. The four-tiered *varṇa* order is, admittedly, a theoretical view of society from the top of the hierarchy, but the way society functioned at the grassroots level was more varied and, in fact, appears to have been more differentiated. The emergence of socio-economic categories such as the *gahapatis* and *dāsas* and *karmakaras* in early historic times and many more strata subsequently reflect on the inadequacies of *varṇa* centred analyses.

Ritual status did not necessarily always subsume worldly competence and it led to the problem of reconciling the two.[220] It was ostensibly acute in the case of the upwardly mobile who sought recognition and confirmation of their assumed and accrued status. The ingenious theory of *varṇasaṁkara*[221] provided the ideological rationale for the incorporation of the swelling ranks of the peasantry of diverse origins within the framework of the Śūdra fold. However, the assertion of their formal superiority by the dominant peasant castes is noticed, especially in south India where they went on to acquire a *sat-śūdra* status.

Caste formation and the hierarchization of regional societies may be best understood with reference to other contemporary processes of change such as the emergence of agrarian regions and the evolution of state societies. To illustrate, while state formation was dependent on agrarian expansion and the spread of rural settlements, the growth of state societies had a bearing on the growing complexity of village communities. In the course of such developments undifferentiated communities could witness the rise of a stratum of ruling elite and consequently experience fission.[222] Differentiation and relations of domination and subordination thus emanated from diverse sources.

Sculptural art, religious ideas, mythologies and the organizational principles of monastic establishments, including tantricism, articulate inequality and hierarchy and thus seem to explicate the social world and cultural ethos of the early medieval times.[223] Stein's is perhaps the lone dissenting voice in contemporary historiography which extrapolates the fanciful theory of a brāhmaṇa-peasant alliance and envisages a world of 'peasants without lords'[224] in the face of incontrovertible evidence to the contrary. The pervasive influence of *dharma, karma* and *bhakti* ideology permeated rural society together with the spread of *śāstric-purāṇic* ideas, mediated through the institutionalised network of *tīrthas, maṭhas* and temples. These ideas and institutions organized diversity and provided validation to the asymmetrically structured hierarchical society.[225]

NOTES

1. For a historiographical survey of early Indian economic history see R.S. Sharma and D.N. Jha, 'The Economic History of India up to AD 1200: Trends and Prospects', *Journal of the Economic and Social History*

of the Orient (hereafter *JESHO*), vol. XVII, pt. 1, 1974, pp. 48-80.

For an updated statement see D.N. Jha, 'Trends in Early Indian Historiography', in *Economy and Society in Early India—Issues and Paradigms*, New Delhi, 1993, pp. 1-31.

2. D.D. Kosambi, *An Introduction to the Study of Indian History*, Bombay, 1956, idem, *The Culture and Civilization of Ancient India in Historical Outline*, London, 1965; also see A.J. Syed (ed.), *D.D. Kosambi on History and Society: Problems of Interpretation*, Bombay, 1985. Among the early works of R.S. Sharma one may mention *Sudras in Ancient India*, Delhi, 1958; *Aspects of Political Ideas and Institutions in Ancient India*, Delhi, 1959; *Light on Early Indian Society and Economy*, Bombay, 1966; *Indian Feudalism c. AD 300-1200*, Calcutta, 1965; and *Social Changes in Early Medieval India (circa AD 500-1200)*, Delhi, 1969.
3. N.C. Bandyopadhyaya, *Economic Life and Progress in Ancient India*, Allahabad, 1980 (rpt); K.M. Gupta, *The Land System in South India between AD 800-AD 1200*, Lahore, 1933; Pran Nath, *A Study in the Economic Condition of Ancient India*, Allahabad, 1980 (rpt); U.N. Ghoshal, *Contributions to the History of the Hindu Revenue System*, Calcutta, 1929; idem, *The Agrarian System in Ancient India*, Calcutta, 1930; A.N. Bose, *Social and Rural Economy of Northern India c. 600 BC-AD 200*, 2 vols, Calcutta, 1942-5.
4. For a discussion see Ronald Inden, *Imagining India*, Oxford, 1990, particularly chs. 2 and 4.
5. For an explanation of the changing British perceptions see Bernard S. Cohn, 'African Models and Indian Histories', in Richard G. Fox (ed.), *Realm and Region in Traditional India*, New Delhi, 1977, pp. 90-113.
6. A good discussion of the manipulation of even early European history to suit the imperial designs is available in Martin Bernal, 'The Image of Ancient Greece as a tool for Colonialism and European Hegemony', in George C. Bond and Angela Gilliam (eds.), *Social Construction of the Past: Representation as Power*, London, 1994.
7. Op. cit.
8. Op. cit.
9. K.A.N. Sastri, *Studies in Chola History and Administration*, Madras, 1932; idem; *The Cōḷas*, (2nd edn), Madras, 1955; A. Appadorai, *Economic Conditions in Southern India (AD 1000-1500)*, 2 vols, Madras, 1936.
10. Morris D. Morris and Burton Stein, 'The Economic History of India: A Bibliographic Essay', *Journal of Economic History*, vol. xxi, 1961, p. 185.
11. The problem was recognized by the middle of the 1970s. See, for example, Romila Thapar, 'The Scope and Significance of Regional History', Presidential Address to the Punjab History Conference, Patiala, 1976, reprinted in *Ancient Indian Social History—Some Interpretations*, (rpt), Delhi, 1987, especially pp. 362-4.
12. In fact, sub-phases have been worked out in the early historical context.

See Sharma, *Aspects of Political Ideas and Institutions in Ancient India* (3rd revd and enld edn), Delhi, 1991, chs XXII and XXIII, and also his 'Stages in Ancient Indian Economy', in *Light on . . .* op. cit., pp. 52-89.

To make a general statement the post-Gupta centuries have, however, been usually perceived as one undifferentiated entity.

13. See, for example, Devangana Desai, 'Social Dimensions of Art in Early India', Presidential Address, Ancient India Section, Gorakhpur Session, *Proceedings of the Indian History Congress* (hereafter *PIHC*), 1989, pp. 21-56.
14. R.S. Sharma, *Indian Feudalism* (2nd edn.), Delhi, 1980, ch. VI, pp. 170-212.
15. R.N. Nandi, 'Growth of Rural Economy in Early Feudal India', Presidential Address, Ancient India Section, Annamalainagar Session, *PIHC*, 1984, especially pp. 45-71.
16. See Sharma, *Indian Feudalism*, op. cit., pp. 53-6; idem, *Urban Decay in India (c. 300–c. 1000)*, New Delhi, 1987, particularly chs. 8 and 9 and also his 'The Kali Age: A Period of Social Crisis', in S.N. Mukherjee (ed.), *India: History and Thought, Essays in Honour of A.L. Basham*, Calcutta, 1982, pp. 186-203. See also B.N.S. Yadava, 'The Accounts of the Kali Age and the Social Transition from Antiquity to the Middle Ages', *The Indian Historical Review* (hereafter *IHR*), vol. V, nos 1-2, pp. 31-63.
17. The alternative framework was provided in the early 80s. See H. Kulke, 'Fragmentation and Segmentation versus Integration: Reflections on the Concept of Indian Feudalism and the Segmentary State in Indian History', *Studies in History*, vol. IV, no. 2, 1982, pp. 237-63 and B.D. Chattopadhyaya, 'Political Processes and the Structure of Polity in Early Medieval India: Problems of Perspective', Presidential Address, Ancient India Section, Burdwan Session, *PIHC*, 1983, pp. 25-63.

    A more comprehensive discussion of this perspective is available in Chattopadhyaya's *The Making of Early Medieval India*, Delhi, 1994, 'Introduction'.
18. Brendan O'Leary, *The Asiatic Mode of Production: Oriental Despotism, Historical Materialism and Indian History*, Oxford, 1989, p. 284, fn. 33.
19. For a survey of the problem see ibid., pp. 319-22; G.M. Bongard-Levin, 'Some Problems of the Social Structure of Ancient India', in Bongard-Levin's *A Complex Study of Ancient India—A Multi-Disciplinary Approach*, Delhi, 1986, particularly pp. 115-27. See also Devraj Chanana, *Slavery in Ancient India*, Delhi, 1960.
20. For some good account of the picture as presented in the early Buddhist canonical literature and the Jātakas see N. Wagle, *Society at the Time of the Buddha*, Bombay, 1966; and Uma Chakravarti, *The Social Dimensions of Early Buddhism*, Delhi, 1987.

21. See B.D. Chattopadhyaya, *The Making of Early Medieval India*, Delhi, 1994, especially the 'Introduction'.
22. See, for example, Kosambi, *An Introduction* ..., op. cit., pp. 11, 14-15. Also see his 'The Basis of Ancient Indian History', in A.J. Syed (ed.), *Kosambi on History and Society* ..., op. cit., pp. 27-63.
23. Such linkages date back to the time of the peninsular Indian neolithic-chalcolithic cultures and the Harappan civilization. For example see B.P. Sahu, *From Hunters to Breeders (Faunal Background of Early India)*, Delhi, 1988, pp. 164-5, 227-8.
24. See *The Making* ..., op. cit., 'Introduction'.
25. See H. Kulke, 'Fragmentation and Segmentation ...' op. cit., particularly p. 245 onwards; B.D. Chattopadhyaya, 'Historiography, History and Religious Centres: Early Medieval North India, *circa* AD 700-1200', in Vishakha N. Desai *et al.*, (eds.), *Gods, Guardians and Lovers: North Indian Temple Sculptures, c. 700-1200*, Ahmedabad, 1993, especially pp. 37-8 and also his 'State and Economy in North India: Fourth century to Twelfth century', in Romila Thapar (ed.), *Recent Perspectives of Early Indian History*, Bombay, 1995, particularly pp. 328-37.
26. For a recent perspective on the nature and structure of the Mauryan state see Romila Thapar, *The Mauryas Revisited*, New Delhi, 1987, pp. 1-31. See also her 'The State as Empire', in H.J.M. Claessen and Peter Skalnik (eds.), *The Study of the State*, The Hague, 1981, pp. 409-26.
27. Even a cursory comparison of the traditional works of the nationalist historians with those of the 'Indian feudalism' school clearly demonstrates the shift in the terrain of discussion. Supra, n. 1.
28. See, for example, Makkhan Lal, *Settlement History and Rise of Civilization in Ganga-Yamuna Doab*, Delhi, 1984; and N. Karashima, Y. Subbarayalu and Toru Matsui, *A Concordance of Names in the Chola Inscriptions*, 3 vols., Madurai, 1978.
29. Not only are their dates disputed but the nature of the texts are also a moot point. It is doubtful whether the *Arthaśāstra* reflects the reality of the Mauryan period. The text that has reached us is said to have been written at the beginning of the Christian era. Similarly, a section of the *Manusmriti* has been dated to the seventh century. See T.R. Trautmann, *Kauṭilya and the Arthaśāstra: A Statistical Investigation into the Authorship and Evolution of the Text*, Leiden, 1971; Bongard-Levin, *A Complex Study of Ancient India* ..., op. cit., pp. 152-5, and R.S. Sharma, *Śūdras in Ancient India*, revd. edn., Delhi, 1980, Appendix I.
30. Bongard-Levin, *A Complex Study of Ancient India* ..., op. cit., p. 154.
31. See Guenther D. Sontheimer, 'The *Vana* and the *Ksetra*: The Tribal Background of Some Famous Cults', in G.C. Tripathi and H. Kulke (eds.), *Eschmann Memorial Lectures*, vol. 1, Bhubaneswar, 1987, pp. 125-7.
32. Ibid., p. 128.

33. See K.N. Dikshit, 'The Ochre Coloured Ware Settlements in the Ganga Yamuna Doab', in D.P. Agrawal and D.K. Chakrabarti (eds.), *Essays in Indian Protohistory,* Delhi, 1979, pp. 285-99; B.B. Lal, 'The Copper Hoard Culture of the Ganga Valley', in *Antiquity,* vol. 46, 1972, pp. 282-7; T.N. Roy, *The Ganges Civilization,* Delhi, 1983; and V. Tripathi, *The Painted Grey Ware : An Iron Age Culture of Northern India,* Delhi, 1976.
34. See Romila Thapar, 'The First Millennium BC in Northern India (up to the end of the Mauryan Period)', in idem (ed.), *Recent Perspectives of Early Indian History,* Bombay, 1995, p. 95.
35. See R.S. Sharma, 'Material Background of the Genesis of the State and Complex Society in the Middle Gangetic Plains', in *Social Science Probings,* vol. 10, nos. 1-4, 1993, p. 26.
36. See M.K. Dhavalikar, 'Chalcolithic Cultures: A Socio-Economic Perspective', in K.N. Dikshit (ed.), *Archaeological Perspective of India Since Independence,* New Delhi, 1984, pp. 63-80; Supriya Varma, 'Changing Settlement Patterns in Kathiawar', *Studies in History,* vol. 6, no. 2, 1990, pp. 137-61 and Sharma, ibid., pp. 7-10.
37. Supra, n. 33. See also Sharma, ibid.
38. Makkhan Lal, *Settlement History and the Rise of Civilization* ..., op. cit., also see his 'The Development and Dispersal of Agricultural Settlements in the Ganga-Yamuna Doab (2nd and Ist Millennium B.C.)', *PIHC,* Goa session, 1987, pp. 730-40.
39. See Sharma, 'Material Background...', op. cit.
40. The construction of hierarchy of settlements on the basis of surveys, surface measurements of sites and modern ethnographic/demographic parallels, in the absence of excavations, are tricky endeavours. We can have no idea of the geographical distribution of an earlier culture at multi-cultural sites by applying such methods.
41. See R.S. Sharma, *Material Culture and Social Formations in Ancient India,* Delhi, 1983; Romila Thapar, *From Lineage to State,* Delhi, 1984.
42. Supra, n. 38.
43. See Romila Thapar, *From Lineage to State,* op. cit., ch. 3.
44. For recent statements see Makkhan Lal, 'Iron Tools, Forest Clearance and Urbanization in the Gangetic Plains', in *Man and Environment,* vol. X, 1986, pp. 83-90; and D.K. Chakrabarti and N. Lahiri, 'The Iron Age in India: The Beginning and Consequences', in *Puratattva,* vol. 24, 1993-4, pp. 12-32.
45. See R.S. Sharma 'Material Background of the Genesis of the State and Complex Society ...', op. cit., pp. 1-27, including the chart on pp. 14-15 and Supriya Varma, 'Changing Settlement Patterns in Kathiawar', op. cit.
46. Supra, n. 26.
47. See, for example, S. Seneviratne, 'Kalinga and Andhra: The Process of Secondary State Formation in Early India', *IHR,* vol. 7, nos. 1-2, 1980-1, pp. 54-69 and idem, 'Pre-State to State Societies: Transformation in

the Political Ecology of South India with Special Reference to Tamil Nadu', Seminar paper on 'State Formation in Pre-Colonial South India', Centre for Historical Studies, JNU, New Delhi, March 1989 (forthcoming).

48. R.P. Kangle, *The Kauṭilya Arthaśāstra*, pt. II, rpt., Delhi, 1988, 2.1.
49. See S. Bhattacharya, 'Land-System as Reflected in Kautilya's *Arthaśāstra*', in *The Indian Economic and Social History Review*, vol. XVI, no. 1, 1979, pp. 85-95.
50. The works of D.N. Jha and D.R. Das are exceptions in some ways. However, while Jha understandably concentrates almost entirely on the evolution of the revenue system, Das provides useful information without really explaining the historical processes. See D.N. Jha, *Revenue System in Post-Maurya and Gupta Times*, Calcutta, 1967; D.R. Das, *Economic History of the Deccan*, Delhi, 1969.
51. See Romila Thapar (ed.), *Recent Perspectives of Early Indian History*, Bombay, 1995.
52. A good discussion of the process of 'locality' formation is available in B.D. Chattopadhyaya's 'Transition to the Early Historical Phase in the Deccan: A Note', in B.M. Pande and B.D. Chattopadhyaya (eds.), *Archaeology and History*, vol. II, Delhi, 1988, pp. 727-32.
53. See Chattopadhyaya, ibid., S. Seneviratne, 'Kalinga and Andhra ...', op. cit.; Aloka Parasher (ed.), *Social and Economic History of Early Deccan—Some Interpretations*, New Delhi, 1993, ch. 2; and B.P. Sahu, 'Power and the Politics of Patronage: Political and Social Processes in Early Orissa', in *Economic and Political Weekly* (forthcoming).
54. See M.G.S. Narayanan 'The Role of Peasants in the Early History of Tamilakam in South India', in *Social Scientist*, no. 184, September 1988, pp. 17-34; Rajan Gurukkal, 'Towards the Voice of Dissent: Trajectory of Ideological Transformation in Early South India', *Social Scientist*, nos. 236-7, Jan.-Feb. 1993, pp. 2-22; and T.K. Venkatasubramanian, *Societas to Civitas: Evolution of Political Society in South India* (*Pre-Pallavan Tamilakam*), Delhi, 1993.
55. See H.P. Ray, 'Bharhut and Sanchi—Nodal Points in a Commercial Interchange', in B.M. Pande and B.D. Chattopadhyaya (eds.), *Archaeology and History*, vol. II, Delhi, 1988, pp. 623-5 and her 'Early Historical Settlement in the Deccan: An Ecological Perspective', in *Man and Environment*, vol. XIV, no. 1, 1989, p. 104. See also Seneviratne, 'Kalinga and Andhra ...,' op. cit.
56. See Romila Thapar, *The Mauryas Revisited*, op. cit.
57. See H.P., Ray, 'Early Historical Settlement in the Deccan ...', op. cit., pp. 105-6.
58. See B.P. Sahu, 'Situating Early Historical Trade in Orissa' in K.M. Shrimali (ed.), *Indian Archaeology Since Independence*, Delhi, 1996, particularly pp. 99-101.
59. See H. Sarkar, 'Emergence of Urban Centres in Early Historical

Andhradesa', in B.M Pande and B.D. Chattopadhyaya (eds.), *Archaeology and History*, vol. II, op. cit., especially pp. 634-6 and B.D. Chattopadhyaya, 'Urban Centres in Early Bengal: Archaeological Perspectives', *Pratna Samiksha*, vol. II, Calcutta (forthcoming).

60. See Supriya Varma, 'Changing Settlement Patterns in Kathiawar', op. cit., particularly pp. 152-3.
61. For details see B. Rajendra Prasad, 'Early Historic Andhra Desa—A Perspective', Presidential Address, Section I, *Proceedings of the Andhra Pradesh History Congress*, vol. XVIII, pp. 8-12.
62. H.P. Ray, 'Early Historical Settlement in the Deccan ...', op. cit., p. 106. For the spatial and chronological distribution of the term *āhāra* and its variants see D.N. Jha, *Revenue System in Post-Mauryan and Gupta times*, op. cit., pp. 141-3.
63. *Gāthā-Saptaśatī*, edited and translated by R.G. Basak, Calcutta, 1971, 1.9, 6.43, 6.67-8, etc.
64. See V.K. Jain, 'Dynamics of Hydraulic Activity in Mauryan and Post-Mauryan Times', in *PIHC*, Delhi Session, 1992, pp. 162-9.
65. Ibid. Also see S. Bhattacharya, 'Land, Soil, Rainfall, Irrigation—Some Aspects of the Backdrop of Agrarian Life in the *Arthaśāstra* of Kauṭilya', in *Indian Economic and Social History Review*, vol. XV, no. 2, 1978, pp. 211-19.
66. See H.P. Ray, 'Bharhut and Sanchi ...', op. cit., p. 627.
67. See for example Luders' list, *EI*, vol. X, no. 1124 and *EI*, vol. VIII, pp. 73ff.
68. See H.P. Ray, *Monastery and Guild: Commerce under the Satavahanas*, New Delhi, 1986.
69. See B.D. Chattopadhyaya, 'Geographical Perspectives, Culture Change and Linkages: Some Reflections on Early Punjab', Presidential Address, Ancient Section, Punjab Historical Conference, Patiala Session, March 1995 (forthcoming).
70. R.S. Sharma, *Urban Decay in India*, op. cit., p. 168.
71. See B.D. Chattopadhyaya, 'Historiography, History and Religious Centres ...' op. cit., particularly pp. 37-41. See also Vijay Nath, 'Tirthas and Acculturation: An Anthropological Study', in *Social Science Probings*, vol. 10, nos. 1-4, 1993, especially pp. 37-42.
72. For examples see B.D. Chattopadhyaya, 'Origin of the Rajputs: The Political, Economic and Social Processes in Early Medieval Rajasthan', *IHR*, vol. III, no. 1, 1976, pp. 59-82; and H. Kulke, 'Early State Formation and Royal Legitimation in Late Ancient Orissa', in M.N. Das (ed.), *Side-Lights on History and Culture of Orissa*, Cuttack, 1977, pp. 104-14. See also Romila Thapar, *Clan, Caste and Origin Myths in Early India*, New Delhi, 1992.
73. See Surajit Sinha, 'State formation and Rajput Myth in Tribal Central India', in *Man in India*, vol. 42, 1962, pp. 35-80; K.S. Singh, 'A Study in State Formation among Tribal Communities', in R.S. Sharma and V.N.

Jha (eds.), *Indian Society: Historical Probings*, 2nd edn., New Delhi, 1977, pp. 317-36. See also relevant papers in Surajit Sinha (ed.), *Tribal Polities and State Systems in Pre-Colonial Eastern and North-Eastern India*, Calcutta, 1987; and J.B. Bhattacharjee's *Social and Polity Formations in Pre-Colonial North East India*, New Delhi, 1991.

74. See K.M. Shrimali, *Agrarian Structure in Central India and the Northern Deccan (c. AD 300-500)*, New Delhi, 1987, particularly pp. 22-8 and maps 2-4.
75. Ibid., p. 27.
76. See K.V. Ramesh and S.P. Tewari (eds.), *A Copper-Plate Hoard of the Gupta Period from Bagh, Madhya Pradesh*, New Delhi, 1990; also K.M. Shrimali 'Land Relations in Central India, *c.* AD 350–*c.* AD 450', (mimeographed).
77. Cited in M.S. Randhawa, *A History of Agriculture in India*, vol. 1, New Delhi, 1980, p. 430.
78. See Rajan Gurukkal, 'Non-Brahmana Resistance to the Expansion of Brahmadeyas: The Early Pandya Experience', *PIHC*, Annamalainagar Session, 1984, pp. 161-3.
79. See R.S. Sharma, '*Rājaśāsana*: Meaning, Scope and Application', *PIHC*, Calicut Session, 1976, pp. 76-87.
80. See Nandini Sinha, 'State and the Tribe: A Study of the Bhīls in the Historic Setting of Southern Rajasthan', in *Social Science Probings*, vol. 10, nos. 1-4, 1993, pp. 55-67.
81. For example see Rajan Gurukkal, 'Towards the Voice of Dissent ...', op. cit.; Kesavan Veluthat, 'Religious Symbols in Political Legitimation: The Case of Early Medieval South India', *Social Scientist*, nos, 236-37, Jan-Feb 1993, pp. 23-33; and B.P. Sahu, 'Power and the Politics of Patronage ...', op. cit.
82. See Vijay Nath, 'Tirthas and Acculturation ...', op. cit.
83. For a discussion of the historical processes see B.D. Chattopadhyaya, *The Making of Early Medieval India*, op. cit., 'Introduction'.
84. See R. Tirumalai, 'Land Reclamation of Flood-Damaged and Sand-Cast Lands—A Study in Prices, Rentals and Wages in Later Chola Times(From AD 1070 to AD 1210)—Based on Srirangam Inscriptions', in *Journal of the Epigraphical Society of India*, vol. 11, 1984, pp. 65-87; M.D. Sampath, 'Agricultural Guild', in D.C. Bhattacharya and Devendra Handa (eds.), *Praci-Prabha: Perspectives in Indology*, New Delhi, 1989, particularly pp. 67-8.
85. See K.V. Raman and P. Shanmugam, '*Settlement Pattern in Lalgudi Taluk*', in N. Karashima (ed.), *Socio-Cultural Change in Villages in Tiruchirapalli District, Tamil Nadu*, India Part I, Tokyo, 1983, pp. 2-12.
86. R. Champakalakshmi, 'The Study of Settlement Patterns in the Chola Period: Some Perspectives', in *Man and Environment*, vol. XIV, no. 1, 1989, pp. 91-101.
87. Ibid., p. 95.

88. Ibid.
89. See B.P. Sahu, 'Aspects of Rural Economy in Early Medieval Orissa', *Social Scientist*, nos. 236-7, Jan-Feb. 1993, pp. 48-68; and Chitrarekha Gupta, 'Evolution of Agrarian Society in Kamarupa in Early Medieval Period', *IHR*, vol. XIX, nos. 1-2 (forthcoming).
90. B.P. Sahu, ibid., particularly pp. 54-5.
91. See N. Lahiri, *Pre-Ahom Assam: Studies in the Inscriptions of Assam between the 5th and the 13th Centuries AD*, New Delhi, 1991, pp. 106-7.
92. See P.K. Mohan Reddy, 'Agriculture in Ancient Andhra', in *Proceedings of the Andhra Pradesh History Congress*, vol. XVIII, pp. 16-19.
93. See Y. Gopal Reddy, 'Agriculture Under the Kakatiyas of Warangal', in *Itihas*, vol. 1, no. 1, 1973, pp. 57-71.
94. B.D. Chattopadhyaya, 'Irrigation in Early Medieval Rajasthan', *JESHO*, vol. XVI, pts. 2-3, 1973, pp. 298-316.
95. Nandini Sinha, 'Rural Society and State Formation in Early Medieval South-Western Rajasthan', *PIHC*, Aligarh Session, 1994, pp. 123-31.
96. See K.S. Shivanna, 'Some Aspects of the Agrarian System During the Hoysala Period', in *Srikantika, S. Sastri Felicitation Volume*, Mysore, 1973, pp. 292-8; and Shivanna and G.R. Rangaswamiah, 'Agriculture During the Ganga Period', in the same volume, pp. 299-303. See also A. Settar, 'Aspects of Agricultural Expansion in Early Medieval Southern Karnataka', in K. Veerathappan (ed.), *Studies in Karnataka History and Culture*, Mysore, 1987.
97. See Kesavan Veluthat, *The Political Structure of Early Medieval South India*, New Delhi, 1993, ch. 6; M.D. Sampath, 'Agricultural Guild', op. cit., pp. 67-74; Kesavan Veluthat, 'Landed Magnates as State Agents: The Gavudas under the Hoysalas in Karnataka', *PIHC*, Gorakhpur Session, 1989, pp. 118-23, and the same author's 'The Nature of Agrarian Corporations in South Canara Under the Alupas and Hoysalas', *PIHC*, Delhi Session, 1992, pp. 108-14.
98. See Rajan Gurukkal, 'The Socio-Economic Milieu of the Kerala Temple: A Functional Analysis *c.* 800-1200 AD', in *Studies in History*, vol. II, no. 1, 1980, pp. 1-13. Also Kesavan Veluthat, *Brahmana Settlements in Kerala*, Calicut, 1978.
99. See B.D. Chattopadhyaya, *Aspects of Rural Settlements and Rural Society in Early Medieval India*, Calcutta, 1990, pp. 28-9.
100. See Chitrarekha Gupta, 'Evolution of Agrarian Society in Kamarupa ...', op. cit.
101. See Chattopadhyaya, *Aspects of Rural Settlements* ..., op. cit., pp. 21-4.
102. See N. Lahiri, 'Landholding and Peasantry in the Brahmaputra Valley *c.* 5th-13th Centuries AD', *JESHO*, vol. 33, 1990, p. 164 and *Pre-Ahom Assam* ...', op. cit., pp. 93-5.
103. See Chattopadhyaya, *Aspects of Rural Settlements* ..., op. cit., pp. 77-83. Also see idem, 'Markets and Merchants in Early Medieval Rajasthan',

in *Social Science Probings*, vol. II, no. 4, 1985, pp. 413-40.

104. See R. Champakalakshmi, 'The Study of Settlement Patterns in the Chola Period ...', op. cit.; B.P. Sahu, 'Aspects of Rural Economy ...', op. cit.; N. Lahiri, *Pre-Ahom Assam ...*, op. cit., pp. 106-7; and Neeraj Sahay, 'Water Resources and the State in Early Andhra and Orissa *Circa* AD 350-1000', unpublished M.Phil Dissertation, University of Delhi, 1995, ch. II.
105. Ibid., See also Shyam N. Lal, 'An Aspect of Rural Landscape in the Rashtrakuta Kingdom', *PIHC*, Mysore Session, 1993, particularly pp. 91-2.
106. For such details in a regional context see Annapurna Chattopadhyay, 'Some Aspects of the Village in Ancient Bengal: Size and Periphery', *PIHC*, Aligarh Session, 1994, pp. 108-14.
107. See for example R.N. Misra, 'Village Life and Settlements in the Light of Vakataka Inscriptions', in B.M. Pande and B.D. Chattopadhyaya (eds.), *Archaeology and History*, op. cit., p. 645.
108. See Rajan Gurukkal, 'Aspects of Warrior Power in Localised Agriculture: The Case of the Pandya Region During the Early Medieval Period', *PIHC*, Srinagar Session, 1986, pp. 195-6.
109. See V.S. Elizabeth, 'Hero-stones in the Rashtrakuta Period: Their Implications for Society and Polity', *PIHC*, Gorakhpur Session, 1989, pp. 828-30.
110. See, for example, M. Krishna Kumari, *History of Medieval Andhradesa*, Delhi, 1989, pp. 47-52; and B.K. Pandeya, *Temple Economy Under the Colas*, New Delhi, 1984, pp. 41-3.
111. Cited in Nandini Sinha 'State and the Tribe ...', op. cit., p. 62.
112. See Chitrarekha Gupta, 'Evolution of Agrarian Society in Kamarupa ...', op. cit.
113. In early medieval Orissa there were administrative units such as Oṅgataṭaviṣaya and Telataṭaviṣaya which were named after the rivers Ong and Tel respectively. See S.N. Rajaguru's *Inscriptions of Orissa*, vol. IV, Bhubaneswar, 1966, line 4, p. 106 and line 25, p. 192.
114. See Shyam N. Lal, 'An Aspect of Rural Landscape in the Rashtrakuta Kingdom', op. cit., pp. 89-100.
115. B.D. Chattopadhyaya, *Aspects of Rural Settlements and Rural Society in Early Medieval India*, op. cit.
116. See, for example, L. Gopal, 'Technique of Agriculture in Early Medieval India (*c.* AD 700-1200)', *University of Allahabad Studies*, 1963-4, pp. 1-37 and R.S. Sharma, *Urban Decay in India*, op. cit., pp. 172-4.
117. A.S. Altekar, *A History of Village Communities in Western India*, Bombay, 1927.
118. A.K. Choudhary, *Early Medieval Village in North-Eastern India: AD 600-1200*, Calcutta, 1971.
119. For detailed discussions see ibid., ch. 3.
120. See K.M. Shrimali, *Agrarian Structure in Central India and the Northern*

Deccan, op. cit. and R.N. Misra, 'Village Life and Settlements in the Light of Vakataka Inscriptions', op. cit.

121. For a discussion of some of the problems see V.M. Jha's review of K.M. Shrimali's *Agrarian Structure* ...; in *Social Science Probings*, vol. 5, nos. 1-4, 1988, pp. 150-2.

122. See S.K. Acharya, 'Rural Settlements in South Kosala', *The Journal of Orissan History*, vol. XIII, 1995, particularly pp. 49-51.

123. For a meticulously reconstructed picture of the successive changes in the village see Chattopadhyaya, *Aspects of Rural Settlements*, op. cit., ch. 4.

124. For settlements in Lalgudi taluk see n. 85. On the issue of the study of settlement complexes in the early historic context see Chattopadhyaya, 'Urban Centres in Early Bengal ...', op. cit.

125. See R. Champakalakshmi, 'The Study of Settlement Patterns in the Cola Period', op. cit., p. 98.

126. K.V. Raman and P. Shanmugam, 'Settlement Pattern in Lalgudi Taluk', op. cit., p. 6.

127. B.D. Chattopadhyaya, *Aspects of Rural Settlements* ..., op. cit. See also Kishore K. Singh, 'Changing Landscape of Rural Settlements in Early Medieval India', a review article, in *Social Scientist*, nos. 242-3, July-Aug. 1993, pp. 79-88.

128. See B.D. Chattopadhyaya, ibid., ch. 3 and 'Conclusion'.

129. For details see Kesavan Veluthat, *The Political Structure of Early Medieval South India*, op. cit., chs. 6 and 7.

130. For details of the argument see Chattopadhyaya, *Aspects of Rural Settlements*, ch. 2, particularly pp. 51-7. For early medieval south India see N. Karashima, 'The Village Communities in Chola Times: Myth or Reality', in *Journal of the Epigraphical Society of India*, vol. 8, 1981, pp. 85-96.

131. See, for example, Nandini Sinha, 'Rural Society and State Formation in Early Medieval South-Western Rajasthan', op. cit., especially p. 128.

132. Ibid., p. 129.

133. See Y. Subbarayalu, 'The Place of Ur in the Economic and Social History of Early Tamilnadu, AD 750-1350', in A.V. Narasimha Murthy and B.K. Gururaja Rao (eds.), *Rangavalli: Recent Researches in Indology*, Delhi, 1983, p. 171.

134. Puspa Niyogi's *Brahmanic Settlements in Different Subdivisions of Ancient Bengal*, Calcutta, 1967; Kesavan Veluthat, *Brahman Settlements in Kerala*, Calicut, 1978; Shanthakumari Leela, *History of the Agraharas in Karnataka, 400-1300*, Madras, 1986; Swati Datta, *Migrant Brahmanas in Northern India*, Delhi, 1989; and Upinder Singh's *Kings, Brahmanas and Temples in Orissa: An Epigraphic Study (300-1147 C.E.)*, New Delhi, 1994, are some of the important works.

135. See Brendan O'Leary, *The Asiatic Mode of Production*, op. cit., pp. 265-7, including n. 7. See also R.A.L.H. Gunawardana, 'The Analysis of Pre-

Colonial Social Formations in Asia in the Writings of Karl Marx', in *IHR*, vol. II, no. 2, 1976, especially pp. 368-70.

136. Baden-Powell's study gave strength to the nationalist writings insofar as it argued that individual ownership of land prevailed all through Indian history. Baden-Powell, *The Origin and Growth of Village Communities in India*, London, 1899. See also A.S. Altekar, *History of Village Communities in Western India*, op. cit., pp. 80ff. The question has been critically looked into in Lallanji Gopal's 'Ownership of Agricultural Land in Ancient India', in *JESHO*, vol. IV, 1961, pp. 240-63.

137. For a detailed discussion see S.K. Maity, *Economic Life of Northern India in the Gupta Period*, Calcutta, 1957, pp. 11-28; A. Appadorai, *Economic Condition of Southern India*, vol. 1, op. cit., pp. 99-121; D.N. Jha, *Revenue System in Post-Maurya and Gupta Times*, op. cit., ch. 2; and R.S. Sharma, 'How Feudal was Indian Feudalism?', in *Social Scientist*, no. 129, Feb. 1984, pp. 16-41.

138. The question has been addressed by G.M. Bongard-Levin, in *A Complex Study of Ancient India*, op. cit., pp. 109-11, 175 in the early historic context and G.R. Kuppuswamy, 'Land-Ownership in Medieval Karnataka', in *Journal of Karnatak University, Social Sciences*, vol. 8, 1972, pp. 1-7, in the later period. See also R.S. Sharma, *Indian Feudalism* (2nd edn., rpt.), Delhi, 1985, pp. 111-14.

For the early British position on the matter see Louis Dumont, 'The 'Village Community' from Munro to Maine', in *Contributions to Indian Sociology*, 1967, pp. 67-89.

139. See R.S. Sharma, *Indian Feudalism*, op. cit., pp. 92-6, 124-6 and 'How Feudal was Indian Feudalism?', op. cit.

140. Ibid.

141. See R.S. Sharma, *Material Culture and Social Formations in Ancient India*, op. cit.; Romila Thapar, *From Lineage to State*, op. cit., See also Irfan Habib, 'The Social Distribution of Landed Property in Pre-British India (A Historical Survey)', in R.S. Sharma and V.N. Jha (eds.), *Indian Society: Historical Probings*, op. cit., pp. 264-75; and idem. 'The Peasant in Indian History', General Presidential Address, Kurukshetra Session, *PIHC*, 1982, pp. 3-16.

142. Supra, n. 20. Also see Suvira Jaiswal, 'The Changing Concept of Grihapati', *PIHC*, Warangal Session, 1992-3, pp. 87-96.

143. See R. Thapar, *From Lineage to State*, op. cit., ch. 3; and G.M. Bongard-Levin, 'Republics in Ancient India', in *A Complex Study of Ancient India*, pp. 61-106.

144. R. Fick and A.N. Bose had perhaps exaggerated the role of the brāhmaṇa landholders. See R. Fick, *The Social Organization in North-East India in Buddha's Time*, English trans., Calcutta, 1920, p. 241; and A.N. Bose, *Social and Rural economy in Northern India* (rpt.), vol. 1, Calcutta, 1970, pp. 173ff, vol. II, 1967, p. 261. For a substantial part of the land being in possession of the *gahapatis* and *kutumbikas* see Sharma,

Light on Early Indian Society and Economy, op. cit., p. 62; and idem, *Material Culture and Social Formations*, op. cit., p. 108.

145. See S. Bhattacharya, 'Land System as Reflected in Kauṭilya's *Arthaśāstra*', op. cit.
146. See Bongard-Levin, *A Complex Study of Ancient India*, op. cit., pp. 109-10 and 175.
147. See Suvira Jaiswal, 'The Changing Concept of Grihapati', op. cit., p. 93.
148. See B.N.S. Yadava, 'Some Aspects of the Changing Order in India During the Saka-Kushana Age', in B.G. Gafurov *et al.* (eds.), *Central Asia in the Kushana Period*, vol. II, Moscow, 1975, p. 126.
149. Ibid., pp. 126-7.
150. See Marlene Njammasch, 'Social Structure of the Village in Kathiawar in the 6th-7th Centuries AD', in *Social Science Probings*, vol. 9, nos. 1-4, 1992, pp. 1-7.
151. Ibid., p. 5.
152. See N. Karashima, 'Allur and Isanamangalam: Two South Indian Villages of the Chola Times', in *IESHR*, vol. II, no. 2, 1966, pp. 150-62.
153. See Y. Subbarayalu, 'The Place of Ur in the Economic and Social History of Early Tamilnadu, 750-1350', op. cit.; idem, 'Quantification of Inscriptional Data with Special Reference to the Study of Property Rights in Medieval Tamil Nadu', Paper presented at the Symposium on 'Quantitative Methods in Indian History', Indian History Congress, Dharwad Session, 1988 (mimeographed).
154. See Subbarayalu, 'The Place of Ur...', ibid., p. 173.
155. Ibid.
156. See Kesavan Veluthat, 'Landed Magnates as State Agents: The Gavudas Under the Hoysalas in Karnataka', op. cit.; idem, 'The Nature of Agrarian Corporations in South Canara Under the Alupas and Hoysalas', op. cit.
157. Kesavan Veluthat, 'Landed Magnates as State Agents ...', ibid.
158. *EI*, vol. VIII, no. 10, pp. 78ff.
159. See D.C. Sircar 'Kraya-Śāsana and Kara-Śāsana', in *Studies in the Political and Administrative Systems in Ancient and Medieval India*, Delhi, 1974, pp. 66-75.
160. See Y. Subbarayalu, 'Quantification of Inscriptional Data with Special Reference to the Study of Property Rights ...', op. cit.
161. Mercantile groups are normally considered to be outside the orbit of rural society, but during early medieval times they emerged as landholders and donors. However, such individual donations were usually small. See B.P. Mazumdar, 'Merchants and Landed Aristocracy in the Feudal Economy of Northern India (8th to 12th century AD)', in D.C. Sircar (ed.), *Land System and Feudalism in Ancient India*, Calcutta, 1966, pp. 62-71.
162. Y. Subbarayalu, 'Quantification of Inscriptional Data ...', op. cit.

163. For a detailed discussion see D.N. Jha, 'Temples as Landed Magnates in Early Medieval South India (*c.* AD 700-1300)', in R.S. Sharma and V.N. Jha (eds.), *Indian Society: Historical Probings*, op. cit., pp. 202-16. See also B.K. Pandeya, *Temple Economy Under the Cholas*, op. cit.
164. See Marlene Njammasch, 'From the Ancient Labour Tax to the Feudal Corvee: A Marxist Approach to the Study of *Viṣṭi*', in *Social Science Probings*, vol. 1, no. 4, 1984, pp. 563-78.
165. See ibid., p. 578 and B.N.S. Yadava, 'Problem of the Interaction Between Socio-Economic Classes in the Early Medieval Complex' in *IHR*, vol. III, no. 1, 1976, p. 53. See also D.N. Jha, 'Indian Feudalism: The Early Phase', in D.N. Gupta (ed), *Changing Modes of Production in India—An Historical Analysis*, Delhi, 1995, pp. 32, 37.
166. See Kesavan Veluthat, 'Labour Rent and Produce Rent: Reflections on the Revenue System Under the Cholas (AD 850-1279)', in *PIHC*, Dharwad Session, 1988, p. 141.

Earlier works on revenue system by nationalist historians mixed up evidence from smṛti literature and inscriptions and provided an ideal picture. However, some of them painstakingly enumerated the revenue terms. See U.N. Ghoshal, *Contributions to the History of the Hindu Revenue System*, op. cit. Writings within the dominant historiography focus on the rising taxes and impositions in the context of the feudal social formation. See, for example, D.N. Jha, *Revenue System*, op. cit.; idem, 'Early Indian Feudalism: A Historiographical Critique', Presidential Address, Ancient India Section, *PIHC*, Waltair Session, 1979, pp. 15-45; and B.P. Mazumdar, 'Land Revenue in Early Medieval North India (*c.* 600-1200)', in R.S. Sharma (ed.), *Land Revenue in India—Historical Studies*, Delhi, 1971, pp. 20-3. For a list of the taxes in early medieval times also see Lallanji Gopal, *Economic Life of Northern India, c. AD 700-1200*, Banaras, 1965, pp. 32-70.

The use of statistical methods by Karashima, Subbarayalu *et al.* in south India seems to provide more definitive statements about the nature and quantum of revenue, their spatio-temporal spread and the role of the state. See N. Karashima, *South Indian History and Society: Studies from Inscriptions—AD 850-1800*, Delhi, 1984; idem (ed.), *Socio-Cultural Change in Villages in Tiruchirapalli District, Tamilnadu, India*, Tokyo, 1983.
167. Although the untouchables surfaced in the middle of the first millennium BC, their ranks swelled enormously in the post-Gupta centuries. See V.N. Jha, 'Stages in the History of Untouchables', in *IHR*, vol. II, no. 1, 1975, pp. 14-31.

For the ideological rationale and benefits, to the various strata of rural society, from landless ostracized *jatis* see Irfan Habib, 'The Peasant in Indian History', General Presidential Address, Kurukshetra Session, *PIHC*, 1982, pp. 14-15, 18; idem, *Caste and Money in Indian History*, Bombay, 1987, p. 6.

168. See Nayanjot Lahiri, 'Landholding and Peasantry in the Brahmaputra Valley ...', op. cit., pp. 160-3.
169. M.G.S. Narayanan and Kesavan Veluthat, 'The Traditional Land System in Kerala: Problems of Change and Perspective', paper presented at a Seminar on Land Reforms in Kerala, Calicut, 1981 (mimeographed).
170. See K.K. Gopal, 'Assignment to Officers and Royal Kinsmen in Early Medieval India (*c.* 700-1200)', *University of Allahabad Studies*, 1963-4, pp. 75-103.
171. See B.D. Chattopadhyaya, *Aspects of Rural Settlements* .., op. cit., pp. 85, 94-5. Also see K.K. Gopal, ibid., pp. 92-3.
172. G.R. Kuppuswamy, 'Land-Ownership in Medieval Karnataka', op. cit.; idem, 'Land Succession in Medieval Karnataka', in *Journal of Karnataka University, Social Sciences*, vol. IX, 1973, pp. 106.
173. It has been posited that landgrants were made in the periphery to tide over the systemic crisis in the Gangetic plains in course of the transition from antiquity to the Middle Ages. See D.N. Jha, 'Early Indian Feudalism: A Historiographical Critique', op. cit., pp. 20-2. However, the exact relationship between such grants and the resolution of the said crisis remains unclear.
174. See H. Kulke, 'Fragmentation and Segmentation versus Integration ...', op. cit., p. 247.
175. See, for example, Marlene Njammasch, 'Social Structure of the Village in Kathiawar ...', op. cit., p. 3.
176. For some instances of scattered grants see B.P. Mazumdar, 'Epigraphic Records on Migrant Brahmanas in North India (AD 1030-1225)', in *IHR*, vol. V, nos 1-2, 1978-9, p. 74.
177. For a different but related argument see H. Mukhia, 'Marx on Pre-Colonial India—An Evaluation', in D. Banerjee (ed.), *Marxian Theory and the Third World*, New Delhi, 1985, pp. 182-4.
178. For the politics and a general critique of this construct see Jan Breman, *The Shattered Image: Construction and Deconstruction of the Village in Colonial Asia*, Amsterdam, 1988. See also M.N. Srinivas, 'The Indian Village: Myth and Reality', in *The Dominant Caste and Other Essays*, Delhi, 1987, pp. 20-59.
179. See for a recent discussion of Marx's use of contemporary sources Brendan O'Leary, *The Asiatic Mode of Production* ..., op. cit., pp. 262-7.
180. A good discussion of the meanings and motivations is provided in Louis Dumont's, 'The 'Village Community' From Munro to Maine', op. cit.
181. For an assessment of their contribution see Aloka Parasher, 'Writing on Villages and Peasants in Early India: Problems in Historiography', in V.K. Thakur and A. Aounshuman (eds.), *Peasants in Indian History*, vol. I, Patna, 1996, pp. 66-76.
182. See, for example, T.V. Mahalingam, 'Village Communities in South

India', in *Transactions of the Archaeological Society of South India*, vol. I, Madras, 1955, pp. 33-46.

183. D.D. Kosambi and R.S. Sharma envisage the emergence of self-sufficient units by the end of the Gupta Period. See Sharma, *Indian Feudalism*, op. cit., pp. 52 and 103-5; idem, *Social Changes in Early Medieval India*, op. cit., pp. 2-6.
184. G.M. Bongard-Levin, 'Some Problems of the Social Structure of Ancient India', in *A Complex Study of Ancient India*, op. cit., particularly see pp. 107-15. The problem has also been briefly addressed by Irfan Habib in his 'The Peasant in Indian History', op. cit., pp. 20-2.
185. For the early historical period see Bongard-Levin, 'Some Problems of the Social Structure ...', op. cit.
186. For early medieval south India and especially for the spatial segregation of groups in the villages see N. Karashima, 'The Village Communities in Chola Times ...', op. cit., pp. 87-8 and 91.
187. See Guyla Wojtilla, 'Indian Village Community According to the *Krisiparasara* and Some Other Contemporary Literary Sources', *Les Communautes Rurales*, Troisieme Partie: Asie et Islam, Paris, 1982, pp. 119-29.
188. Ibid., pp. 122-3.
189. N. Karashima, 'The Village Communities in Chola Times ...', op. cit.
190. B. Stein, *Peasant, State and Society in Medieval South India*, Delhi, 1980.
191. See Y. Subbarayalu, 'The Chola State and the Agrarian Order—Some Clarifications', Seminar paper on 'State Formation in pre-Colonial South India', Centre for Historical Studies, JNU, New Delhi, March 1989 (forthcoming). See also D.N. Jha, 'Validity of the Brahmana-Peasant Alliance and the Segmentary State in Early Medieval India', in *Social Science Probings*, vol. 1, no. 2, 1984, pp. 270-96.
192. See Louis Dumont, 'The 'Village Community' from Munro to Maine', op. cit., n. 18, p. 76.
193. *EI*, vol. XIV, no. 23, lines 31-2.
194. See B.D. Chattopadhyaya, 'Urban Centres in Early Medieval India: An Overview', in S. Bhattacharya and Romila Thapar (eds.), *Situating Indian History*, Delhi, 1986. For south India see R.N. Nandi, 'Growth of Rural Economy in Early Feudal India', op. cit.

    Inter-local economic exchanges in northern India and the northern Deccan have been pointed out in a recent study of monetary history. See John S. Deyell, *Living Without Silver: The Monetary History of Early Medieval North India*, New Delhi, 1990.
195. See B.D. Chattopadhyaya, *Aspects of Rural Settlements ...*, op. cit., 'Conclusion'.
196. For a historiographical survey of the early writings see R.S. Sharma, 'Historiography of the Ancient Indian Social Order', in *Light on Early Indian Society and Economy*, op. cit., pp. 1-18.

197. Ibid. For an updated and more comprehensive survey see Suvira Jaiswal, 'Studies in Early Indian Social History: Trends and Possibilities', in *IHR*, vol. VI, nos 1-2, 1979-80, especially pp. 1-24.
198. Ibid.
199. See, for example, A.N. Bose, *Social and Rural Economy of Northern India*, 2 vols., op. cit.; and B.N. Dutt, *Studies in Indian Social Polity*, Calcutta, 1944.
200. See R.S. Sharma, 'Problems of Peasant Protest in early Medieval India', in *Social Scientist*, no. 184, September 1988, p. 4.
201. B.N.S. Yadava, 'Problem of the Interaction Between Socio-Economic Classes in the Early Medieval Complex', op. cit., p. 44.
202. See B.N.S. Yadava, 'Immobility and Subjection of Indian Peasantry in Early Medieval Complex', in *IHR*, vol. I, no. 1, 1974, pp. 18-27; idem, 'The Problem of the Emergence of Feudal Relations in Early India', Presidential Address, Ancient India Section, Bombay Session, *PIHC*, 1980, pp. 19-78. See also R.S. Sharma, 'How Feudal was Indian Feudalism?', op. cit.
203. For peasant protests see B.N.S. Yadava, 'Problem of the Interaction Between Socio-Economic Classes ...', op. cit., pp. 54-8; R.S. Sharma, 'Problems of Peasant Protest in Early Medieval India', op. cit., pp. 3-16; R.N. Nandi, 'Growth of Rural Economy in Early Feudal India', op. cit., pp. 71-7; and D.N. Jha, 'Early Indian Feudal Formation: The State of the Art', in *Social Science Probings*, vol. 3, no. 3, 1986, particularly pp. 317-19.
204. B.D. Chattopadhyaya, *Aspects of Rural Settlements and Rural Society in Early Medieval India*, op. cit.
205. See Sanjeeb K. Behera, *Evolution of the Structure of Polity in Orissa, AD 350-1100*, Ph.D. Thesis submitted to Jawaharlal Nehru University, New Delhi, 1996, ch. 7.
206. For stratification within the peasantry in south India see Kesavan Veluthat, 'The Structure of Land Rights and Social Stratification in Early Medieval South India', in V.K. Thakur and A. Aounshuman (eds.), *Peasants in Indian History*, vol. 1, op. cit., pp. 312-30.
207. See M.D. Sampath, 'Agricultural Guild', op. cit., p. 69. See also Kesavan Veluthat, 'The Nature of Agrarian Corporation in South Canara Under the Alupas and Hoysalas', op. cit., p. 112.
208. See B.N.S. Yadava, 'Historical Investigation into Social Terminology in Literature: A Problem of the Study of Social Change (Mainly in the Context of Early Medieval Northern India)', General Presidential Address, Warangal Session, *PIHC*, 1992-3, pp. 1-35.

    Yadava provides substantial evidence for differentiation, but does not elaborate on their implications.
209. In addition to what has been already stated earlier see Irfan Habib, 'The Peasant in Indian History', op. cit.; V.K. Thakur, 'The Peasant in Early India: Problems of Identification and Differentiation', in *Peasants*

in *Indian History*, vol. I, op. cit., pp. 123-49.

210. See Uma Chakravarti, 'In Search of the Peasant in Early India: Was the *Gahapati* a Peasant Producer?', in *Peasants in Indian History*, op. cit., pp. 150-78.

211. See M.G.S. Narayanan, 'The Role of Peasants in the Early History of Tamilakam ...', op. cit., n. 15, p. 29.

212. See Ranabir Chakravarti, '*Kuṭumbikas* of Early India', in *Peasants in Indian History*, op. cit., p. 190.

213. Statements about ideal relationships of power in society were made through ritual means. For the validation of the ideal *varṇa* and gender hierarchy through the mediation of rituals see Kumkum Roy, 'Legitimation and the Brahmanical Tradition: The Upanayana and the Brahmacarya in the Dharmasutras', in *PIHC*, Amritsar Session, 1985, pp. 136-46.

214. See Uma Chakravarti, 'Conceptualising Brahmanical Patriarchy in Early India: Gender, Caste, Class and State', in *Economic and Political Weekly*, 3 April 1993, pp. 579-85.

215. For the importance of *varṇa* as a legitimising ideology see Suvira Jaiswal, '*Varna* Ideology and Social Change', *Social Scientist*, vol. 19, nos. 3-4, 1991, pp. 41-8.

216. See Irfan Habib, 'The Peasant in Indian History', op. cit., pp. 18, 45, n. 107.

217. See B.D. Chattopadhyaya, 'Origin of the Rajputs: The Political, Economic and Social Processes in Early Medieval Rajasthan', op. cit.

218. Chitrarekha Gupta, 'The Writers' Class of Ancient India—A Case Study in Social Mobility', in *IESHR*, vol. 20, no. 2, 1983, pp. 191-204.

219. For some of the regional details see B.D. Chattopadhyaya, *The Making of Early Medieval India*, op. cit., pp. 24-8.

220. See B.N.S. Yadava, 'Some Aspects of the Changing Order in India during the Saka-Kushana Age', op. cit.; idem, 'Problems of the Interaction Between Socio-Economic Classes in the Early Medieval Complex', op. cit.

221. See V.N. Jha, '*Varṇasaṁkara* in the Dharma Sūtras: Theory and Practice', *JESHO*, 1970, pp. 273-88.

222. See B.D. Chattopadhyaya, 'Origin of the Rajputs ...', op. cit.; and Irfan Habib, 'The Peasant in Indian History', op. cit., pp. 12-13. See also Romila Thapar, *Clan, Caste and Origin Myths in Early India*, op. cit., particularly the concluding portions.

223. See R.S. Sharma, 'The Feudal Mind' (mimeographed).

224. B. Stein, *Peasant State and Society in Medieval South India*, op. cit. For a critique see D.N. Jha, 'Validity of the Brahmana-Peasant Alliance and the Segmentary State in Early Medieval India', op. cit.; R. Champakalakshmi, 'Peasant State and Society in Medieval South India', A review article, *IESHR*, vol. XVIII, nos. 3-4, pp. 411-26.

225. See Romila Thapar, 'Society and Law in the Hindu and Buddhist

Traditions', in *Ancient Indian Social History—Some Interpretations*, op. cit., pp. 26-39; D.D. Kosambi, 'Social and Economic Aspects of the *Bhagvad-Gita*', *JESHO*, vol. IV, pt. 2, 1961, pp. 198-224; Vijay Nath, 'Tirthas and Acculturation: An Anthropological Study', op. cit.; B.P. Sahu, 'The Brahmanical Model Viewed as an Instrument of Socio-Cultural Change—An Autopsy', in *PIHC*, Amritsar Session, 1985, pp. 180-9; and B.D. Chattopadhyaya, 'Historiography, History and Religious Centres: Early Medieval North India, Circa AD 700-1200', op. cit., particularly pp. 41-3.

SECTION I

Rural Settlements

1

Land-System as Reflected in Kauṭilya's *Arthaśāstra*

Sibesh Bhattacharya

The *Arthaśāstra* evidences reflecting a unified attitude of a single text[1] may be looked into for elucidation of certain aspects of early Indian land-system. As our real concern is with the actual functional aspects of land-system we are refraining from discussing here the purely conceptual issues like the question whether the king was the ultimate owner of all land or not. In the *Arthaśāstra* scheme there were two primary categories of land: state land and private land. 'It is quite clear that all unoccupied land is supposed to belong to the king, that is to the state.'[2] However it is not unlikely that a distinction was made between the state land and king's personal estate or crown land. *Svabhūmi* used in the *sūtra* 2.24.2 appears to refer to king's personal land.[3] Thus the director of trade (*paṇyādhyakṣa*) was required to keep separate the produce of king's personal estate (*svabhūmija*) from produce received from 'other places' (*parabhūmija*)—obviously these were received by way of revenue in kind—and he had to make different arrangements for their sale.[4] Royal goods (*rājapaṇyāh*) from king's estate was to be sold at one centre (*ekamukhaṁ*) and goods from other places at many centres (*anekamukhaṁ*). The term *parabhūmija* has been rendered by Kangle as goods from foreign countries and he maintains that the state engaged in foreign trade also. But the fact that *parabhūmija* goods were sold at a number of selling centres and *svabhūmija* goods at one centre would imply, if Kangle's

* R.P. Kangle's *The Kauṭilīya Arthaśāstra*, Part I and Part II, Bombay, 1969, 1972 have been followed for the text and translation of the *Arthaśāstra*.

interpretation is accepted, that state trading involved more foreign goods than indigenous products. This does not seem very reasonable. Perhaps the terms *svadeśīyānāṁ* and *paradeśīyānāṁ* were used for indigenous and foreign goods respectively.[5] Foreign trade appears to have been mostly in the hands of private traders, the director of trade had of course a supervisory and controlling role.[6] Anyway, we do not have enough evidence to say whether a difference was made in the manner of land utilization, tillage, tenancy, etc., between the state lands and crown lands.

State lands, managed and operated by the director of state farming (*sītādhyakṣa*), were mostly put to cultivation directly by the state. It was mainly labour-employment oriented operation in which *dāsa* (slaves-servants), *karmakara* (wage labourers), *daṇḍapratikartṛ* (convicts paying off fines through labour),[7] etc., were employed. *Dāsas* and *karmakaras* were paid some small cash wages besides food.[8] The quantity and quality of food supplied to them do not appear to have been much above the bare subsistence level.[9] *Daṇḍapratikartṛ* of course received no payment.

The state, however, found it impossible to put to direct cultivation all its land; the remainder had to be leased out. There seems to have been two categories of lessee—the *ardhasītikas* and *svaviryopajivins*. The former were clearly peasants cultivating on half-share basis[10] and the latter seem to have been sharecroppers paying one-fourth or one-fifth of the produce to the state.[11] Even though we have perhaps a rough preferential scale of the different modes of cultivation of state lands[12] we cannot form any idea regarding the relative quantity of state lands cultivated directly by the state agency and lands leased out on sharecrop basis. The extent of the direct state farming in the *Arthaśāstra* generally seems to have been overestimated.[13] If the state had the requisite administrative infrastructure for large-scale direct farming, then it would not depend so heavily on private enterprise for bringing virgin land under cultivation (*śūnyaniveśa*).[14] The amount of state land leased out to cultivators thus could not have been very small.

Kauṭilya's *Arthaśāstra* has been regarded by a number of scholars as heralding a new and radical socio-economic policy. It has been asserted that Kauṭilya made a conscious attempt to habilitate landless Śūdra agricultural labourers and raise them to the status of peasant proprietors.[15] Similarly it has been argued that Kauṭilya's economic policy had an open anti-landlordism stance and that he took several measures not only to discourage the growth of landlordism but also to undermine the economic position of existing landlords and that he favoured the growth of peasant proprietors.[16]

It is true that in establishing new settlements Kauṭilya showed a clear preference of 'lower *varṇas*' (*avaravarṇa*) and 'farmers' (*karṣaka*) over others as more desirable settlers because they were likely to make greater economic returns. Industrious farmers (*karmaśīla karṣaka*) were counted among the excellences of a country.[17] Kauṭilya thus clearly perceived the fact, and appreciated the economic implication of it, that agriculture was the backbone of state economy and that agriculture depended to a very large measure on the labour of Śūdras and *avaravarṇas*. But it cannot be definitely asserted that Kauṭilya advocated a conscious policy to bring about any substantial economic improvement in the situation of Śūdra agriculturists or to cause any large-scale change in the existing land distribution and ownership patterns. To advocate the employment of *dāsa, karmakara, daṇḍapratikartṛ*, etc., against a little or no payment in state farms on the one hand and to discourage the employment of landless labourers in private farming on the other appears to be too contradictory for a systematic thinker or a practical politician. Habilitation of Śūdras as independent peasants would ultimately work against the interest of state farms dependent to a very large extent on slaves and wage labourers.

In the *Arthaśāstra* the expression *karṣaka* has been used simply to signify 'a tiller of soil' without any status content. Merely from the word, unless otherwise specified, it is not possible to determine whether the *karṣaka* was a hired farm labourer or a slave or a tenant cultivator or an owner cultivator. *Gṛhapatikavyañjana*, the seeming householder, a class in the elaborate Kauṭilyan espionage system, has been described as a *karṣaka*.[18] The context would indicate that he was expected to look like an independent farmer with his own land. In connection with the maintenance of record of villagers by the revenue department *karṣakas* are distinguished from *dāsa-karmakaras*.[19] It is well-known that *dāsa-karmakaras* were put to wide use as agricultural labourers[20] and normally they were landless. But from these alone it would not be correct to conclude that *karṣakas* should always and inevitably be distinguished from landless agricultural labourers and be identified with peasant proprietors. In some places the text clearly refers to *karṣakas* working in employment of others for fixed wages (*vetana*). 'He should receive a wage as agreed upon, in conformity with the work and time (if the wage is not agreed upon). A cultivator (*karṣaka*), a cowherd (and) a trader should receive one-tenth part of the crops, of butter (and) of the goods dealt in by them (respectively) if the wage is not agreed upon. But if the wage is agreed upon, then as agreed upon.'[21] We also find *karṣakas* accepting collective employment as a union (*saṁghabhṛta*) or a joint undertaking (*saṁbhūya samutthāna*) against payment (*vetana*) to the collective body.[22] In these cases the *karṣakas* were clearly hired labourers and presumably landless.

If we keep in mind this neutral status connotation of the term *karṣaka* in the *Arthaśāstra*, Kauṭilya's attitude that Śūdra/lower *varṇa* 'farmers' (*karṣakas*) should be preferred for agricultural operations assumes a new dimension. Sections and *sūtras* dealing with 'new settlements' (*janapada niveśa and śūnya niveśa*) are highly instructive from this angle.[23] Villages were to be settled 'consisting mostly of Śūdra farmers'.[24] But *brahmadeyas*, exempt from taxes and 'fines' (*daṇḍa*, some kind of state levy here), were to be granted to learned and religious Brāhmaṇas as 'freeholds',[25] and estates without the right of alienation to certain categories of state officers.[26] Arable fields were to be allotted to 'taxpayers' alone and an unarable field was not to be taken away from one who was making it arable. If a field was kept uncultivated it was to be taken away from the defaulting allottee and was to be allotted afresh. 'Or village servants (*grāmabhṛtaka*) and traders (*vaidehaka*) should till it. Or those who do not till should make good the loss (to the treasury).'[27] In these rules there is nothing to suggest that land was allotted to Śūdras; cultivable land was to be normally allotted to taxpayers alone. It is unreasonable to interpret the expression *akṛṣatāṁ ācchidya* as taking away a field from one who does not personally till it. The clear intention of the rules described above is to prevent the possibility of loss to state revenue—Kauṭilya displays almost a morbid obsession with the fear of loss to revenue—caused by keeping a productive land inactive. That these rules had nothing to do with discouraging 'absentee landlordism'[28] is clear from the remedies suggested by him. It seems unlikely that a *vaidehaka* would till the land personally, nor would perhaps a *grāmabhṛtaka* who was a state employee of some status.[29] Moreover, Kauṭilya would not even mind keeping a field idle if the consequent loss to the treasury was compensated. '*Or those who do not till should make good the loss (to the treasury).*' Kauṭilya's scheme of new settlements thus made ample provisions for landholders of different kinds who engaged others to till their lands. The advice that 'the king should enforce discipline on slaves (*dāsa*), persons kept as pledges (*āhitaka*) and kinsmen who do not obey'[30] shows the authoritarian character of Kauṭilya's concept of agricultural management. It is interesting that this advice occurs in the section on new settlements. In the face of his dictum that if one who was not an owner of landed property (*asvāmī*) made a bid to buy such a property he was to be punished,[31] it cannot be maintained that Kauṭilya endeavoured to transform landless Śūdra labourers into owner cultivators.

There is no valid evidence for believing that Kauṭilya took steps to curb the growth of large landholders. We have already seen earlier that he had no compunctions in making landgrants to Brāhmaṇas and some state employees in newly settled areas. It would be wrong to assume that it was a special policy followed in some selected areas which were being developed and that it was a temporary measure. Under perfectly normal conditions also landgrants were made in favour of important dignitaries and people who mattered for the government and administration. Gift of land has been recommended as an important instrument in Kauṭilyan diplomacy. It has been specially recommended as a bait for winning over the supporters of enemies. 'And if an enemy in the rear—a forest chieftain, a principal officer of the enemy or the enemy (himself)—be found capable of being secured by gift of land, he should win his support with (the grant of) land without excellences....'[32] Then follows a hair-splitting analysis of the different kinds of lands to be given to different categories of seducible sections of enemies which include such persons as 'forest chiefs', 'pretender from the family of the enemy', 'a prince in disfavour of the enemy', etc. Obviously such VIPs could not be lured by promises of paltry lands. That large fiefs were sometimes granted to important people is recorded in the following *sūtras*: 'He should overcome with energy, a son, a brother or another member of the family, planning to seize the kingdom; if lacking in energy, by acquiescing in what is seized and by entering into a pact (with him), for fear that he might join the enemy. *Or, he should create confidence in him by grants of land to others like him.*'[33] The above advice to the king was given as a measure to overcome any internal revolt, or the threat of revolt, by members of the royal family or important state officers. Moreover, *akṣapatalādhyakṣa* was asked to enter in his record book 'the receipt of favours, *lands*, use, exemptions, and food and wage by those who serve the king; the receipt of jewels and *land* (and) the receipt of special allowances and (payments for) remedial measures against sudden calamities by the *king* and his *queens* and *sons*'.[34] It clearly proves that estates were granted to members of royal household. State grants of land and village are also referred to elsewhere.[35] Such grants it may be assumed amounted to creating rentfree landed estates. In this context villages exempt from taxes which the administrator (*samāhartṛ*) was required to make a record of[36] appear to refer to such rentfree estates.

Our evidences therefore do not suggest that Kauṭilya envisaged any plan to abolish or even weaken landlordism. What then is the real meaning of his statements that Śūdra *karṣakas, avaravarṇas,* etc., were to be preferred for settling in new areas? It appears that Śūdra labour was extensively used for agricultural operations generally in capacity as hired workers, sometimes as sharecroppers, and more rarely as owner cultivators. In the traditional *varṇa* theory the occupation of agriculture and cattle-farming was assigned to Vaiśyas but certain economic factors, especially the growth of trade, commerce and industry from sixth century BC onwards necessitated some departure from the occupational distributions of the classical *varṇa* scheme. As trade and commerce began weaning away a substantial number of Vaiśyas from agriculture and farming, more and more Śūdras had to be called in for manning these jobs.[37] Thus according to the *Milindapañha*[38] agriculture and cattle-keeping were the occupations of 'ordinary Vaiśyas and Śūdras'. In the same vein the *Arthaśāstra*[39] includes *vārttā* and *kārukuśīlavakarma* among Śūdra's occupations along with service of the twice-borns (*dvijātiśuśrūṣā*) which alone constitutes their proper vocation according to the Smṛtis. And *vārttā* according to the definition in the *Arthaśāstra* included agriculture.[40] Thus a large class of Śūdra farmers arose but the majority of them seem to have been landless cultivators. In this context the following extract appears interesting: '. . . capable of bearing fines and taxes (*daṇḍakara-sahah*), with farmers devoted to work (*karmaśīlakarṣaka*), with a wise master (*abāliśasvāmī*), inhabited mostly by the lower *varṇas* (*avaravarṇaprāya*), with men loyal and honest (*bhaktaśucimanuṣya*)—these are the excellences of a country (*janapada*).'[41] The passage has three important constituent parts (which are the excellences): (i) capacity to yield revenue to the government, (ii) industrious farmers with a wise master, (iii) a large obedient and honest *avaravarṇa* population. Meyer, following Kāmandaka,[42] suggested the reading *bāliśasvāmī* for *abāliśasvāmī* and had interpreted the expression as 'having foolish lords'.[43] The emendation and interpretation of Meyer may be rejected as unreasonable[44] but he seems to have grasped the essence of the meaning of the term *svāmī* in this passage; *svāmī* here stands for a landlord or a local governor and not for the king himself. The *svāmī* in this passage seems to be a kin of *grāmasvāmī*, the village lord.[45] *Svāmī* in this passage cannot refer to the king himself because the excellences of the king have already been mentioned earlier separately;[46] because it does not make sense to misconstrue what really is the excellence of the king (if *abāliśasvāmī* signifies the king as Kangle interprets it) as the excellence of the *janapada*; because the king was the *svāmī* of more than a mere *janapada* whereas the expression *svāmī* in this passage refers only to a *janapada*. It is also not entirely unlikely that the word *svāmī* refers to landowners. Anyway the overall impression that the passage leaves on the reader as far as the farmers and the lower *varṇas* are concerned is that of a dependent peasantry and obedient labourers. *Karmaśīla karṣakas* appear to be just another shade of *karmakaras*. It is practically the same impression that one gathers also from the section on *janapadaniveśa*, where farmers have been distinguished from taxpayers, where land is found allotted to traders and *grāmabhṛtakas* also.

Employment of labour under direct management or the leasing out of lands were the two usual methods of cultivation followed by landholders. Big landholders either got their estates cultivated directly by labourers working for wage (*karmakara*)[47] or by slaves (*dāsa*). Standard wage for such labourers (*karmakara*) seems to have been one-tenth of the produce. However, a different rate could be fixed on mutual agreement between the employer and employee. Apparently in these bargains the advantage generally lay with the landlord. Perhaps in order to improve their bargaining power agricultural labourers sought employment on contract basis collectively as unions (*saṁghabhṛta*); the union undertook to complete the work and distribute wages to individual labourers.[48] There is no direct reference in the *Arthaśāstra* of the employment of *dāsas* in agriculture by private landowners. But since it is clearly stated that *dāsas* were employed by the state in its agricultural operations,[49] and since the employment of *dāsas* was a common feature of early Indian agrarian life,[50] it may be assumed that private landowners also engaged *dāsas* as farmhands.[51]

Landholders also obviously leased out lands. This is clear from some legal injunctions. It was obligatory to fulfil the terms of lease for both the landowner as well as the lessee. But the contract appears to have been generally valid for a very short duration covering presumably a single crop-season and the nature of the contract appears to have been rather loose. Annulment does not seem to have been very difficult. This must have generally worked to the advantage of landowners. It was an offence for both the *kṣetrika* (the owner of field) to take away the field from the *upavāsa* (lessee) and for the lessee to leave the field before sowing.[52] This indicates that at other periods the contract could be cancelled. The distinction made between the *kṣetrika* and *upavāsa* is highly significant and implies that only a full title to ownership would qualify a person to be called a *kṣetrika*.[53] The 'owner' of land seems to have been also technically called the *svāmī*,[54] and his rights differed from the one enjoying mere possession (*bhuktika*).[55] It appears that lessee enjoyed some right of enjoyment, *bhuktika* might signify a lessee, and he could not be evicted at will by the landlord.[56] but what was the nature and extent of this right cannot be fully determined. Whether the term *bhuktika* also covered sharecroppers is not clear. Although sharecroppers are not directly mentioned in relation to private farming, a *sūtra* referring to the wives of sharecroppers (*ardhasītikas*) as liable for debts incurred by their husbands probably indicates that sharecropping was not confined to state farming alone.[57] It may be surmised that the responsibility of fulfilling the obligation of his contract did not lie alone on the sharecropping farmer individually, but on his whole family. Since private irrigation works were leased out (*prakraya*), hired (*avakraya*) or given on share-produce basis (*bhāga*),[58] it may be assumed that similar practices were current in land-system also.

Independent owner cultivators and sharecroppers represented the intermediate zone between the big landholders and landless farm labourers. It is not possible to form any idea about the proportions of land held by these different categories (i.e. big landholders, independent owner cultivators and sharecroppers),[59] but there must have been a considerable number of owner cultivators. *Gṛhapatikas* who were also cultivators (*karṣaka*),[60] and *kuṭumbins* who might be described in modern terminology as medium farmers[61] are referred to in such a manner in the text that it leaves the impression that their number could not have been very insignificant. A normal *gṛhapati* whose means of livelihood was not 'depleted' (*vṛttikṣīṇah*) appears to have been a prosperous landowning cultivator.[62] Although *kuṭumbins* are mentioned in the *Arthaśāstra* in relation with city planning,[63] the context makes it clear that they were agriculturists of some means and stability; and it may be surmised that every *kuṭumbin* was not a city dweller. If the term *kṣetrika* was also used for farmers of this category, it may further be surmised that many of them also employed tenants (*upavāsa*), sharecroppers and hired labourers.[64]

It hardly needs to be emphasized that Brāhmaṇa donees of gift land or state servants who were granted lands would engage others for tilling. It is not unlikely that many of them, particularly the state officers, gave their lands on short-term basis to tenants for cultivation. Such a kind of temporary tenancy is indicated in the following *sūtra*: 'If one does not till land that is inalienable, another may use it for five years and return it after receiving compensation for his exertions.'[65] We have already noted above that land granted to state officers was not alienable.[66] At the time of the termination of this five-yearly tenancy some payment was made to the erstwhile tenant.[67] The *sūtra* succeeding the above quoted one is also interesting. It reads: 'Non-taxpayers living in a different place may live on the produce (of their fields).'[68] As the donees of the *brahmadeya* gifts and officers receiving land-grants did not have to pay taxes,[69] the 'non-taxpayers' of the above rule, to our thinking, refers to such Brāhmaṇas and officers. Many of the Brāhmaṇas and state employees thus were perhaps absentee landlords.[70]

Some restrictions were imposed on free sale of lands. As we have seen above, a *brahmadeya* land could be sold only to a similar recipient of *brahmadeya* grant. The obvious intention was to prevent passing of non-taxable land to people who were not exempted from land revenue and causing loss to state income. We have no means to ascertain whether the restriction would still be imposed if the prospective buyer agreed to pay the normal land revenue. If we are allowed to speculate we might say that the general tenor of Kauṭilyan thought and his great keenness for augmenting state income would suggest that such a measure would meet with his approval. We have also noted above another kind of restriction that one who was not already an 'owner' (*svāmī*) could not make a bid for buying immovable property. Within these broad rules there were other smaller restrictions. 'Kinsmen, neighbours and creditors, in this order, shall have the right to purchase landed property (on sale). After that, others who are outsiders (may bid for purchase)' declare the first two clauses of the rules concerning the sale of immovable property.[71] May be Ghoshal is right in concluding that 'the law of sale of agricultural holdings was purposely designed to prevent the acquisition of estates by capitalists'.[72] But the same rules also would drastically reduce the chances of a landless peasant, even if he could muster the requisite resources through extreme frugality, to acquire land through purchase.

It appears therefore that king's personal estate, state farms and big landholders together must have accounted for a very substantial amount of total holdings. Besides there were a large number of owner cultivators. Sharecroppers and tenants were engaged not only by the state and big landlords but also by the more prosperous owner cultivators. Slaves and hired workmen provided the main labour force for agriculture to both private landholders as well as to state farms. In other words the picture of land distribution that emerges from Kauṭilya's *Arthaśāstra* does not seem to differ substantially from the general pattern that characterized ancient India.

NOTES

1. However, counter to the general view, T.R. Trautmann finds the *Arthaśāstra* a compilation of works by different hands. Trautmann, *Kauṭilya and the Arthaśāstra (A Statistical Investigation of the Authorship and Evolution of the Text)*, Leiden, 1971, pp. 70-8, 118-19, 169-87.
2. R.P. Kangle, *The Kauṭilīya Arthaśāstra,* Part III, Bombay, 1965, p. 168.
3. E.H. Jhonston, *JRAS,* 1929, pp. 90-1; Kangle, op. cit., pt. II, p. 149, n. 2; cf., *svāpateyaṁ, Mahāvastu,* R.G. Basak (ed.), vol. I, Calcutta 1963, p. 464.
4. *Artha.*, 2.16.4, 8, 11, etc.
5. *Artha.,* 4.2.28.

6. *Artha.*, 4.2.24-36.
7. For *daṇḍapratikartṛ*, see *Artha.*, 2.23.2, 3.13.18.
8. *Artha.*, 2.24.2, 2.24. 28-9.
9. *Artha.*, 2.15.43-6.
10. Cf. *ārdhika*, Manu., IV. 253.
11. *Artha*, 2.24.16; Kangle, op. cit., II, p. 150, n. 16 is of the opinion that *svavīropajīvins* paid three-fourth or four-fifth of the produce to the state and that whereas the *ardhasītikas* had to bring their own implements, equipments, seeds, etc., these were provided to the *svavīryopajīvins* by the state. In that case the *svavīryopajīvins* were just another category of agrarian labourers and their employment would be preferred as more economical over leasing out land to *ardhasītikas*. But the impression one gathers from the section on the *sītādhyakṣa* is that the descending order of preference by the state machinery for the disposal of state agricultural land was: (i) employment of wage labourers (*dāsākarmakara*, etc.), (ii) giving land to *ardhasītikas*, and (iii) to *svavīryopajīvins*. These categories are also mentioned in the above order, *Artha.*, 2.24.2, 16. However, the term *svavīryopajīvin* reminds one of the expression *śūdrāṁśca ātmopajīvin* in Manu. VII. 138, which according to commentators means free Śūdra labourers working for wage.
12. See above note.
13. See, e.g. U.N. Ghoshal, *A History of Indian Public Life*, vol. II, Oxford University Press, 1966, ch. V; Jaimal Rai, op. cit., pp. 50-1.
14. *Artha.*, 2.1.
15. R.S. Sharma, *Śūdras in Ancient India*, Varanasi, 1958, pp. 147, 173; R.S. Sharma, *Light on Early Indian Society and Economy*, Bombay, 1966, p. 66.
16. Jaimal Rai, *Rural Urban Economy and Social Changes in Ancient India*, Varanasi, 1974, pp. 46-57; 'The position of the nobility, comprising aristocrats thriving on agrarian economy from the early Vedic age, was seriously undermined', ibid., p. 57; cf. U.N. Ghoshal, op. cit., pp. 88-9. The present author was also till very recently of the same view (S.C. Bhattacharya, *Some Aspects of Indian Society*, Calcutta, 1978, pp. 159-61).
17. *Artha.*, 2.1.2, 6.1.8, 7.11.21.
18. *Artha.*, 1.11.9-10; cf. 2.35.8.
19. *Artha.*, 2.35.4; they are also distinguished from *gorakṣaka*, *vaidehaka*, and *kāru*, some of the other occupational groups, all presumably belonging to Śūdra *varṇa*.
20. *Artha.*, 2.24.2, see note 8; Cf. R. Fick, *Social Organisation in North-East India in Buddha's Time*, Delhi, 1972 (rpt.), p. 305; K.M. Saran, *Labour in Ancient India*, Bombay, 1957, p. 25; D. Chanana, *Slavery in Ancient India*, New Delhi, 1960, p. 108.
21. *Artha.*, 3.13. 27-9.
22. *Artha.*, 3.14. 18-22.
23. *Artha.*, 2.1.

24. *Artha.*, 2.1.2; Cf. 6.1.8, 7.11.21.
25. Gift, passed in inheritance, could also be sold to a similar grantee of *brahmadeya*, *Artha.*, 3.10.9.
26. *Artha.*, 2.1.7.
27. *Karadebhyah kṛtakṣetrānyaikapuruṣikāṇi prayacchet, akṛtāni kaṛtṛbhyo nādeyāni. akṛṣatāṁācchidyānyebhyah prayacchet. grāmabhṛtakavaidehakā va kṛṣeyuh. akṛṣanto vāvahīnaṁ dadyuh, Artha.*, 2.1.8-12.
28. Jaimal Rai, op. cit., pp. 48-9.
29. *Artha.*, 5.3.23, he got a salary of five hundred; Cf. Kangle, op. cit., II, p. 56, n. 11.
30. *Artha.*, 2.1.25.
31. *Artha.*, 3.9.7.
32. *Artha.*, 7.16.16.
33. *Artha.*, 9.3.15-16 (my emphasis).
34. *Artha.*, 2.7.2 (my emphasis).
35. *Artha.*, 2.35.3.
36. *Artha.*, 2.35.13.
37. Sibesh Bhattacharya, 'The Rise of the Vaiśyas in the Post Vedic Period', *South Asian Review*, October, 1973, pp. 46-9.
38. V. Trenckner (ed.), London, 1928, p. 178.
39. *Artha.*, 1.3.8.
40. *Artha.*, 1.4.1.
41. *Artha.*, 6.1.8.
42. *Kāmandaka*, 4.54.
43. Cited by Kangle, op. cit., 11, p. 315, n. 8.
44. Kangle, ibid.
45. *Artha.*, 4.13.8; for the importance of the village lord in the rural society during this period, see B.N.S. Yadava, 'Some Aspects of the Changing Order in India during the Śaka-Kuṣāna Age', *Kusana Studies*, G.R. Sharma (ed.), Allahabad, 1968, pp. 81-3.
46. *Artha.*, 6.1.2-6.
47. *Artha.*, 3.13. 26-9.
48. *Artha.*, 3.14. 19-24.
49. *Artha.*, 2.24.2.
50. See note 20.
51. *Dāsa* and *karmakara* are usually coupled together, *Artha.*, 2.24.2, 2.35.4; chs. 13 and 14 of the third book are called *dāsakarmakarkalpah.*
52. *Artha.*, 3.10.8.
53. Kangle, op. cit., pt. III, p. 170.
54. *Artha.*, 3.9.7. 17; in 3.9.32 the ownership of a *Setubandha* is indicated by the team *Svāmyṁ.*
55. Distinction between 'ownership' and 'possession' was made by the use of terms *svatva, Svāmītva* on the one hand and *bhuj* and its derivatives on the other (U.N. Ghoshal, *The Agrarian System in Ancient India*, Calcutta, 1973 rpt., ch. V, especially pp. 109ff; Cf. *Mitaksara* on *Yaj*, II 27).

56. *Artha.*, 3.10.8.
57. *Artha.*, 3.11.23.
58. *Artha.*, 3.9.35-6.
59. A.N. Bose thinks that land was mostly concentrated in the hands of Brāhmaṇa landlords, *Social and Rural Economy in Northern India*, vol. I, Calcutta 1970, pp. 173ff, vol. II, Calcutta, 1967, p. 261. R.S. Sharma, however, feels that peasant proprietors and well-to-do peasants had more land in their possession than Brāhmaṇa and Kṣatriya landlords, *Light on Early Indian Society and Economy*, p. 62.
60. *Artha.*, 1.11. 9-10; 1.12.22; 2.35.8.
61. G.P. Mishra, *Some Aspects of Change in Agrarian Structure*, Institute for Social and Economic Change (Bangalore), Monograph 4, New Delhi, 1977, pp. 3-5.
62. *Artha.*, 1.11.9-10.
63. *Artha.*, 2.4. 24-5.
64. In the Buddhist literature *gahapatis* and *kuṭumbikas* appear to have been considerable landholders. *Gahapatis* in fact were both business magnates and big landholders. Sibesh Bhattacharya, 'The Meaning and Significance of the Term Gahapati', *Archiv Orientalni*, vol. 44, 1976, pp. 149ff. However, it is not quite certain whether the *gahapati* of the Buddhist texts and early Brahmi inscriptions ought to be identified with the *gṛhapatika* of the *Arthaśāstra*.
65. *Artha.*, 3.10.13.
66. *Artha.*, 2.1.7.
67. If the *Arthaśāstra* is accepted as a text of the Mauryan period, it may be suggested that this rule was made to protect the interest of the 'officer-landowners' who, as Asokan inscriptions indicate (Third Major Rock Edict), used to go on long tours every fifth year. During the absence of an officer serving his tenure elsewhere away from the place of his landed property such temporary five-yearly tenancy might have been given to a peasant. This, however, is a mere hypothesis.
68. *Artha.*, 3.10.15.
69. *Milindapañha*, p. 146, clearly indicates that state officers were exempt from taxation; Cf. Kangle, op. cit., III. p. 171.
70. Kangle, op. cit., II, p. 223, n. 15, seems to have missed the real import of the *sūtra* and remarked that 'the implication may be that tax-paying farmers cannot be absentee landlords'.
71. *Artha.*, 3.9.1-2.
72. U.N. Ghoshal, *A History of Indian Public Life*, vol. II, p. 89.

2

Village Life and Settlements in the Light of Vākāṭaka Inscriptions

R.N. Mishra

The Vākāṭakas represent the rise of a dynasty (in the Vindhya and Vindhya *pṛishṭha*[1] regions) which eventually became largely instrumental in spreading the Brahmanical Great Tradition in the region under their control by following an aggressive policy of establishing settlements most of which were given to practising agricultural pursuits on one hand and Vedic and Śāstric rituals on the other. These settlements, variously designated in the Vākāṭaka inscriptions as *kheṭaka, vāṭaka, pallī, grāma, pura, gulma* and *nagara,* seem to have carried out activities which are sometimes metioned explicitly and sometimes can be inferred from the contexts occurring in the inscriptions.

The Vākāṭaka grants, of which 34 have been discovered so far,[2] refer to donations of 23 villages[3] besides certain measures of land referred to in terms of *nivartana.*[4] In all the cases, donees were brāhmaṇas of various *Śākhās, Charaṇas*[5] and *Gotras.* As regards the villages, they have been mentioned in different contexts, sometimes as the ones that were donated, sometimes as denoting boundaries of the donated village and sometimes as situated on the different *mārgas.* The inscriptions refer to 10 such *mārgas,* namely Uttaramārga, Padmapurā-pūrvamārga, Padmapurā-parāmārga, Śailapuramārga, Jamālakheṭakamārga, Kosikamārga, Gepurakamārga, Varadākheṭakamārga, Yaśapuramārga and Sundhātimārga.[6] Location of villages on the *mārgas* seems to denote their economic importance, though it would perhaps be conceded that trade was neither brisk nor rich during the period under review and the *mārgas* represented internal routes of communication, if not administrative units, in some cases.

The names of the villages are interesting in that they seem to reflect some kind of hierarchy in terms of the size of the settlements. As against six capital towns or *nagaras* namely Nandivardhana, Pravarapura,[7] Padmapura,[8] Vatsagulma[9] Aśvatthanagara[10] and Lohanagara[11], 103 villages are mentioned in 34 inscriptions of the Vākāṭakas.[12] To this list of six cities we may add the names Purikā and Chanakā[13] which are associated with the Vākāṭakas in the Purāṇas. The names of some of the settlements seem to have been derived from the flora of the region (e.g. Sirīsagrāma,[14] Vilavaṇaka,[15] Vaṭapūraka,[16] Ārāmaka,[17] Kadambasāraka,[18] Kokilāra,[19] Aśvatthakheṭaka[20] or from their mineral resources or occupational associations (e.g. Charmāṅka,[21] Hiraṇyapura,[22] Karmakāra,[23] Lohanagara,[24] Lekhpallikā,[25] Śailapura).[26] The suffixes added to the names seem to grade the settlements in some kind of hierarchical position depending upon density of population. Their relative density of population is indicated by their names with the suffixes like *kheṭaka, pallī, vāṭaka,* etc. The details follow:

(1) *Kheṭaka* : Kinihikheṭaka,[27] Aśvatthakheṭaka,[28] Varadākheṭaka.[29]
(2) *Vāṭaka* : Bonṭhikavāṭaka,[30] Dhuvavāṭaka,[31] Añjanavāṭaka,[32] Brāhmaṇa-vāṭaka,[33] Pavarajjavāṭaka.[34]
(3) *Pallī* : Chinchapallī,[35] Vijayapallī (vāṭaka),[36] Lekhapallikā,[37] Maṇipallikā.[38]
(4) *Grāma* : Sirīsagrāma,[39] Niligrāma,[40] Griddhagrāma,[41] Maṇḍūkigrāma,[42] Badarīgrāma.[43]
(5) *Pura* : Kolipura,[44] Chandrapura,[45] Hiraṇyapura,[46] Brahmapuraka,[47] Gepura,[48] Yaśapura,[49] Sudhāpura,[50] Pravarapura, Padmapura.
(6) *Nagara* : Aśvatthanagara, Lohanagara.
(7) *Gulma* : Vatsagulma.
(8) *Vardhana* : Nandivardhana.

Some remark may be necessary to explain the suffixes, occurring in the cases of the units of settlement mentioned above. According to Pāṇini, *kheṭaka* was a suffix of contempt denoting smallness of a settlement.[51] However, a later work *Bṛihatkathā* defines *kheṭa* as surrounded by rivers or hills.[52] *Vāṭaka* may refer to settlement having some kind of a surrounding enclosure. This boundary or enclosure may have sometimes been only notional, as in case of the 'Pravareśara-shaḍvimśati vāṭaka' mentioned in the Belora plates of Pravarasena II.[53] As regards *pallī*, it is equated with *ghosha* in the *Amarakośa*. *Ghosha* denoted a pastoral or cowherd settlement.[54] Grāma(s) are profusely mentioned in the texts, and they could vary in size as regards their population they could consist of one *kuṭi* or 2 or 3 or 4 according to the *Vinayapiṭaka*, or could, on the other hand, have 100 to 500 families, according to Kauṭilya.[55] Villages were also known as *padra*; in one instance, a Vākāṭaka grant refers to Ākāsapadda[56] as the name of a village. As regards the words *pura* and *nagara*, they seem to have been synonymous, as is seen in the *Rāmāyaṇa* in reference to Ayodhyā, which is described as *Ayodhyānāmanagari-Yāpurī*.[57] In two cases in the Vākāṭaka grant *pura* occurs for the capital town, viz., Pravarapura and Padmapura. The suffix *gulma* in the name Vatsagulma is also quite interesting. Manu regards *gulma* as a station where an army unit was posted for protection of the kingdom.[57] Vatsagulma could therefore have been a garrison-town as well as a capital.

It would appear from these details that Vākāṭaka villages were of different sizes, and that in the settlement complex the village-town ratio stood at 6:103. As mentioned earlier, some of these villages were variously situated and included those located on the *mārgas* or routes of communication.

Inscriptions do not yield much information about the residents of these villages, though it seems that they contained a fairly large number of śūdra cultivators. Kauṭilya says that the population of a village should mostly consist of śūdra cultivators and this position has been accepted by Ghosh as representing a realistic situation in view of the villages' role vis-a-vis that of cities in terms of production and consumption patterns.[59] Large landholdings of individual brāhmaṇa donees in the Vākāṭaka grants[60] seem to confirm this position. These grants refer to donation of 23 villages to individual brāhmaṇas.[61] Somārya was twice a donee.[62] Sometime 25 to 400 *nivartanas* of land were donated to single individuals.[63] The connotation of the *nivartana* measure is uncertain; it is variously explained as anything from 3/4 to 4 acres of land.[64] Baudhāyana (3.2. 1-4) refers to householders subsisting on 6 *nivartanas* of land, which would suggest that a donation of this size was just enough for subsistence.[65] Larger measures consisting of 50 or more *nivartanas* must have required śūdra cultivators, who, it may be concluded, lived in particular villages donated to brāhmaṇas. There is yet another piece of evidence to suggest the presence of śūdra cultivators in the villages. The Ridhpur plate refers to grant of a village together with four huts of cultivators—*sakarṣakaniveśanāni.*[66] This would indicate employment of śūdras in agricultural operations by the owner of land. Besides brāhmaṇas, these village settlements also contained peasants (*brāmaṇādyān-grāmakuṭumbin*)[67] or 'other residents'[68] who were sometimes 'commanded' in the grant as addresses. Among other addresses occur such officials as *sarvādhyaksha,*[69] soldiers, policemen,[70] and *grāma-mahattara*[71] who might also have lived in the villages.

As regards economic and other activities in a Vākāṭaka village, it appears that the brāhmaṇas carried on their religious and ritual activities from the villages unhindered and greatly patronized by the state. Different kinds of economic operations were pursued in the villages which is indicated by references in the grants. There does not seem to have been much pressure on land, which in turn indicates a low density of population. Land granted to donees was in the range of 25, 50, 60 and 400 *nivartanas* to individual brāhmaṇas;[72] 2000 *nivartanas* to 4 brāhmaṇas in one case[73] and 8000 *nivartanas* to 1000 brāhmaṇas of whom only 49 have been named.[74] Mirashi says that these 49 'perhaps represented others or were the heads of the families' or, the number would perhaps refer vaguely to a 'large number of brāhmaṇas, so benefited'.[75] Presence of śūdra cultivators, however, would indicate that agricultural operation was the chief economic activity of the Vākāṭaka villages. Some of them, as their names seem to indicate, could have been centres of production involving manufacture and sale of objects made of iron, stone, gem, gold and leather. This may be inferred from the villages having names like Lohanagara, Śailapura, Maṇipallikā, Suvarṇapura, Charmāṅka, etc.

In the administrative dispensation in regard to grants, certain concessions and immunities are offered to the donees in the Vākāṭaka charters. These may indirectly refer to the normal activities in the villages, of which the benefit was transferred by state to the donees; even as such activities generating revenue continued. These activities included purchasing and fermenting liquor, digging salt, presenting grains, supplying flowers and milk, cows, grass, hides, charcoal and using mines and Khadira trees.[76]

This would indicate that agriculture and animal husbandry were the main economic activities in the Vākāṭaka villages, which must have been of varying size, existing sparsely and inhabited by the brāhmaṇa donees and śūdra cultivators. In comparison, there was perhaps less of trade and industry; there is only one instance of a merchant named *vāṇijaka* Chandra who is mentioned as having purchased half of a Vākāṭaka village and donated it to a brāhmaṇa.[77] In the Hisse Borela inscription a reference is made to Ārya Svāmilladeva, the *ajñākara* of the Vākāṭaka Devasena, who excavated a Sudarśana lake for the welfare of all human beings.[78] It may or may not have been an irrigation tank.

The Vākāṭakas thus appear to have founded village settlements in the territory under their rule on a fairly large scale which perhaps led to a considerable increase in agricultural production.

NOTES

1. B.N. Mukherjee (1984), 'A Note on the original Habitat and Kingdom of Vākāṭakas', read in the U.G.C. Seminar on 'The Age of the Vākāṭakas' held at Nagpur University from 28 to 31 January 1984 (hereafter *VSN-84*).
2. Cf. a paper of K.M. Shrimali read in VSN-84. The number of these grants is now 40. The reference to villages and their names occur in connection with donations, or as places of residence of brāhmaṇas, or in reference to boundaries, etc.
3. Ibid.
4. V.V. Mirashi (1963), *Vākāṭaka Inscriptions, Corpus Inscriptionum Indicarum*, vol. V, Ootacamund, inscription nos. 6, 10, 12, 13, 14 which respectively refer to grant of 8000, 25 and 60,400 and 2000 *nivartana* of land to various brāhmaṇas of different *Sākhās* and *Gotras. Nivartana* was a royal measure. The Pandhurua Plates of Pravarasena VI refer to a gift of 25 *nivartana* of land with one additional *nivartana* for a residential house '*rājamānena bhumeḥ pañchaviṁśatiḥ niveśana nivartatena saḥ*'. This would indicate that one residential house required the space of a *nirvartana* of land. Shrimali (op. cit.) similarly quotes Baudhāyana to indicate that 6 *nivartanas* were sufficient for a householder's subsistence.
5. Malati Mahajan (1984), 'Administrative Divisions under the Vākāṭakas', a paper read in VSN-84. Mahajan says 'sometimes roads leading to different towns are named (in Vākāṭaka inscriptions) after those towns. In the early period these roads ran either through the forests or through the waste land. In course of time human habitation came into existence on either side of these roads and later on these roads were probably

recognized as administrative units. Sometimes these were named after the direction in which they lay and sometimes were named after the city to which they ran.'

6. Mirashi (1963), insc. nos. 2, 3, 4 and 5; ibid., insc. nos. 6, 10, 13.
7. Ibid., insc. nos 6, 10, 13.
8. Ibid., insc. no. 17.
9. Ibid., insc. nos. 23, 24.
10. Ibid., insc. no. 8, p. 36 line 12.
11. Ibid., insc. no. 13, Mirashi (1963), p. 59 describes it as the headquarters of an ancient division ...; represented by Lori about 9 miles south-west of Warud. When pura-ending names are further added to these six nagarā-ending cities, the number of the cities will increase. The problem needs reconsideration.
12. For the total number of villages as 103, reference is to the figure as quoted in K.M. Shrimali, op. cit.
13. Cf. Mirashi (1963), pp. XI-XII.
14. Ibid., insc. no. 2.
15. Ibid., insc. no. 2.
16. Ibid., insc. no. 7.
17. Ibid., insc. no. 9.
18. Ibid., insc. no. 12.
19. Ibid., insc. no. 12.
20. Ibid., insc. no. 13.
21. Ibid., insc. no. 6.
22. Ibid., insc. no. 10.
23. Ibid., insc. no. 10.
24. Ibid., insc. no. 13.
25. Ibid., insc. no. 14.
26. Ibid., insc. nos. 4-5, p. 19.
27. Ibid., insc. no. 7.
28. Ibid., insc. no. 13.
29. Ibid.
30. Ibid., insc. no. 3.
31. Ibid., insc. no. 14.
32. Ibid., insc. no. 9.
33. Ibid., insc. no. 14.
34. Ibid., insc. no. 7.
35. Ibid., insc. no. 3.
36. Ibid., insc. no. 14.
37. Ibid.
38. Ibid., insc. no. 15.
39. Ibid., insc. no. 2.
40. Ibid., insc. no. 12.
41. Ibid.
42. Ibid., insc. no. 3.

43. Ibid., insc. no. 14.
44. Ibid., insc. no. 7.
45. Ibid., insc. no. 10.
46. Ibid.
47. Ibid., insc. nos. 15, 7.
48. Ibid., insc. no. 9.
49. Ibid., insc. no. 15.
50. Ibid., insc. no. 15.
51. Cf. A Ghosh (1973), *City in Early Historical India*, Simla, p. 37.
52. Ibid.
53. Mirashi (1963), insc. nos. 4-5.
54. Ghosh (1973), p. 37.
55. A. Ghosh (1973), p. 36.
56. V.V. Mirashi (1963), insc. no. 23.
57. A. Ghosh (1973), p. 45, fn. 1, quoting from the *Rāmāyaṇa*, I, 5. 6.
58. A. Ghosh (1973), p. 48.
59. Ibid., p. 36 quoting Kauṭilya.
60. Mirashi (1973), insc. nos 2, 3, 4-5, 7, 9, etc.
61. K.M. Shrimali, op. cit.
62. Ibid., also Mirashi (1963), insc. nos 6 (p. 25) and 14.
63. 400 *nivartana* of land was granted to Brāhmaṇa Rudrārya; (Mirashi insc. no. 12), 2000 *nivartana* of land to different brāhmaṇas and Somārya (ibid., insc. no. 14), 8000 *nivartana* of land to 1000 Brāhmaṇaṣ 25 *nivartana* to Yakshārya, and 60 *nivartana* to Kaliśarman were also granted; Cf. Mirashi, insc. nos. 6, 10.
64. K.M. Shrimali (1984), quoting *EI*, 28 p. 245.
65. Ibid. See also above, n. 4.
66. Mirashi (1963), p. 36, line 15 'We have in this town donated the field enjoyed (so far) by Bhuktaka together with a farm house situated in it (and four huts of cultivators, to the brāhmaṇas . . .).' Mirashi 1963, p. 37.
67. Ibid., insc. no. 2.
68. Ibid., insc. no. 15.
69. Ibid., insc. no. 10.
70. Ibid., insc. no. 11.
71. Ibid., insc. no. 8.
72. Ibid., insc. nos. 10, 14, 13; Cf. also Shrimali, op. cit.
73. Ibid., insc. no. 14.
74. Ibid., insc. no. 6.
75. Ibid., p. 23, fn. 1.
76. Ibid., insc. no. 2 (p. 9), no. 3 (p. 14), insc. nos. 4-5 (p. 20), etc., also Shrimali, op. cit.
77. Mirashi (1963).
78. K.M. Shrimali, op. cit.

3

Settlement Pattern in Lalgudi Taluk, Tiruchirapalli District, Tamil Nadu

K.V. Raman and P. Shanmugam

The present study is an attempt to analyse the settlement pattern in the Lalgudi taluk from the earliest times to the end of the thirteenth century AD. The study is based on epigraphs and monuments, supported by field survey. About 70 villages,[1] distributed in the wet, dry and intermediate zones, were visited to assess the archaeological wealth of the area.

The earliest settlers of the area seem to have occupied the Southern parts of the taluk, adjacent to the river Kollidam (Coleron). Evidence of their occupation is attested to by the presence of a kind of pottery—Black and Red ware—used by the people. Pieces of such pottery were collected on the surface in the following 9 villages situated along the northern bank of the river: (1) Sirukambur, (2) Gopurappatti (Paccur), (3) Panamaṅgalam, (4) Melavaladi, (5) Nagar, (6) Tirumaṅgalam, (7) Pachchampettai, (8) Pinnavasal and (9) Komakudi. At Sirukambur, Panamaṅgalam, Nagar, Tirumaṅgalam, Pachchampettai and Pinnavasal the present habitation is located just above the low mound, yielding the ancient pottery. In Melavaladi the ancient mound has been disturbed to a greater extent and very little of the ancient remains are now available. The mound is reduced to a flat field and is now under active cultivation. In Komakudi, the mound is situated on the side of a big tank. On the basis of surface indications it may be suggested that the mound was not disturbed much. At Gopurappatti, the

*We are grateful to Mr. Shyam Narayan Lal for having drawn afresh the accompanying map.

ancient site is put under intensive cultivation and much of the low mound is disturbed.

The Black and Red ware is associated with ancient settlers of Tamil Nadu. This pottery was first used by the iron using megalithic folk and continued to be in use in the early centuries of the Christian era. The pottery was unearthed in all the megalithic levels in south India.[2] Further in the excavations at Uraiyur,[3] a suburb of Tiruchirapalli, just on the opposite bank of Lalgudi taluk, Black and Red ware was unearthed at the lowest levels. The excavations at Tirukkampuliyūr and Alagarai,[4] places situated on the northern and southern banks of Kaveri in the Musiri and Kulittalai taluks respectively, have yielded Black and Red ware at the early levels. This pottery has been dated to the end of the first century BC on the basis of dated antiquities at Arikamedu.[5] At Uraiyur this pottery is dated to pre-second century BC on the basis of relative chronology. At a few places in Tamil Nadu the Black and Red ware has been dated to pre-third century BC on the C^{14} showing.[6] However, in Lalgudi, also such an earlier date is possible but can not be confirmed as they were all collected on surface. The settlements can however be dated to a period not later than the first few centuries of the Christian era.

The choice of these ancient settlements of the ancient people seems to have depended on the irrigational facilities, since all these habitations were situated in the wet zone, and along the Koḷḷidam river. It is difficult to suggest when these settlements came to an end. The accumulation of the ancient habitation deposit seems to be very thin, indicating a shorter period of occupation. It can be surmised that the people have abandoned the settlements in some places while in others continuity could be seen. The suggestion is based on the evidence, that in some of the early historical settlements the present habitations are situated just above the ancient habitations without any intervening period of habitation. The reason for the abandonment of the settlements could be the floods in the river, which was not a rare phenomenon in ancient times.

Settlements of the Pallava times are known from literature and epigraphs. The Śaiva Nāyanmārs, who visited the religious centres in this area have glorified them with their songs. The Dēvaram hymnists have praised the deities in the villages at Tiruppaṅgili, Pachchil, Manturai and Anbil, all situated along the course of the river Koḷḷidam.[7] The existence of temples presupposes settlements nearby. These settlements could be older than seventh century AD. It may be observed that the Pallava settlements were situated very near the early historic settlements discussed above. The Dēvaram hymns do not throw any light on the composition of these settlements.

Some Pallava settlements are known from epigraphs. The earliest Pallava settlement seems to be Nichchavinita-mangalam.[8] Nichchavinita may be a corrupt form of Nityavinita, a title of Pallava Mahendravarman I (AD 610-30). The Chola inscriptions use the correct form Nityavinita[9] and it may be concluded that this Brāhmin settlement was established during the days of Mahendravarman I. Pallava settlements were at Tiruveḷḷarai, Tiruppaṅgili, Pallapuram (hamlet of Pervalanallur), Naḷḷimaṅgalam, Tiruttavatturai (Lalgudi), Tiruvisalur, Javantinathapuram (Tirumayilrangam), Idaiyarrumaṅgalam, Sirugavur, Tenkankudi and Alambakkam. In these settlements, the name Nallimaṅgalam[10] seems to be a corrupt form of Nandimaṅgalam probably named after Nandivarman II (AD 731-96). Both the settlements, Tiruvisalur and Alambakkam had the name Dantivaramamaṅgalam. Probably these settlements received the name from the Pallava king Dantivarman (AD 796-846).[11] Peruvalanallur seems to be a settlement known at least from the times of Paramesvaravarman (AD 670-91), as this place is mentioned as a battlefield where the king Paramesvaravarman defeated his enemy western Chāḷukya Vikramāditya I (AD 675).[12] Idaiyarrumaṅgalam and Tirumayilrangam are mentioned in the inscriptions of the Pāṇḍya king Maranjadaiyan (AD 862-85) at Javantinathapuram.[13] At Tiruveḷḷarai,[14] inscriptions of Dantivarman are known. A Pallava rock cut cave at Tiruppaṅgili suggests the existence of a Pallava settlement.

A study of the above settlements would indicate an increase in the number of settlements during the Pallava times. The Pallava settlements were established somewhat far away from the ancient settlements. At the same time the settlements were established in the dry zone also. Peruvalanaḷḷur, Alampakkam, Tiruveḷḷarai and Tiruppaṅgili, though situated very near to the Koḷḷidam river they are all located in the dry zone and on an elevated plan. About the size and composition of these settlements we have very meagre information. Tiruppaṅgili and Tiruveḷḷarai seem to be big and important settlements. To this may be added Pallapuram, though a comparatively smaller settlement but later it enlarged into a big complex. All these places have rock cut shrines. These settlements have big tanks, probabl excavated during the Pallava rule. The lands of these villages, were mostly cultivated by tank irrigation. The Pallavas have excavated few tanks in this area. At Tiruveḷḷarai, a chief of Dantivarman constructed a tank and named it after the king as Marppidugu-eri.[15] At Alampakkam another tank was excavated by a chief during the days of Nandivarman III.[16] These tanks were used for irrigational purposes as well as for providing drinking water. Though such instances of excavation of tanks were not numerous, with the available evidence it can be suggested that royal patronage was extended to the population for the excavation of tanks away from the old or ancient habitations.

A large number of new settlements were occupied by the Brāhmins. These settlements were established by the Pallavas probably from the time of Mahendravarman I. About the size and hamlets of the settlements we have little information. Tiruveḷḷarai, had a hamlet with the name Tennur.[17]

During the Early Chola times also some new settlements were established. Apart from the Pallava settlements, new settlements like Anittiramaṅgalam, Saṭṭamaṅgalam, Kalvanmaṅgalam, Gundasilamaṅgalam, Kottamaṅgalam and Panamaṅgalam were established under the patronage of kings. Other settlements like Adigudi, Karandai Padala Pudukkudi, Kattur, Sirumaruvur, Tiruvaypadi, Pooalūr, Ingaiyūr, Sattanpadi, Turaiyūr and Manakkal are known from epigraphs in the early tenth century AD. Most of the settlements were established near the older Pallava settlements. These settlements could have been in existence even in the Pallava times or even earlier but became prominent only in the early Chola times. New settlements were also established on the dry areas. Settlements like Tiruppidavūr (Tiruppattur), were established during Rājendra I's time (AD 1012-44).

In the late Chola period also numerous settlements were established. More than 60 settlements are known from the epigraphs. Many of these settlements were located in the dry zone. In the wet zone, new settlements like Apputikurai, Iśāṇaikurai, Udaramaṅgalam, Ulundankudi, Kiramaṅgalam, Kurrur, Sirrambur, Sattamangalam, Chempalani Chentinai, Tandankurai, Talakkudi, Pangayach Chelvinallur, Piraikkudi kumaramaṅgalam and Paingani were known. These settlements seem to be smaller in size than the earlier settlements. In the dry zone many new settlements were established. Idaimalai, Urrattur, Garuvidamaṅgalam, Kallaikudaiyan Kudī-iruppu, Kurukkai, Sangendi, Sanmaṅgalam, Siruvalaippur Tattankurichi, Tirunedungur, Tiruppidavur and Nerkulam were a few settlements established in the dry zone. These settlements seem to be bigger than the settlements in the wet zone. Some of the settlements in the intermediate zone were Venganattam, Muvarayinallur and Kannanur.

A few of these Chola settlements have *piḍāgai* or hamlets. Madhurantaka Chaturvēdimaṅgalam[18] (Nattamankudi) had three *piḍāgais*: (1) Tirunārāyaṇanallur; (2) Mangudi alias Tyagasamudranaḻḻūr, and (3) Nottur. Sangendi,[19] Tiruppidavūr (Tiruppattur), Todaiyur and Srikanta Chaturvēdimaṅgalam had each one *piḍāgai*. Chirusattamaṅgalam,[20] a hamlet of Todaiyūr, was separated from the village some time about AD 1224. Panamaṅgalam[21] had a hamlet called Senguṇḍai situated on the west of the village. Tiruveḻḻarai[22] had five hamlets: On the west two hamlets (a) Avaninārāyaṇamaṅgalam and (b) Muttam alias Nadaripugalanallur were located; Muvayiranallur seems to be another western hamlet (Muvarayanpalayam). This and Manpirai, another hamlet were separated from Tiruveḻḻarai sometime in AD 1132. Adatkudi was later added to Tiruveḻḻarai in AD 1200 as a hamlet.

Realignment of a few of the settlements are known from epigraphs. A few instances of bifurcation of *piḍāgai* (hamlets) are also known. In one instance[23] the hamlet Alaivay was separated from Sattamaṅgalam to be added with Kulōttuṅga Choḻakkurrur. In another instance, Adattkudi[24] was made a hamlet of Tiruveḻḻarai. Muvayiranallur and Manpirai, two hamlets, were separated from Tiruveḻḻarai.[25] Chirusattamaṅgalam, a hamlet of Todaiyur, was separated from it in AD 1224.[26] During Rājarāja II's time about nine hamlets were added to form a big village Kulottuṅga Choḻakkurrur[27] (Gaṇḍarāditya Chaturvēdimaṅgalam). They are: (1) Chembiyanmadevinallur, (2) Rājarājankurrur, (3) Karkudi, (4) Karikudichcheri, (5) Vinnamaṅgalam, (6) Rajagambirakkurrur (Korramaṅgalam), (7) Valavankurrur, (8) Butippattamaṅgalam alias Pagaiaruttukkoṇḍa Choḻanallur, and (9) Alaivay (separated from Sattamaṅgalam). The reason for the realigments are not clearly known. It could have been for the easy assessments and collection of land taxes.

About the composition of the settlements some information is available. The village settlement was known by the name *ūrnaṭtam.* Different groups of people lived at various quarters. The settlements of the merchants were known as *puram* or *ūr.* The settlements on the bank of the river Koḷḷidam were named as *kurai.* The settlement of the Paraiyas was known as *Paraichchēri.* A *paraichchēri*[28] for Kilur, a hamlet of Srikanta Chaturvēdimaṅgalam, is mentioned. Another *Paraichchēri*[29] is known for Nerkkulam. The Pulaiya quarter[30] at Valadi was known as *pulaichchēri.* Another *pulaichchēri nattam* is mentioned for Chembiyankurrur.[31] The settlement of the brāhmins was known by the name *chaturvēdimaṅgalam* or *agaram.*[32] A part of the village was known by the name *chēri* (Ilattuvaniyachcheri).[33] Streets in the settlements are known as *vidi* and *perunteru.* The Śiva temple at Pachchil was known as *merrali* indicating that the temple was located on the western side of the village settlement.[34]

The Chola state took steps for the establishment of new settlements. The Brāhmin settlements were established on two different lines. Old settlements were granted to brāhmins and the name was suitably modified. In the second instance, new settlements were created and gifted to brāhmins. The village Tirukkarambanturi was given to brāhmins with the new name Guṇasilamaṅgalam.[35] In another instance, Dantivarmamaṅgalam (Alambakkam), a Pallava brāhmin settlement, was renamed twice as Gaṇḍarāditya Chaturvēdimaṅgalam[36] and Madhurantaka Chaturvēdimaṅgalam.[37] Apart from these changes some new settlements were also created for the brāhmins during the Chola period. The villages Korramaṅgalam (Kottamaṅgalam), Komaṅgalam, Sendamaṅgalam, Sattamaṅgalam, Sanmaṅgalam, Kiramaṅgalam, Udaramaṅgalam, Vinnamaṅgalam and Chembiyanmadevinallur could have been newly established since their old names as villages are not referred to in the epigraphs.

New settlements of the merchants were also established by the Chola kings. Kattur, Turaiyur, Puvalur and Parāntakapuram were new merchant settlements created by the early Chola kings. In another instance, the village Sirukavur was transformed as a trading centre with the name Parāntakapuram during the time of Parāntaka.[38] Together a few other commercial centres were also established at distant places. Urrattur seems to be an important commercial centre situated in the north in the dry area. Another important commercial centre seems to be Tiruppidavūr probably established during the days of Rājēndra I. Another such centre would be Nagar located in the intermediate zone.

In the post Chola times also some new settlements are known. Adanur, Edumalai, Kalliyur, Seppalaikkudi, Palaiyur, Periya Kallikudi and Malavaichchirmai are known from epigraphs. On the wet zone also some new settlements were created.

A late Chola inscription[39] speaks about the settlements of Apputikurai (Appadurai) and Iśāṇaikurai (Esanakorai). Whether the present settlements were established during the Chola times could not be said with certainty. In the village Appadurai, near the present village settlement no medieval pottery is traceable. However, a late Chola temple in a dilapidated condition could be located on the left side of the main road near Appadurai. Potsherds assignable to the medieval times are also available at this place. Probably the village was situated near this place and at a later time the settlement was shifted to the present place.

In a few villages, remains of pottery are available indicating village settlements. The potsherds were of mostly red ware and red polished ware. No definite date can be assigned to these potsherds. However a broad date ranging from ninth to fourteenth century can be given to this type of medieval pottery. Villages like Kariyamanikkam, Talutalappatti, Pullambadi, Tiruppattur, Ulundankudi, Udaiyarnattam, Kannanur, Kiramaṅgalam, Poovalūr and a few other places yield this kind of pottery. In some places medieval pottery is available on the surface of the present settlement. But in a number of other places, the pottery is available away from the present settlement. At Talutalappatti and Pullambadi, the medieval settlements were situated away from the present settlements indicating a shift in the settlements. At Poovalūr, Tiruppattur, Nagar and Tirumaṅgalam the potsherds are available near the present village settlements.

The number of village settlements were on the increase from the time of the Pallavas. It had almost doubled during the late Chola time. In early Chola times there seems to be an increase in the new settlements. The density of the population seems to be more in the wet zone rather than in the dry zone since the number of settlements were more in the wet zone. In the dry zones the settlements are separated by long distances and consequently the population was sparse.

The settlements were grouped into several *kūrrams* during Pallava times. Two such *kūrrams* are known for the Lalguḍi area. They are Pachchil *kūrram* comprising the western parts adjacent to the river Koḷḷidam and Killar *kūrram* comprising the eastern parts of the taluk adjacent to the river Kaveri. Later, during Chola days also the names were retained but the territories underwent a change. To this two *kūrrams* were later added Idaiyarrunāḍu and Vadavalināḍu. Idaiyarrunaḍu comprised the territory between Pachchil *kūrram* and Killar *kūrram*, and Vadavalināḍu comprised the portion around Tiruveḷḷarai. A few villages in Musiri taluk were also included in the *nāḍu*.

During Chola times, the eastern-most part of the Taluk along the Kaveri river was made Poygaināḍu, including some of the territories south of the river Kaveri. With this the northern parts of Pachchil *kūrram*, Idaiyarrunāḍu, Killar *kūrram* and Poygaināḍu were grouped in the *nāḍus*. In this way Venkonkudikkandam and Chemburai kandam emerged. With this during later Chola times were added Valluvappadinadu, Vellalaiyurkkandam, Kanakkiliyanallurnadu, Tiruppidavurnadu and Uratturnadu.

The number of villages contained in these *nāḍus* and the size of the *nāḍus* were not uniform. The *nāḍus* adjacent to the river Koḷḷidam had more village settlements than the *nāḍus* in the dry or northern part of the taluk.

The settlements of the brāhmins (*Brahmadēya* villages) seem to be more on the southern side of the taluk. In the wet zone the eastern villages were now redistributed among the brāhmins. During the time of the Pallavas all the brāhmin settlements were located in the wet area of the Lalgudi taluk. The same phenomenon can be seen during the early Chola times. However, more brāhmin settlements were established in the northern parts (dry zone) of the taluk during the Late Chola times. Karuvidaimaṅgalam (Garuḍamaṅgalam), Srikanda Chaturvēdimaṅgalam (Nambikurichi), Pagaiyaruttuk-kondachola Chaturvēdimaṅgalam (Sangendi) and Sanmaṅgalam were some of the brāhmin settlements established in this period. Even in later Chola period the brāhmin settlements were numerous on the wet zone.

We shall try to find out the reasons for the spread of people from one area to the other. The vestiges of settlement of the early period are limited in number. The incidence of occupation seems on the whole to be sparse when compared to the number of settlements of later times. The area of settlement tend to increase from the Pallava times onwards. One of the reasons could be the increased facilities extended by the king for irrigation and other agricultural operations. Another reason could be the keen competition between two rising kingdoms—the Pāṇḍyas and the Pallavas—to control the Kaveri basin. The area assumed greater importance during the seventh to ninth centuries on account of the need of greater resources by the expanding kingdoms. This process was further expanded during the Chola rule when the Kaveri basin formed the nerve centre of political, economic and cultural history of Tamil Nadu. The movement from wet zone to dry zone was probably due to the abundant land available in the northern part of the taluk. Another reason for their movement may be an increase in the population. The brāhmin residents were given land in the wet zone and were encouraged by the state. The increase in the population probably increased the pressure on land in the wet zone, and the state could have come forward to ease the pressure by providing resources for cultivation. During the Pallava and Chola times there was increased activity regarding tank irrigation by a network of canals which could have encouraged people to move to dry zones also without the fear of losing their wealth. This may be another reason for the establishment of numerous settlements of the late Chola period in the dry zone.

The foregoing analysis has indicated some of the features of the early settlements in Lalgudi taluk and can not be considered as complete. Exploring some more villages would throw a good amount of light on the problem of the early historical settlement pattern in this area. Further, a comparison with the existing settlements will also indicate the aspects of development from the ancient settlements.

NOTES

1. Appendix I.
2. B.K. Gururaja Rao, *The Megalithic Culture in South India*, Univeristy of Mysore (1972), pp. 257, 258.
3. Excavations at this site was carried out by the Department of Ancient History and Archaeology, University of Madras in the years 1964-8 and the report is awaited.

4. T.V. Mahalingam, *Report on the Excavations in the Lower Kaveri Valley*, University of Madras, Madras (1970).
5. R.E.M. Wheeler, 'Arikamedu: an Indo-Roman Trading station on the east coast of India', *Ancient India* (1946), p. 50.
6. K.S. Ramachandran, *Archaeology of South India, Tamil Nadu*, Delhi (1980). p. 76.
7. *Devaram*, Section nos. 57 (Anbil); 58 (Mandurai); 61 (Tiruppangili) and 62 (Tiruppachchil).
8. *ARE*, 105 of 1929.
9. *ARE*, 103 of 1929.
10. *ARE*, 98 of 1929.
11. *ARE*, 723 of 1909.
12. T.V. Mahalingam, *Kanchipuram in Early South Indian History*, Bombay (1969), p. 100.
13. *EI*, XXVIII, no. 6, pp. 38-42.
14. *EI*, XI, p. 154.
15. Ibid.
16. *ARE*, 723 of 1909.
17. *EI*, XI, p. 154.
18. *ARE*, 148 of 1928-9.
19. *ARE*, 494 of 1912.
20. *ARE*, 216 of 43-4.
21. *SII*, IV, 434.
22. *ARE*, 594 of 1908.
23. *ARE*, 128 of 1929.
24. *ARE*, 40 of 1937-8.
25. *ARE*, 164 of 1938-9.
26. *ARE*, 157 of 1938-9.
27. *ARE*, 128 of 1929.
28. *ARE*, 512 of 1912.
29. *ARE*, 500 of 1912.
30. *ARE*, 37 of 1937-8.
31. *SII*, IV, 424.
32. *ARE*, 148 of 1929.
33. *SII*, IV, 424.
34. *SII*, IV, 537.
35. *SII*, VIII, 199.
36. *ARE*, 715 of 1909.
37. *ARE*, 208 of 1938-9.
38. *ARE*, 109 of 1929.
39. *SII*, VIII, 336.

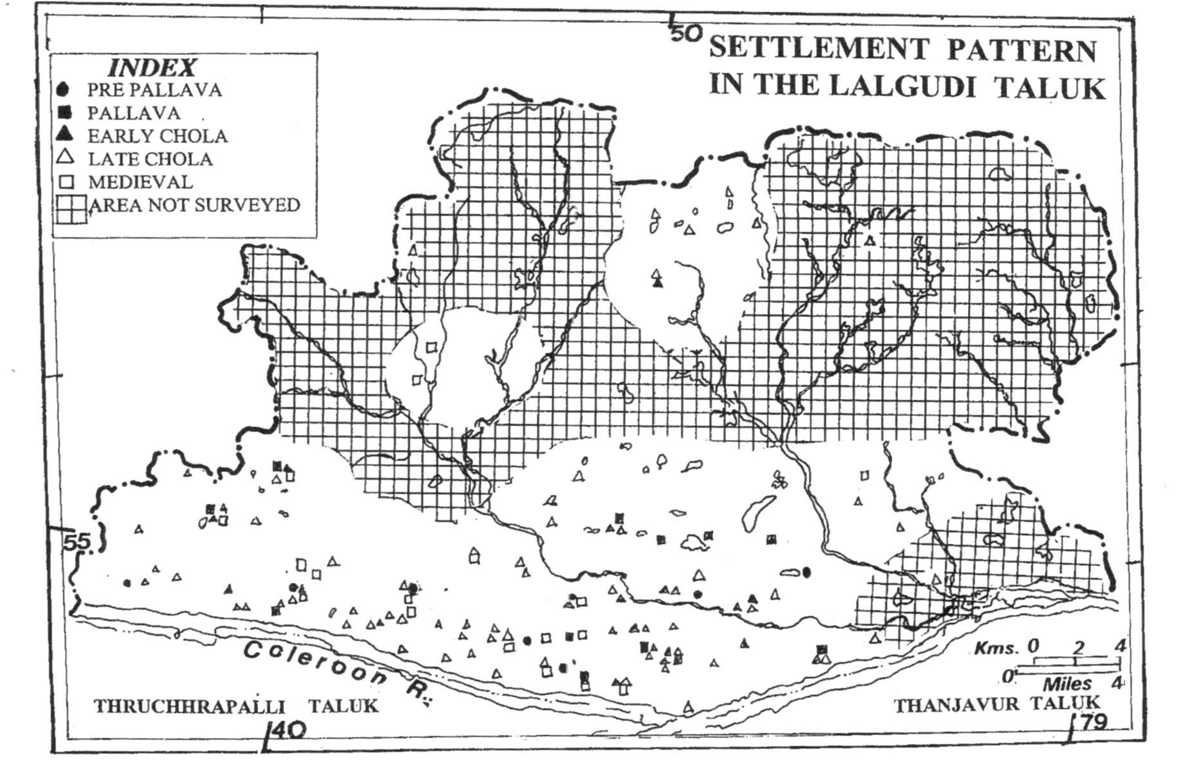

(Courtesy: Shyam Narayan Lal)

MAP 1: SETTLEMENT PATTERN IN THE LALGUDI TALUK

APPENDIX 1

List of Places Visited

Sholanganallur
Sirukambur
Sengudi
Kariyamanikkam
Pandiyampuram
Todaiyur
Gopurappatti
Bitchandarkoil
Talakkudi
Sempalani
Valadi
Kilavaladi
Appadurai
Esanakorai
Tandankorai
Tirumanamedu
Pachchampettai
Mayilrangam
Idaiyattumangalam
Kukur
Anandimedu
Kil Anbil
Jengamarajapuram
Ariyur
Vaimanapalayam
Tiruppangili
Ulundangudi
Alagiyamanavalam
Palur
Panamangalam
Kurrur
Nagar
Tirumangalam
Mandurai
Angarai
Lalgudi
Sirudaiyur
Manákkal
Mummudichcholamangalam
Sattamangalam
Adigudi
Poovalur
Pinnavasal
Kattur
Kottamangalam
Sirumayangudi
Nattamangudi
Mannachchanallur
Marudur
Kannanur
Mahilambadi
Purattakkudi
Peruvalanallur
Pudur Uttamanur
Pallavaram
Vellanur
Komakudi
Venkatachalapuram
Alambakkam
Tiruvellarai
Tattankurichchi
Sangendi
Pullambadi
Kariyamanikkam
Taluttalappatti
Kumunur
T. Valavanur
Keeramangalam
Neikuppai
Oothathur
Nedungur
Tiruppattur
Periyakurukkai
Neikulam

SECTION II

The Concept of Village Community and General Problem of Ownership of Land

4

Ownership of Agricultural Land in Ancient India

Lallanji Gopal

The various theories on the subject[1] may be broadly divided into three, according to whether they emphasize the claim of the community, the king or the peasant as the owner of the soil.

V.A. Smith[2] and, following him, J.N. Samaddar[3] express the view that the soil was the property of the king. Others who support this theory are B. Breloer,[4] Shamasastry,[5] Hopkins[6] and Bühler.[7] Maine[8] is the chief propounder of the view that agricultural land was owned and cultivated by men grouped in village communities. The theory of individual ownership has been advocated among others by Baden-Powell,[9] K.P. Jayaswal[10] and P.N. Banerjee.[11]

Here we do not discuss the communal ownership of land, which is little referred to in classical Hindu legal texts. We hope to consider this at length in a later publication. For the present the claims of peasant and king are evaluated.

We have some evidence which points to the existence of private ownership of cultivated land even in the Vedic period.[12] Firstly, we have references to the measuring of fields,[13] and to their being separated by strips (*khilya*).[14] Again, we find expressions meaning 'lord of a field' and 'the winning of a field' (*urvarāsā, urvarāpati, urvarājit, kṣetrasā, kṣetrapati*).[15] The reference by Apālā[16] to her father's field and the hair on his head as personal possessions, coupled with prayers[17] for fertile fields and for worthy sons and grandsons, indicates private proprietorship. In the *Atharvaveda*,[18] the *Taittirīya Saṁhitā*[19] and the *Chāndogya Upaniṣad*[20] the sense of separate and individual fields is more clear.

The Pāli canonical works, reflecting the practice in the Age of the Buddha, show a developed sense of individual ownership, when peasant proprietors called *khettapati*, *khettasāmika* or *vatthupati* cultivated the arable land. There cannot be any doubt that the conception of ownership in land had developed.[21] Boundaries were set up to distinguish the plots of land possessed by different owners.[22] The canonical literature[23] reveals that land was classed with cattle and other movable and immovable property as the personal property of a householder. The sale and mortgage, etc., of land are also referred to.[24] Besides the donation of parks by Anāthapiṇḍika, Ambapāli and Jīvaka, there are some other instances of gifts of lands.[25] The *Cullavagga*[26] describes a law-suit relating to the Jetavana, a significant instance illustrating individual ownership of land. The stealing of another's plot is referred to in the *Dīghanikāya*.[27]

In this connection no study has been made of the evidence supplied by the Jain canon. The *Uttarādhyayana Sūtra*[28] mentions land (*khetta*) along with cattle, gold, dwelling places, etc., as means of obtaining pleasure. According to the *Bṛhatkalpa Bhāsya*[29] agricultural land or *khetta* is considered among the ten kinds of external possessions, others being buildings, gold, conveyances, furniture, etc. There are many references[30] showing that lands and houses formed the main possessions of a householder.

There are indications in the *Arthaśāstra* too which show private ownership of land. Firstly, Kauṭilya uses the word *svāmyam* or ownership while dealing with disputes about the sale of land[31] and about a person driving cattle through a field without informing the owner.[32] The fields of the different holders were demarcated by boundaries, an encroachment upon which was an offence. The *Arthaśāstra*[33] deals with boundary disputes between individuals. The private ownership of land is further clear from the rules[34] relating to the construction of irrigation-works on another cultivator's plot. The cultivator had the right of alienating his field. He could lease it to others for cultivation. The land could also be sold by the cultivator. Dispossessing a person of his field was a penal offence. Kauṭilya gives detailed rules regarding all these points.[35] Making improvements on another's plot did not create any right of ownership.[36] An important evidence in favour of private ownership is the rule[37] that a person who steals images of gods or of animals, abducts men, or takes possession of the fields, houses, gold, gold coins, precious stones or crops of others, shall be beheaded or compelled to pay the highest amercement. At another place the *Arthaśāstra*[38] discusses the question of the fatherhood of a child: whether it belongs to the husband or to him from whom the seed is received? The analogy on which the two alternative claims are based is that of the ownership of the crop: does it belong to the owner of the field or to the person who sows the seed in the field?

The traditional Indian point of view on the question of the ownership of land is best reflected in the legal texts.

It has been maintained by some that the Indian legal system had no distinct notion of ownership.[39] But, as has been rightly shown by Jolly,[40] there was a clear distinction between the concepts of ownership and possession. The pronoun *svam* and its derivatives are used to express ownership, while the derivatives of the root *bhuj* indicate mere possession or enjoyment. Later works basing their conclusions on earlier Smṛtis define ownership (*svatva*) as property capable of being disposed of as one likes.[41] There is also a discussion about the nature of ownership, as to whether it is a separate category (*padārtha*) or a capacity.[42] Likewise the commentaries and digests discuss in minute detail whether ownership is to be apprehended from Śāstra alone or is a matter of worldly usage.[43] In the Dharmasūtras and Smṛtis the different modes of acquiring ownership[44] have been noted in detail.

Indian legal works clearly distinguish between possession and legitimate title, the two constituents of ownership, and emphasize their due importance in determining it.[45] Bṛhaspati[46] says that possession coupled with a legitimate title constitutes proprietary right. Yājñavalkya[47] makes the relative importance of the two factors quite clear. In his opinion even title, if not accompanied by some slight possession, has no strength; while title is stronger than possession not handed down hereditarily. Nārada[48] also regards as a thief the man who enjoys a property even for hundreds of years without title. The abiding claim of ownership of an individual over his arable land is apparent best from a set of rules in Nārada[49] to the effect that if the owner of a field is unable to cultivate it, is dead, or is not heard of, and a stranger cultivates the field without objection from anybody, the stranger shall enjoy the produce of the field; if the owner or his son returns while the field is being tilled by a stranger, he can get his field back on repayment to the stranger of all the money expended on making the land ready for crops; if the owner is unable to return the expenses, the stranger may retain seven-eighth of the produce every year for eight years, giving one-eighth to the owner every year, and should hand over the field to the owner when the eighth year arrives.

But the second factor of enjoyment was not less important in determining ownership, particularly in the case of immovable property.[50] Nārada[51] and Kātyāyana[52] state that possession needs to be supported by title only in cases within human memory, but in cases beyond the memory of man possession extending over three generations is proof of ownership even in the absence of a document or other title. The Smṛtikāras seem to be divided on the minimum period of adverse enjoyment amounting to ownership. The earlier writers, such as Gautama[53] and Manu,[54] appear to regard ten years' adverse enjoyment of land as sufficient to create ownership. Yājñavalkya[55] extends the period to twenty years. But later writers like Bṛhaspati,[56] Viṣṇu,[57] Kātyāyana[58] and Nārada[59] require a period of sixty years. An attempt to reconcile this conflict in the precepts of the legal texts was made by later writers of commentaries and digests.[60] However, the Smṛtis tried to safeguard the rights of the owner of land in certain cases, even when the period of adverse enjoyment would have deprived him of it.[61]

Land, like other objects of private ownership, was a subject of legal dispute. Kātyāyana gives six causes of land disputes: claiming more land, claiming that another person is entitled to less than he possesses, claiming a share, denying a share, seizing possession when previously there was none, and, lastly, boundaries.[62]

The prevalence of peasant proprietorship follows from many other rules relating to legal problems connected with agricultural land. Manu, while treating the question of a right over crops, says that if a man sows his seed in another's field,[63] or when the seed is carried by water or wind and germinates there,[64] he has no right over the crop, which belongs to the owner of the field. Then there was the question of the settlement of boundary disputes. The Smṛtis give elaborate rules on this point. Manu[65] refers to boundary disputes regarding fields, wells, tanks, gardens and houses. Nārada[66] uses the expression boundary dispute to refer to a dispute in regard to landed property, whether it is a dike or bridge, a field, a tilled piece of land, or waste. Yājñavalkya[67] prescribes punishment for making breaches in the boundary between two or more fields and for ploughing a field beyond the boundary of one's own field. In Viṣṇu the fine for transgressing the whole of the boundary of a field is 1008 *paṇas*.[68] How keen was the sense of ownership is again shown by the rules regarding the right to enjoy the fruits and flowers of trees that grow on the boundary between two fields.[69]

The rules about dispossession of a cultivator's plot by another person also imply a recognition of the claims of the owner of a field. Manu[70] places a field in the category of other immovable properties which were undoubted objects of private ownership, such as a house, a tank, a garden or a field, and prescribes a heavy fine for a person who by intimidation possesses himself of these objects belonging to another man. Yājñavalkya[71] also treats dispossession of another's field as a penal offence. The fear of religion was also brought to bear on the question. Theft of land was viewed as one of the four great sins.[72] Hell is mentioned as the punishment for this sin,[73] and lunar penance has been prescribed to expunge its guilt.[74] The proprietary right of a cultivator over his field is again manifested by the rules[75] prescribing the compensation to be paid to the owner of agricultural land for damage caused to his field by a negligent herdsman in charge of cattle.

The right of cultivators to do with their fields as they liked establishes full individual right over agricultural land. According to Indian tradition itself, as recorded in late medieval commentaries and digests, ownership implies the quality of the object owned to be used by the owner according to his pleasure.[76] This test of ownership, when applied to agricultural land, proves it also to have been an object of private proprietorship. The *Āpastamba Dharmasūtra*[77] grants to cultivators the right to lease their fields against half or any other fixed share of the produce. Vyāsa and Bṛhaspati[78] also refer to the leasing of fields.[79] Further a cultivator had the right to use his field as a pledge. Manu[80] and Nārada[81] place lands, houses, etc., in the category of pledges which can be used. Bhāradvāja gives a list of debtor's possession, by selling which a creditor is to be paid if the debtor has no cash; these properties in order are: grain, gold, iron, cattle, clothes, land, slaves, and conveyances, in the absence of his fields his garden, and lastly his house.[82] An epigraphic corroboration of this is found in the Jaunpur brick inscription of AD 1217 which records a certain Gaṅgadeva borrowing an amount of 2,250 *drammas* from two bankers and as security for this sum giving in pledge the cultivated land which was his own share.[83] Likewise, though certain restrictions were imposed, land could be sold. The rules of ownership and sale in earlier works[84] were motivated by many considerations, into the details of which we need not enter. However, they in no way deprived a cultivator of his right to dispose of the land as he liked. Moreover, even these restrictions were gradually removed. We see later Smṛtis like Bṛhaspati and Nārada[85] allowing immovable property as an article of trade. The right to sell one's land is implied by Bṛhaspati;[86] two out of the seven classes of legal documents mentioned by him are concerned with the sale and mortgage of landed property. Kātyāyana says: 'what is decided by the neighbours assembled together, who know (the land, etc., and its value) and who are afraid of committing sin, as the price of fields, gardens, houses and the like, of bipeds and quadrupeds, is declared to be the proper price; a price which is less or more than it by one-eighth is declared to be improper; what is sold for an improper price may be annulled even after a hundred years.[87] This same authority allows a period of ten days for repentance to sellers and purchasers in case of land; when *sapiṇḍas* are parties in the sale the period of repentance is twelve days; in other cases the period is even shorter.[88] Kātyāyana also contains rules on an *uktalābha* sale[89] which has been defined by Bhāradvāja[90] as a conditional sale, where the seller borrows only a portion of the proper price of a plot of land, promising to repay the borrowed money on a certain day, failing which his ownership over the land will come to an end. A right similar in nature is that of giving away land as charity.[91] Even the Dharmaśāstras[92] permit such a practice. Manu[93] also refers to the practice of the gift of land to Brāhmaṇas. Bṛhaspati's[94] description of a deed of gift also implies a right to grant one's landed property. Viṣṇu[95] says that by giving land one obtains heaven, by giving it to the extent of a bull's hide only one is purified from every sin. Manu also refers to the merit of land gifts.[96] Thus we find that Indian legal texts grant a peasant all the rights of sale, gift, mortgage, etc., which form ownership.[97]

The best treatment of the question of the proprietary claims of cultivators and the State is found in the Mīmāṁsā works.[98] The Mīmāṁsā writers anticipate the points that a modern writer on the subject discusses. The discussion starts on the injunction that in the Viśvajit sacrifice a votary should give away all his belongings to the officiating priests. The natural question is: 'What can a man legally give as his own?'[99] Jaimini[100] initiates the discussion by stating that land is not to be transferred, for it belongs equally to all. Śabarasvāmin[101] explains the aphorism thus:

> Land is not to be given because men are found enjoying lordship over fields, and not over the whole earth. It is said that then he who is the sovereign lord gives it. Even he cannot give the land because in the case of fields of which he is the lord by actual enjoyment there is no speciality in him. The difference due to his paramountcy is in this that by virtue of his protecting the rice and other crops that grow on the earth he is entitled to a share of them as his remuneration, but not to the lordship of the soil.

Two points which stand out in this discussion are: first, a distinction between the entire territory of the state and private fields, the former being incapable of individual ownership; and second, a recognition that a king receives taxes not because of a title of ownership but through his function of protection as sovereign. This discussion has been carried into greater detail by subsequent writers. Mādhava[102] and Khaṇḍadeva,[103] belonging respectively to the fourteenth and the seventeenth centuries, are two important Mīmāṁsā commentators whose discussions bring into relief the functional nature of sovereignty and the distinction of private and common property. The testimony of these later commentators is further remarkable as showing that the earlier view of Jaimini as explained by Śabara held ground as authoritative throughout the period. Mādhava arguest thus:

> A king cannot give away the State territory. It may, however, be claimed that, according to the Smṛti injuction, a king is the lord of (the property of) all excepting Brāhmaṇas, and land is the property of the paramount ruler. But the purport of the Smṛti text is that the king's lordship is for the purpose of correcting the wicked and supporting the virtuous. Land is not the property of the king but is the common property of all beings enjoying the fruit of their labour on it. Therefore, although there can be a gift of private (*asādhāraṇa*) land, there can be no gift of the State land.

Khaṇḍadeva also declares that even a paramount sovereign has no proprietary right over the land, for even conquest produces proprietary right only with regard to the personal property, houses, fields, etc., of the enemy; the conquest of land merely produces the title of sovereignty, which is limited to protecting the kingdom and eradicating evil, and for that purpose only the realization of taxes from cultivators and of fines from offenders is legitimate, but no proprietary right on the land arises therefrom. Houses, fields, etc., acquired by purchase and so forth, may, however, become objects of gift.

This Mīmāṁsā standpoint on the subject has been accepted as authoritative by later commentators on legal works. Medhātithi[104] repeats the Mīmāṁsā arguments. Nilakaṇṭha in his *Vyavahāra-mayūkha*[105] quotes Jaimini with approval and follows the discussion of the proprietary rights of a conqueror as found in Khaṇḍadeva.

It may be claimed by the opposite group of scholars, though not with much justification, that the legal texts only lay down a norm or ideal. So we have to substantiate our study of the question with a thorough examination of the epigraphic evidence, which cannot be accused of being unfaithful in reflecting the practice of a particular period. The inscriptions, however, only corroborate the testimony of the Smṛti literature and reveal that arable land was divided into plots over which farmers had proprietary rights. A Nasik cave inscription[106] records the gift of a field for providing clothes for certain ascetics living in one of the Nasik caves. The Junnar inscriptions supply significant instances of private transfers of land and of the gift of small units of agricultural land, owned by individual proprietors.[107] The evidence of the two Kangra inscriptions of AD 804[108] may also be profitably utilized here. These record, among many donations by private individuals to a Śiva temple, the gift of agricultural land. This evidence provides an example of the ownership of land by merchants, and thus shows that land was owned even by classes other than those to whom grants or assignments of lands were generally made by the State. This is also supported by some later inscriptions[109] mentioning pieces of agricultural land owned by corporate bodies.

A large number of inscriptions attest to the practice of kings' assigning villages to brāhmaṇas. On a superficial view such grants would appear to be infringing the proprietary right of individual cultivators. But a careful perusal does not warrant this view. Really what was assigned as gifts in such cases was the revenue which the State received from the village and often certain other rights, but not the agricultural land in the village. The earlier inscriptions on the subject are brief and so do not throw any light on the problem, but those later in date are full of details and show that such grants of villages did not imply a transfer of the proprietary rights over fields. These inscriptions, often addressed to the villagers, require them simply to give to the donee the revenue and other dues, which they owed to the State.[110] There is nothing whatever in the inscriptions to show that cultivators were to transfer to the donee their ownership over the land. They were affected only to the extent that the person to whom they paid their dues was now changed. Likewise, the lists of the rights of a donee include only the different taxes and dues which he was to receive from the village. Here also we do not find any expression which may suggest that he acquired even a limited proprietary right in the agricultural land. Further, where the land-grants, in addressing future officers and kings, require them not to interfere with the donee's right over the village[111], any reference to his right to occupy the agricultural land of the village is conspicuous by its absence. It may, however, be objected that the use of the terms *kṛṣataḥ karṣayataḥ* in the expression '*bhuñjataḥ kṛṣataḥ karṣayataḥ pradiśato vā*' in some grants implies the donne's proprietary rights over village fields. But as cultivation of land requires attention and time, it would really have been adding to the burdens of a learned brāhmaṇa if the land granted by the king as a favour was required to be cultivated by him. This was even more relevant in the case of religious institutions like temples and monasteries. The difficulty can further be realized in cases where the donees lived in villages, towns or districts situated at a great distance from the village granted.[112] As we have already seen the grants contemplate in passages addressed to villagers, state officials or future kings a right to the enjoyment of revenue payable by the villagers to the king. The terms in question, therefore, may be taken to refer to the cultivatory rights of a donee to fields which hitherto had been under the ownership of the donor king (in later usage called *sīr*), and also included ownerless lands reverting to him. From I-tsing we learn how the monasteries managed to get the fields owned by them cultivated, by leasing them to monastic servants or other families.[113] The evidence of the inscriptions would suggest that such pieces of land were cultivated by men who received half the produce.[114]

That the grant of a village did not amount to an assignment of the proprietary rights over arable land in the village is further evident from inscriptions[115] which mention the grant of a village together with some particular tract in that very village or elsewhere. If the State had proprietary right over all the agricultural land in the village the grant of the village would have implied that of the particular tract as well. It seems that what was granted in the case of villages was a right to revenue, whereas in the case of a particular field it was the proprietary right over it. The State had proprietary right only over certain fields. Agricultural land in general belonged to him who cultivated it. There are besides instances in which kings grant small plots of cultivable lands of various sizes situated in different parts of a village or even in different villages.[116] If the State owned all the land in a village, we cannot explain the necessity of granting tracts scattered over a large area, situated at a distance from one another. It could very well have granted a field of requisite area consolidated in a particular part of the village. This would have been more convenient both for the donor and the donee. It appears, therefore, that the State did not own all the arable land in a village. The fields generally belonged to peasants, though there were some tracts owned by the State, which alone it could grant.

It thus follows that the references to the grant of a single field[117] as against a village really amount to a grant of the field which the king owned in that village. Such tracts were known as the Royal land (*rājakam khettam*).[118] In the Nasik Cave Inscription of Gautamīputra Sātakarṇi[119] the king mentions a field in a village as 'my own land' (*amhasatakam*). The Chendallur paltes[120] of Pallava Kumāraviṣṇu II mention that in the village of Chaṇḍalūra in Kavacakarabhoga subdivision of the districts of Kammaṅka-raṣṭra, the king's domain in the four directions amounts to eight hundred *paṭṭikās,* and that out of this a field amounting altogether to four hundred and thirty-two *paṭṭikās* has been given as a *brahmadeya.* These grants do not imply that the State had a right to eject a tenant and lease the field to another. When the State had no land of its own in a particular village, before making a grant it had first to purchase land from some cultivator. The Nasik Cave Inscription of Uṣavadāta[121] records that he gave a field which he had bought of a Brāhmaṇa named Aśvibhūti for the price of four thousand *kārṣāpaṇas.* The inscription very significantly adds that Aśvibhūti had received this field from his father. A late inscription from Tirukkoyalur, dated AD 961,[122] mentioning a Vaidumba king purchasing 3 *velis* of land from the local assembly in order to grant it to a temple, shows that throughout the period of our study there was no fundamental change in the position as regards the ownership of agricultural land.

Our survey would, however, remain incomplete if we did not consider the opposite view and did not give it its due meed.

Firstly, it is claimed that a king had the right to confiscate land and, in certain cases, to transfer it from one person to another. To support this argument two passages from the *Arthaśāstra*[123] and a statement of Bṛhaspati[124] have been cited. An often-quoted passage in the *Arthaśāstra* is: 'lands may be confiscated from those who do not cultivate them, and given to others'.[125] It has been taken to imply State ownership of land. A thorough investigation would not support this view. The *Arthaśāstra* implies two distinct types of land: one may be called the royal farm while the other is revenue-paying land in general. The difference is indicated by the *Arthaśāstra* employing two separate terms for incomes derived from the two types.[126] *Sītā* denotes the various incomes from the first category of land. *Bhāga* stands for revenue from lands other than state farms. The *Arthaśāstra* uses the term *sītā* to include all kinds of crops that are brought in by the superintendent of agriculture.[127] An analysis of the chapter dealing with the duties of this officer clearly shows that he got the royal farms cultivated either directly by state officers or through tenants under his supervision.[128] Moreover, the reference to the right of the State to confiscate lands does not apply to private fields.[129] The passage occurs in the chapter dealing with the formation of villages and refers to the newly settled or colonised lands, which were obviously ownerless and to which the State had full proprietary rights. An analysis of the passage in the context in which it appears also shows that it cannot be taken to describe the position of the cultivators of non-crown lands. At first provision is made for *brahmadeya* lands and assignments to some of the state officers. Next, there are rules about revenue-paying cultivators. Fields, prepared obviously at State expense, are to be allotted to tax-payers only for the life of immediate settlers. Unprepared lands are not to be taken away from cultivators who have made them fit for cultivation. But the fields of those who do not cultivate them properly should be confiscated and given to others, or such fields may be cultivated by village labourers and petty traders (*vaidehikas*). Later in the text rules are given for concessions and remissions of taxes, granted on the occasion of opening new settlements or on any other emergent occasion. The rules show that the State had not a limitless right to do with the land what it willed. In disposing of new lands under schemes of colonization the king had the right to limit the grant of a field to a cultivator's life only in case of prepared lands. He could evict tenants only when they neglected plots assigned to them. The rule, guaranteeing against eviction, or in other words giving the right of hereditary possession to cultivators who prepared plots of newly colonized lands at their own expense, implies that hereditary occupation of fields was the rule in the case of settled villages. The second passage from the *Arthaśāstra* [130] too goes against State landlordism, for it warns that if the king sometimes confiscated land, it caused resentment and alarm. It is clear that such cases only go to show the proprietary right of the cultivator to his land. Bṛhaspati[131] also implies private ownership and says that the king had no right to dispossess a rightful owner. If he does so, it is not considered valid. Bṛhaspati[132] in the next passage, explains himself: 'when land is taken from any man by a king actuated by avarice, or using a fraudulent pretext, and bestowed on a different person as a mark of his favour, such a gift is not valid.' The rule in question evidently applies to cases where the king takes away land from one possessing it without a title and gives it to another of superior merit. But what, continues Bṛhaspati, is taken away by the king from one possessing it without a title and is given to another of superior merit cannot be rescinded.[133] In this context we may add an illuminating verse from the *Nārada Smṛti*: 'A householder's house and his field are considered as the two fundamentals of his existence. Therefore let not the king upset either of them; for that is the root of householders.'[134]

There are, however, certain verses which attribute to the king the lordship of all the land. First, there is a verse in the *Manusmṛti*[135] to the effect that of ancient treasure troves found underneath the ground and of the produce of mines the king is entitled to a share, because he affords protection and because he is lord of the earth. Next, Bhaṭṭasvāmin, commenting on a passage in the *Arthaśāstra*,[136] quotes a verse meaning that those who are well-versed in the sacred books declare the king to be the lord of land as well as water; the householders have the right of ownership over all other things except these two.[137] According to Kātyāyana,[138] who is also quoted to support state landlordism, the king has always been declared to be the lord of the soil and not of other things, for otherwise, he would not receive one-sixth of the produce; since creatures inhabit the land, the king is also declared to be their lord, and thus he acquires the right to the agricultural tax. But we do not see how all these verses can be taken to justify the theory that agricultural land belonged to the State.[139] U.N. Ghoshal[140] has very correctly pointed out the mistake in basing a theory of State landlordism on these verses. According to him, 'the statements are laid down not as definite heads of law, but as arguments for justifying or explaining the king's right to levy specific branches of the revenue from land. They are, in other words, essentially of the nature of legal maxims in whose general and comprehensive character they fully share.' These extracts, however, undoubtedly contain a statement of the sovereignty of the king implying his general lordship over everything in his kingdom.[141] This does not amount to the king being the universal landlord. The king does not dispute the right of a cultivator to ownership; the view of peasant proprietorship of land holds ground.

It has, however, to be admitted that, of the three passages referred to above, the one quoted in the commentary of Bhaṭṭasvāmin expressly refers to the State ownership of land. The importance of its testimony lies in giving evidence of a period when a group of thinkers supporting State landlordism undoubtedly existed. But then it is difficult to determine the date of Bhaṭṭasvāmin[142] and still more difficult in the case of the unknown authority quoted by him.

Thus, though the general opinion of legal authorities favoured the theory of peasant proprietorship, it would be wrong to suppose that there was no dissenting voice. It appears that a group of thinkers, not considerable in number, advocated State landlordism. The treatment of the point in Mīmāṁsā works indicates that the question was not free from some amount of controversy and discussion.

This standpoint on the problem quite easily explains the account of the agrarian system as given by foreign writers. The earlier advocates of peasant proprietorship used to discard the statement of Megasthenes[143] as incredible. B. Breloer[144] has, however, explained the so-called contradiction in his statement. Of the two versions in which the statement of Megasthenes has reached us

Strabo[145] evidently describes the condition of the crown lands while Diodorus[146] refers to non-crown lands. It appears that Megasthenes took the theory of the overlordship of the king over all sorts of property in his realm as meaning the actual State ownership of land[147] The two Chinese travellers, Fā-hsien[148] and Hsüan Tsang[149] while describing land-tenure in India, used the expression 'royal land' for the whole territory of the State. Dr. U.N. Ghoshal has shown that the use of this expression indicates that the Chinese travellers believed the soil in India to be State-owned, as in contemporary China.[150] However, in view of the express statement to the contrary by authoritative Indian sources, we cannot accept their testimony as correct. It is just possible that the foreign travellers could not appreciate the fine points of the agrarian system and read their own native customs in the things they described; or interpreted the general theoretical claim of the king to all the property in his kingdom as proof of his ownership in practice. The possibility, however, cannot be ruled out that they were influenced by those Indian thinkers who believed in State landlordism. These foreign accounts, because of the ambiguity and confusion associated with them, are not such that any great reliance can be placed upon them in matters of this kind.

It has been claimed that 'the king had certain transcendent authority over all land which prevented untrammelled disposal or enjoyment of land by private owners'.[151] To prove this contention the rule of Nārada,[152] that immovable property held for three generations is incapable of being alienated without the king's sanction, has been cited. But this rule only shows that enjoyment of an immovable property for three consecutive generations creates in the person enjoying it a proprietary right which can be set aside only if the king decides a land-suit in favour of a person having a title of greater merit. The rule of the intestate and ownerless land reverting to the king,[153] which has been quoted in support of this view, does not amount to the proprietary right of the State but only implies that a king had a general claim over all property in his realm. Such an explanation finds support from Bṛhaspati[154] who, while discussing the law of inheritance, propounds the rule of escheat and in its justification adds the expression: 'for he is the lord of all; except in the case of a Brāhmaṇa'.

The right of a king to revenue has also been taken to support the regal claims over agricultural land. The cultivators' right to the free enjoyment of his land was no doubt restricted to some extent by rules which were the logical extension of the royal right to land revenue. Of these two are significant. The first is the rule regarding the imposition of a fine on a cultivator who negligently destroys his crops.[155] The fine was in respect of the loss sustained by the king as a result of the action of the cultivator.[156] Allied to it is the rule about the sale of land by the State in case of non-payment of land revenue.[157] But the details of these rules themselves show that no abiding claim of the king to ownership was recognized. Kātyāyana, for example, says that if such a sale is inequitable it may be set aside within ten years, and a compromise or exchange may be set aside within three generations.[158] Prajāpati[159] remarks that the original owner could get back his property sold for the royal dues by paying the full price to the purchaser up to three generations. The statement in the *Arthaśāstra*[160] that the king could prevail upon the peasantry to raise a second crop was applicable only in emergencies when the State, according to the *Arthaśāstra* itself, might assume very wide powers; and so it would not be safe to base any theory on it.

But these rights of the State in no way imply a proprietary right. It is not clear how A.N. Bose[161] could take the 'fiscal term *bhāga* or *rājabhāga* which denotes king's regular and legitimate share as opposed to controversial and additional imposts on land produce' to 'indicate a partnership of title between the peasant and the king'. Such a view, it is submitted, reveals a gross misunderstanding of the Indian theory of taxation. According to Indian thought the revenue received by the king is his wages for his affording protection to the subject.[162] Even the late *Śukranīti*, which generally favours an increase in the control of the State over agriculture and other industries, acquiesces in such a view and states[163] that the ruler has been made by Brahmā a servant of the people, getting his revenue as remuneration, and his sovereignty is only for protection. The theory was so deep-rooted that even literary works refer to it without implying any scope for doubt or discussion.[164] In the earlier stages of the development of society people made quasi-voluntary contributions to the king for his services, but with the passage of time, as institutions were standardized, the revenue became fixed and compulsory.[165]

Thus our investigation shows that the peasant was the proprietor of the land in every sense of the term. The king, as the universal sovereign of every thing in his State, had, no doubt, some claim over the land. He received revenue from the peasant as the wages for the protection he afforded to the people; but this in no way amounted to a proprietary right over the land. But the question was not entirely free from discussion even in ancient times, and supporters could be found for the not much favoured view of State ownership of land.

These are the facts; they may be labelled by any convenient modern phrase or theory that suits them.[166]

It has been contended[167] that Indian theory combines universal landlordism of the king and peasant proprietorship, and that the agrarian system meant a sort of perpetual lease held on the annual performance of an obligation. No authoritative text belonging to our period combines the facts of the agrarian system in a theory resembling this view. The originality of the theory is the chief argument against it. The only passage which we have been able to find in its support is by the commentator of the *Narasiṁha Purāṇa.*

By conquest, the earth became the property of the holy Paraśurāma; by gift, the property of the sage Kaśyapa; and committed by him to Kṣatriyas for the sake of protection, became their protective property successively held by powerful conquerors and not by subjects cultivating the soil. But an annual property is acquired by subjects on payment of annual revenue: and the king cannot lawfully give, sell or dispose of the land to another for that year. But if the agreement be in the form 'you shall enjoy it for years', for as many years as the property is granted, during so many years the king should never give, sell or dispose of it to another. Yet if the subjects do not pay the revenue, the grant, being conditional, is annulled by the breach of the condition and the king may grant it to another.[168]

NOTES

1. *Report of the Indian Taxation Enquiry Committee* (1924-5), vol. II, Appendix IV.
2. *Early History of India,* pp. 137ff; *Oxford History of India,* p. 90.
3. *Economic Condition in Ancient India,* p. 168.
4. See U.N. Ghoshal, *Hindu Revenue System,* p. 168.
5. *Kauṭilya's Arthaśāstra* (tr.), p. 144n.
6. *India, Old and New,* p. 223.
7. *S.B.E.,* XXV, p. 259 — note on *Manu,* VIII. 39.

8. *Village Communities of the East and West,* pp. 76f, 103, 107, 113, 160, 226f.
9. *Indian Village Communities,* pp. 2f, 36ff, 98-139.
10. *Hindu Polity,* pp. 343ff.
11. *Public Administration in Ancient India,* p. 179.
12. Competent authorities like Schrader (*Prehistoric Antiquities,* p. 289) and Macdonell and Keith (*Vedic Index,* I. 210f) admit that the idea of individual ownership was recognized even as early as the Vedic Age, Bandyopadhyaya—*Economic Life and Progress in Ancient India,* pp. 114f; cf. U.N. Ghoshal—*Hindu Public Life,* pt I, p. 60.
13. *R.V.,* I. 110.5.
14. Pischel quoted in *Vedic Index,* I, p. 100.
15. *Vedic Index* I, p. 99. Also *R.V.,* IV. 38.1; VI. 20.1.
16. *R.V.,* VIII. 91.5.
17. *R.V.,* IV. 41.6.
18. IV. 18.5; V. 31.4; X.i. 18; XI. 1.22.
19. II. 2.1.2.
20. VIII. 42.2.
21. *Jātaka,* III. 301f.; *Dīgha,* XII. 7; *Mbh.,* V. 36.5.
22. *Jātaka,* IV. 281f.; *Dīgha,* XXVII. 18.
23. *Mahāvagga,* III. 11.4ff. *Suttanipāta,* IV. 10.11; *Kāmasutta,* IV. 1, Theragāthā 957.
24. *Jātaka,* III. 293; Vinaya II. 158, 159.
25. *Jātaka,* 484; IV. 281.
26. VI. 4.9.
27. XXVII. 19.
28. 3.17.
29. I. 825.
30. *Uttarādhyayana,* XIII. 24; IX. 49; *Ācārāṅga,* I. 2.3. 3; II. 7.2.4-6; *Ovāiya,* 1. Almost all passages in the Jain Canonical works having a bearing on agricultural tenure seem to suggest the existence of separate cultivation by farmers, *IHQ,* X. 291.
31. *Artha.,* III. 9—*Asvāmīpratikrośe caturviṁśatipaṇo daṇḍaḥ; praṇaṣṭasvāmikañca yathopakāraṁ vā vibhajet.*
32. *Artha.,* III. 10—*Svāminaścānivedya cārayato dvādaśpaṇo daṇḍah.*
33. III. 9.
34. *Artha.,* III. 18.
35. *Artha.,* III. 9.
36. *Artha.,* III. 10.
37. IV. 10 cf. *Artha.,* III. 17—*mahāpaśumanusyakṣetragṛhahiranya-suvarṇasūkṣmavastrādīnāṁ sthūlakadravyāṇāṁ dviśtāvaraḥ pañcāśataparaḥ.*
38. III. 7.
39. Moreland, *Agrarian System of Moslem India,* p. 4.
40. *Hindu Law and Custom,* p. 196.
41. Kane, *History of Dharmaśāstra* III, p. 555. Also see infra, p. 247, n. 1.

42. Ibid., p. 547.
43. Ibid., pp. 548ff; also Jolly, *Hindu Law and Custom*, pp. 198f.
44. *Gautama*, X. 39-41; *Vasiṣṭa*, XVI. 16; *Bṛhaspati*, IX. 2; *Nārada*, quoted by *Smṛticandrikā*, II, p. 70.
45. *Smṛticandrikā* (ed. Gharpure), II, pp. 70ff; *Mitākṣarā* on *Yājña*, II. 27.
46. IX. 3. Later on *Bṛhaspati*, IX. 22 elaborates his statement and says that it is not by mere force of possession that land becomes a man's property; a legitimate title also having been proved it is converted into property by both possession and title, but not otherwise. See also *Yājña*, II. 29; *Nārada*, I. 85-6.
47. II. 27.
48. I. 87.
49. XI. 23-5.
50. *Nārada*, I. 77.
51. I. 89.
52. 321.
53. XII. 37.
54. VIII. 147-8.
55. II. 24.
56. IX. 26-31.
57. V. 187.
58. 318, 327.
59. I. 91; XI. 27.
60. Kane, *History of Dharmaśāstra*, II, pp. 322ff.
61. *Vasiṣṭha*, XVI. 18; *Manu*, VIII. 149; *Kātyāyana*, 330-5; *Bṛhaspati*, IX. 11, 12; *Nārada*, 1. 81, 83 IV. 7-10.
62. 732.
63. IX. 49.
64. IX. 54; also *Nārada*, XII. 56.
65. VIII. 262.
66. XI. 1.
67. II. 155.
68. V. 172; also *Manu*, IX. 291.
69. *Nārada*, XI. 13-14; *Kātyāyana*, 760-1.
70. VIII. 264; *Matsya Purāṇa*, CCXXVII. 30.
71. II. 155.
72. *Manu*, XI. 58; *Viṣṇu*, XXVI. 13.
73. *Gautama*, XIII. 17.
74. *Manu*, XI. 163, *Viṣṇu*, LII. 6.
75. *Manu*, VIII. 240-1; *Nārada*, XI. 28-9, 34; *Yājña*, II. 159-61; *Kātyāyana*, 664-5, 667.
76. Jimūtavāhana, Nīlakaṇṭha and Mitramiśra quoted by U.N. Ghoshal, *Agrarian System in Ancient India*, pp. 85f. A similar view has been expressed by *Vyavasthācandrikā* (ed. S.C. Sircar), I(i) cl. 51 and *Smṛticandrikā*, I cl. 25.

77. I. 6.18; II. 11.28; II. 21.1; II. 28.1.
78. Quoted by *Vyavashāramayūkha* of Bhaṭṭa Nilakaṇtha, notes, p. 226.
79. Cf. reference to *ardhasītikas-Gautama,* XVII. 6; *Manu,* IV. 253; *Viṣṇu,* LVII. 16; *Yājña,* I. 166; *Parāśara,* XI. 19. According to *Manu* (IX. 52-3), if by a special contract land is made over to another for sowing, the owner of the seed and the owner of the soil both are considered as sharers of the crops; if, however, no agreement has been made the benefit clearly belongs to the owner of the field. A rule in *Yājñavalkya* (II. 158) provides for the case where a person does not cultivate a field leased to him.
80. VIII. 143.
81. I. 125.
82. Quoted by *Parāśaramādhavīya,* III. p. 259.
83. *JUPHS,* XVII, pp. 196ff.
84. Cf. *Gautama,* VII. 15.
85. Quoted by *Vivādaratnākara,* p. 189.
86. VIII. 7-8.
87. 705-6.
88. 685.
89. 711-12.
90. Quoted by *Vyavahāranirṇaya,* p. 351.
91. Cf. sale of land to be clothed in the formalities of a gift—Kane, *History of Dharmaśāstra,* III. p. 567, no. 1063.
92. *Gautama,* XIX. 17; *Baudhāyana,* III. 10. 15.
93. X. 114.
94. VIII. 6.
95. XCII. 3-4. Cf. *Purāṇa Index,* S. V. Pañcalāṅgalakam.
96. IV. 230. Cf. *Mbh.,* XIII. 34.67—one should make a gift of land even after purchasing it.
97. Cf. Jolly—*Tagore Law Lectures,* pp. 88f.
98. Colebrooke (*Miscellaneous Essays* I, pp. 320f) drew the attention of the scholars to this important source. K.P. Jayaswal (*Hindu Polity,* pp. 344ff) — as the first to assess its value. Cf. also A.S. Nataraja Ayyar—*The King's Right to the Soil*—Lecture II delivered at the Faculty of Law, Delhi University—*Vyavahāra Nīrṇaya,* vol. IV, no. 1.
99. *Mīmāṁsā Sūtra,* VI. 7.1-2.
100. VI. 7-3.
101. *Mīmāṁsā - Darśana* (B.I.), VI. 7.3.
102. *Nyāyamālāvistara* (A.S.S.), p. 358.
103. *Bhaṭṭadīpikā* on *Pūrvamīmāṁsā Darśana* (Mysore), II, p. 317.
104. On *Manu* VIII. 99.
105. p. 91.
106. *EI,* VIII, 8 (no. 9).
107. Lüders 1163, 1166, 1167. One inscription records the gift of a field measuring fifteen *nivartanas* in the Puvānada village by a certain Palapa

(A.S.W.I. IV, p. 96, no. 20). According to another inscription from Junnar, Āḍuthuma, the Śaka, invested the income of two fields measuring twenty and nine *nivartanas* respectively with a guild at Koṇācika (Lüders 1162). Another record again from Junnar mentions the gift of a field by a certain Vāhata Vaceḍuka (ibid., 1164).

108. *EI*, I. 16 (nos. I and II). Cf. Mulgund inscription dated AD 902 —*EI*, XIII. 15 (K). It records three donations: (a) a field measuring 1000 betel-creepers by a merchant who bought it for a very great sum from three persons (b) a field measuring 1000 betel-creepers by four headmen of certain guilds and (c) a field measuring 1000 betel-creepers by a brāhmaṇa family.

109. *EI*, I, 20 (no. II); I. 21.

110. *Yuṣmābhirasyājñāśravaṇavidheyairbhavitavyaṁ samucitāśca pratyāyāḥ meyahiraṇyādayo deyāḥ*—*EI*, II. 30. Also *EI*, XXVIII. 47, IV. 16, XII. 1, XXVI. 18, XXIII. 3, IX. 21, 39. *Gupta Ins.*, 40, 26, *EI*, III. 21; XXI. 5; XXII. 22; XXVIII. 2; XII. 17; XXVIII. 39; XXIII. 9; XV. 4.

111. *Putrapautrānugāmī bhuñjato na kenacid vyāghātaḥ karttavyaḥ sarvvakriyābhissaṁrakṣitavyaḥ parivarddhayitavyaśca yaścāsmacchāsanamagaṇayamānassvalpāmapi paribādhāṁ karyāt kārayedvā tasya brāhmaṇaiḥ veditasya sadaṇḍaṁ nigrahaṁ kuryyāma*—*EI*, XXII. 27; XXII. 14; XXVI. 21. *Taṅgrāmamasau brāhmaṇaḥ putrapautrānukrameṇopabhuñjāno na kaiścitkiñcidvaktavyaḥ*—*EI*, XIII. 6 (p. 105); *Gupta Inscrptions*, 56. *Ye cāsmadvaṁśotpadyamānakarājānaḥ tairiyaṁ dattirnna vilopyānumodanīyā samucitarājābhāvyakarapratyāyā na grāhyāḥ*—*ibid.* 26. *Brāhmaṇena cātmanograhāraḥ putrapautrikamupabhujyamāno na kaiścidvallabhadurllabhairupahantavyaḥ*—*EI*, XXIII. 9.

112. *EI*, XV. 11 (B), 12; XVII. 7 (B); XIX. 20; XI p. 108; IX. 45; III. 3; V. 16 (A); XVIII. 15, 27, 31; XIV. 8; I. 13; VIII. 20 (A). Cf. *Artha.*, III. 10—*akaradāḥ paratra vasanto bhogamupajīveyuḥ*.

113. Takakusu, pp. 61-2.

114. Cf. *addhiyamanussāṇaṁ* in the Plates of Śālaṅkāyana Vijaya Devavarman —*EI*, IX. 7; addhikā in Hirahadagalli plates of Pallava Śivaskandavarman—*Select Inscriptions*, p. 440. Cf. also *kṛṣikarmānuṣṭhāna* in Talesvara plates of Dyutivarman—*EI*, XIII. 7 (A).

115. *EI*, VI 4; VII, p. 203; XXVI. 23, 47; III. 8; XXVIII. 1,3; *IA* VII p. 301; IX p. 102.

116. *EI*, III. 46; IV. 8; XI. 5 (p. 83f), 9 (p. 108); XXI. 30 (B), 36; XVII. 7 (B) and XIX. 20; XV. 12; *IA*, IX p. 238; also *EI*, 27 (p. 279); Sanjan Plates of Buddhavarṣa—*EI*, XIV. 8; Dayyamdinne Plates of Vinayāditya Satyāśraya—*EI*, XXII. 7 Dudia Plates of Vākāṭaka Pravarasena—*EI*, III. 35; Sankheda grants of Dadda IV Praśāntarāga—*EI*, V. 5 (nos. I and II); Devageri Plates of Kadamba Mṛgeśvaravarman—*IA* VII. p. 35; Banpur grant of Śailodbhava Dharmarāja Mānabhita—*EI*, XXIX. 5 (B); Mulgund Inscription of Kanna—*JBBRAS*, X, p. 119.

117. *EI*, XXIII. 10; VIII. 20 (A and B); XXVIII. 34 (B); IX. 7, 45; II. 4 (I);

III. 20; VI. 2 (A); XVIII. 31; VI. 16 (A); *IA*, VI. pp. 28, 29.

118. *EI*, VIII. 8 (no. 3). Cf. *rājakīyakṣetram* in the Dabok inscription dated 813 AD—*EI*, XX. 13.
119. *EI*, VIII. 8 (no. 5).
120. *EI*, VIII. 23. Cf. Fā-hsien (p. 67)—Several *le* north-east from the city was the king's field.
121. *EI*, VIII. 8 (No. 10).
122. *SII*, III., pp. 104-6.
123. II. I—*akṛṣatamācchidyānyebhyaḥ prayacchet;* I.14— . . . *paryāttabhūmiḥ . . . iti bhītavargaḥ.*
124. XIX. 16-18.
125. II. 1.
126. II. 3—items under the income group rāṣṭra; II. 15—incomes looked after by the superintendent of store-house.
127. II. 15—*sītādhyakṣopanītaḥ saṣyavarṇakassītā.*
128. II. 24; Ghoshal, *Hindu Revenue System*, pp. 29ff.
129. Cf. K.T. Shah, *Ancient Foundations of Economics in India*, pp. 79-82; A.N. Bose, *Social and Rural Economy*, p. 32, n. 1.
130. I. 14.
131. XIX. 16-18.
132. XIX. 22.
133. XIX. 23.
134. XI. 42.
135. VIII. 39.
136. II. 24.
137. *JBORS*, XII, p. 138.
138. 16-17.
139. The laborious efforts of K.P. Jayaswal (*Hindu Polity*, pp. 343, 348, 350) to revise the text of these verses to suit individual ownership of land are without any justification (U.N. Ghoshal, *Beginnings of Indian Historiography*, pp. 158f). We have already seen that legal works propound the theory of peasant proprietorship over land. It may again be pointed out that Manu at least among the authors quoted here does not seem to subscribe to the view of State landlordism, as is clear from his other verses dealing with this question, P.V. Kane—*History of Dharmaśāstra*, II, p. 867.
140. *Agrarian system in Ancient India*, pp. 98-9.
141. It seems that the overlordship of the king over all property in the State was first advocated clearly in the *Mahābhārata*, which refers to this view in a number of passages. A passage speaks of the Vedic utterance that the king is the owner of the wealth of all save the priest (*Mbh.*, XII. 77.2). Another passage, which says that all the wealth of the earth is the Kṣatriyas' and no one else's (*Mbh.*, XII. 136.3), evidently refers to the king's sovereign right. Elsewhere Daśaratha (*Mbh.*, III. 275.23) is reported as claiming that all property in his domain, excepting that of

Brāhmaṇas, belongs to him. The Smṛti literature also makes statements voicing the overlordship of the king. Thus *Gautama* (XI. 1) states that the king is master of all,with the exception of Brāhmaṇas.

142. Cf. P.K. Gode, *Studies in Indian Literary History*, vol. I, pp. 144ff.—*Manuscripts of Commentaries on the Kauṭilya Arthaśastra*. One indication about the date of Bhaṭṭasvāmin is his quoting Bṛhaspati several times on the blemishes of diamonds and on *prakāśā-taskaras*. (Kane, *History of Dharmaśāstra*, I, p. 104). His reference to the treatises on agriculturue by Vṛddhā-Parāśara and others is also significant (On *Artha.*, II. 24; *JBORS*, XII, p. 134—*Kṛṣitantraṁ Vṛddha-Parāśarādipraṇitaṁ kṛṣiśāstram*). That a considerable period elapsed between Kauṭilya and Bhaṭṭasvāmin would appear from many previous commentators whose words he quotes. (Kane, loc. cit.). He seems to have been followed by the Tamil-Malayalam Commṇentary of an unknown author (P.K. Gode, loc. cit., pp. 145f).
143. Frag. I (McCrindle, p. 42); Frag. XXXIII (McCrindle, p. 84).
144. *Kauṭalīya Studien* I, pp. 52ff. quoted by U.N. Ghoshal, *Hindu Revenue System*, pp. 168f.
145. XV. 1.40.
146. II. 40.
147. It is remarkable that Kauṭilya, the Mauryan Minister, does not assert royal ownership of all land. K.A.N. Sastri suggests that the *Arthaśāstra* stretches the right of regulation to its utmost limit and that the detailed rules of supervision and control made agriculture a vast State regulated enterprise which to Hellenistic eyes implied that the king was the owner of the soil (*Age of Nandas and Mauryas*, p. 177).
148. pp. 42-3.
149. *Si-yu-ki*, I, p. 176.
150. *Hindu Revenue System*, pp. 167-70, 191-2, 225-6.
151. A.N. Bose, *Social and Rural Economy*, p. 31.
152. XI. 27.
153. *Artha.*, III. 9; *Vyavasthā Candrikā* (ed. S.C. Sircar), VII. CI. 173-5.
154. XXV. 67-8.
155. *Manu*, VIII. 243.
156. The rule in the *Arthaśāstra* (III. 10) that a tax-payer and an owner of a *Brahmadeya* should sell or mortgage his field to his own class was intended to check the decrease in the income of the State which otherwiśe would have resulted.
157. These provisions have been elaborately dealt with in the *Vyavahāranirṇaya*, pp. 348ff. Also *Sarasvatīvilāsa*, p. 324.
158. 704.
159. Quoted by *Vyavahāranirṇaya*, p. 350.
160. V. 2.
161. *Social and Rural Economy*, p. 32.
162. *Baudhāyana*, I. 10.1; *Gautama*, X. 28-9; *Manu*, VII. 128, VIII. 306-8;

Nārada, XV. 48; *Artha.,* I. 13; *Bhāgavata Purāṇa,* I. 13.40-1; *Brahmāṇḍa Purāṇa,* II. 31-48; *Vāyu Purāṇa,* LVIII. 48; *Mārkaṇḍeya Purāṇa,* XVIII. 6-7.

163. I. 375.

164. *Raghu,* II. 66—*ṣaṣṭhāṁśam urvyāh iva rakṣitāyāḥ, Śākuntala,* II. 14—*rakṣāyogāt ayam api tapaḥ pratyahaṁ saṃcinoti.* Also *Raghu,* 1.18; XVII. 65; *Śākuntala,* p. 76.

165. That the proprietary right of the sovereign derives no warrant from the ancient laws or institutions of the Hindus had been demonstrated earlier by Chief Justice Sir Michael Westropp (*Vyakunta Bapuji* v. *Govt. of Bombay* 12 *Bom. H.C.R.,* pp. 30-53, Appendix) as also by Wilkes—*History of Mysore,* vol. I, ch. V, pp. 65-138.

166. Prof. K.V.R. Aiyangar accepts individual ownership of a permanent character (*Ancient Indian Economic Thought,* p. 104) and maintains that the cameral feeling of an implied partnership of the state in all wealth-producing activities when carried to extreme practice and theory and under secular influence urged the theory of State property in land, etc. (*Indian Cameralism,* p. 160).

167. M.H. Gopal, *Mauryan Public Finance,* p. 62; F.W. Thomas, *Cambridge History of India,* vol. I, p. 475.

168. Quoted by M.A. Buch, *Economic Life in Ancient India* II, pp. 24f (quoting from Lees, *Land and Labour of India,* pp. 111-14). Also Sen, *Hindu Jurisprudence,* pp. 52f.

5

Assignment to Officers and Royal Kinsmen in Early Medieval India *c.* AD 700-1200

Krishna Kanti Gopal

Unfortunately there are not many references directly bearing on the mode of payment to officers during the early medieval period. The legal texts and *nīti* works such as the *Yuktikalpataru* and the *Mānasollāsa* are totally silent on this point. We have only a very brief observation by Medhātithi. Commenting on the passage in Manu[1] postulating payment to officers of administrative units by grants of land, he observes that all this is only recommendatory and should not be literally applied to and that it only means that a salary commensurate with the position and responsibilities of each officer should be granted. The remarks of Medhātithi are not very explicit but they can be construed to imply that payment in cash was also in vogue.

At least, it would follow from the combined testimony of Hsüan Tsang[2] and the *Harṣacarita*[3] that in the seventh century the state officers were mostly paid in the form of land-grants. This would appear to have been the common practice in our period as well.

There is a complete absence of the coins of some of the dynasties, such as the Pālas and the Senas. Some others, such as the Gāhaḍavālas, the Cāhamānas, and the Chālukyas, etc., do not seem to have issued a regular and complete currency in all the three chief metals and in all the denominations. Further, it is only a few kings, sometimes only one in a dynasty, who issued coins. It is quite likely that sometimes older coins remained in circulation. But there is always the possibility that the paucity of the coins available for this period would make a case against the prevalence of coins in paying the state officers.[4]

From the ninth century we get epigraphic references to land-grants made to state officials and these increase in number from the eleventh century.[5] But the records which have come down are few compared with the number of officers in the different kingdoms of the period. The difference appears all the more striking in view of the much larger number of epigraphs recording religious grants. The reason is to be attributed to the fact that whereas the religious grants, meant to secure spiritual merit, were intended to last for ever and were therefore recorded on durable material, there was no corresponding need to preserve the land-grants made to an officer. It follows from the smṛtis of Yājñavalkya[6] and Bṛhaspati[7] that the secular grants were written on perishable material. In the *Lekhapaddhati*[8] also the term used for assignments made to a *rāṇaka* and a *rājaputra* is *bhūrja-pattalā*. It is clear that these assignments were made on perishable material such as the birch-bark. In a story from the *Bṛhatkathākośa*[9] similar assignments made by a king to his *sāmantas* appear to have been on cloth or some such other material. We read in the *Tilakamañjarī*[10] that the charter for the enjoyment of certain provinces which a prince received was conveyed on a piece of cloth. It is likely that in some cases the recipients of these secular grants were quite influential and strong and, taking a lesson from their religious counterparts, could press the king to issue these grants on durable material especially when the grants were meant to last long.

We have some inscriptions recording the grant of villages made to different state officials in different parts of northern India. Thus Bhavadeva, who was a minister of king Harivarmadeva (*c.* AD 1075-1125), claims that one of his ancestors had been granted a village by the king of Gauḍa.[11] From three land-grants we know that the Somavaṃśī king Mahābhavagupta I (*c.* AD 935-70) had assigned four villages to his brāhmaṇa chief minister Sādhāraṇa.[12] Devānanda III, the Nanda ruler, granted a village to his kāyastha minister for peace and war.[13] An astrologer named Jagadhara Sarman received two villages, one from king Yaśabhañjadeva of Khiñjalī[14] and the other from the latter's younger brother.[15] King Anantavarman Coḍagaṅga assigned to one of his trustworthy agents a village with a hamlet.[16] King Nṛsiṃha II granted two villages to his minister *kumāra mahāpātra* Bhīmadeva.[17] King

Yaśaḥpāla of the Pratihāra dynasty gave a village to a certain Māthura Vikaṭa[18] who was most probably a kāyastha official. The Gāhaḍavāla records reveal that the chief priest Jāguka received in all the grant of ten *pattalās,* while the son, who succeeded him to the same office, obtained eight *pattalās* more.[19] Kṣatriya Rājyavardhana, who also probably had the official designation of a *mahāmahattaka* like his father and grand-father, is found receiving six land-grants in the reign of king Jayacandra.[20] From the Ajayagadh inscription of Bhojavarman[21] we learn that king Gaṇḍa granted by a charter a village to Jājūka of a distinguished kāyastha family whom he had appointed to superintend at all times all the affairs of the state and that king Kīrtivarman likewise gave to Māheśvara, another member of the same kāyastha family, for rendering service to Kīrtivarman in the Pitaśaila *viṣaya,* the title of *Viśiṣa* [22] of Kalinjar and the grant of the village of Pipalāhikā to be his for ever. According to the Devapattana inscription of Śridhara[23] king Cāmuṇḍa bestowed a village on *mahāmantrin* Mādhava.

It appears that such grants were generally permanent as has been clearly recorded in some cases. We feel that these cases are not those of state officers being granted the villages in lieu of salaries. If such had been the case there was not much sense in making a special mention of it in the records when village grants went along with their services as a matter of course. Moreover, in most cases the recipients appear to have been occupying their position long before they got the village. Some of the grants make it quite clear that the officers received the villages as a special favour of the king. Thus an inscription of the tenth century from Gorakhpur clearly says that the village which the minister (*saciva*) Madoli granted to the goddess Durgā, had been received by him through the favour of king Jayāditya,[24] most probably a feudatory of the Gurjara-Pratihāras. It would appear that sometimes the king pleased with an officer for some valuable service performed by him gave a village over and above the usual remuneration he was receiving. It has been suggested in a recent study[25] that the *pattalās* which Jāguka, the chief priest of the Gāhaḍavālas, received were the annual payments for his services. We feel, however, that the suggestion could not have worked out in practice because the number of *pattalās* being obviously limited such annual grants even to the important officers of the state would have soon exhausted the number of *pattalās* at the disposal of the emperor.

Though it is doubtful whether the grants mentioned here were a form of remuneration for state service, they indicate some kind of feudal practice. These assignments gave to the officers the status of feudal chiefs as the lords of the villages granted to them. The relatively few recorded cases can also mean that land-grants constituted a special favour by the king. In any case the existence of such grants suggests a society where coined money was not in much circulation which in turn makes a strong case for land-grants and not cash being the usual mode of payment.

We have other evidence which indicates more clearly that the regular officials were often remunerated in the form of village grants.[26] In an inscription of the Cāhamānas of Śākambhari[27] we have a reference to the religious grant of a village which a *duḥsādhya*[28] made out of his fief. It is significant that the record mentions it along with other grants made by members of the royal family from their estates and feudal assignments. As the *duḥsādhya* had to seek the permission of his master his right to the assignment was obviously limited. According to a copper plate dated AD 1260[29] king Jayavarman II caused a certain *pratihāra* (head of the palace-guard) to donate a village to three brahmaṇas. Obviously this officer possessed the village as his assignment because it is he who is said to have performed the religious ceremonies connected with the grant but he had to do it with the permission of his master who signed it and made it a royal charter. An inscription of Mahendrapāla II[30] which records the grant of a village by the emperor in the possession of *talavarggika* Hariṣaḍa indicates that the officer had been given the village but had only a limited right in the sense that the king could give it to another person. A more abiding claim of these officers is suggested by the inscription[31] in which king Vākpatirāja is said to have re-granted to a goddess a village when requested by the wife of the *mahāsādhanika* Mahāika who obviously had received it as an assignment earlier. A regent of five districts under king Vajrahasta of the Gaṅga dynasty is found giving a village to the bridegroom on the occasion of the marriage of his daughter.[32] This naturally suggests that this high officer had received more than one village from his emperor. A similar inference can be drawn from the claim made by Bhavadeva, a minister, that he increased his land by military feats.[33] The land which a brāhmaṇa officer of king Vigrahapāla III is said to have granted out of his own possession with the permission of the king[34] was most probably part of the land assigned to him as a service tenure. The Pāla records refer to the land allotted to the *kaivarttas* as remuneration for their services.[35]

We have some literary references also which corroborate these epigraphic records in making a case for the grant of land to state officers as service tenure. The *Rājataraṅgiṇi*[36] informs us that king Avantivarman divided his kingdom among his relatives and officers, most probably in the form of estates and feudal assignments. The village which Suyya, the engineer, granted to the brāhmaṇas[37] would appear to have been out of his service assignments. The *Kumārapālacarita*[38] mentions the minister of the king as enjoying seven hundred villages. The title *mahāmaṇḍaleśvara* applied to the minister of Pṛthvīrāja III Cāhamāna in the *Kharataragacchagurvāvali*[39] can be taken to indicate that he had been granted a whole *maṇḍala* as his assignment. In some cases at least the service tenure would appear to have been of a permanent nature. Thus, in the *Udayasundarīkathā*[40] we have a reference to a kāyastha officer enjoying a tenure which was permanent and hereditary.

There are some indications to suggest that sometimes some of the state officers were assigned shares in the revenue from a village. It is not clear whether they received part of the usual share of the state or an additional charge on the part of the villagers. The latter possibility seems more likely. It is also not clear if these charges were in place of regular salaries or were additional assignments. We would prefer to take them as assignments in place of salaries. In any case it is apparent that state servants were remunerated with land rather than with salaries in cash. Thus, the taxes for *paṭṭakilas* (village headmen) and *duḥsādhyas* (police officers) are included in the list of rights and incomes transferred to the donee in a grant of Jayasiṃha.[41] In the copper plates of *mahārājaputra* Govindacandra of the Gāhaḍavāla dynasty we have references to three terms *akṣapaṭalaprastha* or *akṣapaṭalādāya*, *pratihāraprastha* and *viśatiaṭhūprastha* or *viṃsaticchavatha*.[42] These were the shares of the produce, most probably a *prastha* from every household, which the officers known as *akṣapaṭalika*, *pratihāra* and *viśatiaṭhu* received.[43] There is nothing to indicate the mode in which these state servants used to collect these charges for themselves. It is natural to suppose that those on the spot such as the *paṭṭakilas* would have collected their shares themselves along with the state dues. In the case of others it would appear more likely that the state machinery for the realization of taxes collected the dues meant to remunerate these officers also which they subsequently received from their respective headquarters. From the Candella inscriptions we learn that petty state servants, forest officials and the village police had some rights in the villages which they were required to transfer to a donee in case of a religious grant.[44] From these references it may be inferred that these rights of state officers were of a very limited type and could never have developed into anything like a fief. In some cases, however, even such rights to revenues would appear to have acquired a more lasting character. Thus, we see in an inscription from Marwar[45] that under king Aśvarāja the *mahāsāhaṇiya* (Great Master of Stables) granted to a temple his share of barley realized from every one of the Persian wheel wells *(arahaṭa)* of four villages. It is fair to suggest that the share of barley which this officer received was like the *prastha* charges attributed to three Gāhaḍavāla officers. What is significant in this case is the fact that the state officer had such a right over the item of revenue that he could transfer or donate it to others without having to seek permission from his master.

In the administrative set-up of northern India in the early medieval period the feudal hierarchy and the bureaucracy appear to have got jumbled together in a curious manner.[46] With the growing tendency to remunerate the officers in the form of assignments of land and to appoint feudatories to different posts in the empire the demarcation line between officers on the one hand and the feudatories and feudal chiefs on the other tended to get blurred. This amounted to a general weakening of the traditions of bureaucratic administration and the growing emphasis on the feudal elements in the administrative system.

In the epigraphic records from different parts of northern India we often find that the state officers had titles of *rāuta*, *ṭhākkura* and *rāṇaka* attached to their names. These titles stood for feudal chiefs, which position the officers came to occupy through land assignments in lieu of their salaries. We also find that *rājānaka*, which was originally a title of a feudal chief, was extended to the ministers in the Chamba state.[47] It is interesting to note that the *Rājataraṅgiṇī*[48] also employs *rājānaka* as the usual title of ministers in Kashmir. There are also examples where *rājaputra* and *mahārājaputra*, which were titles of feudal chiefs, were used for officials also.[49] It has to be noted that the *Kharataragacchagurvāvali* mentions the minister of Pṛthvīrāja III as a *mahāmaṇḍaleśvara*.[50] Two explanations can be given. It is likely that this minister was assigned a *maṇḍala* for enjoyment as his service tenure. The second possibility is that he was a feudatory who had been appointed as a minister at the imperial court. *Maṇḍaleśa*, which was often used as a title by independent feudatories, significantly appears in the *Rājataraṅgiṇi* [51] as the designation of provincial governors.

At the same time we find that the feudal chiefs were being looked upon as a part of the administrative machinery of the state. In the *Samarāṅgaṇasūtradhāra*[52] *sāmanta* has been mentioned in the midst of different officers of the state. In the *Varṇaratnākara*[53] also *sāmantas, māṇḍalikas* and forest chiefs (*vana-rāutas)* are enumerated as servants of the king (*rājasevaka*).

There was now no sharp distinction between the officers and the feudal chiefs.[54] The practice of conferring honour on a feudal chief by various devices was being extended to officers also. From the *Aparājitapṛcchā*[55] we learn that like the different grades of feudatories and feudal chiefs there were distinct rules for the houses and conveyances of the high officials. How the state officers with feudal rights gradually tended to become feudal chiefs is indicated in the *Kathāsaritsāgara*[56] which speaks of a royal priest enjoying a thousand villages and the privilege of *chattra* and *vāhana* just like a *sāmanta* (*sāmanta-tulya)*. In the *Bṛhatkathākośa*[57] also a warrior appointed to the post of a *sahasrabhaṭa* had many villages as assignments and is called a *sāmanta*. We have many records in which the *mahāsāndhivigrahika* officers are also styled *sāmantas* and have the special feudal honour of the *pañcamahāśabda*.[58] The records of the Chālukyas of Gujarat provide us with an instance of an officer being made a feudatory with distinctive feudal honours attached to his name. Vaijalladeva appears in some earlier inscriptions as a military governor (*daṇḍanāyaka*) but in a later inscription he is called *mahāmaṇḍaleśvara*, had attained the *pañcamahāśabdas* and was governing the Narmadātaṭa-*maṇḍala* through the favour of his overlord king Ajayapāla.[59]

We thus see that the officers were remunerated in terms of feudal assignments, though there is no specific reference in the legal texts and the epigraphic and literary records of the period. The paucity of coins and the references to kings awarding villages to officers when pleased with them indicate a feudal economy. The officers are found owning villages which they most probably received as remuneration from their king who had a superior right over them. Some of the lower officers would seem to have received specific shares in revenue as their remuneration. All this naturally gave a semi-feudatory status to the officers. Some of the feudatories were probably given some of the higher posts in the empire. Thus we find that the line of demarcation between officers and feudatories was gradually becoming dim.

Another practice which in our period resulted in the kingdoms being parcelled out into a number of feudal estates was that of granting villages or land assignment to members of the royal family in particular and to other chiefs of the same tribe in general. Such grants were more common in the clan monarchies of our period.[60] The system naturally weakened the central power by reducing the area under the direct control of the state.

We find that bestowing honour on the kinsmen and providing for their maintenance was definitely regarded as the ideal for a king.[61] Lakkhana in his *Aṇuvayarayaṇa Païba* (AD 1257) praises king Āhavamalla for maintaining his kinsmen with honour and presents.[62] According to the Acaleśvara inscription dated AD 1319 when the Asuras (i.e. the Muslims) had destroyed the kṣatriyas Lāvaṇyakarṇa of the Cāhamāna family of Candravati and Abu devoted himself to the protection of his tribesmen and their land.[63] The *Agni Purāṇa*[64] says that the friends of the king's relatives should receive the remuneration fixed by his ancestors. Somadeva discusses the policy to be pursued in the case of kinsmen in some detail. He appears to have realized the baneful effect of the policy of granting feudal assignments to kinsmen. In his *Nītivākyāmṛta*[65] he warns the king against granting positions which may lead to an increase in their military force and their revenue. He suggests, however, that the king may favour a kinsman or a son who does not make a false show of loyalty and has never gone against him, and likewise appoint him to a suitable post. The king should bring under his control kinsmen with a large following by winning their confidence through trustworthy persons or by setting spies on them and should turn away an evil-minded son or a kinsman from his purpose by proper reasoning.

Though kingship normally descended to the eldest prince and was not shared by other princes as a patrimony to be divided among all the sons, there are many instances in the history of our period when brothers and near relatives were assigned virtually independent kingdoms.[66] The classic example comes from the Kalacuri dynasty. From the Kalacuri records we learn that king Kokkala had eighteen sons the eldest of whom became the king of Tripuri and made his seventeen brothers feudatory chiefs in neighbourhood.[67] In Kashmir this mistake was often committed by rulers with very disastrous results for the unity of the kingdom. Queen Diddā nominated Saṅgrāma-rāja to succeed her to the throne and appointed Vigraharāja as ruler over the fortress of Lohara. The mistake was rectified by Utkarṣa who united the two kingdoms. Once again there was a division after the death of Hārṣa with Uccala ruling in Kashmir and his brother Sussala in Lohara. In AD 1112 Sussala once again amalgamated the two kingdoms. For some time Jayasiṃha managed to control Lohara with great difficulty but in the end he found the solution of the problem by crowning his son Gulhaṇa as the ruler of Lohara.[68] In Orissa we find that king Uddyotakesarī Mahābhavagupta IV of the Somavaṃśī dynasty appointed Abhimanyu as the sub-king of the western part of his empire.[69] The *Padmānanda Mahākāvya*,[70] written towards the middle of the thirteenth century, relates the story of king Vajranābha who distributed his kingdom among his four brothers.[71]

The *Kathākoṣa*[72] gives a story about a king who established his elder son as a crown-prince and gave to the younger a kingdom in Ujjayinī as an 'apanage for a prince' (*kumārabhukti*). In another story in the same text the father of prince Amaracandra, pleased with the extraordinary courage of his son, is said to have given him the apanage of a prince.[73]

It was very common in our period for kings to grant feudal assignments to their relations and kinsmen. According to the *Rājataraṅgiṇī*[74] king Avantivarman of Kashmir divided his kingdom, presumably in the form of feudal assignments, among his relatives and officers. From the *Chachnāma*[75] it would appear that in Sind it was quite usual for a king to assign to his relations the rulership over different parts of the kingdom or chieftainship of the forts which controlled different areas.

With the appearance of the clan monarchies we find many references to assignments made to the kinsmen. It would appear that the tribe had an important hand in the formation of these monarchies and hence their chiefs had to be appeased. It is also likely that these had a high sense of loyalty towards their kinsmen and so the other members of the tribe had some claim over the king. This bond of community in these tribes is suggested by the Indian Office plate of Vijayarājadeva[76] which on paleographic considerations can be assigned to the eleventh or twelfth century. It records the grant to two men Vigrahapāla, son of Dusala, and Mūladeva, son of Kusuara, belonging to the Palha clan. The grant is said to have been of those parts of the feudal estate of Kesarikoṭṭa which were hitherto not enjoyed by Mūladeva. Another part of the same plate records that out of this the village of Potā was to be enjoyed by Vigrahapāla and his descendants alone. In one case the plate specifically lays down that no tribesman has any claim over the assignment and in the other that no other than of the Palha tribe has any claim to it. These clauses would suggest that usually the other members of the tribe also had some claim over a feudal assignment but have been waived aside in the present case.

An inscription from Rajasthan dated AD 725[77] speaks of the estate of Dhavagarttā enjoyed by Dhanika a chief of the Guhila tribe under king Dhavalappadeva. It appears that division of the kingdom among tribesmen was recognized even in those times as a characteristic feature of the Pratihāras, and it was therefore natural that they formed the main strength of the Pratihāra army. It is interesting to note that the Begumra plate[78] of the Rāṣṭrakūṭas which records the defeat of king Bhoja I of the Pratihāra dynasty at the hands of Dhruva, the Rāṣṭrakūṭa chief of the Gujarat branch, in lauding the power of the former describes him as 'united to fortune and surrounded by crowds of noble kinsmen'. We learn from an inscription from Rajor (Alwar) dated AD 958[79] that under the imperial Pratihāra dynasty a chief named Mathanadeva belonging to this lineage had received the estate named Vaṃśapotaka as an allotment for his enjoyment.

The system of making assignments to chiefs of the tribe continued under other clan monarchies which emerged into power during the decline of the Pratihāra kingdom. An inscription dated AD 973 from Harsha (Jaipur)[80] indicates that under the Cāhamānas of Śākambharī the kinsmen of the king had in their private possession villages and hamlets which they had received as assignments from the king (*svabhogāvāpta*) and which they could dispose of at will. The personal estates referred to in this inscription include those of king Siṃharāja, his two brothers, Vatsarāja and Vigraharāja, and his two sons Candrarāja and Govindarāja. Under the Cāhamānas of Nadol there are several records testifying to the apportionment of land among the kinsmen of the ruling chief. In an inscription from Sevāḍī (Jodhpur) dated AD 1143[81] we find that under king Kaṭudeva the crown-prince Jayatasīha was enjoying the possession of Samīpātī (Sevāḍī). The extent of decentralization appears from the fact that even in a small kingdom like Nadol the epigraphs indicate that in the reign of Kelhaṇa only the central portion of the empire was directly administered by the king himself, whereas the outposts of the kingdom were governed by his sons and near relatives.[82] The Bamnera grant[83] mentions *mahārājaputra* Kumārasiṃha who was enjoying the village of Koreṭa as his assignment. D. Sharma[84] seems to be convincing when he suggests that he was another son of Alhaṇa. According to the Nadol plates dated AD 1161 king (*rājakula*) Ālhaṇadeva and the crown-prince (*kumāra*) Kelhaṇadeva jointly granted a group of twelve villages to a junior member of the family *rājaputra* Kīrtipāla.[85] We find that in the Cāhamāna kingdom of Nadol in the reign of Alhaṇa, Māṇḍavyapura was under Kelhaṇa's younger brother Gajasiṃha, but under Kelhaṇa himself it was respectively in AD 1183 and 1192 under Kelhaṇa's sons Siṃhavikrama and Soḍhaladeva.[86] This may indicate that the feudal assignments to tribesmen were not necessarily always hereditary and permanent. The overload would appear to have an abiding title to these feudal assignments and could transfer parts of it to others. We have seen that Kīrtipāla had been assigned twelve villages by king Ālhaṇa and the heir-apparent Kelhaṇa and these were in the possession of Kīrtipāla's sons Ābhayapāla and Lakhaṇapāla but it is to be noted that Sonāna, one of these twelve villages, was temporarily assigned to a certain *thākura* Anasīha.[87] It is to be noted that in the Cāhamāna records *rājaputra* is mostly used in the sense of a scion of a royal family, which is the literal and original meaning of the term, and not a military chief enjoying some land assignment, which meaning it came to acquire in the records of other contemporary dynasties. But it would appear that the term was not slow to get associated with some kind of land assignment even in the records of the Cāhamānas. In one of the inscriptions of this family[88] we have a reference to a *sejā* (allotment) of a *rājaputra* named Ajayadeva. In an inscription from Jalor dated AD 1181[89] Jojala, the maternal uncle of Samarasiṃha, the Cāhamāna ruler of Jalor, is described as *rājyacintaka rājaputra* Jojala, which may suggest that he had received some feudal assignment. Another grant of the family dated AD 1176[90] informs us that during the reign of Kelhaṇa the two sons of Kīrtipāla, the *rājaputra* Lakhaṇapālha and the *rājaputra* Abhayapāla, were the estate-holders (*bhoktṛs*)[91] of Sināṇava. In the same inscription Lakhaṇapālha and Abhayapāla along with the queen granted their share in the barley realized from the *araghata* of a village. This would suggest that the three enjoyed the village together. We have other records of the family to demonstrate clearly that the queens also received independent assignments of land. Thus, in one inscription dated AD 1143[92] a village is said to have been enjoyed by queen Śrī Tihuṇaka as her *girāsa* (=*grāsa*). Another inscription dated AD 1179[93] refers to the *bhukti* (feudal assignment) of queen Jālhaṇadevī.

It appears that the later Cāhamānas of Bhṛgukaccha also made assignments to members of the royal family. We thus find that the port of Cambay was under the personal enjoyment of Sindhurāja, the younger brother of Siṃha, the Cāhamāna ruler of Broach.[94]

Though we do not have so many records testifying to the land apportionment among the royal kinsmen, we have some indications that they were by no means unknown under other dynasties also. Thus, the Modasa plate dated AD 1011[95] speaks of a *bhoktāra mahārājaputra* Vatsarāja under king Bhoja of the Paramāra dynasty. It would appear from the title *mahārājaputra* that Vatsarāja was a son of king Bhoja, unknown from other sources. *Bhoktāra* may be a mistake for *bhoktṛ* and thus it would follow that this prince enjoyed Mohaḍavāsaka or a part of it as the estate under his possession.

Under the Candellas we find that some members of the royal family were given the rulership over a district. Thus, Kaṇhapa or Kṛṣṇapa, the brother of king Dhaṅga, had in his charge a district near Jhansi and Dudhai and called himself a *nṛpa*. His successor Devalabdhi continued to rule the district under his uncle Dhaṅga and his cousin Gaṇḍa.[96]

The colophon of a manuscript dated AD 1150 informs us that during the reign of the Gāhaḍavāla king Govindacandra prince Vijayacandra enjoyed the possession of Baḍaharadeśa on the southern bank of the Yamunā.[97]

The practice in the clan monarchies in later medieval times in Rajasthan[98] and the Rajput kingdoms of medieval Chhatisgarh[99] indicate that the characteristic unit granted to a chief was a group of 84 villages. U.N. Ghoshal[100] takes the references in the records of our period to the unit of 84 villages and its sub-divisions to indicate the survivals of chiefs' allotment in a system of clan monarchies. The practice of apportioning state territory into groups of 84 villages is unknown to the literature on law and polity.[101] Some reference to this practice is, however, found in the works of our period.[102] The *caurāsiā* holders of villages formed the basic unit in the division of empire among the feudal chiefs. The *caurāsiā* or holders of 84 villages are mentioned as a well-known class of chiefs in the *Visaladeva Rāso*[103] assigned to the latter part of the fourteenth century AD.[104] There is some epigraphic corroboration of the suggestion that the unit 84 represented the division which the chiefs used to receive.[105] In a Gurjara-Pratihāra[106] record we have one of the earliest references to the system of 84 villages. In it a chief is said to have acquired 84 villages by the might of his own arm, probably suggesting thereby that it was not because he belonged to the same tribe that he received it but in the sense that his overlord had to accept his claim in view of his military strength. The testimony of Kalavan plates of the Paramāras[107] belonging to the second half of the eleventh century AD is more to the point. It speaks of a chief (*sāmanta*) of the Gaṅga family enjoying a district which was a feudal grant of 84 villages. An inscription from Rajasthan[108] belonging to the twelfth century refers to Ratnapura-*caturāśika*. It would appear that Ratnapura was a feudal estate of 84 villages which originally some king had apportioned to a chief of his tribe. In a record of the Rāṣṭrakūṭa king Kṛṣṇa II dated AD 910-11[109] from Gujarat a group of 84 villages appears in the midst of other administrative divisions of larger and smaller number of villages which would suggest an attempt to incorporate the unit of clan monarchies into the existing territorial system. In the Set-Mahet grant of the Gāhaḍavāla king Govindacandra[110] we have a reference to a *pattalā* of 84 villages (*caturāśīti*). Likewise the Badera plates of Madanapāladeva,[111] a feudatory of the Gāhaḍavālas, mention a *caturāsikā pattalā*. *Pattalās* came to be used in some parts of northern India as the term for a territorial divison, but basically it meant the territory which the king gave to chiefs as their *jāgirs*. It is quite likely that the *pattalās* of 84 villages in the above-mentioned Gāhaḍavāla records were granted to the other chiefs of the tribe by some early Gāhaḍavāla king.

Sometimes in order to suit the size of the state and possibly also the number of kinsmen claiming such estates the king often reduced the number of villages in them to 42. As the size of the states in our period was often limited we find that the village-groups given to kinsmen and other chiefs under the clan monarchies generally consisted of 12 or its multiples. The unit of 42 villages is mentioned in a Paramāra inscription dated AD 1055[112] and two records of the Chālukyas of Gujarat dated respectively AD 1051[113] and 1175.[114] It is interesting to note that a Gāhaḍavāla grant dated AD 1133[115] mentions a *pattalā* of 42 villages (*bayālisī*). In a grant dated AD 1091[116] we find that the number of villages in the unit attached to Ānandapura under the Chālukya king Karṇa I was 126, which being a multiple of 42 suggests that originally the unit was granted to some chief belonging to the ruling tribe. The references to units of 12 villages or their multiples are many. Thus Kīrtipāla, a junior prince of the Cāhamāna family, is said to have been granted 12 villages by the Cāhamāna king Ālhaṇadeva and the crown-prince Kelhaṇadeva.[117] A unit of 12 villages is mentioned in a Cāhamāna inscription[118] of the tenth century. An inscription in Gujarat dated AD 1192[119] records the grant of 12 villages to a Guhila chief. In the inscriptions of the Paramāras we find references to groups of 48, 36 and 12 villages.[120] A unit of 12 villages is referred to in an inscription of the Candella king Paramardideva.[121] There were also units of many other numbers of villages, which are not covered by the systems of 84 and 12 but which appear to have been fashioned after them by kings to suit their convenience.

In the Rajput type of monarchies organized on clan lines the king keeps the central, or the best, part of the kingdom to himself, distributing the outlying portions to the other chiefs of the clan. In the clan monarchies of the early medieval period the picture resembles that of later times insofar as in some records some specific parts of the kingdom are stated to have been under the direct enjoyment of the king, implying thereby that the other parts had been apportioned to others. Such portions under the personal enjoyment of the king are introduced as *sva-bhoga* in the records of the Candellas[122] and the Cāhamānas[123] whereas the grants of the Chālukyas,[124] and the Paramāras[125] have *sva-bhujyamāna.*[126] In some of these records there are references to show that these areas under the possession of the kings were formed after the units granted to other chiefs of the tribe and thus suggesting that the apportionment was done at the time of the foundation of the clan monarchy. Thus, we find that it was a unit of 126 villages (multiples of 42) which is said in the Sunak grant[127] to have been under the personal enjoyment of Karṇa I. Likewise in the Harsha stone inscription[128] one of the possessions of king Siṃharāja is Tūnakūpaka, a group of 12 villages.

There are not many relevant references indicating the relationship between the king and the tribal chiefs enjoying the assignments in the clan monarchies. The practice prevailing in later medieval times was that the kinsmen receiving these assignments were practically independent rulers in their areas but owed only two obligations to the king, of contributing aids in times of war, and of paying him fees on succession to their estates.[129] The first obligation in any case is mentioned in the *Agni Purāṇa.*[130] It requires the relations receiving remuneration from the king to arm themselves with the complete suit of arms, keep in their service armed soldiers and supply the king with horses, elephants and armed men in times of emergency. For the obligation of the kinsmen to pay fee on inheriting his estate we have no evidence. In many of the records referring to this type of assignment to royal kinsmen we have some indication to their abiding right to their estates in the sense that they are found making grants of portions of these. It would appear that they were not required to secure the permission of the king before making the grant. In the Harsha stone inscription[131] of the Cāhamāna king Vigraharāja we find that whereas the *duḥsādhya* officer had to seek the permission of the king (*svāmyanumata*) for making a grant out of the assignments enjoyed by him, the royal kinsmen had not to undergo any such formality. The Nadol plate of the Cāhamānas dated AD 1161[132] indicates that the fief of 12 villages was granted to prince Kīrttipāla by king Ālḥaṇadeva and crown-prince Kelhaṇadeva with absolute rights and in perpetuity in the sense that in making a grant of a sum from each of these villages he enjoins his descendants to observe the terms of the grant made by him. We can get some idea of the conditions of the grant from the India Office plate of Vijayarājadeva[133] in which the grant is made to two members of the Palha tribe. The grant is said to be made in perpetuity (*sadāthityā*) as long as the moon,the sun and the stars endure and to be enjoyed by the sons, grandsons, great-grandsons and other such descendants of the donee. Such assignments appear to have been small administrative units in themselves and were not to be interfered with by any military officer (*kenāpi balādhikṛtena na paripaṃthanīyā*). The donees had the right to enjoy the assignment and to transfer them to another person (*sahastaprahasatena bhoktavyā*).

In this connection it should briefly be considered whether these feudal assignments to royal kinsmen were administrative units or personal estates rewarded for administrative service in a wider territorial unit. R.S. Sharma[134] favours the latter view. But, the difficulty is, however, that in Indian texts we do not have any direct evidence bearing on the question. We would support the former possibility on the ground that in all these records mentioning the apportionment to royal kinsmen the latter are simply said to be enjoying those estates. The records which often refer to the posts held by the donors, donees and other connected persons do not give any indication of the royal kinsmen being in charge of any bigger administrative units. So it would appear that the estates were given to the royal kinsmen to be ruled as administrative units.

We have no means of determining the areas which in the different clan monarchies of our period were apportioned to the royal kinsmen. Generally the records do not indicate whether any given area was in the nature of a grant to a kinsman. We could have formed some idea if we had known all the different administrative units in these kingdoms. In any case, all attempts in this connection will have to be treated as tentative in the sense that we cannot say to have recovered all the records granting such estates. It would appear, however, that the region under the personal enjoyment of the king was relatively small in proportion to the total area of the kingdom as would follow from the fact that in our records very few regions are described as being under the personal possession (*svabhujyamāna*) of the king. We feel that apportionment to kinsmen had become quite common in our period. It appears that Sulaimān[135] refers to the fact that the monarchies of our period were established on clan lines when he observes that in the kingdoms of India the nobility is considered to form but one family in which alone power resides.

Here we may refer to assignments made to refugee princes. In a royal family the succession being reserved for the eldest son the other ambitious princes would often have migrated to other courts to try their luck. As polygamy was the rule among kings this must have been the case more so in our period because the issues of the king's wives belonging to different tribes could not have been reconciled to the idea of losing succession to another member of the royal family. We learn from the *Harṣacarita*[136] that Kumāragupta and Mādhavagupta, two such princes from Mālava, had sought refuge at the court of Sthāṇīśvara to be brought up as playmates of the sons of Prabhākaravardhana. Such princes were given lucrative assignments by the king to whose court they went. The *Mānasollāsa*[137] reveals how common this practice had beome in our perid when it advises a king to follow a definite policy of welcoming a ruling king who seeks protection, to give him a seat befitting his position, to please him with kind words, present him fine clothes, gold ornaments, jewels, horses and elephants, villages, cities or even small countries and make him stay in the best houses. The *Tilakamañjarī*[138] speaks of princes who flocked from different directions for help from a powerful king in recovering their state which had been snatched from them by their wicked kinsmen. Another passage in the same text[139] refers to a son of the king of Kaliṅga living at the court of another king. We learn from the *Prabandhacintāmaṇi*[140] that Jagaddeva was received by the Candella king Paramarddi who granted him the rulership of a *deśa* (region). Likewise, we know that Cāhaḍa, the son of Siddharāja, went to the Cāhamāna kingdom where he joined the Cāhamāna army in order to take vengeance upon the Chālukya king Kumārapāla.[141] These refugee princes were for all practical purposes treated as kinsmen and assigned feudal estates of a similar nature. As marriage relations could easily be established with these princes, there was not much difficulty in such a practice. It is interesting to note that a Guhila chief, who took refuge in Surāṣṭra in about AD 1193 after being uprooted from his territory, is said to have been granted 12 villages which we have seen above was the unit of villages granted to royal kinsmen in monarchies founded on the lines of clans.

NOTES

1. VII. 118-19.
2. Watters, *On Yuan Chwang*, I, p. 176.
3. *Bhṛtyopayogāya vyabhajateva vasudhāṃ bahudhā*, p. 93.
4. *JESHO*, IV. 99f.
5. Ibid., 70f.
6. I. 318-20.
7. Quoted in *Vyavahāramyūkha*, pp. 25-7.
8. p. 7.
9. IX.21-3. These are referred to as *grāmapattanadeśānāṃputrikāśāsanāsi*. Later on *śāsasāni* and *patrikā* are split. Another verse refers to *patrikāguṇḍikādikam*. The use of the word *patrikā* is contrasted with śāsana which is generally known to have been on copper-plate.
10. p. 103—*Rājñā samādiṣṭaḥ Sudṛṣtināmākṣapaṭalikaḥ praviśya paṭṭakāropita-niravaśeṣviśeṣamabhyarṇavartibhiranekaiḥ Kaśmīrādimaṇḍalapratibaddhaiḥ pradhānanagaragrāmairupetaṃ kumārabhuktāvakhilapratibaddhaiḥ pradhānanagaragrāmairupetaṃ kumārabhuktāvakhilamuttarā-patha-marpayāṃbabhūva.*
11. *EI*, III, no. 4, vv. 6-7.
12. Ibid., no. 47.
13. Ibid., XXIX, no. 26.
14. Ibid., XVIII, no. 29.
15. Ibid., XIX, no. 43.
16. *EI*, III. 174.
17. *JASB*, LXI. 254-6.
18. *JRAS*, 1927, p. 694.
19. *JESHO*, IV. 82f.
20. R. Niyogi, *History of the Gāhaḍavāla Dynasty*, p. 223.
21. *EI*, I. 333-5.
22. The Ajayagadh rock inscription of Candella king Kīrtivarman (*EI*, XXX, no. 17, v. 8) records the grant of the village of Pipalā hika and the authority over the gates of the Kalanjar fort (*Kālañjarādvāravarādhikāra*) to Māheśvara by Kīrtivarman in recognition of the services which the former rendered when the latter was in distress at Pītādri. This new Ajayagadh inscription thus makes it clear that viśiṣa was the designation of the officer who had authority over the gates of a fort and may be considered to be the commander of a fort, ibid., p. 88.
23. *EI*, II. 439-46, v. 12.
24. *IA*, XXI. 170-71.
25. *JESHO*, IV. 82f.
26. It has been inferred from the expression *vikara-grāmāh* in the Chandravati grant of Candradeva dated AD 1093 (*EI*, XIV no. 15, p. 195, 11. 27-30) that even some regular officials were granted villages—*JESHO*, IV. 85f. Kielhorn (*EI*, VII. 96ff) took the term to be the proper

name of a village. D.R. Sahni (*EI,* XIV. 196) translates it to mean villages given to persons deprived of hand. But such a suggestion looks improbable because it envisages too many men deprived of hands to need several villages for their maintenance and because it suggests a lopsided emphasis on the maintenance for persons thus disabled and not for others who stood in greater needs. The expression has no doubt to be translated as meaning tax-free villages; there is, however, nothing to indicate that these villages were granted to officials. The inscription records the grant of a *pattalā* to 500 brāhmaṇas the people in which are required to pay the state dues to the donees. But an exception is made in the case of villages formerly given to temples or brāhmaṇas or as *vikaras* (*devadvijavikaragrāmāḥ*). The inscription goes on to enumerate the names of villages under three heads, *devagrāmas, dvijagrāmas* and *vikaragrāmas.* The clear implication of the inscription is that like the *devagrāmas* and *dvijagrāmas* the *vikara-grāmas* were also exempted from paying the dues to the donees. We would prefer to take the term as referring to villages which had earned freedom from taxes due to some kind of service performed to the kingdom.

27. *EI,* II, no. 8.
28. The precise meaning of the term is doubtful. It may mean one who catches dangerous robbers, thus having been a police officer.
29. *EI,* IX. no. 13 (B).
30. *EI,* XIV. 182-4 (pt. I).
31. *IA,* XIV. 160.
32. *EI,* III, no. 31.
33. Ibid., no. 4, v. 12.
34. *EI,* XXIX, no. 8.
35. *JASB* (L), 1951, p. 121; *EI,* XXIX, no. 5.
36. V. 21—*Vibhajya bandhubhṛtyeṣu bubhuje pārtrivaḥ śriyam.*
37. V. 120.
38. (N.S.P.) Introduction, p. x.
39. D. Sharma, *Early Chauhān Dynasties,* p. 198.
40. p. 152-*pūrvapuruṣakramāgatāyā dhruvavṛtteḥ prabhuḥ.*
41. *CII,* IV, no. 63.
42. R. Niyogi, *History of the Gāhaḍavāla Dynasty,* p. 167.
43. *JESHO,* IV, 86f.
44. *EI,* XVI. no. 2—*Rāja-rājapuruṣā-ṭavikācāṭādibhiḥ svaṃ svamābhāvyaṃ parihartavyam.*
45. *EI,* XI, no. 4 (III)—*Arahaṭaṃ arahaṭaṃ prati dattaḥ javahārakaḥ ekaḥ.*
46. The *Śukranīti,* I. 377-84 says: 'Those servants who have been appointed equal with *sāmantas* and others are also to be known as *sāmantas,* etc., in succession and to be sharers of the royal income. Those who have been deprived of the post of the *sāmantas,* etc., but who are maintained by the *mahārājas* and others at the same salary are called *hīnāsā-manta.* The man who is appointed over 10 *grāmas* is known as nāyaka. The

āśāpāla is he who enjoys the revenue of 10,000 *grāmas* also known as *svarāṭ*.'

47. Vogel, *Antiquities of Chamba State*, pt. I, p. 114.
48. VI. 117, f.n.
49. *IA*, XVIII. 212, f.n. 3.
50. D. Sharma, *Early Chauhān Dynasties*, p. 72.
51. VI. 73; VII. 996; VIII. 1228, 1814, 2029.
52. I, p. 275.
53. p. 64.
54. Cf. *Śukranīti*, I. 377-8: Those servants who have been appointed equal with the *sāmantas* and others are also to be known as *sāmantas*, etc., in succession and to be sharers of royal income.
55. pp. 203f, vv. 14-15, 30.
56. *Lambaka* 3, *Taraṅga* 18, vv. 124-6. It is interesting to note that in the Kākatiya kingdom the appointment of a person to the office of a minister was invariably accompanied by the conferment of special insignia like the palanquin, the white umbrella and a special dress and the grant of the *jivita* or *vṛtti* (land) pertaining to that office (*niyoga*) besides presents of costly ornaments and perfumes. See G. Yazdani, *Early History of the Deccan*, p. 673.
57. p. 59 (XXXV, 1ff).
58. *EI*, X. 89; *CII*, IV. 137-45.
59. *IA*, XVIII. 81-5. Cf. A.K. Majumdar, *Chalukyas of Gujarat*, pp. 225f.
60. Baden Powell, *Land System*, I, p. 250; *Indian Village Community*, pp. 196ff uses the term clan monarchies for monarchies organized on clan line and thus differing from the type of single rulership. Under this system the king has the best or the central part of the kingdom for himself and assigns remaining portions to the lesser chiefs of the clan.
61. The *Śukranīti* says: If in the king's family there be many males, the eldest among them is to be the king, the others are to be his assistants and auxiliaries. More than all other assistants these members of the aristocracy help forward the interests of the state—I. 684-6. The king should station them in various quarters by paying them one-fourth of the royal revenues or make them governors of provinces. He may appoint them as the heads of cows, elephants, horses, camels, treasure, etc. The mother and the lady who is of the same rank as the mother should be appointed in charge of the kitchen. Cognate kinsmen and brothers-in-law are to be even appointed in the military department. Critics of one's own faults are to be appointed in the overseeing of clothes, ornaments and vessels—I. 697-704. Later on it says that the king should always be accompanied by his kinsmen, friends and the state officers who have been made equal to him through qualifications—I.747-8.
62. Rāhula Sāṃkṛtyāyana, *Hindī Kāvya Dhārā*, p. 446, *Saṃmāṇadāṇa-posiya sabaṃdhu*.

63. V. 25, *Nīte Kṣayaṃ kṣatravare'surairyaḥ svagotragopālaparāyaṇobhū* quoted by D. Sharma, *Early Chauhan Dynasties*, p. 175, f.n. 13.
64. CCXXXIX. 31-*Pitṛpaitāmaho vaśyaḥ saṃhato dattavetanaḥ.*
65. XXIV. 57-64. It uses *kulya* and *dāyāda* indiscriminately.
66. Cf. *Śukranīti*, I. 695-6; By the partition of kingdom there can arise no good. Rather the kingdom divided into parts is exposed to enemies. In the preceding passage (I. 691-4) the *Śukranīti* calls the members of the royal family as *dāyāda* (sharers of inheritance) and says: Unity of opinion among them is good for the king. Differences among them are dangerous to both the state and the family. Hence the king should arrange for them the same kind of comforts as for himself, and should be strict in command to the servants in satisfying them with umbrellas and thrones.
67. Cf. *CII*, IV. 401ff, v. 6—*Tatrāgrajo nṛpavarastripuriśa āsitpārṣve ca maṇḍalapatin sa cakāra bandhūn.*
68. B.P. Mazumdar, *Socio-Economic History*, p. 15.
69. *JOHRS*, I. 279.
70. V. 45.
71. The *Padmānanda Mahākāvya* written by Abrayacandra at the request of minister Padma under Vīsaladeva is not a historical text but such a theme in the literary texts suggests that it was not an unusual phenomenon for the period.
72. pp. 117f.
73. p. 38.
74. V. 21-*Vibhajya baṃdhubhṛtyebhyaḥ bubhuje pārthivaḥ śriyam.*
75. Elliot and Dowson, I. 142, 151, 158, 174, 175.
76. *EI*, III. 313f.
77. *EI*, XII, p. 11. The inscription is now deposited in the Victoria Hall, Udaipur.
78. *IA*, XII. 189. In the *Śukraniti*, I. 707-21 the members of the royal family are contemplated as playing important part in the deliberations. The text lays down fixed seats in the assembly-hall for the several relations of the king.
79. *EI*, III. 266f—*svabhogāvāptavaṃśapotakabhoga.*
80. *EI*, II. 119ff, 11. 33-40. R.S. Sharma, *JESHO*, IV. 87 suggests that Jayanīrāja of the record was a distant kinsman of the king Siṃharāja. But the inscription does not give any such indication. On the other hand if the use of *svabhoga* in the case of the members of the royal family and that of *svabhujyamāna* in the case of *duḥsādhya* officer Dhaṃdhuka and Jayanīrāja are deliberate,then the possibility would be just otherwise.
81. *EI*, XI, p. 34.
82. D. Sharma, *Early Chauhān Dynasties*, p. 202.
83. *EI*, XIII. 208.
84. Loc. cit., p. 136.

85. *EI*, IX. no. 9 (B).
86. D. Sharma, loc. cit., p. 138.
87. *EI*, XI, p. 48. See also D. Sharma, op. cit., p. 142.
88. *EI*, XIII, no. 18 (B).
89. *EI*, XI, p. 53.
90. *EI*, XI, no. 4 (XV).
91. *Bhoktṛ* literally means one who enjoys and thus seems to have been used, like *bhogin* and *bhogika* of other records, in the sense of a man who enjoys a feudal assignment.
92. *EI*, XI, no. 4 (V). R.S. Sharma, *JESHO*, IV. 87 explains girās as being for food and clothing. But it is to be noted that in modern usage girās stands for the landed property of a ruling tribe, *DHNI*, II. 1110, n. 5.
93. *EI*, XI, no. 4 (XVII).
94. *Kirtikaumudī*, IV. 75, 84-7.
95. *EI*, XXXIII. 196-8.
96. N.S. Bose, *History of the Candellas*, p. 133.
97. *Jaina Pustaka Praśasti Saṅgraha*, p. 106—*Śrimad-Govindacandradevarāje Jānhavyā daksine kūle śrīmad—VijavacandradevāBadaharadeśabhvjamāne.* It has been suggested by R. Niyogi, *History of the Gāhadavāla Dynasty*, p. 117, that Ādakkamalla who in the fragmentary stone inscription from Nagod dated AD 1237 (*EI*, XXIII. 186-9) is mentioned as belonging to the Gāhadavāla dynasty and ruled probably over the area between the Yamunā and the Sone belonged to a branch line of the main Gāhadavāla dynasty which was made by Govindacandra to rule as a feudatory of the imperial family in the Vindhyan region conquered from the Kalacuris.
98. *JASB*, 1919-20, p. 197.
99. Baden-Powell, *Land System*, I. 250f; *The Indian Village Community*, pp. 196ff.
100. *Hindu Revenue System*, pp. 241, 259.
101. Ibid., p. 241.
102. In the *Aparājitapṛcchā* (p. 203; also pp. 194, 196) the list of the grades of feudatories has, besides the holder of 50, 20, 3, 2 and 1 villages, the *caturaṃśika* at the bottom. *Caturaṃśika* has been corrected by V.S. Agrawal, *Harṣacarita: eka śaṃskṛtika adhyayana*, p. 220 as *caturāśika* or holder of 84 villages, who thus argues that the chiefs holding 84 villages formed the basic unit in the division of empire among the feudal chiefs. But we do not approve of the amendation. *Caturaṃśika* literally means one possessing one-fourth portion and this suits the context. The grade immediately preceding *caturaṃśika* in the list given in the text is *laghūsāmanta* defined as a feudatory having 5000 villages. The number of villages possessed by a *caturaṃśika* is 1,000 which is thus roughly one-fourth of that owned by a *laghūsāmanta*.
103. pp. 68, 243.
104. Ibid., Introduction, p. 5.

105. D.C. Sircar, *Studies in the Geography of Ancient and Mediaeval India*, pp. 198-205.
106. *EI*, IX, no. 1 (A).
107. *EI*, XIX, no. 10, 11. 8-9—*caturāśīti - mānyaka - paṭṭa - Āudrahādiviṣaye.*
108. P. Peterson, *Collection of Sanskrit and Prakrit Inscriptions*, p. 206—*Ratnapuracaturāśikāyāṃ mahārājabhūpālāśrī - Rāyapāladevānmahāsana-prāptaśrī -Pūnapākṣadevaḥ.*
109. *EI*, I, no. 8.
110. *EI*, XI, pp. 20-6.
111. *JUPHS*, XIV. 69-79.
112. *EI*, III, no. 7.
113. *IA*, XII. 196ff.
114. *IA*, XVIII. 83.
115. *EI*, IV. 111f.
116. *EI*, 1, no. 36.
117. *EI*, IX, no. 9 (B).
118. *EI*, II, no. 8.
119. *DHNI*, II. 1201.
120. D.C. Ganguly, *History of the Paramāra Dynasty*, p. 237.
121. *EI*, IV, no. 20. Also see *CII*, IV, no. 42.
122. Charkhari plate of Devavarmadeva dated AD 1051—*EI*, XX. 127.
123. Harsha stone inscription of Vigraharāja dated AD 973—*EI*, 11. 119f, 11. 33-40.
124. Balera paltes of Mūlarāja I dated AD 995—*EI*, X. 78f.; Sunak grant of Karṇa I dated AD 1091—*EI*, 1, no. 36. It would appear that the Chālukya king Kumārapāla after defeating Arṇorāja kept Nadol in the first instance under has direct control. This would follow from Ojha grant no. 1 (*Silver Jubilee Volume of the ABORI*, pp. 314n) which mentions Sadol as the *svabhujyamānamāṇḍala* of Kumārapāla. See D. Sharma, *Early Chauhān Dynasties*, p. 134.
125. Grant of Sīyaka II dated AD 949—*EI*, XIX, no. 39 (A).
126. R.S. Sharma *JESHO*, IV, p. 91 suggests in connection with the reference in the Paramāra grant that the districts under the personal enjoyment of the king belonged to the personal estates which the king had received as crown-prince.
127. Loc. cit.
128. Loc. cit.
129. Baden-Powell, *The Indian Village Community*, pp. 196ff.
130. CCXXXIX. 32.
131. *EI*, II. 119f.
132. *EI*, IX, no. 9 (B).
133. *EI*, III. 313f.
134. *JESHO*, IV. 90.
135. Elliot and Dowson, I. 6.
136. (N.S.P., 1925) pp. 137ff.

137. II, p. 106.
138. p. 103—*Duṣṭadāyādasamavaṣṭabdharājyairāgatyāgatya diṅmukhebhyo nijapadarthibhiḥ pārthivakumāraiḥ.*
139. p. 111.
140. p. 115. 1.4—*Śrī Paramarddiprasādato deśadhipatye sañjāte sati.*
141. Ibid., p. 79.

6

Merchants and Landed Aristocracy in the Feudal Economy of Northern India: Eighth to Twelfth Century

B.P. Mazumdar

The disintegration of the Gupta empire coincided with the rise of a number of independent powers and disturbed political economy. The classical tenor of life ended and fresh movements ushered in a new age both in the political and socio-economic history of India. Early medieval inscriptions acquaint us with a number of Brāhmaṇas, poets and artisans who left their original homes in search of fortune and received grants of land from the rulers or their feudatories in their new environments. Bengal poets like Śaktisvāmin, Lakṣmīdhara, Madana and Gadādhara went to the courts of the Paramāra and Candella kings and of Lalitāditya of Kashmir. They wrote dramas, poems and *praśastis* in their new environment. Bilhaṇa, a native of Kashmir, became the court-poet of the Chālukya monarch Vikramāditya VI. The Brāhmaṇas of Uttar Pradesh, Gauḍa and south India received grants of many tax-free lands from the kings and feudatories of Madhya Pradesh, Andhra and Orissa.[1] Many Gauḍa Karaṇa-kāyasthas wrote inscriptions of the Candella, Cāhamāna and Kalacuri kings. Some of those inscriptions, e.g. Khajuraho (AD 954), Nādol (AD 1141) and Delhi-Siwalik (1163), throw considerable light on the then political and socio-economic history and local administration.[2] Similarly, the Māthurānvaya and the Vālabhya Kāyasthas wrote the charters of the Cāhamāna and Paramāra kings.[3] In short, early medieval epigraphs refer to large-scale migration in the post-Gupta period. The medieval period was not only an age of feudalism but also the age of mobility of intellectual people on a large scale.

Amongst those personages who left their ancestral homes in search of better prospect, the movement of military leaders and their soldiers caused significant changes in the politico-economic set-up. Bengal and Bihar possibly proved to be the most favourable and lucrative areas for those adventurers. D.C. Sircar has rightly shown that the number of mercenaries from different parts of India went on increasing in the Pāla army. The Nalanda plate of Dharmapāla mentions mercenary soldiers, who not only belonged to Gauḍa, but also were Mālavas, Khaśas, Kulikas and Hūṇas.[4] Inscriptions of the times from Devapāla to Vigrahapāla III add the names of Karnāṭas and Lāṭas to the list (vide Monghyr, Bhagalpur and Bangaon copper-plates). The Manahali plate of Madanapāla (AD 1144-61) further adds the name of the Coḍas.[5] Besides these soldiers, the names of war-lords like Sāmantasena and Nānyadeva (*c.* AD 1097-1147) who established themselves in Bengal and Bihar, came from the Karṇāṭa country. The Belāva plate of Bhojavarman tells us that the Varmans originally came from Siṁhapura and Vajravarman was 'the welfare (incarnate) of the victorious war expedition of the Yādava armies'.[6] Sirhhapura is not in Bengal. R.C. Majumdar suggests a probable location of this place in Kaliṅga.[7] The Rāmpāl copper-plate of Śrīcandra informs us that his great-grandfather Pūrṇacandra was a ruler of Ṛohitāgiri which has been identified by some scholars with Rohtaṣgarh in the Shahabad District, Bihar.[8] The ancestors of Dommaṇapāla, an independent chief of Pūrvakhāṭikā, in the Sunderbans, are described in an inscription dated AD 1196 as having migrated from Ayodhyā.[9]

South Bihar, with its hills and river valleys, also attracted many outsiders. The Dudhpani rock-inscription of the eighth century and the Govindapur stone inscription of AD 1137-8 taken together tell us of the Māna rulers of western Gaya and north Hazaribagh. The founders of this dynasty, Udayamāna and his two brothers, were originally merchants engaged in trade between Ayodhyā and Tāmralipti. The Ujjainiyā Rajputs also travelled from Malwa and established themselves as a political power in the Bhojpur-Dumraon region in Shahabad in the fourteenth century. In that locality ruled Pratāpadhavala and his successors (inscrs. dated AD 1159 and 1169) in the second half of the twelfth century. Wherefrom they hailed is not known but *Mahāmāṇḍalika* Udayarāja, a feudatory of Indradhavala, is described in the Sone East Bank copper-plate as belonging to the Kadambā-kula.[10] The Kadambas of Kaliṅga and their overlords the Gaṅgas, came from the Karṇāṭaka country to Ganjam. Besides these families of Karṇāṭa origin, D.C. Sircar has traced numerous other Karṇāṭis outside Karṇāṭa.[11] He believes that the Rāṣṭrakūṭas like Mahana or Mathana ruling over Aṅga and those ruling at Pathari, 40 miles north-east of Bhilsa in Madhya Pradesh (AD 760-865), at Kanauj (1050-1210), Hastikuṇḍi in Jodhpur and Dhanop in Udaipur (900-1000), Bithu near Pāli in Jodhpur (1200-1815), Mānapura (sixth-seventh centuries), Berar (seventh-eighth centuries) and Orissa (eleventh-twelfth centuries) originally hailed from Karṇāṭa.

During such a period of large-scale movements and frequent wars, land becomes the dominant form of wealth and the chief instrument of economic power. Kings and feudatories were not unmindful of the fact that land and its products should not go beyond their control. In our present state of knowledge we can assert that the Gāhaḍavālas did not make any single land-grant in favour of feudatories holding a status higher than the *Thakkuras* and *Rāutas* in the fertile Ganges-Yamunā Doab.[12] In a large number of other cases, kings made their sons, brothers, nephews and close relatives their fief-holders. The Cāhamānas of Naḍḍūla followed this practice. Kaṭukarāja made his son Jayatasiṁha a fief-holder of Samipati.[13] Ālhaṇa (AD 1145-63) made his third son Kīrttipāla a feudal proprietor of 12 villages belonging to Naḍḍūlāī.[14] Kīrttipāla's sons, Lokhanapāla and Sonapāla, were made joint proprietors of Sonānā by their cousin-brother *Mahārājadhirāja* Kelhaṇa, the eldest son of Alhaṇa.[15] Kelhaṇa (*c.* AD 1163-93) also granted the fiefdom of Bāmnerā to Ajayasiṁha, son of Kuṁvarasiṁha who seems to be identical with *Mahārājaputra* Kumārasiṁha, the proprietor of the Koreṭā village during the reign of his father Ālhaṇa[16] Kelhaṇa also gave the *jāgir* of Ghaṁghāṇakapadra to his son Soḍhadeva.[17] The Kalacuri kings adopted the same practice as that of the Naḍḍūla Cāhamānas. Kokkalla I made each of his 17 younger sons *Maṇḍalapatis* or feudatory chiefs in his kingdom. The Kalacuris of Tuṁmāna trace their descent from one of those sons, named Kaliṅgarāja, and they remained feudatories of their relatives at Ḍāhala till at least *KS* 831/AD 1079.[18] The Gaṅgas of Kaliṅganagara conferred the title of *Rāṇaka* on their relative the Kheḍis (Bhīmakheḍi, Dharmakheḍi, Ugrakheḍi, Udayakheḍi), who belonged to the Kadamba-kula. Those Kheḍis were *Pañcaviṣayādhipatis* or in charge of five districts and issued their grants from Jayantīpura in the modern Chikati Taluk in Ganjam.

Early medieval epigraphs also acquaint us with the fact that queens and wives of feudatories sometimes were made fief-holders by their husbands. Possibly those grants were motivated by love or the decision to make arrangements for their sustenance in the eventuality of the ladies outliving their husbands. But the digests of our period do not indicate that the wives were allowed to get shares on the partition of property during the lifetime of thier husbands. However, a few Cāhamāna kings are found to make their queens *bhoktṛs*. Kelhaṇa's queen Jālhaṇadevī was the *bhoktṛ* of Saṇḍeraka which was the westernmost frontier province of the Naḍḍūla kigdom. Pratāpadevī, queen of Harirāja, enjoyed a fief at Tantoṭi in the Ajmer District in AD 1194.[19] About 250 years earlier, contiguous to that area, a queen named Citralekhā granted 2 villages in the old Jaipur State out of her fief to the temple of Nārāyaṇa.[20] The Bali inscription, dated *VS* 1200/AD 1143, informs us that *Rājñī* Tihuṇaka, queen of Jayatasīha or Jayasiṁha Chālukya, was enjoying the village Vālahī as a *grāsa*.[21] According to the Machhlishahr inscription, dated *VS* 1258/AD 1197, the village Pamahai was granted by *Mahārājñī* Saṁnaṁdarī to king Hariścandra, who subsequently donated it to Rāhīhīyaka, son of *Thakkura* Madanū.[22] The queen who was issueless, as the inscription records, must have been one of the queens of Jayaccandra Gāhaḍavāla. She is alone among the Gāhaḍavāla queens who had been given the privilege of enjoying proprietary rights over a village. All other queens, as known from inscriptions, gave charities with the consent and at the expense of their reigning husbands. In the kingdom of the Paramāra king Naravarman, Mahādevī, the *vadhū* (wife, may also mean daughter-in-law) of *Mahāmaṇḍalika* Rājadeva granted 4 *halas* of land out of her *bhukti*, to a Brāhmaṇa.[23] N.P. Chakravarti translates the words *Mahāmāṇḍalikā-śrī-Rājadevāvadhū-śrī-Mahādevyā-pūrvvākalpe dattā* in lines 15 and 16 as (4 *halas* of land) 'given by the illustrious Mahādevī from her previous settlement (?)'. If we accept the interpretation of Chakravarti. there seems a probability that the aforesaid Mahādevī had landed properties elsewhere also. Thus the fiefdoms enjoyed by the queens and wives of feudatories were acquired by them not in a state of widowhood but during the lifetime of their partners. So the possibility of application for the recommendation of Jimūtavāhana that a widow has the right to inherit her husband's entire property in the absence of any male issue, does not arise at all in these specific cases.

As in Europe so also in India the merchants and nobility of wealth tried to become landed nobles. In ancient times merchants holding land are not known to have been vassals of persons for the land they held. We have already seen how three merchants became masters of three villages in the Hazaribagh District through the favour of Ādisiṁha, king of Magadha.[24] In the neighbouring state of Orissa, during the reign of the Gaṅga king Madhukāmārṇava, Lakṣmaṇa Rāmadeva, holding the privilege of *pañcamahāśabda,* granted three villages to Eṛapanāyaka who was the ornament of the spotless family of merchants. What is more interesting in this Chicacole plate is that though those villages were termed as *vaiśya agrahāra,* yet the donee had to pay an annual rent to the extent of 150 rupees[25] or purchase the villages by paying 150 rupees, according to Sircar. The donee was at the time of the grant living as a resident of Dantapura which was a port as old as the time of Ptolemy.[26] Thus, a merchant, who must have been engaged in active service in that city-port of Dantapura, was not satisfied with movable property alone, but arranged for his security of wealth against lands. The same tendency of merchants to become proprietors of land on a feudal basis is also noticeable in Ajmer. Verse 10 of the Barla inscription of the time of Pṛthvīrāja III dated *VS* 1234/AD 1178 records that *Thakkura* Pālhuka was a trader by profession.[27]

The inclination of some active merchants towards vassaldoms is also noticeable among the goldsmiths of Orissa during the rule of the Gaṅgas of Kaliṅganagara and Ṣvetaka. *Kāṁsyakāra Śreṣṭhī* Svayambhu and Khaṇḍimalla enjoyed the feudatory status of *Sāmanta.*[28] As a word of caution, it may be stated that the post of an engraver did not carry a fiefdom either in Orissa or any other part of northern India. Under the Gaṅgas of Kaliṅganagara there were such merchants who engraved copper plates and have described themselves simply as *Śreṣṭhī* Prabhākara, *Vaṇikputra* Hari.[29] Again, none of the engravers of the Pāla and Sena copper plates, except the engraver of the Deopara inscription, held a feudatory status. Sūlapāṇi, who engraved the Deopara inscription of Vijayasena, alone has the unique distinction of holding the title of a feudatory, *Rāṇaka,* in the history of numerous engravers who lived in Bengal and Bihar, since the ascendancy of Gopāla to the throne.[30]

Commerce was a risky venture throughout the middle ages. Roads were unsafe. Temper of rulers was unpredictable and the political stability was uncertain. Some merchants therefore were tempted to exchange their profession with that of a landed nobleman. Mere *Baniās* or *Seṭhs* never commanded so much social prestige as the feudal lords. A few examples of the behaviour of early medieval kings with the commercial classes are given here. The grant of half of the town of Selluka and 1500 villages by the Paramāra king Bhoja to his subordinate Yaśovarman[31] shows that the ruling kings allowed their feudatories to control even the urban economy. Sometimes the kings levied additional taxes on merchants. During the reign of Rāyapāla, his sons, who were feudatories, issued an order that 2 *palikās* of oil due to them were to be collected from each oil-mill (*ghāṇaka*) in *VS* 1189/AD 1132. Again in *VS* 1200/AD 1143 another feudatory of the same king, asked also for 2 *palikās* of oil, due to him, from each oil mill. Thus within the course of eleven years during the reign of one king alone, each of the oil millers were asked to contribute at double the rate for the temple of Ādinātha at Nādlāi. Not only the dealers in oil were taxed,but merchants in general, were forced to pay taxes at enhanced rates at Nāḍlāi. In *VS* 1195/AD 1137 they were asked to pay some dues on every cartload of goods passing through the roads. Again, an additional impost was levied at the customs house in *VS* 1218/AD 1161. In the neighbouring kingdom of Gujarat, Bhima II levied fresh taxes on a large number agricultural products in AD 1220.[32] The misery of the business community did not end by payment of taxes. Their hearths and homes were also insecure. In eastern India, the Bhāṭerā plate tells us that as many as 296 houses, including those of oil millers, ivory and bell-metal workers and shops were allotted by Govindakeśava, ruler of Sylhet, to a Śiva temple[33] Anaṅgabhīma III (AD 1216-35) the Eastern Gaṅga king of Orissa, acted in a similar manner. He granted a township (possibly Jayanagara-grāma) which is 11 miles from Cuttack, and was then inhabited by goldsmith, brazier, 2 weavers, 2 oilmen, 3 fishermen, dealers in perfumery goods, conch-shells, etc., to Lord Puruṣottama in *c.* AD 1230.[34]

Donations of merchants of the period under survey convey an impression that they were poorer in comparison to the landed aristocrats. Not a single merchant has been found to donate a whole village or construct big temples, except under the Chālukyas and Vāghelas. At most, they have caused the excavation of channels and machine-wells and sometimes gave portions of their merchandise in charity. In order to construct or defray the expenses of temples, not one but several merchants pulled their resources together. As many as 9 chiefs of oil millers of four villages and all the members of the guild of oil millers came to an agreement that each one of them would give I *palikā* of oil on the ninth day of the bright half of every month for the illumination of the Vaillabhaṭṭasvāmin temple at Gwalior in *VS* 933/AD 876. On the date of the agreement amongst the oil millers, the guild of gardeners also decided to give 50 flower garlands for the worship of the above-mentioned deity at the same time.[35] Even in the Chālukya kingdom where the merchants were in more affluent condition, the *śreṣṭhi* and other *mahājanas* of Timbāṇaka, near Bhavnagar, agreed among themselves to donate one *rūpaka* per shop per year and each merchant of the same town undertook to give one dramma annually to the Śiva temples at Talājha in *VS* 1264/AD 1207.[36] It is interesting to note here that the earlier-mentioned images of Viṣṇu and Śiva in Gwalior and Saurāṣṭra respectively, were not installed by the merchants, but by feudatories. The Vaillabhaṭṭasvāmin temple at Gwalior was built by Alla, the *Koṭṭapāla* or Guardian of the fort of Gwalior. The Śaiva temple was installed by the feudatory ruler Jagamalla. Thus it might not be unreasonable to suggest that the merchants of Bhavnagar and Gwalior were forced to give charities by the ruling overlords.

In early medieval India feudalism triumphed over the ideas of united realm and over-royal authority. The formation of territorial principalities had great impact on the politics, administration and economy of this country. Landed aristocrats held many of the superior posts and became members of the governing body. Of course, enfeoffment did not bring the concession of an office. The feudatories also directed the rural and urban economy. With the exception of Gujarat, they gained control over production and distribution. As some merchants became more interested in transforming themselves as feudatories, landed aristocrats gained a measure of control of the investment-capital. When feudalism was firmly established in north India by the end of the twelfth century, capital to a large extent, ceased to be invested in commercial enterprises outside the confines of the territories of the landlords. Much wealth therefore seems to have been utilized over building of temples and creation of religious endowments.

NOTES

1. *Hist. of Bengal,* vol. I, pp. 686-7; Mazumdar, *Socio-Economic History of Northern India,* pp. 99-100.
2. *Hist. of Bengal,* vol. I, p. 688.
3. Mazumdar, op. cit., p. 101.
4. *EI,* XXIII, p. 291.
5. Maitreya, *Gauḍalekhamāla,* p. 153.
6. Inscriptions of Bengal, vol. III, p. 19, verses 5 and 6.
7. *Hist. of Bengal,* I, p. 198.
8. This location has not been accepted by R.C. Majumdar who observes in *HB,* vol. I, p. 194, that 'it is more reasonable to hold that Rohitāgiri ... was somewhere in Eastern Bengal, and probably near Comilla'.
9. *IHQ,* X, pp. 321ff; *Ind. Cult.,* vol. I, p. 679; *Hist. of Bengal,* vol. I, p. 222. The Pāla family acquired possession (*upārjita*) of Pūrvā-khāṭikā.
10. *EI,* XXIII, pp. 225-9; vol. XXVII, pp. 119ff.
11. *J. N. Banerjea Volume,* pp. 211-19.
12. Cf. grants in favour of *Rāuta* Rājyadharavarman, *Thakkura* Jayapālaśarman, *Rāuta* Jāṭaśarman, *Thakkura* Devapālaśarman, *Thakkura* Vasiṣṭha, *Rāuta* Paharājaśarman, etc. (*DHNI,* vol. I, pp. 517, 519, 528).
13. *EI,* XI, pp. 32-3 (Sevadi inscr. AD 1144-5).
14. *EI,* IX, pp. 68,60.
15. *EI,* XI, p. 73.
16. Sharma, *Early Chauhān Dynasties,* pp. 139,142; *EI,* XIII, p. 208.
17. *JPASB,* X, p. 407 (Pal inscr. 1241 *VS*/AD 1185).
18. Amoda inscr. (*Dynastic Hist. of N. India,* II, p. 805).
19. *EI,* XX, p. 62.
20. Bayana inscr. dated 1012 *VS*/AD 956 (*IA,* XIV, p. 10; XV, p. 36). H.C. Ray in *Dynastic Hist. of N. India,* I, p. 591; II, p. 823, identifies her husband Maṅgalarāja, a feudatory of the Gurjara-Pratihāra king Mahipāla II, with the Kacchapaghāta prince of an identical name mentioned in the Gwalior Sāsbahū temple inscription dated *VS* 1150.
21. *EI,* IX, pp. 32-3. *Grāsa* means *girās,* signifying landed possession of a ruling tribe (*Dynastic Hist. of N. India,* II, p. 1110).
22. *EI,* X, p. 99.
23. Ibid., XX, p. 108.
24. *Dynastic Hist. of N. India,* I, p. 349 (Dudhpani rock inscr.).
25. *Inscriptions of Orissa,* ed. S.N. Rajaguru, vol. II, pp. 177ff.
26. Majumdar, *Classical Accounts of India,* p. 380; Raychaudhuri, *PHAI,* pp. 89, 305n.

27. *EI,* XXXIII, pp. 299ff. D.C. Sircar observes at p. 301, 'it is uncertain whether he actually belonged to the mercantile class as well'.
28. *Inscr. of Orissa,* vol. II, pp. 120, 124, 130, for Khaṇḍimalla pp. 284 and 300 for Svayambhu.
29. Ibid., vol. II, pp. 40, 235.
30. *Ins. of Bengal,* vol. III, p. 49.
31. *EI,* XIX, pp. 69ff (Kalvan plate).
32. *IA,* VI, p. 202.
33. *EI,* XIX, pp. 27ff.
34. *EI,* XXVIII, pp. 244, 256 (Nagari plate).
35. *EI,* I, pp. 154ff (Vaillabhaṭṭasvamin temple inscr.).
36. *EI,* I, p. 272 (Cintra *Praśasti*).

7

Property Rights in Medieval Tamil Nadu as seen from the Saledeeds in Chola Inscriptions

Y. Subbarayalu

Quantitative methods are only now becoming popular in the studies in ancient and early medieval Indian history even though they were introduced long back by D.D. Kosambi in his now famous study of the punch-marked coins.[1] The main reason for the diffident use of the quantitative methods may be that we do not get many purely economic documents prior to the thirteenth century as we do for the Mughal and modern periods. But in recent years scholars are paying more and more attention to the large volume of inscriptions for using it as a major source for economic history of medieval south India. Therefore some kind of quantification of the inscriptional data has become inevitable to avoid errors arising from impressionistic judgements. There are several thousands of inscriptions throughout India from the third century BC to the eighteenth century AD. They are, however, not distributed evenly, some area and some periods having larger concentrations than others. The Chola period (AD 850-1250) in early medieval history of Tamil Nadu has the largest single group of inscriptions running to nearly ten thousand, mostly in Tamil language. About a third of those inscriptions has been published with properly edited texts in the epigraphical volumes of the Archaeological Survey of India. The sheer volume of these inscriptions has been a great attraction as well as a challenge to students of Chola history.

*This is a revised version of the paper presented at the symposium 'Quantitative Methods in Indian History', Indian History Congress, Dharwad Session, 1988.

The great efforts of the pioneering epigraphist-scholars and historians to digest this huge volume of inscriptional data and to give a meaningful historical picture using the conventional methods deserve all praise and respects. For further progress in the studies the conventional methods alone are not sufficient as a sort of arbitrariness is naturally built in in the old methods. It is to steer clear of this inbuilt weakness that Noboru Karashima started applying quantitative methods to analyze the Chola-period inscriptions and now there are several followers.[2] So far only the basic statistical methods have been employed, just to construct frequency distributions of clusters of related variables over time and space. Given the fragmentary nature of the inscriptional data such basic methods alone can give some meaningful results in the initial stages.[3] The frequency tables have been found very useful to see through the tendencies in the disparate data in a large number of disjointed and fragmentary records.

Using the same methodology an analysis is made here of the land sale inscriptions of the Chola times, spread over four centuries from about 850 to 1250, to understand their socio-economic implications. The data which is summarised in Table 1 has been collected using nearly ninety per cent of the published inscriptions[4] running to about 3,500, and which come mostly from the central and northern districts of Tamil Nadu. Omitting the badly mutilated inscriptions, there are 276 sale transactions relating mostly to agricultural land and a few relating to house-sites.

TABLE 1: STATISTICAL SUMMARY OF SELLERS AND BUYERS OF LAND

Period	*Sabhā*	*brāhmaṇa Ind.*	*Ūr*	*Non-Brāh. Ind.*	*Temple*	*Total*
I						
Seller:	73(52.5)	40(28.8)	23(16.5)	2(1.4)	1(0.7)	139
Buyer:	2(1.4)	21(15.1)	1(0.7)	89(64.0)	26(18.7)	
II						
Seller:	22(40.0)	6(10.9)	17(30.9)	3(5.5)	7(12.7)	55
Buyer:	0	5(9.1)	1(1.8)	34(61.8)	15(27.3)	
III						
Seller:	26(49.1)	8(15.1)	13(24.5)	4(7.5)	2(3.8)	53
Buyer:	0	0	0	41(77.4)	12(22.6)	
IV						
Seller:	6(20.7)	2(6.9)	7(24.1)	13(44.8)	1(3.4)	29
Buyer:	0	0	0	19(65.5)	10(34.5)	

Note: Numbers within parentheses denote the percentage.

The Table, which is more or less self-explanatory, gives both the absolute numbers and the percentages of both the sellers and purchasers for each of the four sub-periods into which the Chola period is divided. Column 3 'Ūr' includes mostly the communal assemblies of the peasant or *veḷḷānvagai* villages, besides a few of those of the mercantile villages called *nagaram*.[5] As far as column 4 'non-brāhmaṇa individual' is concerned, it includes also the royal members among the purchasers. There are no royal sellers. Merchants who figure as individuals are also included in this column.

Period I alone has 139 sales, i.e. nearly a half of the total instances for all the periods put together. Period II has 55, period III, 53 and period IV has just 29. In period I the communal assemblies (*sabhā, mūlaparuḍai*)[6] of the brāhmaṇa settlements account for 52.5 per cent of the total sales, brāhmaṇa individuals for 29 per cent, the communal assemblies of the non-brāhmaṇa peasant settlements for 16.5 per cent. The sales by the non-brāhmaṇa individuals are not significant. There is only one sale by temple. During period II the sales by the brāhmaṇa assemblies (40 per cent) and the brāhmaṇa individuals (11 per cent) show a decrease whereas those by the other categories show an increase. During period III the brāhmaṇa assemblies and the brāhmaṇa individuals again show some increase in their sales while the assemblies of the peasant villages show some decrease. In period IV the brāhmaṇas show a remarkable decrease while the non-brāhmaṇa individuals show quite an opposite trend. During periods I and III the brāhmaṇas, individual as well as a community, were the major sellers. During period II they share nearly a half of the total sales and during period IV they share only about a fourth of the total.

The lands sold by the brāhmaṇa assemblies are all said to be their village common, while those sold by the brāhmaṇa individuals are specified as their individual possessions. That means, in the brāhmaṇa settlements individual ownership was very much in vogue. On the other hand in the non-brāhmaṇa villages no individual landownership seems to have prevailed in the beginning and it emerges slowly, to become very conspicuous only during period IV when we find the individual non-brāhmaṇa sellers constituting 44.8 per cent.

The sales by the peasant assemblies (*ūr*), though not

inconsiderable, do not seem to be proportionate to the total number of the peasant settlements as compared to that of the brāhmaṇa settlements. Because only about twenty per cent of the villages of the study area were brāhmaṇa villages, the rest being generally peasant settlements.[7] Two hypotheses may be offered for this skewed distribution. One, most of the available inscriptions which record land sales come from canonized temples associated with Brahmanical rituals and situated well within the brāhmaṇa villages or under their control. Two, the landholders of the peasant villages were very reluctant to alienate their property since it was their mainstay. It is found that the sales by the brāhmaṇas show a downward trend but for some slight increase during period III. The reason may be that the brāhmaṇas gradually became less influential economically. There is another point to be explained in the case of the brāhmaṇa sellers. The large number of sales by the brāhmaṇas may be construed to show that their economic position was weak, right from the beginning. But if we look at the other side of the picture this doubt becomes clear. Not only there were many brāhmaṇa sellers, there were also many purchasers. Therefore the sales, particularly those of the early phase, should be considered as the activities of normal times only. We come across some distress sales in periods III and IV, but they are found to be a general phenomenon at that time.

The sales by the assemblies of the mercantile villages, taken separately, steadily increase in number (percentage-wise 5.8, 7.2, 7.4 and 10.3 respectively for the four periods), though not very appreciably. Curiously no individual merchant is found to sell his land. The sales by the temples are found to be not so significant. It seems temples were always at the receiving end as far as the Chola period is concerned.

The purchasers' side has its own interesting picture. The brāhmaṇa assemblies figure as purchasers in a very few instances only whereas brāhmaṇa individuals are found purchasing land more often during periods I and II. The non-brāhmaṇa individuals were the major purchasers from the beginning. About one-third to a half of them belonged to the upper stratum, comprising influential persons holding titles of honour and government offices, royal personages and merchants. In period IV their increase is considerable. The queens figure as purchasers during all the four periods. In period IV their increase is considerable. In one clear instance the king is said to be purchasing land. Merchants are found in considerable number in the fourth period. Temples are found prominently as purchasers during all the four periods.

The purpose of the purchase was 'donation' almost in all cases. Most of the purchased lands were donated to temples or some religious institution like *maṭha* attached to temples. In a few cases they were meant for the upkeep of a tank or channel. The temples were thus becoming big landowners throughout the Chola rule. Though most of the sales and purchases were meant for religious purpose there are some instances to show that secular transactions were taking place regularly side by side with the religious ones. These are only rarely mentioned in the inscriptions since the central purpose of the inscriptions is to record religious charities.

The largest number of sales during period I may suggest some important changes in the agrarian structure and also in the socio-religious practices in the ninth and tenth centuries. For the seemingly gradual decrease of the sales of land in course of the four periods the following hypotheses may be considered: (1) Saturation point was being reached in the availability of alienable lands as well as in the donations made to temples. (2) There were some other ways and means for donating land or some equivalent thing to temples. These points need not be mutually exclusive. The second seems to be true of the later half of period III and the whole of period IV. There figure many grants of taxes levied on land rather than those of lands themselves.

The important conclusions that may be derived from the foregoing analysis are as follows: (1) brāhmaṇas individually as well as a community had become influential landholders by the tenth century. Private landownership prevailed in the purely brāhmaṇa villages. The alienation of landed property was very common among the brāhmaṇas. The influence of the brāhmaṇas as landholders, however, decreased in the course of the Chola rule and reached a low ebb by the end of the thirteenth century. (2) In the non-brāhmaṇa villages communal land rights were the norm in the beginning and consequently alienation of land was not so popular. But during the later half of the Chola period private landownership gradually entered into the system. (3) Canonized temples became landowners by accumulating more and more lands in their possession from the beginning, both by way of donations as well as purchase. (4) Taken as a whole, land alienation by sales shows a gradual decrease through the four centuries under study. This may be symptomatic of some significant changes that were going on in the socio-economic system.

The above findings are of course subject to verification by other similar studies relating to various other aspects. Land gifts made without prior purchase have to be studied independently. Similarly the agrarian structure of the different settlements should be studied separately. Karashima by some of his independent studies has already made the significant discovery that in the peasant villages of the tenth century communal holdings of land was the prevailing norm and that private holdings emerged only in the later half of the Chola rule for various reasons, whereas in brāhmaṇa villages private ownership prevailed from the beginning of the Chola rule. This statement is confirmed to some extent by the present analysis of land-sales.[8]

The motivation behind the sales is only rarely mentioned. Some of the sales for which the reason is mentioned explicitly are found to be made to pay off the tax arrears failing other means due to failure of crops or natural calamities. Such cases are found conspicuously in the twelfth and thirteenth centuries. The other sales, where explicit reasons are not forthcoming, may have generally economic motives behind them. The fact is that these inscriptions are not strictly legal documents, though they generally appear so in their format. The main purpose of the inscriptions is to proclaim to the outsiders the accomplishment of certain charities. Other details like the exact extent of the land, the sale price,[9] etc., are only incidental and they are ignored in several cases. So to find out the 'secular' counterpart of the land-sale inscriptions is rather difficult, though not impossible. At times we get interesting glimpses like the following: 'A merchant had first purchased land from some *sabhā*, his son who inherited the property gave it in turn to his own son-in-law as *strīdhana* (dowry) and the last one sells it now to somebody else who buys it for a temple charity' (*SII*, 19, No. 113).

An interesting fact that is obtained from the land-sale analysis is the finding about the position of the king vis-a-vis landownership. There are a good number of purchases by queens and one purchase by the king himself. In this latter case dated AD 1141 it is said that the king purchased land from some previous owner (*paṇḍuḍaiyān* —*SII*, 7, No. 780) for instituting some special service in a temple by way of celebrating his son's birthday. The purchased land was renamed in the name of the son and made over to the temple as the god's absolute property (*tirunāmattu-kāṇi*). So there is no question of considering the king as the 'owner' of all the land under his rule.

The question as to the different rights included in this 'ownership' can be clarified only to certain extent. Usually it is believed that only certain rights to the income of the land and not the absolute rights of the land were transacted. Though there were occasions when certain income rights were sold, most of the sales listed may be ascertained to be sales of absolute rights, of course absolute rights as defined in the contemporary society. The rights of 'use, mortgage, resale and gift' are mentioned along with the land. That the purchaser can use the acquired land in whatever way he wishes is also confirmed by certain inscriptions. For instance in an inscription a fertile land under cultivation was converted on purchase into a drainage canal (*SII*, 6, No. 292).

TABLE 2: REFERENCES TO SELLERS AND BUYERS OF LAND

PERIOD I

Refer.			*Seller/ Buyer*	*Refer.*			*Seller/ Buyer*
SII	3	110	NB/ NB	SII	6	286	B / U
SII	3	150	N / NB	SII	6	287	B /B
SII	3	151	S /NB	SII	6	290	B / S
SII	3	181	S / T	SII	6	290	S / NB
SII	3	204	S / NB	SII	6	291	S / T
SII	4	531	B / T	SII	6	292	B / S
SII	4	547	S / NB	SII	6	297	B / NB
SII	5	570	B / B	SII	6	314	U / B
SII	5	573	B / NB	SII	6	323	B / NB
SII	5	574	B / T	SII	6	368	S / NB
SII	5	575	S / R	SII	6	370	S / B
SII	5	593	S / T	SII	7	33	S / B
SII	5	679	S / NB	SII	7	64	U / NB
SII	5	684	S / NB	SII	7	420	S / B
SII	5	711	B / M	SII	7	499	S / NB
SII	5	713	S, N/NB	SII	8	9	S / B
SII	6	12	B / B	SII	8	241	B / NB
SII	6	285	B / B	SII	8	547	U / T

SII	8	550	U, S / T
SII	8	558	U / T
SII	8	570	U1 / T
SII	8	572	U / T
SII	8	587	U / NB
SII	8	604	B / NB
SII	8	605	S / T
SII	8	607	S / B
SII	8	609	S / B
SII	8	612	B / NB
SII	8	617	B / NB
SII	8	618	S / NB
SII	8	619	B / NB
SII	8	629	S / NB
SII	8	634	S / M
SII	8	646	S / NB
SII	8	651	S / NB
SII	8	652	S / NB
SII	8	688	U / T
SII	8	689	U1/ NB
SII	8	692	U1 / NB
SII	8	698	U / NB
SII	8	699	U / NB
SII	12	63	NB/ NB
SII	12	95	B / NB
SII	12	102	U / NB
SII	12	105	S / NB
SII	12	110	U / M
SII	12	111	U / NB
SII	13	26	S / T
SII	13	44	S / NB
SII	13	46	S /T
SII	13	50	S,U/NB
SII	13	51	S / NB
SII	13	64	S / M
SII	13	66	B / NB
SII	13	67	S / NB
SII	13	102	B / T
SII	13	109	S / B
SII	13	110	S / NB
SII	13	162	S / B
SII	13	164	S / NB
SII	13	183	U / NB
SII	13	187	S / NB
SII	13	193	B / ?
SII	13	202	B / NB
SII	13	204	S / T
SII	13	211	S / B
SII	13	231	S / NB
SII	13	240	S / R
SII	13	260	S / T
SII	13	262	S / B
SII	13	273	B / B
SII	13	281	U / NB
SII	13	301	B / NB
SII	13	302	S / NB
SII	17	636	S / B
SII	17	656	S / B
SII	19	6	S / NB
SII	19	25	S / NB
SII	19	26	S / T
SII	19	27	B / T
SII	19	60	S / NB
SII	19	63	S / T
SII	19	95	S / NB
SII	19	113	S / M
SII	19	114	S / T
SII	19	127	S / B
SII	19	131	S / NB
SII	19	134	S / NB
SII	19	139	B / NB
SII	19	162	S / NB
SII	19	165	S / T
SII	19	170	S / T
SII	19	181	S / NB
SII	19	183	B / NB
SII	19	191	S / R
SII	19	222	B / NB
SII	19	235	B / R
SII	19	281	S / B
SII	19	290	BN / NB
SII	19	305	B / NB
SII	19	309	B / NB
SII	19	318	B / NB
SII	19	321	S / NB
SII	19	335	B /B
SII	19	339	U / NB
SII	19	342	T / NB
SII	19	352	S / NB
SII	19	357	B / NB
SII	19	359	B / NB
SII	19	365	N / NB

SII	19	370	S / T	SII	19	404	B / R
SII	19	371	S / T	SII	19	407	S, B/R
SII	19	376	B / NB	SII	19	408	S / R
SII	19	379	B / R	SII	19	452	S / M
SII	19	391	U / T	TASSI'	59	84	N / M
SII	19	400	S / M				

PERIOD II

EI	27	27	S / NB	SII	7	139	S / B
IPS		90	S / T	SII	7	141	S / T
IPS		96	S / T	SII	7	156	B / NB
SII	3	3	S / NB	SII	7	440	U / NB
SII	3	10	S / NB	SII	7	442	S / T
SII	3	15	N / T	SII	7	842	U / T
SII	3	51	U / NB	SII	7	854	U / NB
SII	3	54	S / NB	SII	7	872	S / B
SII	3	56	S / NB	SII	7	886	U / NB
SII	4	327	U / B	SII	7	889	U / NB
SII	4	537	S / NB	SII	7	1047	U / T
SII	4	555	S / B	SII	8	1	U / T
SII	5	31	S / R	SII	8	66	T / U
SII	5	32	S / NB	SII	8	67	U / T
SII	5	140	B / T	SII	8	316	U / NB
SII	5	267	B / T	SII	8	521	B / NB
SII	5	465	N / T	SII	8	754	N / NB
SII	5	489	T / NB	SII	13	30	NB / NB
SII	5	518	T / R	SII	13	79	U / NB
SII	5	641	B / NB	SII	13	83	S / B
SII	5	644	T / NB	SII	13	115	S / T
SII	5	667	NB / T	SII	13	124	S / NB
SII	5	677	S / NB	SII	13	144	S / R
SII	5	722	NB / T	SII	13	167	N / NB
SII	5	1409	S / NB	SII	13	182	T / NB
SII	6	31	S / R	SII	17	442	T / NB
SII	6	32	S / NB	SII	17	579	S / NB
SII	6	267	B / T	SII	19	29	T / NB
SII	7	110	B / NB	TAS	6	103	U / NB

PERIOD III

IPS		122	N / NB	SII	3	31	B / NB
IPS		139	S / NB	SII	3	64	S, U / NB
IPS		190	U / NB	SII	3	71	S / NB

SII	4	133	S / NB	SII	7	542	S / NB
SII	4	134	S / NB	SII	7	748	S/ NB
SII	4	540	T / T	SII	7	774	N / T
SII	5	457	S / NB	SII	7	776	N / T
SII	5	702	S / NB	SII	7	780	NB / R
SII	5	703	B / NB				(King)
SII	5	879	U / NB	SII	7	832	U / NB
SII	5	986	B / NB	SII	7	944	NB / T
SII	5	993	S / T	SII	7	1034	B / NB
SII	5	997	B / NB	SII	7	1037	S / NB
SII	5	1358	T / NB	SII	7	1040	B / NB
SII	5	1381	S / NB	SII	8	226	U / NB
SII	6	340	B / NB	SII	8	303	S / M
SII	6	351	S / T	SII	8	304	S / NB
SII	6	434	S / T	SII	8	305	S / NB
SII	6	435	N / M	SII	8	324	U / T
SII	7	96	U / NB	SII	8	458	S / NB
SII	7	97	U / NB	SII	8	701	S / NB
SII	7	409	S / NB	SII	17	540	NB / NB
SII	7	417	S / NB	SII	17	586	S / T
SII	7	443	B / NB	SII	17	590	NB / NB
SII	7	497	S / T	SII	17	598	S / T
SII	7	540	U / NB	SII	17	607	S / T
SII	7	540	U / NB	SII	17	608	S / NB

PERIOD IV

IPS		158	N /M	SII	7	1028	NB / M
IPS		165	U / T	SII	7	1039	NB / NB
IPS		170	N / M	SII	8	289	NB / T
SII	4	226	NB / NB	SII	8	336	NB / T
SII	4	381	T / NB	SII	8	337	NB / NB
SII	4	424	NB / T	SII	8	338	U / T
SII	5	227	S / NB	SII	8	339	NB / T
SII	5	632	NB / NB	SII	8	340	NB / T
SII	5	983	B / NB	SII	8	577	NB / M
SII	5	984	NB / T	SII	17	463	N / NB
SII	6	437	NB / NB	SII	17	519	S / NB
SII	7	415	S / NB	SII	17	595	U / NB
SII	7	430	S / M	SII	17	600	B / NB
SII	7	853	U / T	SII	17	731	S / T
SII	7	942	S / NB				

ABBREVIATIONS USED IN THE TABLE

EI	—	*Epigraphia Indica*
IPS	—	*Inscriptions of the Pudukkottai State*
TAS	—	*Travancore Archaeological Series*
SITI	—	*South Indian Temple Inscriptions*
TASSI	—	*Transactions of the Archaeological Society of South India*
B	—	Brāhmin individual
M	—	Merchant
N	—	Nagaram
NB	—	Non-Brāhmin individual
R	—	Royal Family
S	—	Sabhā /Mulapardai
T	—	Temple
U	—	Ūr
Ul	—	*Talaivāy-chānrār* (a corporate group of cultivators)

NOTES

1. Most of his articles are now reprinted in D.D. Kosambi, *Indian Numismatics*, ed. B.D. Chattopadhyaya. Orient Longmans, 1987.
2. The earliest serious attempt to use statistical methods in south Indian studies was made by R. Sathianatier, *Studies in the Ancient History of Tondaimandalam*, Rochhouse & Sons Ltd, Madras, 1944. It is rather unfortunate that he had no immediate successors. A systematic start was made only by Professor Karashima of University of Tokyo in 1960s. See, for the revised articles, N. Karashima, *South Indian History and Society: Studies from Inscriptions*, Oxford University Press, New Delhi, 1984. Having been a student to and co-worker with Professor Karashima the present writer closely followed Karashima in his Ph.D. dissertation on 'State in Medieval South India' (Unpublished, Madurai Kamaraj University, Madurai, 1976). Another work that followed the lead was P. Shanmugam, *The Revenue System of the Cholas, 850-1279*, New Era Publications, Madras, 1987 (Originally Ph.D. thesis in Madras University, 1977). Among the works of American scholars that by E. James Heitzman is outstanding: 'Gifts of Power: Temples, Politics and Economy in Medieval South India' (Ph.D. thesis University of Pennsylvania, 1985).
3. Only in Heitzman's work some sophisticated methods like chi-square test are introduced. In any case the basic frequency tables are a prerequisite.
4. The accuracy of 90 per cent is assured as hole-sort cards were used for studying this corpus of inscriptions.

5. The *nagaram* or mercantile settlements were mostly rural in nature in medieval times and not much different from contemporary peasant villages but for the fact that the leading landholders of these settlements were also merchants.
6. There is very explicit evidence to assert that these assemblies were composed exclusively of the brāhmaṇa landholders of the respective settlements.
7. Y. Subbarayalu, *Political Geography of the Chola Country,* Madras, 1973, p. 34.
8. N. Karashima, *South Indian History and Society: Studies from Inscriptions, AD 850-1800,* pp. 1-15.
9. Regular money transactions appear only from period III. Earlier they were partly in money and partly in gold bullion.

8

Landownership and Succession in Medieval Karnataka

G.R. Kuppuswamy

INTRODUCTION

Of the various problems connected with land system[1] it is proposed to consider in the following pages the different forms of landownership and the question of land succession which prevailed in medieval Karnataka, roughly covering the period *c.* 1000 to 1336. These are of particular significance here as there are some Hoysaḷa and other inscriptions throwing light on the problems.

Baden-powell[2] and Appadorai[3] have made a clear distinction between common or joint-ownership and individual ownership, the former being more known than the latter. In the case of common ownership, the land was held in common, the community having the collective ownership. Varieties of this were possible. Very often arable lands were divided among the members of the community, while the waste-land, for grazing purposes, was kept in common. In the case of the individual ownership, the different portions of the village were taken up or held separately or individually.

While it is not proposed to go into the question of individual ownership which may have existed side by side with the other forms of ownership,[4] it is the common ownership which has attracted the attention of scholars and therefore deserves consideration. Fortunately a detailed study of inscriptions will throw sufficient light on this interesting problem.

*Here two brief chronologically coterminus articles by the author, on land-ownership and succession in Karnataka, have been cobbled together. They touch upon interrelated problems and make a symbiotic whole.

SUB-DIVISIONS OF COMMON OWNERSHIP

On the basis of the study of the inscriptions it is possible to think of three further sub-divisions of common ownership,[5] viz., (*a*) complete ownership in common; (*b*) part (separation) rotation and part common and (*c*) part severalty and part common. In the first category, the degree of control exercised by the community was almost complete and each member was entitled to receive only a share of the produce. In the second, the community retained the right of periodical redistribution. In the last category, the control of the community extended over pasture-land only and the rest held by individuals according to some agreement.

The position may now be examined with reference to some select inscriptions belonging to Hoysaḷa rulers.

Common Ownership

The best instance of the common ownership, i.e. complete ownership in common, is provided by the Hirenallur inscription of 1215.[6] It is related to a settlement made among the brāhmins of the immemorial *agrahāra* of Hirenallur in 1215. As the settlement runs, 'Of the 30 shares of wet land under the Heggade tank in Tuyyalūrkere all the money-rent and grain-rent belongs to the brāhmins who hold these shares. The fixed rent that is received from palace for the two villages will be divided equally between the holders of sixty shares.'

While the above inscription does not give a complete picture of all the conditions governing this sub-category of common ownership a unique copper-plate inscription[7] of 1106 belonging to Kadamba Tribhuvanamalla from Goa makes up this deficiency. It relates to the establishment of a Brāhmin settlement at Gōpaka of 12 families, belonging to various *gōtras*. As the stipulations of the settlement read:

> All the land and houses were to be treated as common property and income accruing therefrom was to be distributed equally among the 12 families. The sellers and purchasers of a part of it were to be liable to a fine of 500 coins. A member was entitled to his share so long as he remained in the settlement. In case he left the place, his portion was to be enjoyed by the rest and the deserter was liable to a fine if he claimed his share. A new person can be accommodated in the vacant house with the consent of the residents in general and neighbours in particular.[8]

It can therefore be concluded that common ownership in this respect was complete and no part of the property could be disposed of except under heavy penalty. Residential qualification was insisted upon and absentee landlordism was never tolerated. Perhaps it was with the expectation of continued co-operation and to preserve the corporate atmosphere that the consent of all the residents and particularly of neighbours was insisted upon before a new person could be accommodated. More than anything else the principle of equal sharing of income or produce prevented the growth of proprietary interests, though it might have killed the spirit of individual initiative and enterprise. An individual either fell or prospered with the community as a whole.

Part-rotation (Separation) and Part Combination or Tattu as the Basis of Distribution

Under this category each shareholder (or a group of shareholders) was allowed a certain portion of land to cultivate and enjoy the fruits thereof. Common tenure was retained insofar as the right of periodical redistribution and control over waste-land were concerned. Of course the same result was obtained by revising the original agreements to bring about a more equal distribution of land. Thus corresponding to the practice in Tamil Nadu, such villages were divided into blocks or *tattus* to each of which shares were allotted. According to T.V. Mahalingam[9] such villages were called *Karai* villages. The system was known as *Karaiyīḍu* system. According to the system, lands were divided into three groups: good, middling and bad and the shareholder received for cultivation a few strips of each of these for a period, after which, there was a redistribution. The principle of combining qualitative and quantitative elements must have prevailed in Karnataka as well.[10]

The Turuvekere inscription of Hoysaḷa Vīranarsimha III, dated 1263,[11] refers to the conversion of the *agrahāra* of Turuvekere by dividing it into 95 shares and as per the agreement there were to be 8 blocks at the rate of 12 shares per block and each block was held responsible for either constructing new tanks or for maintaining the existing ones. A number of regulations governing tenancy, cart-passages and water distribution have been mentioned. Before the division was actually made, all categories of land along with tanks and ponds were pooled together for equal division, each getting something of every variety of land. One of the interesting points in the agreement was that while constructing tanks, care was to be taken to see that no loss or destruction was caused to the neighbouring block. Similarly for old tanks if *mēlaṇkaṇa* was put, nobody should object that it would lead to the pressure of water. Regarding cart-passages, no obstruction was to be caused on the ground of disputed ownership of land over which the passage was made.

Two other instances, one from Karuvīdi[12] and another from Śrīrangapaṭṭaṇa[13] may also be noted here. Even as in the case of Tamilnadu where there was a leader called *Karaikāran* over each *Karai,* there was a leader over each block or *tattu.* His name had the suffix *daśaka.*[14]

Part-Severalty and Part-Common

Under this category were included all instances in which each house-hold had its allotted share which it enjoyed without any common control or regulations effected by common agreement. The best instance is provided by the permanent agreement entered into among the Brāhmins of Kunṭanamaḍuvu dated 1291 and belonging to the reign of Narasimha III. It refers to the distribution of shares in Kētankere, Ubbaravāṇi and other places.[15] The main object of this agreement, executed in the presence of the great minister Harihara *Daṇḍanāyaka,* was to prevent the land from going into ruin[16] by effecting distribution. The agreement covering the villages of Kētankere, Ubbaravāṇi, Pokkunda and Māvinakere divided the lands into 300 shares and the taxes settled at 300 shares were to be defrayed by Brāhmins themselves.[17] It was however the responsibility of the *Mahājanas* to look after the watchman's fees, fines, faults and troubles from *bēḍars* and robbers over which the Brāhmins were not to worry.[18] The interesting part of the agreement related to the settlement of water disputes, equal distribution of water and prevention of wastage.[19] The settlement had a laudable object, viz., to assure that the shareholders might construct tanks, channels in their respective villages, establish gardens and live in peace.[20] It is a very interesting instance of peaceful co-existence and corporate life. Safeguards such as prevention of separation, alteration or exchange of shares, easily identifiable boundary-marks, etc., were provided for in the record itself.

A second instance is connected with the creation of *Sivapura* belonging to the reign of Vīraballāḷa II,[21] dated 1185. It refers to the formation of 34 shares granted to Vīraśaivas. The inheritance is restricted to female heirs only, provided they are *bhaktās.*[22] A clearer illustration of separateness is provided by a record issued by Hoysaḷa Narasimha II in 1226 which speaks of an agreement among the *Mahājanas* of Lakshmīnarasimhapura.[23] The only common hold relates to the issues to *Unḍige* or free permit. The cultivators were permitted to construct tanks and carry on cultivation in the spots assigned separately in accordance with such permits. They were free to plant gardens.[24]

Two other instances of agreement, the one between the Brāhmins of Mallikārjunapura in 1231[25] and of Vijayagōpalapura in 1324[26] will suffice to illustrate the above point.

LAND SUCCESSION

At the outset a statement of the Laws of Inheritance, which the theoretical texts of the time sanctioned for the region, will be made. This will be followed up by an examination of records—lithic and copper plate inscriptions—of the time, to indicate the points of similarity and difference from the theoretically accepted position.

Theoretical Position

According to the system of succession[27] which prevailed in Karnataka, all property of the joint-family, whether immovable or otherwise, was subject to partition, except separate property[28] which was regarded as impartible. This meant that the father could dispose of self-acquired property according to his choice.

The *Mitākṣara* details the line of succession in the following manner. Except in the case of the self-acquired property, the son, grandson and great-grandson succeeded consecutively, to the property of the deceased. If a person died without any male issue, the lawfully wedded wife, the daughters, daughter's sons, parents, brothers, their sons, *gōtrajas*, *bandhus*, a pupil, a fellow-student, on failure of each preceding one, each succeeding one was entitled to the property.[29] Failing all the above claimants, a *Srōtriya* Brāhmin in the same village or any Brāhmin could inherit such properties. It was made applicable to all *varṇas*. In case there was no claimant at all, the king could acquire by escheat, heirless property excluding that of a Brāhmin,[30] after setting apart a portion for the maintenance of the concubines and servants, and for the performance of funeral rites and *śrāddhas* of the deceased. In the case of succession to *Śtrīdhana*[31] preference was given to daughters and if the owner died sonless, her husband was entitled to the property. If the daughter was unmarried it devolved on the brother (full), the mother and father. As regards slaves, Kauṭilya declared that the heirs to the wealth of a slave were his relatives and if none of them existed, the master acquired it.[32]

Evidence of Inscriptions

Keeping the above theoretical background in view, it will be worthwhile to examine the inscriptions of the time to consider the extent to which Inheritance Laws were followed in actual practice and to note deviations, if any, from them.

(*a*) It is clear from an inscription of 1140 from the Hassan District that the slaves had the right to inherit property. It relates to the grant of land with the stipulation that the land may descend to the children of female slaves.[33]

(*b*) Whenever a piece of property was sold, the consent of the near and dear relatives was taken. It is on record that one Hegde's son Ballāḷa sold a piece of land to one Vaidya, Devapiḷḷaiyaṇṇa at Mosaḷe, after obtaining the consent of his wife, son, relatives, dependents and heirs.[34]

(*c*) There are a couple of inscriptions which throw sufficient light on the question of the disposal of property of those who died sonless. An inscription[35] from Kittanahaḷḷi, Bangalore District, dated 1330, details as below the succession among cultivating class which was approved by Hoysaḷa Viraballāḷa: 'If any one among them died without children, his elder or younger brothers were to have possession. If there were no such relatives, the property, was to go to such work of charity as the cultivators would decide. Any transgression of the rules of this caste, cultivators will enquire into and punish the offenders.' The inscription in question does not give details of the entire line of succession. To quote the text: '*makkaḷilladiddaḍe aṇṇatammandirge saluvudu aṇṇatammandiru illadiddaḍe aḷiya mammāgaḷige saluvudu ivarāru nil . . . ā holaṁ dharmakke saluvudu*'. The term *makkaḷilladiddaḍe* may mean failure of male children only. For otherwise, it is difficult to explain how the son-in-law (*aḷiya*) and grand-daughter (*mammagaḷige*) get into the order of succession. Contrary to the scriptures (*Mitakṣara*), the above regulations give preference to brothers and son-in-law over the wives and daughters' children of the deceased respectively. The term son-in-law may refer either to daughter's husband or sister's son (*aḷiya*). In case the term *aḷiya* stands for sister's son, it speaks of the system of *aḷiya santānakaṭṭu.*

A second point of note here is that the entire line of succession is not gone through in the record in question. After the failure of grandson, the property is to be given to the temple as charity, after taking the consent of cultivators.

A second inscription[36] from Kōṭavumachgi states that only 1/10 of the property of those dying sonless is to be used for tank there. It has thereby underlined the scriptural injunction that only a part of the property can be put for any public purpose, the rest being used for the performance of rites. A third inscription from Baḷḷigāve dated 1181 outlines the procedure to be followed in the case of the properties of *baṇajigas* of the place, who die sonless. It will be interesting to note that the decisions were taken in an assembly of great men including the royal officers to be enforced by *mummuridaṇḍas.* As the inscription states, all the property of *baṇajigas* of Baḷḷigāve dying without sons, (to go) for the festival or sacred rites of God Gavareśvara, the property of those who die without sons in the *nagara,* three *puras* and seven *brahmapuris,* in which unclaimed property accrues to the God of that quarter[37]—a very satisfactory arrangement indeed—emphasizing perhaps regional jurisdiction of God's authority.

Another and a more elaborate inscription of Kālachūris throws additional light on the question of succession and disposal of heirless property. It comes from Mangōḷi and is dated 1178. It states,

If any one should die without sons, his wife, female children, divided parents and their children . . . and any kinsmen and relatives of the same *gōtra* should take possession of all his property such as bipeds, quadrupeds, coins, grain, house and fields if none such should survive, (and) the authorities of the village should make over that property, as religious grant to those who hold the grant of God.[38]

From a close examination of the record in question the following points emerge:

(i) While scripture is followed closely in outlining the line of succession, *dauhitras,* i.e. daughter's son and *bandhus* who belong to different *gōtras* (*binnagōtra*) are excluded and immediately after the failure of sons, wife and female children, the property reverts to paternal relatives.

(ii) In keeping with the scriptures, preference is given in the inscription to parents, brothers and their children, who have divided themselves, i.e. separated themselves from joint-family. It has revealed the fact that when the family is not divided the property evidently remains within the fold of the joint-family. It may be recalled here that the scriptures merely mention parents and brothers in the line of succession but the inscription has further clarified the position.

(iii) The word *stri* invariably stands for lawfully wedded wife and not for any other women kept by the deceased for whom separate provision was made and they were not in any case entitled to a place in the line of succession.

(iv) A redeeming feature in this and other inscriptions examined so far, is that in practice the property of those who were issueless would be donated to the temple or put to any other public use. The manner of the disposal of the property is not indicated in the theoretical scriptures quoted earlier.

(*d*) Of the other lithic records referring to the line of succession, a Hoysaḷa inscription from Mysore district dated 1265 states exhaustively thus, 'The property of those who die without children should go to elder brother, younger brother,[39] father's elder brother or their children.' The inscription extends the line of succession to include son-in-law and father-in-law while the wife and daughter have no place. Son-in-law is preferred to daughter and father-in-law puts in his claim, perhaps as a *bandhu. Gōtrajas* and *dāyavādins* have preponderating influence over others, in keeping with patriarchal system.

(*e*) Another curious inscription from Bangalore District states[40] 'If there is *a tammaḍi* or priest, the elder brother's property will go to the younger brother and younger brother's property to elder brother. If there is no elder or younger brother, the nearest relatives and children by female servants will have the chief claim. If there are no such claimants, the childless ones' (property) will be given to temple. If there is no provision for *tammaḍi* without the payment or any others, free from all imposts, a fair will be established in that Mugulāṇḍanahaḷḷi, as a city for *nānādesi's* to continue.'

A few points of clarification are required to be made here. The term *oḍave* is used in the inscription which evidently stands for movable property. The phrase '*aṇṇana oḍave tammage tammana oḍave aṇṇage*' implies that if the elder brother is survived by the younger brother, the latter inherits the former's property and *vice versa*. In two other respects the inscription is interesting. It gives importance to female servants and their children who do not find a place even in the scriptural injunctions, a very healthy modification of the rules. In the second place, the reference to the establishment of a fair out of the proceeds of heirless property appears to be another purpose for which such properties were put to use. The provisions regarding *tammaḍi* or perhaps priest is to ensure proper management of property, entrusted to the care of the temple.

(*f*) A tinge of matriarchal system of succession is seen in inscriptions from Coorg and other parts of north Karnataka, perhaps reminding us of the *aḷiya santānakaṭṭu* and of its prevalence in Karnataka even earlier than in Tuḷuva country where it had struck deep roots. One of them from Kundoor,[41] Coorg, states, 'It will belong to a female, female children and to children of female slaves.' Another inscription from the same region, permits the succession of property by female descendants in the absence of male issues. An interesting inscription belonging to Kōlāra family referred to by Fleet,[42] records that when Mādiraja was killed in battle his only surviving elder sister (daughter?) Bijjavve succeeded to the lordship immediately. She appears to have treated Gouri (relationship not clear) as her daughter (Fleet says, daughter) and got her married to one Mallikārjuna and the *estate* was given as dowry to her. Mallikārjuna was evidently the son-in-law of Bijjavve and the property of Mādiraja referred to above descended through sister's descendants.

(*g*) *Partition deed:* A unique inscription almost a partition deed from Bantēnahaḷḷi, Belur, dated 1244 outlines the partition of a temple property or properties on the death of one Sōmajiya of Būchēśwara temple, among his relatives. The partition, effected in the presence of and by *Rājaguru* Chandrabūshana and 120 *Sthāṇikas* at Dōrasamudra[43] was based on sound principles of succession and represented the ideal, for, both the daughter and wife of the deceased are given their due shares. Similarly, the wife and son are entitled to a greater share (together 2/3) while daughter, her husband and their sons get only 1/3. It will be interesting to know that partition, though inevitable, was kept to a minimum.

Another inscription from Hantūr, Kadur District, dated 1188[44] supplies a curious instance of equal division of property between sons and daughters, but which was followed by tragic happenings. One Macha (left) in Hannivur for his son and daughter; land valued at 1000 *honnu*. Both dead, through hatred, the daughter's sons encroached upon the lands of son's children. While the inscription corroborated the scriptures on the liberal side, it did not go unchallenged in practice.

(*h*) A curious instance of coparcenary right[45] is provided by an inscription from north Karnataka.

CONCLUSION

A consideration of the above evidences leads to the following important conclusions:

(*a*) The order of succession mentioned in the scriptures was generally followed in practice. Here and there some changes are noticed.

(*b*) Women and female children are given their due share and in the case of female property, succession restricted to females.

(*c*) Slaves and servants particularly female, are not deprived of their shares in the property.

(*d*) The property of those who died sonless was put to public use—in service of temples, tanks or establishment of fairs. Of course care was taken to set apart a portion of it only, for such uses.

(*e*) The rules of succession were framed and enforced in a constitutional manner, after being approved by the king.

(*f*) Coparcenary rights were entertained.

NOTES

1. For instance the other problems relate to types, settlement of disputes, trustees and leases. The general question of landownership itself has engaged the attention of the scholars particularly regarding the claimants. The most considered view seems to be that no private individual could hold land as a matter of absolute right. The state had always the last word to say in this matter. In other words though individuals had wide powers of enjoyment and disposition, the ultimate owner was the sovereign. One may go a step further and say that individual ownership was just a lease or tenure for 999 years with the right of the state to acquire it at any moment. The question has been ably discussed in some of the following works—(*a*) S.K. Maity, *Economic Life of Northern India in Gupta Age*, 1967, pp. 11-28 (*b*) U.N. Ghoshal, *The Agrarian System of Ancient India* 1929—Lecture V, pp. 81-103 (*c*) L. Gopal, *Economic Life of Northern India*, 1965, pp. 1-31 (*d*) Adhya, *Early Indian Economics*, pp. 25-30 (*e*) P.V. Kane, *History of Dharmaśāstras* II (ii), pp. 865-9 (*f*) Appadorai, *Economic Conditions of Southern India* I, pp. 99-121 (*g*) K. M. Gupta, *Land System in South India*, ch IV.
2. To quote Baden-Powell on Joint-Villages 'It is not at all necessary that the joint-village should be actually held undivided. In some cases it is so held . . . but in the majority of cases there is complete separation of the individual or household holdings . . . very often arable is divided and the waste not, either because it is more conveniently kept as common grazing ground, or it is not yet wanted for extension of cultivation.' *The Indian Village Community*, p. 22.
3. Appadorai's views on joint-villages are as set out below: 'In a joint-village the right of land is held in common. Varieties of this are possible and many exist together. In general, the community has collective ownership over the whole or part of the village.' *Economic Conditions of Southern India*, I, p. 124.
4. See Altekar, *History of the Village Communities in Western India*, Bombay, 1927, pp. 80ff, for the rather one-sided view that the ownership of the

lands in Western India was vested in peasant-proprietor or the tenure of land throughout Deccan or Karnatak was *Ryotwāri* one. While sufficient epigraphical evidence is lacking to substantiate the view of the learned scholar, it cannot be totally discarded as unsound. As will be seen later, there seems to have been a tendency even in joint-ownership villages in Karnataka towards greater independence in the distribution of holdings. Or one may say that there is gradual evolution of the idea of peasant-proprietorship noticed in such villages. Similarly, the innumerable grants of *Koḍagi* lands testify to the existence of individual ownership along with the other system.

5. This classification follows that of Appadorai. See his *Economic Conditions of Southern India*, I, p. 125; See T.V. Mahalingam, *South India Polity*, p. 360. According to him *gaṇabhōgaṁ* falls into almost the same three classes, viz., (*a*) complete and unlimited ownership of the community, (*b*) part individual and part-common, (*c*) *Karaividu* lands based on qualitative division of lands into blocks. Karnataka inscriptions refer to *tattus*, an important addition to the classification. See K.M. Gupta, *Land System in South India*, pp. 63ff, for his classification of such lands into *Samudayaṁ*, *Karaiyiḍu* and *Palabhōgam* which roughly correspond to the earlier-mentioned classification.
6. *EC*, VI, Kd. no. 132, p. 118 (Text), p. 2255 (Trans.). The inscription does not mention the ruler's name but it is classified under Hoysaḷas.
7. *EI*, XXX, no. 15, pp. 71-2.
8. To quote the text '. . . *phalam vibhājya bhōktavyaṁ kṣētram sādāraṇam sadā sādaranatvāt kṣētrāṇām grihāṇām dānavikriyau kurvam=pancha śatam danḍyāgrihnan . . . asvāmika=griha(he) sarvaih sthāpita abhyāgatō vasēt pārśvasta grihasammatyā. . . .*'
9. See T.V. Mahalingam, *South Indian Polity*, p. 360.
10. See below.
11. *EC*, XII, Tp. no. 2, p. 117 (Text) p. 42 (Trans.).
12. *EC*, XII, Tp. no. 83. The *Mahājanas* of Karuvādi after pooling together the lands of Haḷḷiyūr and Hiriyūr, had them divided into 125 shares and grouped them into parts. Each party was required to construct its own tank and pond and each village had its own customary boundary.
13. *EC*, XII, Sr. no. 64. This is an instance of equal division based on quality. 112 *vrittis* of land were redistributed in such a way that each had a share of the best, average and inferior land portions.
14. The inscription from Kuṭnaṇamaḍuvu examined under the third category below has references to this term. See *EC*, VI, Tk. no. 55, p. 444 (Text), p. 113 (Trans.). See G.S. Dikshit, *Local Self-Government in Medieval Karnataka*, p. 129 for a similar instance from Tumbula grāma (Advani, Kurnool District) bordering Karnataka. Another inscription from Muroor, Gōkarṇa Taluk; N.K. District, refers to the division of land in units of ten shares—*EI*, XIII, no. 28, pp. 157-63. Also cf. Baden-Powell, *The Indian Village Community*, p. 24. He refers to a system in the

Punjab under which a village is divided into a number of *pattis* and over each section there is a *lambardar*, or the holder of a number. He says in a note (ibid., fn. 2, p. 24) that the number refers to the Collector's list of village landholders with a serial number attached to each name. The Mughal records speak of *muccādam*. It seems, therefore, that this practice of having a head over each block of land was not peculiar to south India but of an all-India character, evolutionary in nature. Unfortunately the functions of such leaders are not clear from these records.

15. *EC*, VI, Tk. no. 55, p. 444 (Text), p. 113 (Trans.).
16. *āraivarillade kiḍutiddaḍe.*
17. *antu vrittimunūru aramaneyim banda sollamabiṭṭi pūrvāya munnūru vrithiya baḷiyoḷuhacchi yati bandaḍam vrittiya baliyalu tiruvaru.* This has reference to levies such as forced labour (*Sollama biṭṭi*) and traditional taxes (*pūrvāya*) and new taxes (*apūrvāya*) which are decided and settled at 300 shares. Regarding Kirukuḷa also it seems that the Brāhmins had to pay it separately and should not treat it as a part of land revenue and deduct it from *Siddāya* or fixed rent, payable, to State. To quote the text—*arasina deseya kirukuḷaabhyāgatīya ādhya paripāntane munurvaradu bhumiya bhāgavendu siddayava hiḍiyalāgadu.*
18. *āvāva sthaḷada danḍaḍōṣa taḷārike bēḍara ko kaḷḷara bādhe ā sthaḷada mahajanangaḷudullude munūravara kāraṇa villa.* Evidently it was the responsibility of the local authorities, namely the *Mahājanas* to protect the shareholders and their lands from such unforeseen calamities.
19. For instance, the Brāhmins of the village of Pokkunda, Māvinkere and Kētanakere, where sixty-one shares belonging to individuals (specified) are located, were not allowed to draw and utilize water by lifting sluice-gate of Basavayya tank beyond sixty-one shares.
20. Text—*munurvaru tamma tamma haḷḷiyalu kerekāluve kaṭṭi tōṭa tuḍikeyanikki sukhadim bāḷvantāgi māḍida sameya śāsana.*
21. *MAR* 1933, no. 48, WEC III, Md. no. 62.
22. Text—*Vrittiyanu vrittivantara heṇṇu makkaḷu henḍiru tottina makkaḷu-bhaktarāgi anubhavisuvaru.*
23. *MAR* 1931, no. 59, p. 168.
24. *Śrī Lakshīminarasimhapurada aśēṣa mahājanangaḷu mahāsabheyāgi neredumāḍida sameyaventendaḍe, puratigeya bhāgu bābuhuli kumaranahaḷḷi tenkatūra inti nisariliyam pratiprathi vibhāgavam māḍiyikkida unḍige druva vunḍige tāva tāvāge vyavasāyavaṁ māḍidaḍe sradhyā pathiya mādalāgadu.*
25. *EC*, V(ii), Cn. no. 170. According to the record, the Brāhmins of Mallikārjunapura, who, considering that the former division of land was unequal, got all the wet and dry lands measured again, and agreeing among themselves on the principle that all were equal and should share alike, made permanent settlement. The shares were 158. To quote the text '*Srimat anādiyagrahāram Śrīmallikārjuna puravāda dinḍigūrada aśēṣa mahājanangaḷu munnina vibhāgavu samavallendu*

madhyastharindam haḷḷigaḷa beddalanasi tammōḷēkamatyavāgi iccha vrittiyāgi nindu kramaventententendaḍe' (Shares of villagers mentioned). The inscription further states that the settlement should be treated as permanent and not transferred at any cost or that the shareholders should not find another excuse in natural calamities for redistribution. To quote further—'*Pariyaā icchā pūrvakavāgi chandrārkatārambaram nischavavāgi nindavaru āhaḷḷigaḷige manneyaru daivakaraṭa vikarabādheyādaḍam matte samavallendu arisālāgadu āva haḷḷiyalu āvanādaḍam krayadānava konḍaḍam saluvudiyarthava naḷiyalāgadu.*'

26. *EC*, XII, Tp. no. 41. The inscription refers to the division of Nirgunda village on a permanent basis. There are altogether 100 shares divided into 4 *tattus* or blocks. Of the two interesting things in the record one is that the former rights of each village and families living therein are fully protected and belonging to the shareholders and the *tattu* in which it is included. Evidently the families here refer to *okkalu* or tenants and it seems further from the record that the *okkalu* came on contract basis and they were attached to the respective *tattus* to which they belonged. While such families were allowed to stay on or leave for another block, the loss or gain was put equally on the shareholders themselves, of the respective *tattus*.
27. Of the two systems of succession, with the exception of Bengal, all parts of India came under *Mitākṣara.* Only Bengal was under *Dāyabhāga.* A detailed discussion of the two systems, the points of difference and similarity have been discussed by Kane in *History of Dharmaśāstras,* III, chs. 26 and 29.
28. Kane, *HDS,* III, ch. 29.
29. Kane, *HDS,* III, p. 701, fn. 1341.
30. Ibid., p. 762, also fn. 1463.
31. Ibid., ch. 33 for detailed discussion of the definition of *strīdhana.*
32. Ibid., II, p. 186.
33. *EC,* V (ii), B1, no. 219, pp. 341-2. Text—*avana tottina makkalige bhūmi saluvudu.*
34. *EC,* V (ii), AK, no. 9, pp. 359-60 (Text) i, p. 115 (Trans.); also see ibid., no. 58 (i), p. 760 (Text) i, p. 254 (Trans.); *EC,* III (i) Sr. no. 110, p. 30 (Trans).
35. *EC,* IX, N1, no. 12, p. 59 (Text), p. 52 (Trans.).
36. *EI,* XX, no. 6, pp. 64-70 *aputrika dravyada das'a vandadolu puṭṭida dravyamum.*
37. *EC,* VIII (i), Sk. no. 119-221 (Text).
38. *EI,* V, no. 3C, pp. 26-8. Text—*managa vaḷḷiyōl aputrakaru sattar appad avara dvipadi chatuspadi dhana dhānya griha—kshetram enib initumaṁ ātana strī mukhyavagi hengūsu makkaḷu vibhaktarāda tangi tande aṇṇa tammandir avara makkaḷu a gilu jnāta gōtra ant avar oḷag āru iddad iddavara kaḷedu kombar ant—anivar olag āru illadidda (r-a) opad ā dhanamam dēva dāyi gaḷige dharma dattavāgi kuḍuvaru.*

39. *EC*, III (i), Tn. no. 21, p. 212 (Text), p. 70 (Trans.).
40. *EC*, II, Cp. no. 73, p. 324 (Text), p. 146 (Trans.).
41. *EC*, IX, Sup.Cg. no. 59, p. 12 (Text), p. 177 (Trans.) *heṇṇige heṇṇu makkaḷige tottina makkaḷige saluvudu.*
42. *JBBRAS*, X, p. 177.
43. *EC*, XV, B1, no. 325, p. 84.
44. *EC*, VI, Mg. no. 24, p. 249 (Text), p. 63 for details.
45. *KI*, II, no. 16, pp. 62ff. See P. V. Kane, *HDS*, III, pp. 561, 591, fn. 1116 and 592ff for an explanation of Coparcenary rights.

9

Village Communities in South India

T.V. Mahalingam

The foundation of any state edifice in Indian administration must necessarily be the village not only on account of its great antiquity but also on account of the fact that people living in it are known to one another intimately and have interests which converge on well recognized objects. Even so late as the early nineteenth century British administrators in our country were so much impressed with the vitality and usefulness of the Indian village communities that they have showered encomiums on them. Elphinstone thought that the secrct of the good things achieved in India in the past is to be sought in the stability and continuity of Indian village life and organization. Sir Charles Metcalfe observes in one of his letters:

> The village communities are village republics, having nearly everything they want within themselves and almost independent of any foreign relations. They seem to last where nothing else lasts. Dynasty after dynasty crumbles down. Revolution succeeds revolution . . . . (But) the union of village communities—each one forming a separate state—by itself—has I conceive, contributed more than any other cause to the preservation of the people of India through all revolutions and changes which they have suffered and it is in a high degree conducive to their happiness and to the enjoyment of a great portion of freedom and independence.[1]

Therefore it is no surprise that the subject of the Indian village communities has attracted a number of scholars particularly after the publication in 1871 by Sir Henry Maine of his stimulating lectures on 'Village Communities East and West'. Scholars like Baden-Powell, Mookerjee, Altekar and Ghoshal to mention only a few have made suggestive contributions to knowledge on the subject. The value of a study of the subject can hardly be exaggerated for in many cases the foundations of the political and administrative institutions of later times have been traced to the ancient village communities. Even the idea of the corporate personality of a group of people is considered to be a development from them. The word community is the same as the French word *commune* which is derived from the Latin word *communalis* or *communis*. The Latin term itself is a compound made up of two words *com* (together) *munis* (bound), i.e. bound together. The word community signifies a fellowship or joint personality, i.e. a body of persons organized for political, economic, social, religious and professional purposes. The village community was therefore not distinct from the village organization which existed in some form from very early times. Though such institutions were not peculiar to south India yet they had certain characteristics with regard to their comprehensiveness and functions on account of which they may be considered unique. They formed a definite part of the administrative machinery in the country and each of them had a homogeneous, individual and continuous personality. But it must be admitted that an integrated study of this fascinating subject has not so far received the attention it deserves, though we are indebted to scholars like Venkayya, Nilakanta Sastri and Appadorai who have approached the subject from specific points of view.

The village communities in south India belonged to a general pattern, bore some common characteristics and served some common purposes and ends. Maine's description of the English township 'as an organized self acting group of Teutonic families exercising a common proprietorship over a definite tract of land, its mark, cultivating its domain on a common system and sustaining itself by the produce' may be taken to be equally applicable to the village communities in south India in its early stages. It was an organism born out of the consciousness among its members of a kinship among them. Its growth was gradual, slow and spontaneous, the community often adapting itself to changing conditions. There were three types of such village organizations namely the *ūr*, *sabhā*, and the *nāḍu* which were essentially agrarian units.

The humble and often unnoticed origins of even mighty institutions are generally shrouded in mystery, and those of the village community of south India are no exception.

We get glimpses of rural administration in the Tamil country from the literature of the Sangam ages where we get reference to two terms, *maṉṟam* and *podiyil.* The *maṉṟam* has been explained to by *Nacciṉārkiṉiyār* as the open place in the centre of the village where the people met together. It was the common public place also called *podiyil* or *poduvil,* usually with the tree of the region or the banyan in the centre. Social festivities and sacrifices to the Gods were conducted there. It was also used for the discussion of public affairs, and the transaction of public business like the administration of justice. In spite of its wide prevalence and popularity we do not know its exact relationship with the village community. But it is from some early inscriptions of south India that we come to know something about the rise of a community feeling in the region. Some of the early inscriptions of the Eastern Gaṅgas and the Pallavas indicate the existence of a feeling of collective recognition of their common interests by the residents in villages, the necessary basis for the rise of a community feeling among them and the evolution of a township. Each village was a community of landholders and land was the primary factor that made the people connected with it to come together for common purposes. Lands were usually held under the three distinct types of tenure: (1) directly from the State, (2) under service tenure by the servants of the government or persons charged with the specific duties, like the recitation of the *Bhārata* in the temple or the maintenance of an *ambalam* and (3) under elemosynary tenure by groups of people or an institution like the temple. To the last group belonged for instance the Brāhmaṇas who were granted the *miyātchi* rights over land or the right of the overlordship of a share of produce. The tenure under which lands were held by groups of persons was known as *gaṇabhogam* as distinct from *ēkabhogam* by which term severality tenure was known. The co-sharers of land in a joint village where they enjoyed all the eight rights of possessions were the absolute owners of land. Such ownership rights consisted

in the exclusive use and absolute disposal of the powers of the soil in perpetuity, together with the right to alter or destroy the soil itself where such an operation is possible. These privileges combined, form the abstract idea of property which does not represent any substance distinct from these elements. Where they are found united there is property, and nowhere else.

Even in the severality villages ownership of land appears to have rested only with the citizens unless the lands were unoccupied ones, and the states' share of the income from land was due to the protection it gave to the people. Wilson's description of the limitations of the titles of the king over land is classical and deserves reproduction. He says:

> He (the King) is not lord of the 'soil'; he is lord of the earth, of the whole earth or kingdom; not of any parcel or allotment of it; he may punish a cultivator for neglect of the crop; and when he gives away lands and villages, he gives away the share of the revenue. No donee would ever think of following such a donation by actual occupancy, he would be resisted if he did. The truth is that the rights of the king are a theory, an abstraction. Poetically and politically speaking he is the lord, the master, the protector of the earth, (*prithvipati, bhūmiśvara, bhūmipa*) just as he is the lord, the master, the protector of the earth (*narapati, nareśvara and nṛipa*). Such is the common title of a king, but he is no more the actual proprietor of the soil than he is of his subjects; they need not have his permission to buy or sell it or to give it away and would be much surprised and grieved if the king or his officers were to buy or sell or give away the ground which they cultivated.

The recognition of private ownership of property in south India is borne out by both literary and epigraphical evidence of a contemporary nature. Vijñāneśvara in his celebrated work, the *Mitākshara* says for instance: It is settled, that ownership in the father's or grandfather's estate is by birth . . . the father is subject to the control of his sons and the rest in regard to the immovable estate, whether acquired by himself or inherited from his father or other predecessor' and thereby suggests that for the disposal of lands son's consent was necessary. This condition need not have been insisted upon if private ownership of land had not been recognized. With regard to the King's control over it the same authority says: 'True it is that this man first got it by gift and also was in possession, but the king gave this very field to me after purchasing from this very man or that this man gave it to me after having obtained by gift, etc.', thereby suggesting that the king, if he wanted to acquire land, had to purchase it as any private individual. The views of Mādhavāchārya on this interesting question may also be referred to here. Commenting on the text of the *Jaiminīya Nyāyamālā vistara* 'namely the *mahābhūmi*, the public land, is an object of gift . . . the king may give it away because he possesses it; the kingdom is the king's only for the sake of protection, and hence it should not be given away'. Mādhavāchārya observes:

But doubts may arise. When an all-powerful king gives away everything he possesses at the commencement of the *Viśvajit* sacrifice, is he to give away the *mahābhūmi* which is inclusive of paths for cattle, highways and tanks? (The doubt arises because the earth is wealth *vide* the *smṛti* which says: 'The king may claim the property of all except that of the Brāhmaṇas').

We reply: The smṛtis enjoin that the king's sovereignty is meant to punish the wicked and to protect the good. No, the earth is not the king's property. But it is the common property of all the living beings for them to enjoy the fruit of their labour. Therefore, though he (the king) has the right to give away that portion of the land that is not common (public—*asādhāraṇa*), he cannot give away the *mahābhūmi*.

Thus ownership of land rested only with the people. This is further supported by inscriptional evidence according to which in a number of cases, lands, which were in the enjoyment of private individuals were purchased by the king and granted to others. The recognition of private property is further indicated by the use of the term *kāṇiātchi* to indicate it. It means hereditary right to land or property and is synonymous with the Sanskrit term *kshetrasvāmya*. Private ownership of property could not rest either in the individuals or in a group of people, jointly. In the *brahmadeya* or *agrahāra* or *chaturvedimangalam* villages the owners of lands held them jointly and created the necessary basis for the evolution of the village organization on the community basis.

As a predominantly agricultural community enjoying their lands under a joint tenure the residents of the *brahmadeya* village looked to the cultivation in common. In such work three different types appear to have been adopted: (1) The members of the village community cultivated land in common and shared the profits among themselves in proportion to the number of shares (*vṛittis*) each possessed. (2) A particular portion of the village could have been enjoyed individually by the shareholders for cultivation purposes, the rest being held by them jointly as under the first type. (3) Lands could have been divided into different grades in accordance with their fertility and every individual member of the joint community given a portion of each of the three classes of lands for a definite period, and after the expiry of that period the lands could be redistributed among the members. This system of periodical distribution of land was for instance known in the present Tanjore district as the *karaiyiḍu*. An important feature of the organization of the joint villages was the extreme exclusiveness of the village communities in them, and their anxiety not to allow outsiders to get any right or share in such villages either by purchase or gift.

For discussing and deciding upon matters connected with agriculture and their obligations to the government the landholders in the joint village had to meet on certain occasions though in a very informal way. But with the advance of time and growing complexity of the social and economic organization of the village, the meeting became frequent leading to the gradual development of custom and precedent in the dealings. With further passage of time such custom and procedure crystallized themselves in such a way that the organization looking after the affairs of the village community became so natural and strong that it was almost impossible to think of such a place without a well recognized and active organization with a well-established and growing tradition behind it. It was such an organization that developed into the perfected self-governing institution during the days of the Pallavas and Cholas in south India. The institution came to be variously called, the *sabhā*, the *mahāsabhā, mahāsabhaiyōm, mahājanas, Kuri, Perunguri*, etc.

By the days of the Pallavas in the north and the Pāṇḍyas in the south the organization in the *brahmadeya* villages had taken a definite shape and was known usually as the *sabhā*. Its emergence as a perfected institution is seen first in the Toṇḍaimaṇḍalam area in the days of the Pallavas. It appears that it functioned at least in twenty different places in the area in the eighth and ninth centuries. However, details regarding their constitution and working are not available. Almost simultaneously the *sabhā* had developed in the Pāṇḍyan country also as may be gleaned from an inscription of Mārañjaḍaiyaṇ at Māṇūr. At a general body meeting of the *mahāsabhaiyār* of the village summoned by beat of drum rules were made fixing the qualifications of property and learning besides the high character required of its members to participate in the proceedings of the assembly, and paticularly in its executive work. Failure to observe the new rules and wilful obstruction to the work of the *sabhā* were made punishable.

But more details are available about the constitution and working of the *sabhā* at Uttaramērūr, which has become justly famous in the history of local self government in south India. Though the two inscriptions relating to the constitution and working of the *sabhā* at the place dated 919 and 921 respectively are considered important on account of the lurid light they throw on its organization and working, it had a long anterior history going back to the days of the Pallavas when it discharged many executive functions through its individual officers or groups of officers known as *vāriyams*. From a study of the inscriptions bearing on the subject it is seen that the *vāriyam* system was an important feature of the *sabhā* organization. But its origin and history are not clearly known nor the import of the word. Some scholars think that the word is derived from the Tamil word *vāram* which means a share or *pangu,* and hence the term *vāriyar* means shareholder, and *vāriyam* a committee of *vāriyars*. Since the *vāriyam* discharged the executive functions of the *sabhā* it may be taken to be its committee. There were different such committees, each of which was entrusted with a specified branch of work. A second suggestion made is that the word may be derived from the Sanskrit word *vara* which means a collection (*samūha*) or group (*gaṇa*). A third suggestion is that it may be derived from *vāra* (meaning income in Tamil and rigorous demand in Kannada). A fourth suggestion and probably the most acceptable is that it is the Tamilised form of the Sanskrit word *varya* meaning 'selected' or 'chosen' [*vṛi* (*var*) to select or choose]. This interpretation is supported by a Tamil inscription of the twelfth year of Kulōttunga III in which the expressions *varaṇam seydal* for the act of choosing and *varaṇam* for the executive body of the *sabhā* are used. The term *vāriyar* would therefore mean a person or a body of persons employed to do a specific work. The Māṇūr inscription referred to above shows that even so early as the ninth century high qualification and integrity were expected of the *vāriyars*. But in the early phases of the history of the institution, it appears that the *vāriyam* was only a temporarily constituted *ad hoc* body or committee for the discharge of some specific duties. In course of time, apparently on account of its usefulness in local administration the *vāriyam* became a regular and integral part of the *sabhā*. Though it is possible that the method of the appointment of the *vāriyam* could have been the same everywhere our knowledge of it is meagre. But from the two celebrated Uttaramērūr inscriptions it may be presumed that each *sabhā* could change the method of the appointment to the *vāriyam* probably taking into account local conditions and requirements. The *sabhā* of Uttaramērūr which had a long history going back to the Pallava period adopted a resolution in 919 with regard to the method of appointment to its executive committees. But for some reason it did not work well, and so two years later, the method of election to the committees underwent another change. According to the second reform the *Kuḍumbus* came to be directly represented on the committees. Each of the thirty *kuḍumbus* into which the village was divided was to nominate for the selection to the committees persons possessing the prescribed qualifications relating to learning, property, age and character. Persons who had served on the committees for the previous three years, those who had served on the committee, but had failed to submit accounts as also their specified relations and men of bad character were excluded from the committees. From among the persons duly nominated one was to be chosen from each *kudumbu* by the *kuḍa ōlai* or lot system in the prescribed manner. Apart from the qualifications specified in the above inscription for membership in the different committees the real importance of the record lies in the fact that the lot system was adopted by the *sabhā* for purposes of election to the standing committees. The system was not however new. In direct democracies worked in ancient Athens for instance the lot system was employed. It was quite popular though there was a chance in it for any person getting elected irrespective of his fitness and qualification. But the Uttaramērūr inscription by fixing a minimum qualification for the *vāriyam* avoided the pitfalls of the lot system.

The committee system which had grown gradually in the course of the previous centuries reached its highest water mark during this period. The Uttaramērūr inscription of 921 mentions five distinct *vāriyams* namely the *tōṭṭavāriyam* in charge of gardens and public places, the *ērivāriyam* in charge of tanks and other irrigation sources, the *samvatsara vāriyam* or the annual committee of twelve members, membership in which required not only experience in the first two committees mentioned earlier but also pre-eminence in learning and age, the *panchavāra vāriyam* connected apparently with the assessment and collection of the tax and the *poṇvāriyam* obviously engaged in examining the fineness and weight of the gold that was invested with the *sabhā* for specific purposes. All the *vāriyams* except the *samvatsaravāriyam* consisted of six persons. In 922 the *sabhā* at Uttaramērūr brought into existence by a resolution a new committee consisting of nine persons for the purpose of assaying gold. Probably without supplanting the old *ponvāriyam* it was intended to help it in its work.

Many other *sabhās* in south India also adopted the *vāriyam* system, but the number of committees under them appear to have differed from place to place, depending probably on local needs. Among the other committees mentioned in inscriptions were the *kuḍumbu vāriyam* (wards committee), *kaḷaṇivāriyam* (fields committee), *kaṇakkuvāriyam* (accounts committee), *kalingu vāriyam* (sluice committee), the *udāsina vāriyaṁ* (committee in charge of foreigners?), *dharma vāriyam* (committee in charge of religious endowments), etc. Probably there were a few others also, of which however we have no idea now. The method of election to the *vāriyam*,the number of such *vāriyams*, the qualifications of their members and such other details must have been decided by the local *sabhās* themselves without interference by the Central Government. Even when the assembly of Uttaramērūr made changes in 919 and 921 with regard to the electoral procedure to be followed by it, it did so of its own accord, and the presence of the royal official on both the occasions appears to have been only for enabling the members of the *sabhā* to settle their constitution and electoral procedure amicably. But interference of the government was not impossible if the working of the village assemblies was not satisfactory. According to an inscription at Talaināyar in the Tanjore district a royal letter was addressed to the *sabhā* and collector (*taṇḍuvān*) of the place at the instance of two officers of King Kulottuṅga III. The document which was written by the *Tirumandira Ōlai* and attested by nine others, all officers of government, contained rules for the election of the executive body (*kūṭṭam*) of the assembly of the village sanctioned by the king. The new rules said that only those Brāhmaṇas who had not been in the assembly during the ten years previous to the year in which the election was held were eligible, the candidates were to be above forty years of age, learned (*vidvān*) and impartial (*samar*). Certain classes of persons were disqualified from serving on the executive of the assembly, for instance those that were guilty of wicked deeds, had defaulted in the payment of land revenue, oppressed docile Brāhmaṇas and respectable tenants, accepted bribes, and had done such other questionable things. Probably all was not well with the working of the *sabhā* at the place, its work was hampered by the rise of a factious spirit among its members and hence the government's interference and insistence. In another place it was ordered by the Government that only persons above forty years of age and who had not served on the executive for the previous ten years were alone eligible for service. Similar rules regarding age and interval between two periods of service were made also at Ayyampēṭṭai in the Tanjore district in 1190. In such cases the age limit of forty must have obviously served as a check against inexperienced and young men getting into the assembly. The interval of ten years between the period of the first election of a member and his second election was probably intended to give an opportunity for all adults in the village to take part in local administration. However when the village assemblies were not able to decide about such important matters they were referred to any other local body like the *mūlaparishat* of the temple of the place, particularly when the rules were not respected and fresh persons who did not possess the requisite qualifications entered the assembly. Actually such an incident is recorded to have taken place at a village in the reign of Rājarāja III and hence when the matter was referred to *mūlaparishat* of the temple of the place it made certain rules with regard to the elections and tenure of the members of the executive, as for instance that members should be elected every year and those who tried to extend their tenure of office for longer periods were liable to punishment as *grāmadrōhins* and those who in violation of the rules got into the assembly by some covert means in collusion with the officers of government or by any other means, were to be treated as traitors and all their property confiscated. But it must be said that on the whole the village assemblies carried on their work in the Chola period without interference either by the central government or by any other agency. The *sabhās* continued to function in the Vijayanagar period also. Some of them consisted of a very large number of members, even 4,000 and were known as *mahāsabhā* or *mahājanas*.

Another body that functioned simultaneously with the *sabhā* was the *ūr*. It appears to have been prevalent only in the non-*brahmadeya* villages in which the proprietors of land were not exclusively Brāhmaṇas, though instances are not wanting to show that it functioned alongside of the *sabhā* either by itself or jointly with it according to the nature of the work to be done. The *ūr* probably consisted of all persons who belonged to the village including agriculturists and professionals, and there is no clear evidence to support the suggestion that 'it is not unlikely that all the conditions pertaining to membership in the brāhmaṇical *sabhās* prevailed except probably knowledge of the Vedas'. If there were two religious groups in a village it appears that there were two *ūrs* at the place probably one representing each of them. From such expressions as *ūrāga iśainda ūrōm* it may be assumed that all the people in the village made the *ūr*. What the *vāriyam* was in the *sabhā*, the *gaṇam*, also called *āḷumgaṇam* and *miyāḷumgaṇam ūrāḷumgaṇam* seems to have been in the *ūr*. It appears to have been a general executive committee of the severality village in which members belonging to different communities could serve. The *gaṇam* had under it officers like the *taṇḍal* (tax collector) and the *niyāyattār* (judge). Another type of territorial assembly was the *nāḍu* which functioned in the territorial unit known by the same name. It is not clearly known how it was constituted. The expression used to denote the *nādu* is *nāḍāga iśainda nāṭṭom* or *nāṭṭavarōm*, but obviously all the residents in a *nāḍu* could not have been its members. The larger Leiden grant seems to suggest that the villages were represented on the *nāḍu* on some principles.

The agricultural community in the country known as the Veḷḷāḷas formed themselves into a corporation called *citramēli* (*meli* in Tamil meaning ploughshare). They were also known as *bhūmiputtirar* and *nāttumakkal*, apparently on account of their dependence on land. Groups of villages under this organization were called *citramēli periyanāḍu*, while some individual villages had the suffix *citrameli-nallūr*, *citramēliviṭankar* and *citramēlichaturvedimangalam*. A number of professionals were attached to them like the goldsmiths, dancing girls, etc. Very probably the *citrameli* organization had control over the production and distribution of the produce from land. It was patronized by the rulers of the time and hence themselves were known by the name of *citramēli*.

Though the members of these different bodies acted jointly still it appears that none of the rural organizations was a corporate body having a single individual personality, but it constituted only a collective body. This is borne out by the evidence of two inscriptions. According to one of them the members of the *sabhā* of a village received an investment of 120 *kāśus* from a Varaguṇa Mahārāja and promised to measure out to the local temple ghee from the interest from the amount. If they failed to do so they undertook to pay individually and as a body double the quantity in default besides a fine to the royal officers. Likewise the *sabhā* of another village undertook to supply ghee to the temple in lieu of interest on money received. If it failed to do so, the Panmāhēśvaras of the temple could ask for a double sum of the dues besides a fine from the *sabhaiyār* both as a body and as individual persons.

The important functions discharged by these assemblies may now be reviewed in brief. The first among them was the control and regulation of landholdings, for as has been said above the members of the village community were a body of landholders either jointly or severally. It was equally interested in the creation and maintenance of facilities for irrigation. This is well borne out by the organization of the *ērivāriyam* or tank committee working under the *sabhā*. It had much to do with the taxation system in the country. Taxes were of two kinds, one levied and collected by the local organizations themselves apparently for being spent on local purposes and the other levied by the government. With regard to the former the local assembly which had absolute control over it had the right of granting remissions of them without any reference to the Government. This is by the assignment in perpetuity made by a *sabhā* to the local temple of the proceeds from a local cess on shops (*angāḍikūli*) in lieu of the interest on a loan which it had taken from the temple. In another case the *sabhā* of a *chaturvedimangalam* decided not to levy any kind of dues on the properties of the temple. Normally the village community could not remit the taxes payable by it to the government, for if it did so it would be a loser to the extent to which the remission was made, for the Government would not accept any reduction in the amount of tax payable to it by the assembly. Hence, if such remissions were made on particular pieces of land, the loss was sought to be made good by the distribution of the amount on other lands in the village. But the assembly at times made remission of taxes in consideration of money received (*kāśukoḷḷa iṛaiyili*) which was the capital sum and the tax money (*vilai poruḷ* and *iṛaiporuḷ*) and thereby made good their obligations to the central government. Such arrangements were made when for instance individuals made provision for charities by setting apart rent-free land and the lands so exempted from the payment of taxes were known as *ūr kiḷ iṟaiyili*. The *iṟaidravyam* was really in the nature of a trust fund for the periodical payment of the *iṟai* which the local bodies usually directed towards some productive capital expenditure, like the provision of irrigation facilities.

A natural right which it enjoyed related to the sale of lands of the people in the village who defaulted in the payment of the taxes. It could decide upon the nature of the land on which taxes were to be levied. Lands for which there was no claimants and hence were not cultivated escheated to the assembly and the taxes *kaḍamai* and *kuḍimai* levied on such lands by the government were paid by it. The *sabhā* could also sell or transfer its right of collection of taxes to a body like a temple. The village organization also influenced the taxation policy of the Government by suggesting what lands could be taxed and probably also what lands could not be taxed.

Apart from its rights relating to lands and their management and taxation it discharged certain other important, ministrant functions. One of them was the supervision of all charitable endowments in the village; and in some places the committee called the *dharma vāriyam* appears to have been in charge of it. On some occasions it exercised control over the administration of temples as well. It provided for the maintenance of peace in the area under its jurisdiction as also administered civil and criminal justice. It also co-operated with the government in the punishment of criminals as for instance by confiscating and selling in public lands that belonged to traitors. Besides it served as a deposit bank and took deposits from people on specified rates of interest. It also patronised scholars by granting them land to be enjoyed by them.

The assembly had under its employment a number of people each of whom was charged with a specific function associated with the administration of the village. Among them were the *karaṇattāṉ* or *kaṇakkaṉ* (accountant), and the *madhyastha* who noted down the proceedings of the *sabhā*. They were appointed either annually or for definite longer periods and remunerated by either gift of land or payment in kind like paddy.

The numerous village communities and their organization which flourished in south India and worked with great success from about 700 to 1400 showed signs of decay and disruption in the fifteenth and sixteenth centuries and finally disappeared by the seventeenth and eighteenth centuries. Though references to the local organizations like the *sabhā* and the *ūr* are found in the late Vijayanagar period these bodies appear to have lost by that time much of their vitality and capacity for initiative. The type of local administrative institutions in south India that attracted the attention of the Anglo-Indian administrators of the last century were entirely different from the type that obtained earlier in the area.

It is not however so easy to enumerate the factors that were responsible for the decline of the old organizations. Probably the most potent cause for it was the growing consciousness among the people of the individual's right as opposed to that of the community. Sir Henry Maine shrewedly observes:

> If I had to state what for the moment is the greatest change which has come over the people of India and the change which has added most seriously to the difficulty of governing them, I should say it was the growth on all sides of the sense of individual legal right; of a right not vested in the total group but in the particular number of it aggrieved, who has become conscious that he may call in the arm of the state to force his neighbours to obey the ascertained rule.

In the course of the fifteenth century the old community feeling among the group of people in a village which was really at the basis of the active functioning of the village assemblies in south India began to decline. Since much of the feeling was due to the joint ownership of land by the community it was its natural anxiety to prevent its own disintegration and hence made rules for preventing for instance the sale of lands to outsiders or the gift of land to women as *stridhana*. Local troubles and factions developed to such an extent that those who created such difficulties were branded as *grāmadrōhins* and *grāma kanṭakans*. But still the conflict between the individual and the community appears to have developed in the course of the fifteenth and sixteenth centuries resulting ultimately however in the success of the latter. The irksome interference of the royal officials in their activities and the bad influence exercised by them could also have partly contributed to the decline of the village assemblies. Again the local organizations failed to receive much encouragement at the hands of the Vijayanagar kings, the administration under whom was based partly on feudal and partly on military principles. The paternal solicitude of the earlier rulers was now replaced by the various forces which was spontaneously working in the village communities. Thus conditions in the country were not conducive to the active functioning of the old village republics. Further the evolution of the *āyagar* system, according to which a number of hereditary functionaries came to look after the administration of the villages and supplied the needs of the people in them brought about the gradual disintegration of the ancient village communities in south India.

Today we see attempts being made to revive active village life in the country with the help of the government. The work brizzles with many difficulties, particularly on account of the allurements of urban life and the disinclination of the people to go to the villages and settle down there. But even if villages are improved and conditions for leading good life are made available in them, the new village structure would be different from one that obtained in south India in the Chola times for, while the revived village life would be largely due to external pressure and government legislation, the old village life was based on a system of village organization which grew spontaneously and was an organism by itself having a living and growing history of its own. The strength, vitality and usefulness of the village organization for effective service were really so great that they should be the envy and the despair of many modern legislators.

NOTE

1. John William Kaye, *The Life and Correspondence of Lord Charles Metcalfe*, II, p. 191.

10

Indian Village Community according to the *Kṛṣiparāśara* and some other Contemporary Literary Sources

Guyla Wojtilla

The role of village communities in the social development of India can hardly be exaggerated. The history of this institution standing several thousand years is full of scantily explored periods. The descriptions done by European travellers in the seventeenth-nineteenth centuries represent an excellent source material, and, due to the historians, sociologists and ethnographers this material has been worked out in details: Marx (1954, 357-8); Engels (1957, 263); Maine (1890); Baden-Powell (1896); Altekar (1927); Heidrich (1959); Chattopadhyaya (1959, 186-9); Alaev (1972, 93-107) and Dumont (1966, 202-12).

If we take to the investigation of the period preceding the seventeenth century we are faced with serious difficulties on account of the strikingly poor material occurring in different sources: Alaev (1975, 23). The searching of data for that time is an urgent task especially if we remember the interesting remark made by Professor Ruben/Ruben (1967, 7): Ruben (1978/: 'Die Dorfgemeinde als solche war den in dischen Autoren... im allgemeinen so selbstverständlich, dass sie sie zu beschreiben nicht als notwendig empfanden.')

In the present paper we would illuminate some problems of the institution in the early medieval period/roughly AD 700-1200/ and for this purpose mostly use the *KṛṣiPa*, a work of the eleventh century: Gopal (1973, 168); Wojtilla (1975); Alaev (1975, 17).

First of all we must deal with the problem of the ownership of land. Although, the long and heavy discussions about the proportional distribution of the different kinds of ownership, state or royal, individual and communal respectively, never ceased to be animated in professional circles: Derrett (1959, 108-23); Gopal (1965, 1-31); Singh (1968, 96); Sircar (1969, 32) and Bongard-Levin (1973, 26), we are of the opinion that the communal rights on land might have been strong enough in the larger part of the total territory due to the existing system of village communities, consequently the role of individual feudal type of ownership has been overestimated by some scholars. This latter view directly leads to the presupposition of an early developed, strong feudal system: Medvedev (1973, 56-96): and the critical remarks done by Il'in (1973, 96-110) and my review going to be published in *JESHO* (1976), vol. XX, pt. II, pp. 247-8.

Our question can be approached by means of the passages referring to the king or kingdom in *KṛṣiPa.* Vers 123: 'The commencement of agricultural operations on Tuesday, Sunday and also on Saturday portends disturbance in the kingdom.' Vers 147: 'If the cultivator falls down /there/ may be trouble at the royal mansion/*rājamandire*/.' Vers 231: 'Enhancement of the honour ... the welfare of counsel, and government—may we have these constantly till a year is completed!' Vers 3: 'One taking to agriculture, can become the lord of the soil/*bhūpati.*' Vers 81: 'Agriculture, the cows, the science of trade, the women and the royal household get spoiled in a moment of lacking of supervision.' As we have learnt from the older tradition the kingdom was regarded as an enlarged household and the term *gṛhapati* might have been equally referred to the king and the head of *gṛha,* the head of the family: *Śat Br,* V, 3, 3, 3; Schlerath (1960, 49); Mylius (1974, 396).

All these data bear witness to the existence of a strong communal system facing to a central power symbolized by the king who might have been authorized to take his share from the total produce in the form of taxes. In this relation we cannot speak of an intermediate person, of a feudatory lord. A similar situation can be found in a satirical story of *Kathāsaritsāgara/KathāSaSāg,* X, 6, 213/ reporting the case of villagers who have eaten the buffalo of an outsider and take the common responsibility for the action before the king. Justly says Ruben/Ruben (1973, 15)/: 'Im

Widerspruch zwischen Dorfgemeinde und Staat trat der Grundwiderspruch der indischen Varienten der altorientalischen und in ähnlicher Weise der "feudalen" Gesellschaft mit all seinen Besonderheiten in Erscheinung.' Similarly, Reddy (1960, 182): 'Most of the conflicts in Indian history had for their objects the exercise of rights over the village, not the exercise of rights within the village.... The issue was always between armed overlords and not between lords and peasants.' The relevant chapter of the book *History and Culture of the Indian People/HCIP*, V, 515/expresses the opinion that the rural economy was centered in the communities of peasant-proprietors in the eleventh-twelfth centuries.

A second feature of village community is the interpenetration of cultivation of land and craftsmanship as well as the bottleneck of trade and money circulation: The *KṛṣiPa* keeps silent about these questions. Among the sources of the early medieval period there are copius references to village craftsmen: *KathāSaSāg* / numerous tales/; *HarṣaC*, 68-9; *ŚukSa*, 9; *PrabaCi*, pp. 3, 6, 57, 63 and so on. All the sources suggest the low position of craftsmen in the community and this situation was pervailing even in the last century: Baines 1912, 58); Kolontaev (1968, 6). The *HarṣaC* 68 speaks of bartering carried out by village women.

The third feature of these units was their isolated position, namely the settlements were mostly surrounded with thick forests. However, *KṛṣiPa* does not refer directly to such position, the great variety of trees occurring in different contexts in the work permit to suppose of large territories covered with forest. A series of other sources unanimously praises this type of villages which the kings often meet during their visitings in the country: *HarṣaC*, 68-9; *DaśKuC*, 157, 197; *SimāDvā* Part VI/southern recension;/ *Gaud*, 607, etc. This aspect is underlined by Ruben (1973, 33), too. In accordance with him we consider this as the main difference between village communities of the Near East and India and this peculiarity may be one of the reasons for the relative stagnation of social development in India since the isolation might serve the preservation of the archaic structure of social units.

A problem of great importance is the existence of castes or social groups in the community. In spite of the epigraphical evidence our knowledge of the inner structure of communities is insufficient: Niyogi (1962, 18-19); Schetelich (1972, 237); Alaev (1973, 118). The question arises: what can the *KṛṣiPa* tell us about castes or social groups? S. Ch Banerji the coeditor of *KṛṣiPa* is of the opinion that the 'purely secular nature of the work' does not afford any scope for the inclusion of the duties of castes: Banerji (1955, 4). L. Gopal in his brilliant study on the date of *KṛṣiPa* emphasized the homogeneous approach of different castes to agriculture as profession, and held it a peculiarity of the works attributed to Parāśara: Gopal (1973, 165-7).

Having analysed the work we easily recognise that the parts of the text accounting festivities arranged on the greatest events of the agricultural year in order to secure the crops show a strong attachment to communal customs. We may find the remains of the archaic features of village community.

There is the festival of cows, *KṛṣiPa*, 100-4:

Cowherds, adorned with ornaments, besmearing the body with saffron and sandalpaste, decorating the cows with cloths and so on, and raising the club in the hand, should, for averting evil to cows, take the chief bull round the village with vocal and instrumental music. Then, accompanied by cultivators, one should, on the first day of *Kārtika*, apply oil mixed with turmeric, over the bodies of cows. On that day cause a piece of hot iron to be put on the bodies of cows, and then cut off/a portion of their tails, hairs and ears. By this/practice/ the entire bovine class doubtlessly becomes healthy, in the cultivators house and free from various diseases for a year.

After sowing the cultivator prays for the welfare and happiness of his farmer-fellows too, and finally they have a common meal with delicious dishes, ghee and *pāyasa* in the field and by this the agriculture becomes free from impediments: *KṛṣiPa*, 177-82. Common meals are mentioned also in other sources: *KathāSaSāg*, X, 6, 213; *ŚukSa*, 46: *Bharat*, 2; *SamaMā*, II,82; *GāSaptaSa*, VII, 3, etc. Regarding the strict taboos regulating meals among people of different castes this custom definitely points to communal traditions.

This idea gets a solid strong statement in the description of Pusyayātrā festival, a festival of hoary antiquity, which is to be carried out.before the harvest in the month Pausa: *KṛṣiPa*, 221-36. The main events are as follows:

Then people should together perform Pusyayātrā near the field, on an auspicious day in Pausa when the paddy is not/ yet/ harvested. Feed all men in due order starting with the old, with *pāyasa* after nicely presenting it on banana-leaves with curries, fish, meat, vegetarian dishes and also with palatable courses/prepared/ with hingu and pepper along with curd, milk, ghee, beverages, various fruits, roots and plenty of sweetmeats and cakes. Then having rinsed of hands and faces there, besmear one another with sandal-paste, *catuhśama* and perfumed oil. Then, having put on new clothes, they should/feed one another with nice fragrant betel-leaves perfumed with camphor. Being adorned with flowers, and saluted Lord of Sacī, perform great merriments there with music, both vocal and instrumental, and dance. Then all, being delighted, should look at the sun, and with folded hands, read the incantation consisting of four verses.

Parāśara gives a wide range of hints as to the people being proud of wealth and not taking part on the Pusyayātrā asking: 'whence is happiness to them in that year'? To the other people he promises the removal of obstacles and the increase of crops: *KṛṣiPa*, 236, 239.

There is only one indication to assign to a particular grade in the community. *KṛṣiPa*, 222 reads: 'feed all men in due order starting with the old'. We are told by other sources that the elders were the leading or influential persons of the traditional community who enjoyed prestige on account of age, experience, learning or wealth: *ŚukSa*, 44, 45, 46; *KathaSaSag*, X, 6, 213. The word *vrddha* used by Parāśara definitely signifies a title as it is seen in *DaśKuC*, 120: *pauravrddha*, and it is an official name of archaic type. A review of the passages concerning cultivators in *KṛṣiPa* shows that *vrddha* or *vrddha's* must belong to a larger group of peoples called *grhin* and *gṛhamedhin*. As pointed out in a study written about the role of *gṛhapatī-grhin* in *DaśKuC* as well as in a paper read in Moscow 1976: Wojtilla (1973 and 1976) these terms include the following aspects: *grhin* or *gṛhapati* is the head of the family, a tenant-holder, free authorized, respectful member of the community. He is either the head of the community/village or city/ or a larger district *janapada*, etc.: *DaśKuC*, 120, 157. They possess the *gṛha*, a socio-economic unit which fairly may be rendered for 'living pattern' consisting of the residential and farm buildings, garden and a piece of land outside the residential area. They are mentioned in *KṛṣiPa* 126, 145 as *pati* and *prabhu*. However, the exact meaning of this term was subjected to change in different ages the people belonging to this group and called *gṛhapati*, *gahapati*, *gehapati or kuṭumbin* formed a ruling class in the community all along Indian history before the end of the last century: Schlerath (1960, 49); Mylius (1974, 396); Fick (1920, 253);

Thapar (1973, 63, etc.). The *KṛṣiPa* was addressed to this class: Wojtilla (1976). They had the Sanskrit language and paid interest for the practical aspects of agriculture, too: Gopal (1963/64, 16). We hear practically nothing of lower strata in *KṛṣiPa* and in spite of the argumentation of Alaev (1975, 25) we do not think of a relation between landholder and farmworkers in *KṛṣiPa,* 126. It is true that the village society had its stratification in the early medieval period: *KathāSaSāg,* X, 61, 117; *gṛhasthasya bhṛtyaḥ,* X, 61, 117: householder sends his servant to the garden, X, 61, 113: a villager goes to the town to get wage-work; *KalāVi,* IX, 53: that the house-servant or hired labourer/ *gṛhadāsa*/being talkative is to be expelled: *ŚukSa,* 47 illustrates the hired work; there are indications of lower position within the joint family, too: *DaśkuC,* 158 and we have to take into account a continuous, however, slow degradation even of the *gṛhapati* class: *AvadāKaLa,* XVII, 14; *SubhāRaK,* 1310, 1317; *VairāS,* 22; Gaud 598; Sharma (1965, 122ff); for the epigraphical evidence: Alaev (1975, 27).

The tendencies to destroy the traditional frames are visible also in the change of the social position of the elders. In our period the hereditary headmen were often replaced with officials appointed by the king or government: Niyogi (1959, 159), 'later... *grāma-vrddhas* come to be known as *mahattaras,* and the headman of the village, probably as *mahattama.* The former was not appointed by the king, probably elected by the villagers or village-elders'. Anyhow this practice was going on in a great number of village settlements: *DasKuC,* 120; *Dvyāśraká,* III, 2; *BrPārāSm* II, p. 113; *SubhāRaK,* 1175, etc. Choudhary (1971, 219) places this change of position in the ninth century AD.

Summarily we may ascertain that the ancient system of village communities which undoubtedly was a predominant factor in the social development of India had preserved a series of archaic features till the upper limit of the early medieval period. These ancient institutions are rather visible in *KṛṣiPa* and the works attributed to Parāśara. The contemporary literary sources make it possible to get a slight knowledge of the modifications of that system, too. At the present stage of researches we can draw only a provisional picture of village communities or of the proportional division of villages of different kinds: communities, royal lands, villages under individual rights or belonging to religious institutions. We may refer only to the main tendency of development.

This is the very slow dissolution of the archaic communities or archaic features constantly existing in the villages and the limited increases of the institutions of feudal type. Additionally the development was unequal in the different parts of the huge Indian subcontinent.

The elaboration of the details of this specially Indian social development mostly relies on the deeper investigation of the village communities in all ages. To do this the first task is to engage in a correct analysis of the sources, without which the conclusions drawn would stand on very shaky grounds: Alaev (1976).

ABBREVIATIONS

AvadāKala: Avadānakalpalatā of Ksemendra. Ed. by P.L.Vaidya, Darbhanga, 1959, Buddhist Text Series.

Bharat: Bharatakadvātrmśka. Hrsg. von J. Hertel, Leipzig, 1922.

BrParāSṃ: Bṛhatparāśarasmṛti, in: *Dharmashastrasmgraha*, II. Ed. by Jibananda Vidyasagara, Calcutta, 1876.

DaśKuC: The Daśakumāracarita of Dandin. Ed. by M.R. Kale, Delhi-Varanasi-Patna, 1966.

DvyāśraKa: Dvyāśrayakāvya of Hemacandra. Ed. by A.V. Kathvate, Vols. I-II, Bombay, 1915-21.

GāSaptaSa: The Prākrit *Gāthā -Saptaśatī*. Compiled by Śātavāhmana king Hāla. Ed by R. Basak, Calcutta, 1971, Bibliotheca Indica.

Gaud: Gaūdavaho of Vākpatirāja. Ed. by N.G. Suru, Ahmedabad, 1975. Prākrit Text Society Series.

HarsaC: The *Harsacarita of Bānabhatta*. Ed. by P.V. Kane, Delhi-Varanasi-Patna, 1965.

KalāVi: Kalāvilāsa of Ksemendra: in: Kāvyāmāla I, pp. 34-79, Bombay, N.S.P.

KathāSaSāg: Kathāsaritsāgara. Ed. by Jagadislal Sastri, Delhi-Varanasi-Patna, 1970.

KṛṣiPa: Kṛṣi Parāśara. Ed. by G.P. Majumdar and S. Ch. Banerji, Calcutta, 1960, Bibliotheca Indica.

PrabaCi: Prabandhacintāmani of Merutuṅga. Ed. by Jinavijaya Muni, Santiniketana, 1933.

SamaMā: Samayamātṛkā of Ksemendra. Ed. by R.S. Tripathi, Varanasi, 1967.

Śat Br: The *Śatapathabrāhmana*. Ed. by A. Weber, Berlin-London, 1855.

SimāDvā: Simhāsanadvātrṃśikā or the Vikrama's Adventures. Ed. by F. Edgerton, Cambridge Mass, 1926, HOS.

SubhāRak: The *Subhāṣitaratnakoṣa*. Compiled by Vidyākara. Ed. by D.D. Kosambi and V.V. Gokhale, Cambridge Mass, 1957, HOS.

ŚukSa: Śukasaptati. Textus ornatior. Hrsg. von R. Schmidt. ABAW I. cl. 21 (1901) 2, Abt. München, 1898.
VairāŚ: The Nīti and Vairāgya Śatakas of Bhartrhari. Ed. by M.R. Kale, Delhi-Varanasi-Patna, 1971.

SECONDARY LITERATURE

L.B. Alaev, 1972: Indiyskaya obstsina v trudah sovetskih issledovately, in: *Problemi Indii, stran srednego vostoka,* red, G.G. Kotovsky, Moskva, Russian, pp. 93-107.
L.B. Alaev, 1973: O haraktere obstsestvennogo stroya srednevekovoy indii in: *Otserki ekonomitseskoy i sotzial'noy istorii Indii,* Moskva, Russian, pp. 110-129.
L.B. Alaev, 1975: Harakter proizvoditel'nih sil v sel'skom hozyaystve indii v dokolonialnoy period in: *Sdvigi v proizvoditel'nih silah sel'skogo hozyaystva stran Yuś noy Azii,* Moskva, Russian, pp. 8-35.
L.B. Alaev, 1976: Etapi evolyutzii indiyskoy sel'skoy obstsini v drevmosti i srednie veka. Paper read at the Second Allunion Conference of Soviet Indologists, Moscow, January, 1976, Russian.
A.S. Altekar, 1927: *A History of Village Communities in Western India,* Oxford.
B.H. Baden-Powell, 1896: *The Indian Village Community,* London-New York.
A. Baines, 1912: *Ethnography,* Strassburg, GIAPA II, 5.
S.Ch. Banerji, 1955: *Krsī-Parāśara,* a Work on Agriculture, *ABORI* XXXVI, pp. 1-27.
G.M. Bongard-Levin, 1973: K probleme zemel'noy sobstvennosti v drevney Indii, *VDI* 1973, 2, pp. 1-26, Russian.
D.P. Chattopadhyaya, 1959: *Lokāyatta: A Study in Ancient Indian Materialism,* New Delhi.
A.K. Choudhary, 1971: *Early Medieval Village in North-Eastern India,* Calcutta.
J. Duncan, M. Derrett, 1959: Bhū-bharana, bhū-pālana, bhū-bhojana: an Indian Conundrum, *BSOAS* XXII, pp. 108-23.
L. Dumont, 1966: *Homo Hierarchicus. Essai sur le systeme des castes,* Paris.
F. Engels, 1957: *Antidühring,* Moscow.
R. Fick, 1920: *The Social Organization in North-East India in Buddha's Time,* Calcutta.
L. Gopal, 1963/64: Technique of Agriculture in Early Medieval India. *University of Allahabad Studies,* Ancient History Section, pp. 1-34.
L. Gopal, 1965: *The Economic Life in Northern India, Circa AD 700-1200,* Delhi-Varanasi-Patna.
L. Gopal, 1973: The Date of *Kṛṣi-Parāśara. JIH Golden Jubilee Volume,* pp. 151-168.
J. Heidrich, 1959: Gemeindeorganization und Sozialordnung im indischen Dorf. Berlin, unpublished diss.

G.F. Il'in, 1973: O feodal'nih otnosenijah v drevnej Indii, in: *Otserki ekonomitsteskoy* . . . , pp. 96-110, Russian.

A.M. Kolontaev, 1968: *Razlos'enie sel'skogo remesla . . . v Indii.* Moskva, Russian.

H.S. Maine, 1890: *Village Communities in East and West,* London.

K. Marx, 1954: *Capital,* I. Moscow.

E.M. Medvedev, 1973: Genezis feodal'noj formatzii v Indii. in: *Otserki ekonomitseskoy* . . . , pp. 56-96, Russian.

K. Mylius, 1974: Die gesellschaftliche Entwicklung Indiens in jungvedischer Zeit nach den Sanskritquellen, IV, Die Institutionen des gesellschafthchen Überbaus, *EAZ* 15, pp. 385-432.

R. Niyogi, 1959: *The History of the Gāhadavāla Dynasty,* Calcutta.

P. Niyogi, 1962: *Contributions to the Economic History of Northern India from the tenth to the twelfth century A.D.*, Calcutta.

P. R. Reddy, 1960: Thoughts on Indian Feudalism, *JIH,* 38.

W. Ruben, 1967: *Die gesellschaftliche Entwicklung im alten Indien,* ed. I. Die Entwicklung der Produktionsverhaltnisse. Berlin.

W. Ruben, 1973: *Die gesellschaftliche Entwicklung im alten Indien*, ed. VI. Die Entwicklung der Gangesgesellschaft, Berlin.

W. Ruben, 1978: W. Ruben, Kulturgeschichte Indiens. Ein Versuch der Darstellung ihrer Entwicklung, Berlin, 1978

M. Schetelich, 1972: Zur Dorfgemeinde in Indien, *EAZ* 13, pp. 237-46.

B. Schlerath, 1960: *Das Konigtum im Rig- und Atharvaveda*, Wiesbāden.

R.S. Sharma, 1965: *Indian Feudalism: c. 300-1200,* Calcutta.

R.C.P. Singh, 1968: *Kingship in Northern India*, Delhi-Varanasi-Patna.

D.C. Sircar, 1969: *Landlordism and Tenancy in Ancient and Medieval India,* Lucknow.

R. Thapar, 1973: *Aśoka and the Decline of the Mauryas*, Delhi

G. Wojtilla, 1973: Ket tisztsegnev a Daśakumāracaritaban. Two official titles in *Daśakumāracarita, AT,* XX, 1, pp. 54-7, Hungarian and its Hindi version in: *Purākalpa,* Benares, 1974, pp. 25-30.

G. Wojtilla, 1975: *Kṛṣi-Parāśara.* Paper presented at the International Sanskrit Conference, Berlin, March 1975. In press.

G. Wojtilla, 1976: Which Class of People Was *the Kṛṣi-Parāśara* addressed to? Paper read at the Second Allunion Conference of Soviet Indologists, Moscow, January, 1976.

SECTION III

Agrarian Change, Structure of Rural Society and Rural Unrest

11

The Peasant in Indian History

Irfan Habib

The momentous events of this century have led to a worldwide recognition that peasants, who constitute the largest single segment of mankind, may have a special part to play in shaping our destinies. In interpreting the historical qualities of the peasantry, Chayanov and Mao Tse-tung offer two widely different, even opposite outlooks. Yet both of them have inspired renewed explorations into the past of the peasantry with a view to discovering its capacities of resistance and change.

In India an endeavour began for reconstructing the history of the peasants as a pre-condition for identifying the main historical periods and processes: D.D. Kosambi and R.S. Sharma, together with Daniel Thorner, brought the peasants into the study of Indian history for the first time. In the following address the debt to these and other scholars for knowledge as well as inspiration would be obvious.

A rigorous definition of the peasant is desirable, though it is naturally elusive. I take the peasant to mean a person who undertakes agriculture on his own, working with his own implements and using the labour of his family. This definition, which would be acceptable to Marxists as well as to Chayanov insofar as it goes, omits any consideration of the extent of use of hired labour and the control over land. The moment these are considered, the peasants seem to fall apart into different strata.

* Only a part of the Presidential Address delivered at the Kurukshetra session of the Indian History Congress (1982) has been reproduced here. The medieval section, though equally significant and thought-provoking, has been omitted because the focus of this volume is on early and early medieval India.

Thus, for example, the Marxists would distinguish the rich peasant (with extensive use of hired labour), the middle peasant (mainly using family-labour) and the poor peasant (with land insufficient to absorb the whole of family labour). But this distinction is accompanied by yet another, based on property relations. We can then recognize the peasant-proprietor; the peasant with some claim to permanent or long-term occupancy; and the seasonal sharecropper, as separate categories. These do not (and need not) directly coincide with the three mentioned earlier, though in practice many poor peasants, and very few rich peasants, are sharecroppers. There is then the distinction by 'wealth' alone: Ownership of more expensive and productive devices, better cattle, more fertile land. This again may partly overlap the other classifications. The 'stratification' that we would be meeting with can be viewed in the context of all these three criteria; and it will be noticed that I would be using evidence of any of the three kinds of classifications to establish differentiation within the peasantry.

While landless labourers are not peasants, they form with the peasants the working agricultural population; and their history too (which in many ways has been different from that of the peasants) remains for me a part of peasant history.

Finally, any study of the peasants must involve an enquiry into how they pay rent or surrender their surplus. This necessitates the shifting of the focus, from time to time, from the exploited to the exploiters. But without seeing the peasants in their actual relation with the exploiting classes there can be no peasant history; the relationship is crucial.

THE ORIGINS: THE INDUS BASIN

The stage at which peasants originate within a society must naturally arrive only after the pursuit of agriculture is established as a major provider of food. A family can then spend the larger part of its labour-time on the cultivation of plants and the harvesting of the seed. In this process not only do the food-gatherers (mainly hunters) turn into producers; the monogamistic family itself evolves as a basic unit of social organization.

When plant seeds are gathered in the wild, there is of course no agriculture. Mesolithic communities like those of Chopani Mando (in the valley of the Belan, a tributary of the Son) among the Vindhyan foothills, who consumed wild rice, belong to the pre-history of agriculture. Domesticated plants came with the Neolithic Revolution; and two zones where crops were raised have been identified within the India of the pre-1947 frontiers. The first is in the Belan valley itself (Koldihwa and Mahagara) where grains of cultivated rice and bones of domesticated 'cattle' and 'sheep-goat' have been found within the period 6500 to 4500 BC. The second zone is that of the Kachhi plain south of the Bolan Pass—an arid area but experiencing seasonal floods from hill torrents. Here at Mehrgarh (sixth to third millennium BC) have been found remains of barley (two-row as well as six-row) and wheat of three varieties (corn-wheat, emmer and bread-wheat). The lowest levels give bones of wild animals only; but the top two metres yield those of domestic cattle, sheep and goats.[1]

The domestication of plants and, possibly later that of cattle, marked a notable stage in human progress; but the full-blooded agricultural revolution was yet to come; the draught potential of cattle was still unexploited, and there was no trace of the plough, which alone could assure a substantial seed: yield ratio. Moreover, given the paucity of the crops cultivated, there could only be one cropping season, 'kharif' in the Belan valley and 'rabi' in the Kachhi plain. The cultivated tracts were in any case very restricted, since there were no means of clearing the dense forests and making land there fit for cultivation. It is difficult to conjecture what the internal structure of these crop-raising communities was like; cultivation might still be a continuation of food-gathering with women as the 'principals', as Gordon Childe had thought.[2] Men had to hunt and, later on, also to tend cattle for meat and milk. The 'sexual' division of labour was not sufficient to produce a surplus which could create any class-divisions or even occupational stratification. In a much more advanced hoe-using neolithic community of Anatolia (sixth millennium BC) W.A. Fairservis, Jr., finds evidence of social 'equalitarianism',[3] this should have been even more true of the Indian communities.

In India the agricultural revolution and the first urban revolution in fact coincide in the Indus (Harappan) civilization, which calibrated carbon dating now places within 2600-1800 BC.[4] The fabric of Indus agriculture rested undoubtedly on plough cultivation. Since the ox had already been converted into a draught animal for pulling the bullock cart, the case for the Indus people using a plough should have been an unanswerable one in spite of Kosambi's strong objection.[5] The discovery of the furrows of a 'ploughed field' at Kalibangan has now met the doubts over the absence of any positive evidence.[6] The plough explains the really large extent of Indus agriculture, covering the north-west plains and extending into Gujarat. The Indus people raised wheat and barley (six-row), both of standard modern Indian varieties; in the Indus sites in Gujarat, rice has been found along with the bajra millet. The field pea represents pulses; and sesamum and a species of brassica, the oilseeds.[7] The most remarkable of the Indus crops is cotton which ushers in the 'industrial' crops.[8] The multiplicity of crops shows that the two-harvest system was now firmly established; agriculture would henceforth be a full-time occupation; and the presence of a peasantry as a social class must therefore be inferred.

But the very moment of the emergence of a peasantry is apparently also that of the emergence of a differentiated society. There seems to be no basis for the belief that there could ever have been a pure peasant society for any period, long or short, such as Burton Stein hypothesizes for south India in another chronological epoch.[9] Full-fledged agriculture meant creation of surplus enough to feed a certain number of food producers. In the arid zone in which agriculture must of need spread first, dykes and embankments to hold and divert flood waters were a pre-requisite; and these demand a certain amount of social and administrative organization—the bed-rock of Marx's Oriental Despotism.[10] Finally, the control over bronze (alloy of copper and tin), an expensive metal, could give a small town-based class an effective sway over a mass of stone-tool using peasantry.[11] Cementing the structure created by these material circumstances was a religion of gods, superstitions and priests, which apparently bound the rulers and ruled alike in an awesome dread of change, giving to the Indus culture its characteristic dull uniformity in geographical terms as well as over time.[12]

The Indus culture then not only gave India its first cities in Harappa and Mohenjodaro, but also its first peasantry. The towns were to disappear with the fall of that culture; but what of the peasants? A 'flood' theory can explain the abandonment of a town or two; it cannot surely postulate the submergence of whole agricultural communities. There has therefore not been any valid or persuasive alternative to the hypothesis first boldly set forth by Wheeler in 1947, which was reinforced by Kosambi in 1956 through a brilliant interpretation of the Rigvedic hymns.[13] This saw the Aryans as directly succeeding the Indus culture, whose authors they destroyed or subjugated.[14]

The success of the Aryans is ascribed to the possession of the horse, and, still more, the horse-drawn chariot.[15] Since compared with all previous armour and weaponry the chariot was an immensely expensive machine, its possession implied a pre-existing aristocracy;[16] it is, therefore, difficult to envision an early egalitarian stage within the Rigvedic society as has sometimes been suggested.[17]

The state of agriculture glimpsed through the *Rigveda* shows the continuance of the ox-drawn plough (*sīra*).[18] The technology was still chalcolithic and the Rigvedic *ayasa* is generally thought to mean copper, not iron. Barley (*yava*) is the chief foodgrain; but rice seems to have begun to be cultivated in the upper Indus basin ('Saptasindhavah') so that the two-crop annual cycle survived in a new form. But wheat, cotton and other crops of the Indus culture are not mentioned.[19] Moreover, the Aryans seem to have regarded with scorn the dyke based agriculture of their enemies: Indra would force open the dams that imprisoned the waters.[20] It is possible that the change in agricultural conditions was linked to the disappearance of the cities with their markets and the supplanting of one structure of control by a completely different one. Pastoralism seems to have become more important, for the Aryans coveted wealth chiefly in the form of cows, horses and camels, along with slaves.[21]

Whatever the mechanism of control, the surplus still came from the peasants. These formed the mass of the community, the *viś*, for the words for 'cultivators', *kriști* and *charsani*, were often employed for the Aryan folk as a whole.[22] The peasants were masters of their own fields (*kșetrapati*).[23] But such 'free' peasants belonged to the superior tribes: a larger population would seem to have comprised the subjugated *dasyu* communities compelled to part with grain and kine.[24] In the lowest levels were the *dāsas* working like 'cattle', presumably on the field, or tending the herds, for their masters.[25] At the apex were the aristocracy (*rājanyas*) proudly driving in their chariots with Indra as their model, and the priests (*brāhmaṇas*) who presided over animal sacrifices and a complex ritual. A celebrated hymn in Book x of the *Rigveda* offers a picture of this class-divided society whose creation the hymn seeks to ascribe to divinity. However simplified, the *varṇa* scheme of the hymn seems to reflect faithfully the deep division of the peasantry into its free *viś* and the servile *dasyus*, who, transmuted as Vaiśyas and Sūdras, from respectively the third and fourth *varṇas*.

THE LONG TRANSITION: THE GANGETIC BASIN

The next stage in the history of the Indian peasantry is dominated by the clearing of extensive tracts in the Gangetic basin. It was undoubtedly a long and tortuous process, with its countless unrecorded heroisms and tragedies; and it could not have taken place without substantial alterations in the mode of social organization.

Down to 2000 BC or thereabouts, agriculture was mainly confined to the Indus basin and its periphery, hardly ever venturing beyond the 30-inch isohyet. The area of the heaviest concentration of rural population in India today, the Gangetic basin, was probably then as densely forested as was the Amazon basin not long ago. But with the appearance of copper and the shafted axe, present in a late stratum at Mohenjodaro,[26] the first clearings could begin. These started naturally enough from the drier or western side. The 'Copper Hoard' people, using ochre-coloured pottery (OCP), first established a few scattered settlements in the Doab and Rohilkhand during the earlier half of the second millennium.[27] The succeeding 'Black and Red Ware' (B & R) culture continued with the copper and stone industry; the settlements now extended, though in the same sparse fashion, up to western Bihar. These were agricultural communities which, like the Rigvedic Aryans, raised rice and barley, but not wheat. Two pulses, gram and khesari, also appear, along with black gram; and an unpublished identification would put even cotton among the OCP-level crops.[28]

These settlements could not, however, multiply until the coming of iron, or rather the coming of the metallurgy which can produce iron tools with steeled edges.[29] Iron being cheaper than copper, iron tools tend to be substituted for bronze as well as stone blades. Moreover, with iron, tools in other materials (such as bone arrowheads) too can be made more easily. The impact of iron is therefore immediately reflected in the archaeological record.

The archaeologists have gradually been pressing back the date of the introduction of iron; on the present evidence, it is likely that its arrival in the upper Gangetic basin took place around 1000 BC near the beginning of the Painted Grey Ware (PGW) culture (*c.* 1100-500 BC).[30] The archaeological evidence has not been precisely reconciled with the literary evidence; but it is practically certain that the PGW represents an 'Aryan' phase, for iron already begins to be mentioned in the late Vedic texts.[31]

In its immediate impact iron seems to have caused a rapid spread of the clearings, as can be established by comparing the large number of PGW and contemporaneous B & R settlements with those of the preceding OCP and B & R cultures over a much longer time-span.[32] Conditions conducive to the raising of wheat reappear; and new pulses and lentils are added to the crop-list.[33]

Agricultural conditions in the Gangetic basin were vastly different from those of the Indus culture. Floodlands and dykes were of only marginal significance here. The bounty of the monsoon liberated the peasant from those narrow strips to which alone the flood gave fresh doses of moisture and silt. In the Gangetic plains the yield would improve if after some years of cultivation one shifted one's field anew to virgin land (claimed from the forest). The 'jhum' method required collective action by groups living in small migratory hamlets; and this was basis enough for the formation of tribes like the Sākyas, who were pre-eminently peasants.[34] 'Free men farmers', possibly answering to the free peasants of the *Rigveda*, are also encountered in the Jātakas.[35]

Conditions of forest clearance also necessitated at the same time a form of non-peasant agriculture. In the freshly cleared ground, full of roots and hard soil (now difficult even to trace owing to centuries of ploughing), a very heavy plough would be needed; it would be heavier still if it was armed with stone, instead of an iron tip. This makes intelligible the reference in the late-Vedic and *Brāhmaṇa* literature to ploughs drawn by six, eight or even twelve oxen.[36] Such ploughs imply masters working with servile labourers. Keith, indeed, stated his impression that during this period, 'for the peasant working on his own field was being substituted by the land-owner cultivating his estate by means of slaves'.[37] The impression is corroborated by the testimony of the Jātakas, where we frequently meet 'big Brāhmaṇa landowners who have their fields cultivated by their slaves or day labourers'; also 'cattle magnates' owning enormous herds (e.g. 30000 heads) with numerous slaves and hirelings (1,250 under one magnate).[38] The evidence closes with Kauṭilya's *Arthaśāstra*, where there are references to slaves and hired workmen of apparently large private landowners.[39] The same text introduces us even more prominently to the ruler's personal demesne, the *sitā* lands, in part cultivated by slaves, wage-earners and convicts, under the supervision of officials, and in part leased to sharecroppers (*ardhasītikas*) and others.[40]

The Gangetic forests also brought in a new element of population which in the Indus basin could not have been very significant—the hunting folk. As the agricultural communities initially penetrated the Gangetic basin, the forests became accessible to the hunting tribes. Copper and, later on, iron-fashioned tools would make hunting more efficient; in the later levels at the PGW sites, iron spear-heads and arrow-heads become common.[41] On the other hand, the expanding populations of the agricultural settlements would provide markets for animals skins, other forest produce, and even meat.[42] In return the hunters could supplement their own forest diet with foodgrains. It is possible then to suggest that all around settled communities and the food-gathering population kept on expanding, and so the Nāgas, Kolis and Nisādas would flourish, and their influence would even begin to permeate the fringes of late Vedic ritual.[43] They were important enough even by the end of the fourth century BC to form with the cattle-herders the third of the seven Indian castes described by Megasthenes, the peasants comprising the second.[44]

By the middle of the first millennium BC the long period of agricultural penetration eastward had created a complex social formation marked by peasant communities created within tribes, interspersed with settlements of servile or semi-servile labourers working under landowning masters, while hunting groups enjoyed a fresh though passing economic importance. These varied social forms probably explain the rather heterogeneous nature of the emerging polities of the *mahājanapadas*, with the rulers' powers strongly circumscribed by powerful aristocracies and by the rising pretensions of the Brāhmaṇa priesthood already in control over large areas of land.[45] The king was called 'the devourer of peasants', since it was the peasants alone, and not the great landowners or the Brāhmaṇas, who paid him the levy in grain.[46]

FORMATION OF THE CASTE PEASANTRY

The conditions I have outlined in the preceding section ultimately proved to be those of a transition—a long transition certainly, but one leading ultimately to a quite different structure of social and economic relations. It seems to me that from around *c.* 500 BC there was an immense acceleration in the process of change for almost five hundred years, which universalized peasant production and also simultaneously created the caste-divided peasantry.

For the universalization of peasant farming, we can perhaps suggest two factors as of crucial importance. The first is the extensive use of iron. As time passed the extraction of the metal increased in volume and the resulting cheapness diversified and generalized its use. Quantity influenced quality. In time iron tools would become directly available to the peasant, and that would be the turning point. The first recorded reference to the plough containing the 'iron point' is apparently in the *Manusmriti* (x, 84), which may be of as early a date as 200 BC, but is probably to be put a little later.[47] But iron 'ploughshares' have been found with the Northern Black Polished Ware (NBPW), beginning *c.* 500 BC.[48] For the effect of this wider use of iron one may invoke Gordon Childe's perceptive observation that 'cheap iron *democratized* agriculture'. 'Any peasant' could now 'afford an iron axe to clear fresh land for himself and iron ploughshares wherewith to break stony ground'.[49]

The other factor which must have contributed to the spread of peasant agriculture was the growing multiplicity of crops. Sugarcane is mentioned in the *Atharva-veda*, cotton and indigo in the Jātakas.[50] Quite a long list could be prepared of the crops noticed in the Indian and Greek sources before the birth of Christ.[51] The growth of the urban markets resulting from the rise of towns from the sixth century BC onwards,[52] was bound to induce an extension in cultivation of market and industrial crops. There were new methods of cultivation too, notably, rice-transplantation by which Kosambi explains a passage in the *Arthaśāstra*.[53] These developments required more intensive and skilled labour, and called for decisions to be made closely on the basis of knowledge of both soil and crop. Extensive agriculture controlled by 'magnates' thus must have tended to become obsolete and competitively unrewarding, since only peasant farming could possess the capacities that were now in demand.

Once the greater efficiency of peasant agriculture was established, pressures for surplus-extraction, whether in the form of tax or 'rent', would reinforce its expansion. Already, as we have seen, the peasants were the basic tax-payers; and the kingdoms of the fifth and fourth centuries BC and, finally, the Mauryan Empire, probably greatly intensified the drive for tax-revenue and so sought to settle more peasants. According to Megasthenes, the peasants paid to the king a 'land-tribute' as well as a fourth of the crop (by another version, 3/4ths).[54] Kauṭilya indeed stressed that settlements in the royal lands should consist overwhelmingly of *śūdra-karṣakas* (Śūdra cultivators/peasants) and other lower classes, being more amenable to exploitation.[55] The large landholders with their own cattle and labourers as also the ruler's labour-tilled lands, significant still in the *Arthaśāstra*, could not easily survive the new conditions. Even where ownership continued with the 'lord' or master (*svāmin*), it was obviously becoming more convenient for him to lease out the land to *karṣakas* rather than till it under his own direct management.[56] There would certainly remain some exceptions: even after the Mauryan period, we encounter in Patañjali (second century BC) a landholder supervising ploughing by five labourers.[57] The modest scale may be noted.

A social change accompanied this 'democratization' of agriculture. The tribes (*janapadas*) disintegrated to be replaced by *jātis* (castes). In the Buddha's time, we begin to hear of *jātis*, 'excellent as well as low'; but the tribe and *jāti* were still only loosely differentiated; the Buddha could be said to belong to the Sākya *jāti* where it surely enough means the tribe.[58] Endogamy characterized tribal organization, a feature which was to be transmitted in such rigorous form to the *jātis*.[59] Megasthenes's descriptions of the seven castes, where the 'husbandmen' form a separate caste by themselves, would seem to be the outcome of a genuine confusion caused by the rise of peasant and occupational *jātis* by the side of the formal *varṇa* system.[60] Manu's codification of the occupational *jātis* as mixed castes, seems to set the lower limit to the period of the formation of the essential elements of the *jāti* system.[61] Once the occupational *jātis* were formed, the tribe naturally broke up into separate endogamous segments, within a larger social system.[62] Such separation of the peasants from superior elements can be inferred by analogy from later known examples. The Badgujars separated from the Gujars out of an original Gujara tribe and the Rajgonds similarly from the Gonds: in each case the superiors claimed a Kshatriya (Rajput) status, while the peasants were relegated to the position of a Śūdra *jāti*.

What resulted from this breakdown of the tribal system, was not a single peasant caste, but a large number of peasant *jātis*. Some perhaps simply retained, like the later Gujars and Gonds, the names of the original tribes.[63] The *viś* peasantry was now a matter of the past. Manu still repeats the formal statement that agriculture was one of the Vaiśya occupations though it was clearly held to be the lowliest of these; and the 'labourer in tillage' was a Śūdra. But Kauṭilya's designation of *Śūdra-karṣakas* more properly defined the actual status of the peasants. By the seventh century AD, Yuan Chwang would classify the peasants simply as Śūdras.[64]

The emergence of 'peasant-castes' was the reflection in part of another development, namely, the further growth of the social division of labour demarcating the peasants more firmly from the artisans. Writing of the second Iron Age in Europe, Gordon Childe stressed the importance of the entry into the 'archaeological record' of 'new tools and labour-saving devices (such as) hinged tongs, shears, scythes, rotary querns'. These laid the basis for 'a number of new full-time specialists' like glass-workers, potters, etc.[65] By the first century AD, the Taxila excavations give us firm indications of the occurrence of some of the technological devices (shears, rotary querns) which Childe has spoken of.[66] The new full time professions must have led to a separation of the artisan communities from the peasantry; the Jāṭakas introduce us to 'manufacturers' villages' exclusively peopled by smiths or carpenters.[67] These formed the basis of the new occupational *jātis*, the 'mixed castes' of Manu, which include those of carpenters, charioteers, and physicians.[68]

There was, finally, the subjugation of the food-gathering population which involves the creation of the 'menial' castes. It is of some significance that in all early texts the ancestors of the later 'Untouchables' are extensively connected with hunting, fishing, working on animal skins and dealing in bamboo.[69] In other words, their origins lay mainly amidst the food-gathering forest folk. I have suggested that during the 'long transition' in the Gangetic basin the size of forest populations increased considerably. At a particular point, reached probably at different times in different localities, this co-existence between agriculture and hunting broke down. The raising of leguminous crops reduced the villagers' dependence on animal meat or fish,[70] and growing use of cotton affected the demand for animal skins. The areas of forest that the hunters had to have for their subsistence had now to go; the clash between the Sākyas and Kolis may well illustrate the conflict between the advancing agricultural pioneers and their opponents in the forests.[71] In the foresters' obstruction of the peasants' quest for more land, there was reason enough for the peasants to entertain a bitter hostility towards the forest peoples. The animal-killing *jātis* are indeed looked down upon with so much scorn in the Buddhist texts as in the Brahmanical works of the period.[72] Manu sets down the code according to which they were to be treated once they were subjugated and reduced to mixed *jātis*. As '*Chaṇḍālas* and *Svapachas*' they were to be kept out of towns and villages and to perform the most menial offices only.[73] Here was the beginning of 'Untouchability' and the creation of the menial castes, forming an ostracised rural proletariat that was henceforth to remain a specific feature of the Indian social order.

The five hundred years preceding the birth of Christ must have been one of the most formative periods of Indian social history. They moulded the basic contours of the caste system, with a peasantry deeply divided into endless endogamous communities and rigorously separated from the artisans as well as 'menial' labourers. This social fabric could not have come of itself; its erection needed direction and sustenance from a whole new system of ideas and beliefs.

This new system is profoundly associated with Buddhism. Kosambi saw in its attack on Brahmanical animal sacrifices the hostility of the 'cattle-raising' Vaiśya against obsolete pastoralism.[74] This seems to reduce the social relevance of Buddhism to a very narrow sphere. With much trepidation, I would venture to suggest that the belief in the *karma* doctrine and the *ahimsā*, the two basic elements of Buddhism, had much profounder relationship with the larger social processes at work.

Gautama Buddha is not known to have preached the excellence of the caste system; and the Aśokan edicts are remarkable for their exclusion of all reference to any obligation imposed by *varṇa* and *jāti*.[75] And yet the *karma* theory, which both Buddhism and Jainism vigorously propagated proved to be the most effective rationalization of the caste system. Whatever the Buddhist notion of the individual soul, the Buddhist tradition saw cycles of birth and rebirth in individual terms.[76] Once the cycle was so conceived, it justified one's present position in a low *jati* by virtue of the deeds in a previous existence, and promised a higher one if one performed the set obligations excellently. By Manu's time, this is firmly a part of the caste doctrine.[77]

The *ahimsā*, in its precise application, might have owed something to the jealousy aroused by the rich, land-controlling Brāhmaṇas, who displayed the power of their ritual by large animal sacrifices. But the prejudice against animal slaughter was likely to have derived in much larger measure from the peasant's hatred of the hunting tribes of the forest. The Aśokan edicts contain express injunctions against hunting and fishing.[78] This explains too the hostility in the Buddhist texts towards the hunting peoples. *Ahimsā* could thus justify the subjugation and ostracism of these communities, the basis of untouchability. But the cycle went on: as the *ahimsā* doctrine came to be accepted by Brāhmanism, even the occupation of the peasant could be termed a sinful and lowly one, for did not the plough with its iron point injure the earth and the creatures living in it?[79] This view came to be shared by later Buddhism as well.[80]

The new social situation, in its own turn, affected the religious world. As the tribal moorings, with their local customs and superstitions collapsed, and the peasant became, as member of a *jāti*, part of a 'general society', he equally stood in need of a general religion. For this there was no provision in the sacred ritual of the Brāhmaṇas and the elitist Saṅgha of Buddhism. But Buddhism developed by first century AD the concept of the Bodhisattva, a benign power whose grace every one could invoke by direct forms of worship.[81] Almost simultaneously, if not a little earlier, came the emergence of Vaiṣṇavism, with its concept of *bhakti*, establishing a personal relationship between the deity and the devotee.[82] The literal significance of the name Kṛṣṇa and the anecdotes of his childhood proclaim vividly the rustic elements in the great cult.[83] This was the beginning of a kind of Peasant Hinduism.

SOUTH INDIA

Southern India deserves separate treatment because in its early social evolution it followed an independent line of development down to the Mauryan conquests (third century BC). The plough appeared in the south in the second millennium BC with a basically neolithic culture,[84] the crops raised were the ragi millet (in two varieties), wheat, horse gram and green gram. Rice and the bajra millet began to be cultivated after the coming of iron, *c.* 1000 BC. Agriculture of this kind implied the existence of a peasantry from the late neolithic times. A large pastoral sector is also suggested by remains of enormous cattle-pens.[85] Almost all pre-Mauryan sites are on the Karnataka plateau, suggesting that cultivation was as yet confined to the drier zone. Here too are concentrated all the eleven rock inscriptions of Aśoka found in the south.[86] Apparently the eastern coastal plains, the home of the Andhras, Cholas and Pāṇḍyas mentioned in Aśokan Rock Edicts II and XIII were still only very partly cleared. It was at this point that, with the Mauryan arms, the northern culture arrived.

The effects of its arrival on the south are important also for understanding what had really been happening in the north. The 'four-*varṇa*' system of the legal theorists failed to be implanted in the south.[87] The peasants were classed as Śūdras, not Vaiśyas, an important index of the contemporary status of the peasants in India generally. The warriors and merchants could not separate and form into distinct castes, and this perhaps suggests that social differentiation in south India had not yet reached a sufficiently high level. But the *jātis* came to be as firmly established in the south as anywhere else in India, possibly by wholesale conversions of the tribes. In such conversion the Brāhmaṇās apparently played a crucial role as high priests of the new order.[88] So too was brought the harsh social division between the peasant (*ulavars or veḷḷaḷar*) and the menial castes. The hierarchical distinction between the two classes is brought out in 'late classical (Tamil) works' of the fifth or sixth century AD.[89]

The absence of the second and third *varṇas* does not necessarily mean that differentiation did not subsequently proceed rapidly enough. In spite of it having been vigorously asserted, it is difficult to admit, even as a hypothesis, that there was ever an 'alliance between the Brāhmaṇās and peasants and that this served as 'the keystone of local south Indian societies'.[90]

THE FIRST MILLENNIUM: THE VILLAGE COMMUNITY AND 'FEUDALISM'

Kosambi propounded a sombre view of the economic and cultural performance of this entire period and ascribed it to a 'complete victory of the village with consequences far deadlier than any invasion'.[91] He believed that agricultural productivity actually declined.[92] For southern India during the same millennium Burton Stein postulates the concept of a 'Peasant Society' with agricultural technology as a 'constant factor.'[93]

The notion of changelessness is, however, not supported by the evidence we can assemble on agricultural technology. The additions to crops continued. Bajra, the bulrush millet, which does not appear in Kauṭilya's *Arthaśāstra,* II, 24, became an important crop in the north along with the Great Millet, Juar (*sorghum vulgare*), which seems to have arrived after the beginning of the Christian era.[94] Together they greatly reinforced 'kharif' cropping in the dry zone of the north-west. Fine varieties of cotton were developed to provide the muslin that won an important luxury market in the Roman world.[95] Kosambi himself pointed out that the first evidence for the coconut on the eastern and western coasts comes from the first century before and after Christ.[96]

The Sudarśana lake in Saurashtra, its history from the Mauryas to the Guptas illuminated by epigraphic evidence, marks the beginning of the recorded history of tank and bund irrigation.[97] The construction of irrigation tanks seems to have become well established in the south by Choḷa times.[98] The 'tremendous' reservoir of King Bhoja (eleventh century) in central India finds a description in Kosambi's own pages.[99] Throughout the Indian Peninsula, the tanks created by bunds have utilized every convenient undulation in the ground;[100] and their construction as it took place must have greatly extended cultivation and improved cropping.

The use of cattle-power for continuous rotary motion too would seem to belong to this period. This is no older in the Chinese and Mediterranean civilizations than the second century BC.[101] In India, the first evidence for even the manual rotary quern and quartzite crushing mill comes from Taxila, about first century AD.[102] It is, therefore, almost certain that the use of cattle to rotate a horizontal drawbar belongs to the succeeding centuries. Once the possibility was known, its applications could be multiple; for threshing;[103] for pressing oil;[104] and for crushing sugar in both kinds of mills, viz., the mortar-and-pestle and the wooden rollers.[105] In all these operations cattle-power would have replaced an enormous amount of human labour, rendered hitherto presumably by slaves or semi-servile labourers.

Agriculture, then, did not remain stable during the first thousand years after Christ; and over this long span productivity probably increased considerably. None of the improvements were, however, of a nature to subvert peasant production; on the contrary, as we have seen, some tended to make agrarian slave-labour superfluous.

In terms of social relations, the period saw the completion of the great division between the peasantry and landless labour. I have argued elsewhere that given the immense seasonal fluctuation in demand for labour on the field, called for a constant reserve of accessible labour-supply.[106] Theoretically, this could have been created by simple free market forces; but these would have enlarged the share of wage costs in the peasant's produce and so reduced correspondingly the size of the surplus. The presence of a specially repressed proletariat was thus of advantage to almost every other class of rural society, the peasant as well as his superiors. This proletariat in India was largely created out of the food-gatherers and forest folk who had been already converted into ostracised *jātis* during the five centuries before Christ.

One would have expected that once these depressed *jātis* accommodated themselves to settled agrarian life, they might have invoked some form of 'Sanskritization' to rise in the hierarchy and turn into peasants themselves. This actually seems to have happened with the Jatts whose history we can follow, though with immense gaps, from the seventh century.[107] But such cases were exceptions. Vivekanand Jha shows that during the two phases that he distinguishes *c.* AD 200-600 and *c.* 600-1200, the number of untouchables went on increasing by the addition of new castes to the category.[108] Excluded from the village and prevented from holding land, the untouchables could never become peasants; they were thus forced to follow the prescribed menial occupations which kept them alive in the slack seasons so as to be available when needed for work in the field. The peasant, sorely exploited himself, joined in practising the severest repression of the menial labourer. This has surely been one of the fatal tragedies in Indian social history.

There was within the peasantry itself a considerable degree of stratification: there were large numbers who were mere sharecroppers on the fields of others. When Manu says that the field belongs to one who 'first cleared away the timber',[109] he is possibly thinking of peasant cultivators possessing their own field. But he says elsewhere that the claims of 'the owner of the field' have precedence over the actual tiller ('owner of the seed');[110] and the latter can only be a sharecropper. Yājñavalkya underlines this when he says that the owner of the field (*kṣetraswāmi*) had the right to assign it to a cultivator of his choice.[111]

The choice to give the land out on lease is implicit in the obligation placed on the donees, in inscriptions from the fourth century AD onward, 'to cultivate the land (themselves) or *get it cultivated*'.[112] I-tsing (seventh century) shows that usually the Buddhist monasteries too leased out their lands to sharecroppers, giving them sometimes oxen, but never anything else. At Tamralipti he saw a third of the produce being brought in by the 'tenants'. It was only some 'avaricious' monasteries which 'do not divide the produce, but the priests themselves give out the works to servants, male and female, and see that the farming is properly done;' but this necessitated the priests 'urging on the hired servants by force'.[113]

Some segments of the peasantry were also subject to various constraints. On this much has been written; but the evidence unluckily is sparse and vague. Fa-hsien (fifth century) says that the Buddhist monasteries were provided by the kings, elders and lay Buddhists with land and 'with husbandmen and cattle';[114] this practically implies a serf-like status of the peasants donated. Other evidence suggests constraints on the peasants' movements only. R.S. Sharma presents epigraphic evidence of uneconomic constraints going back in south India to the third century and in Orissa and Gujarat to the sixth.[115] The evidence becomes a little stronger for the subsequent centuries.[116] A form of subjection is also implied in *viṣṭi* or forced labour, which was almost universally present in India: its use in regular agricultural operations seems, however, to have been limited.[117]

As against the sharecroppers and possible semi-serfs, there is evidence of the existence of an upper stratum among the peasants placed in a position to domineer over the rest. There is the cultivator (*kṣetrikasya)* who appears in Manu as the employer of a hired servant or labourer (*bhritya*).[118] The *Milindapañho* (compiled, first century BC to fifth century AD) tells us of the 'husbandman' (*kassako*) who by successful work is his field becomes 'the owner of much flour and so the lord of whomsoever are poor and needy'.[119] Then there is the 'young son of a peasant (*halotthavritti-putrosya*) in the *Kāmasūtra* (fourth century): Like the village headman (*grāmādhipati*) and official (*āyukta*) he has access to village women as they render forced labour (*viṣṭikarma*), work in his field (*kṣetrakarma)* as also in his house, or taking away cotton and other fibrous material from him, bring him yarn in return.'[120] This is a rare picture that we get of the actualities of the sub-exploitation of peasant by peasant in ancient Indian countryside.

This degree of peasant stratification raises questions about the real nature of the Indian village community, which Marx and Maine both supposed to have been based on a common ownership of the land.[121] It is indeed possible that in conditions of abundance of land, private property in the form of saleable individual right to specific fields might not have arisen, and, as seems to be the case with non-Brāhmaṇa villages of early Choḷa times (ninth and tenth centuries), much of the land might have been held to be vested with the community.[122] But this does not necessarily imply lack of stratification. There would be peasants with seed, reserve of grain, cattle, even possibly slaves; and others bereft of these. It would be the former who would dominate.

In the earliest traceable allusion to the village community it is forcibly brought home to us that only the upper stratum mattered in the community. In a little-noticed passage in the *Milindapañho,* Nāgasena tells king Menander that words do not often signify what they mean on the face of them; and he takes as an illustration the word 'villagers' (*gāmikā*):

Suppose, O king, in some village the lord of the village (*gāmāsāmiko*) were to order the crier saying: 'Go crier, bring all the villagers (*gāmikā*) quickly together before me'... Now when the lord, O king, is thus summoning all the heads of houses (*kutipurise*), he issues his order to all the villagers, but it is not they who assemble in obedience to the order; it is the heads of houses. There are many who do not come: women and men, slave girls and slaves, hired workmen, servants, peasantry (*gāmikā*), sick people, oxen, buffaloes, sheep and goats and dogs—but all those do not count.[123]

It is thus the villagers of substance who alone are summoned by the headman to confabulate with him on matters of the village. Altekar notices that those who gathered at what he styles the Primary Village Assembly, were called '*mahattamas* in U.P., *mahattaras* in Maharashtra, *mahajanas* in Karnataka and *perumukkāl* in Tamil country, all (of which) mean the same thing, Great Men of the Village'.[124] The exclusiveness of the community was naturally still more marked in the Brāhmaṇa villages where all the power lay in the hands of the non-peasant landowners.[125]

Unfortunately, there is very little evidence to answer in specific terms the crucial question: Why need the upper village strata have acted in unison and operated the village as a kind of corporation controlled by themselves? Part of the answer may lie in the economic autonomy of the village, which developed once agriculture had been 'democratized', above all by the iron-pointed plough. Kosambi describes the post-Mauryan villages as yielding surplus in kind to the rulers while being self-sufficient in the minimum requirements for maintaining the continuity of production, very much as Marx had conceived the position of the village in his 'Asiatic' system. Kosambi believed that these conditions first developed in northern India, and later in the Deccan.[126] Artisans had to move to the villages to meet the peasants' need, subsisting on customary shares in grain and allotments of small plots for cultivation. Epigraphic evidence attests to carpenters' plots in northern India in the fifth century[127] and the *Lekhapaddhati* speaks of the five artisans (*pañcha-karuka*), the carpenter, ironsmith, potter, barber, and washerman, as entitled to receive handfuls of grain from the peasant.[128] All this is sound evidence of the artisans fixed association with the village, which in turn strongly implies the existence of the village as a separate but collective unit.

The relationship between the peasants and artisans within the village must largely have depended upon custom but the actual land allotments and settlements of disputes called for a controlling organ. So too the important matter of the hamlet or huts of the 'menial' castes within the village boundaries being kept under proper subjection. The further use of waste land around the village and the terms for admission of non-resident cultivators, had also to be settled by some authority. In other words, the economic unit had to be a social unit as well; and the 'greatmen' of the village by exercising authority in its name enlarged their own income and perpetuated their own dominance by carrying out the social functions.

The benefits of the dominance came mainly through the fiscal system. A large part of the surplus had to be alienated by the village in payment of taxes.[129] The power to distribute this burden upon the individual villagers, gave an immense advantage to the controlling stratum: The strong in the village used to shift the burden on to the 'weak' as it would be said for the early fourteenth century.[130] This fiscal differentiation within the peasantry is seen by some authorities in the distinction between *udraṅga* and *uparikara* already present in fifth century inscriptions.[131] It may well be that it was ultimately its tax-gathering functions that gave the village community at once its firmest basis and oligarchic character.

We may here leave the stratified peasantry and our speculations about the village community to consider the pressures to which the taxation subjected the peasantry as a whole. The view offered often in text books and elsewhere that this amounted normally to one-sixth of the produce has little reality behind it.[132] This was prescribed as the maximum for *bali* in the *Smṛtis*,[133] but the *Arthaśāstra* has *bali* and *saḍbhāga* (one-sixth) as separate taxes.[134] The Rummindei Pillar inscription of Aśoka confirms the existence of this double tax. He remitted the *bali* for the holy village, and continued the other tax at the reduced rate, *aṭhabhāga* (one-eighth). The Greek accounts derived from Megasthenes also speak of two taxes, a 'rental' or 'land-tribute' and a land-tax of one-fourth of the produce.[135] The two taxes occur in Rudradaman's Girnar inscription (AD 150),[136] whereafter there is an increasing multiplicity of taxes.

The fact that *saḍbhāga* (even *dharmasaḍbhāga*) continues to appear among the taxes, hardly justifies the view that agrarian taxation was 'at lower rates in Gupta times than in the Mauryan days'.[137] Indeed the term *bhāga-bhoga* has been held to represent two taxes, the older *saḍbhāga* and an additional levy (*bhoga*).[138] R.S. Sharma states his impression that the increasing number of taxes appearing in later inscriptions indicates a real increase of the fiscal burden on the peasants.[139] A passage ascribed to Varāhamihira (sixth century) describes the sight of desolate villages abandoned by peasants owing to the oppression of the *bhogapati*, tax-collector.[140]

While tax-extraction had an immediate terror for the peasantry, its mode of distribution also affected it in the long term. In its two main versions, Kosambi's and R.S. Sharma's, the theory of Indian Feudalism rests essentially on the mode of alienation of the tax-resources by the rulers.[141] Sharma holds the land-grants made to the Brāhmaṇas, for which epigraphic evidence begins from the first century, to be the forerunner of secular feudalism; but there are difficulties in accepting this, especially owing to a time-gap of some eight hundred years or more before hereditary land-grants to the ruler's kinsmen, vassals and officials begin in northern India (mainly from AD 1000).[142]

A more important source of 'feudalism' was the decay of commerce and decline of towns, which seems to have continued down to the eleventh century.[143] This synchronised with a ruralization of the ruling class, a tendency towards its dispersal at each level, and so the creation of hereditary tax-collecting potentates (*samantas, ṭhakkuras, rānakas, rāutas rājaputras*), etc., placed one over the other in some hierarchical order.[144]

Cavalry supported such dispersed political power. Chariots were obsolete in India by the seventh century.[145] On the other hand, the effectiveness of the horse-rider was immensely improved with the arrival of the saddle some time in the early centuries of the Christian era, and of the (non-metallic) true stirrup by the tenth century.[146] When the Arabs faced Dahar in battle in 712-13, the ruler of Sind was accompanied by '*sons of kings* numbering 5,000 horsemen'.[147] Clearly, the sons of kings represent, through a practically literal translation, the *rājaputras* (*rāutas*), ancestors of the modern Rajputs. These horsemen were the knights of 'Indian Feudalism'.[148] By the tenth century they formed the warrior class in most of northern India and a large part of the Deccan, even if their coalescence into a single caste was a later phenomenon.[149]

The horseman represented an effective single unit of armed force; the warrior clans could lay claim to separate groups of villages (traditionally numbered in multiples of six), their members dispersed among the villages to extract taxes and keep the peasants subjugated.[150] The lower ranks of the warriors would turn into village despots: the village headmen (*khots* and *muqaddams*) who rode horses, wore fine clothes and chewed betel-leaf in the Doab in the early fourteenth century could well have been such proto-Rajputs.[151] The local power and rights that these 'feudal' potentates and warriors carved out for themselves long survived the polities within which they had originated. It was largely out of these deeply entrenched elements that the *zamindar* class of medieval India, continuing into modern times was created.[152]

Our evidence tends to show the peasant as no more than a pliant victim while his superiors fought it out for the control of the surplus he produced. This may however well be due to limitations of our evidence. The epigraphic *praśastis* of rulers were not likely to dwell on agrarian revolts. We owe to R.S. Sharma the identification of one peasant uprising in the eleventh century. The Kaivartas, traditionally a low 'mixed' *jāti* of boatmen,[153] held plots of land on some service tenure in north Bengal. A literary account (*Rāmacharita*) says that upon being subjected to heavy taxation they revolted, fighting naked with bows and arrows and riding on buffaloes. They defeated and killed one Pāla ruler and forced another to mobilise all his vassals, before they could be subdued (*c.* 1075).[154] The revolt was thus also a caste revolt: the Kaivartas might have been trying to throw off their social disabilities as well. A later Sena ruler of Bengal (Ballalasena, *c.* 1159-85) is indeed said to have made a 'clean caste of the lowly Kaivartas'.[155]

NOTES

1. For the information used in this paragraph, I have relied on my colleague M.D.N. Sahi's paper 'Early History of Agriculture in Pre- and Proto-historic India', read at the Indian History Congress, Bodhgaya, 1981 (cyclostyled).
2. V. Gordon Childe, *Man Makes Himself*, London, 1948, p. 123.
3. *The Threshold of Civilization*, New York, 1975, pp. 40ff. Not all the evidence, specially such as inference from art, can be beyond dispute.
4. The simple carbon dates (based on half-life of 5730 years) are given in Bridget and Raymond Allchin, *The Birth of Indian Civilization*, Penguin Books, 1968, p. 140; and there are useful discussions in D.P. Agarwal and A. Ghosh (ed.), *Radio-carbon and Indian Archaeology*, Bombay, 1973, pp. 205-10 and in *Puratattva*, no. 7 (1974), pp. 65-73. Calibration has resulted in pushing back the lower date of the Indus culture and considerably lengthening its span.

5. For the toy clay wheeled carts and bronze oxen found at the Indus sites, see Stuart Piggott, *Pre-historic India*, Penguin Books, 1950, pp. 176-7. The humped ox (*zebu*) of the Indus culture was particularly suited for traction: the hump made possible such an effective harness. Kosambi's objections (*An Introduction to the Study of Indian History*, Bombay, 1956, pp. 63-7) were grounded on the lack of positive evidence for the plough, and a conjectured small size of surplus owing to the presence of only two cities in contrast to Mesopotamia. There are some comments on the negative evidence in D.H. Gordon. *The Prehistoric Background of Indian Culture*, Bombay, 2nd edn,.1960, pp. 70-1.
6. *Indian Archaeology* 1968-69—*a Review*, New Delhi, pp. 29-30 and Plate XXXIV. The ploughed field is described as 'pre-Harappan' since it is covered by Harappan occupation strata.
7. For wheat and barley, John Marshall, *Mohenjodaro and the Indus Civilization*, London, 1931, pp. 586-7. G. Watt says of the six-row barley that it is 'almost the only cultivated form (of barley) in India' (*Economic Products of India*, London, 1890, IV, p. 275). The *hordum vulgare* and *hexatichum* are identical varieties (but Cf. S. Piggott, *Prehistoric India*, p. 153). For other information on the crops, see Piggott, op. cit., and Sahi, 'Early Agriculture . . .', op. cit.
8. Marshall, *Mohenjodaro and the Indus Civilization* I, pp. 31-2. The variety of cotton was found to be 'closely related' to *gossypium arboreum* and thus confirmed a finding, already made on botanical grounds, that this variety was 'quite ancient if not more ancient than any other cotton' (G. Watt, *Commercial Products of India*, London, 1908, p. 577).
9. *Peasant State and Society in Medieval South India*, Delhi, 1980.
10. The classical statement is in Marx, 'The British Rule in India' (1853), reprinted in K. Marx and F. Engels, *On Colonialism*, Moscow, n.d., p. 33.
11. Cf. V. Gordon Childe, *What Happened in History*, Penguin Books, rev. edn., 1954, p. 132.
12. D.D. Kosambi, *Introduction* . . . , pp. 59-61. He possibly overstates the role of religion when he argues that force (through bronze weaponry) was rendered superfluous by the solidifying role of religion (p. 59).
13. R.E.M. Wheeler, 'Harappa 1946, the Defences and Cemetery 38', *Ancient India*, no. 3, January 1947, esp. 78-83; D.D. Kosambi, *Introduction* . . . , pp. 66-90.
14. One should always use the word 'Aryan' with the reservations which Romila Thapar has so cogently urged in her Presidential Address to the Ancient India Section of the Indian History Congress, *Proceedings* of the Congress, Varanasi session (1969), pp. 15-46. There can absolutely be no racial elements involved in it.
15. On the absence of the horse in the Indus culture see Bridget and Raymond Allchin, *Birth of Indian Civilization*, p. 260. The Aryan success seems to parallel that of the Hyksos who overran Egypt with their chariots in the eighteenth century BC.

16. Cf. Leonard Woolley, *The Beginnings of Civilization* (UNESCO History of Mankind, 161, I, pt. 2), London, 1965, p. 190. The point is lightly touched upon by Sarva Daman Singh, *Ancient Indian Warfare, with special reference to the Vedic period*, Leiden, 1965, p. 31, but is specially noted by Sir Mortimer Wheeler in his foreword to the book.
17. R.S. Sharma, *Sudras in Ancient India*, Delhi, 1958, p. 26; see also his article 'Conflict, Differentiation and Distribution in Ṛgvedic Society', *Indian Historical Review*, IV (I), pp. 1-12.
18. S.K. Das, *Economic History of Ancient India*, Calcutta, 1937, pp. 28-9.
19. Cf. ibid., p. 32; and N. Bandyopadhyaya, *Economic Life and Progress in Ancient India*, Calcutta, 1965, pp. 130-1. The word held to mean rice is *dhanaḥ*; see however, Kosambi, *Introduction* . . . , p. 83.
20. Kosambi, *Introduction* . . . , pp. 70-1.
21. Ibid., p. 83.
22. Bandyopadhyaya, *Economic Life* . . . , I p. 125.
23. Das, *Economic History* . . . , pp. 25-6.
24. Cf. Dev Raj Chanana, *Slavery in Ancient India*, Delhi, 1960, p. 20.
25. Kosambi, *Introduction* . . . , pp. 92-3. Women slaves were particularly prized (Chanana, *Slavery* . . . , pp. 20-1); but this does not necessarily mean that they and their children could not be put to work for their masters.
26. Stuart Piggott, *Prehistoric India*, p. 228. It has not so far been found among the tools of the 'Copper Hoard' people, however.
27. B.B. Lal, 'The Copper Hoard Culture of the Ganga Valley', *Antiquity*, XLVI, pp. 282-7; R.C. Gaur, 'The Ochre-coloured Pottery', *South Asian Archaeology*, 1973, ed. van Lohuizen de Leeuw and Ulbagho, Leiden, 1974, pp. 53-62. The dating is on the basis of thermoluminiscence after the calibration of the carbon dates of the Indus culture, the OCP culture can no longer be regarded as contemporaneous with it, excepting its last phase.
28. See K.A. Chowdhury, *Ancient Agriculture and Forestry in Northern India* (a report on plant remains at Atranjikhera), Bombay, 1977, pp. 60-3; and Sahi, 'Early History of Agriculture' . . . , op. cit.
29. For an illuminating survey of the pre-history of iron see Leonard Woolley, *The Beginnings of Civilization*, pp. 277-83.
30. Dilip Chakrabarti, 'The beginning of Iron in India', *Antiquity*, L (1976), pp. 118-19. His date is 800 BC for the Upper Gangetic Basin and 750 BC for 'Eastern India', M.D.N. Sahi, however, argues for as early a period as the thirteenth century BC on the basis of the evidence from Eran and Ahar in Central India (*Proceedings* of the Indian History Congress, Bombay (1980) session, pp. 104-11). The precise time limits of the PGW culture are difficult to set because of the varied Carbon-14 dates at different sites. B.B. Lal has summed up the evidence in a cyclostyled monograph, 'The Painted Grey Ware Culture', 1981, pp. 34-7.

31. For the references to iron in the *Atharvā veda* see Bandyopadhyaya, *Economic Life*. . . , I, pp. 158-9. A synthesis of archaeological and literary materials is offered in R.S. Sharma, 'Class Formation and its Material Basis in the Upper Gangetic Basin', *IHR*, II (1), 1975, pp. 1-13.
32. See B.B. Lal, 'Painted Grey Ware Culture', op. cit., pp. 5-8. About 650 PGW sites are said to have been discovered.
33. K.A. Chowdhury, *Ancient Agriculture* . . . , p. 63; Sahi, 'Early History of Agriculture . . . ', op. cit.
34. Kosambi, *Introduction* . . . , p. 144.
35. Narendra Wagle, *Society of the time of the Buddha*, Bombay, 1966, p. 131.
36. See references in Bandyopadhyaya, *Economic Life* . . . , I, pp. 133-4; Das, *Economic History* . . . , pp. 90-1.
37. *Cambridge History of India*, I, ed. E.J. Rapson, Delhi, reprint 1955, pp. 114-15. The presence of 'serfs' is doubted by R.S. Sharma, *IHR*, II (1), p. 8.
38. R. Fick, *The Social Organization of North East India in Buddha's Time*, English tr., Calcutta, 1920, pp. 243-4; and Atindra Nath Bose, *Social and Rural Economy of Northern India, cir. 600 BC - AD 200*, Calcutta, 1970, pp. 62-93.
39. Cf. Sibesh Bhattacharya, 'Land System as Reflected in Kauṭilya's *Arthaśāstra*', *Indian Economic and Social History Review* (*IESHR*), XVI (1), pp. 85-95.
40. U.N. Ghoshal, *Contributions to the Hindu Revenue System*, Calcutta, 1929, pp. 29-31, 34; Kosambi, *Introduction* . . . , p. 215.
41. B.B. Lal, 'Painted Grey Ware Culture', op. cit., pp. 22-3.
42. Bones of wild animals (stag, nilgai and even leopard), evidently eaten, have been found at the PGW sites of Hastinapura and Atranjikhera (B.B. Lal, op. cit., p. 17). One is reminded of Aśoka's taste for peacocks and deer; he still ate their meat when the number of animals daily killed in his kitchen had been vastly reduced (Rock Edict I).
43. Kosambi, *Introduction* . . ., pp. 121-3. For the Nisādas, see Vivekanand Jha, 'From Tribe to Untouchable; the case of Niṣādas', *Indian Society, Historical Probings*, ed. R.S. Sharma and V. Jha, New Delhi, 1974, pp. 69-75.
44. *The Classical Accounts of India*, ed. R.C. Majumdar, Calcutta, 1960, pp. 225, 237, 264.
45. Fick, indeed, believed on the basis of the evidence of the Jātakas that the land was 'mostly in the possession of Brāhmaṇas' (*Social Organization* . . . , op. cit., 241).
46. Cf. R.S. Sharma in *IHR*, II (1), pp. 8-9.
47. *The Laws of Manu*, tr. G. Buhler, Oxford, 1886, pp. 420-1.
48. B.B. Lal, 'Painted Grey Ware Culture', p. 13. A sickle and hoe-tip have been found at the PGW site of Jakhera (ibid., p. 13); and this suggests a slight modification of the statement that 'iron agricultural implements' begin only with the NBP [R.S. Sharma, in *IHR*, II (1),

p. 2]. Yet the large relative increase in the number of such implements beginning with NBP remains a fact.

49. *What Happened in History*, revd. ed., 1954, p. 183. The first depiction of a peasant in India, driving a plough with a pair of oxen, is in a Kuṣāṇa frieze, *c.* AD 200 (reproduction in D.D. Kosambi, *Culture and Civilization in Ancient India in Historical Outline*, London, 1965, Plate 15). The picture may well be of a twentieth-century Indian peasant ploughing.
50. Das, *Economic History* . . . , pp. 93, 202.
51. For such a list see N.N. Kher, *Agrarian and Fiscal Economy in the Mauryan and post-Mauryan Age*, Delhi, 1973, pp. 379-400. Some individual items on the list, such as maize, groundnut and chilli, are however demonstrably erroneous. Kauṭilya (*Arthaśāstra*, II: 24) specifies the major crops sown for the spring and autumn harvests (Translation by Shamasastry, Mysore, 1956, pp. 127-31).
52. For this second 'urban revolution,' see A. Ghosh, *The City in Early Historical India*, Simla, 1973; and R.S. Sharma's review in *IHR*, I (1), pp. 98-103.
53. Kosambi, *Introduction* . . . , p. 130. One would wish for a more explicit statement of this practice in view of its importance.
54. See accounts of Diodorus Siculus and Strabo, translations in R.C. Majumdar (ed.), *The Classical Accounts of India*, Calcutta, 1960, pp. 237, 264, 287 (n. 20). It is possible that the 'land-tribute' represents the king's traditional levy of one-sixth of the produce also laid down by Kauṭilya.
55. R.S. Sharma, *Śūdras in Ancient India*, Delhi, 1958, pp. 146-9. Cf. Kosambi, *Introduction* . . . , pp. 219-20. Sibesh Bhattacharya, *IESHR*, XVI (1), pp. 85-96) is right in pointing out that Kauṭilya does not recommend peasant ownership but Sharma, whom he criticises on this score, seems quite well aware of the distinction between peasant cultivation and peasant ownership and also of the rather vague connotation of *karṣaka*, which may mean peasant as well as agricultural labourer. But the *Arthaśāstra* in the present case uses the term clearly enough in the sense of peasant-cultivators.
56. Cf. R.S. Sharma, *Sudras* . . . , pp. 230-1; also *Journal of Bihar Research Society*, LXIV, iii and iv, 1958, p. 8.
57. R.S. Sharma, *Sudras* . . . , p. 178.
58. Cf. Narendra Wagle, *Society of the time of the Buddha*, Bombay, 1966, pp. 122-3.
59. Note the Buddha's story of the Sākyas who married their own sisters to avoid marrying outside the tribe; also the legend of the origin of the Lichhavis (Wagle, op. cit., pp. 103-4).
60. The Greek accounts of the Indian castes will be found in the *Classical Accounts of India*, ed. R.C. Majumdar, pp. 224-6, 260-8. The Arab geographers of the tenth century AD and even later continue with this number of seven castes, showing how an error can be perpetuated by

simple autonomous transmission in the face of every opportunity for direct observation.

61. *Manusmṛti,* x, 6-57; tr. Buhler, pp. 493-5.
62. One is reminded here of Kosambi's view of the historical growth of the caste system as a process of 'tribal elements being fused into a general society' (Kosambi, *Introduction* . . . , p. 25).
63. Manu, V, 53, 79; tr. Buhler, pp. 419-20. Cf. R.S. Sharma, *Sudras,* . . . , pp. 232.
64. T. Watters, *On Yuang Chwan's Travels in India,* London, 1904, vol. I, pp. 168-9. Cf. R.S. Sharma, *Sudras* . . . , pp. 232-4.
65. V. Gordon Childe, *Social Evolution,* ed. Sir Mortimer Wheeler, Fontana Books, 1963, p. 110.
66. See John Marshall, *Taxila,* Cambridge, 1951, II, p. 555, for scissors, a developed form of shears; and ibid, p. 486, for rotary querns.
67. R. Fick, *Social Organization* . . . , pp. 280-5.
68. Manu, X, 47-8; tr. Buhler, p. 413. What is difficult to explain is why these artisans should have received a status lower than that of Śūdras in social ranking.
69. This can be seen from Manu's enumeration of the occupations of most of the 'mixed' *jātis*: Nisādas, fishing: Medas, Āndhras, Chunchus and Madgus, 'slaughter of wild animals', Kshattris, Ugras and Pukkasas, 'catching and killing (animals) living in holes'; Kārāvara, Dhigvaṇas, working in leather; and Pāṇḍusopāka, dealing in cane (Manu, X, 39,37,48, 49 tr. Buhler, pp. 411, 413-14). Cf. also Vivekanand Jha, *IHR,* II (I), p. 19. The Chaṇḍālas and Niṣādas (Neṣadas) both appear as hunters in Buddhist texts (ibid., pp. 22-3).
70. Kosambi, *Introduction* . . . , 189.
71. Ibid., p. 122.
72. Vivekanand Jha, *IHR* II (1), pp. 22-3.
73. The basic constraints are given in Manu, X, 40-56; tr. Buhler, pp. 414-15.
74. Kosambi, *Introduction* . . . , 158-9.
75. Modern views of the Buddhist attitude to 'caste' are discussed in Debiprasad Chattopadhyaya, *Lokayata,* New Delhi, 1959, pp. 459-66. The particular negative aspect of the Aśokan edicts has received surprisingly little attention, so also the humane injunction in them to treat well the slaves and wage-earners *(dāsa-bhataka)* (R.E. IX, XI & XIII & P.E. VII; also R.E.V.). These last may refer to domestics, but Asoka might well have in mind the village slaves and labourers. Compare the village *dāsi-dāsa bhataka kammakara* in *Milindapañho,* (ed. V. Trenckner, London, 1962, p. 147; tr. Rhys Davids, I, p. 209).
76. The Jātakas do this for Gautama Buddha himself. The *Millindapañho* recalls that Nagasena and King Milinda had been born in a previous life as a monk and novice (*Questions of king Milinda,* tr. T.W. Rhys Davids, Oxford, 1890, vol. I, pp. 4-6).

77. See, for example, *Manusmriti*, X, 24; tr. Buhler, p. 412.
78. Pillar Edict V and the Qandahar inscription. See Romila Thapar, *Asoka and the Decline of the Mauryas*, 2nd ed., Delhi, 1973.
79. Manu, X, 84; tr. Buhler, pp. 420-1.
80. The Sage is said to have forbidden the monks from engaging in cultivation because this involved 'destroying lives by ploughing and watering field' (I-tsing, *A Record of the Buddhist Religion as practised in India and the Malay Archipelago*, tr. J. Takakusu, Oxford, 1896, p. 62).
81. A late Kuṣāṇa (fourth century AD) sculptured relief shows a Bodhisattva with a peasant driving a plough placed beneath him (Kosambi, *Introduction* . . . , Plate 16). A.K. Warder's essay 'Feudalism and Mahayana Buddhism', *Indian Society: Historical Probings*, ed. R.S. Sharma and V. Jha, pp. 156-74, contains interesting suggestions; but the association with 'feudalism' is rather weakly argued.
82. Suvira Jaiswal, *The Origin and Development of Vaisnavism*, Delhi, 1967, pp. 110-15.
83. Ibid., pp. 151-2. There is support for this in iconography as well. Śaṅkarsaṇa, with whom Krisṇa-Vāsudeva was jointly worshipped in the first century BC, 'invariably figures' holding the pestle and the plough (ibid., pp. 53-4, 56-7, 68).
84. This is deduced from the anchylosis of the hock joints in cattle bones, indicating their use for heavy draught work (M.D.N. Sahi, 'Early Agriculture . . .', op. cit).
85. For the crops and cattle-pens, Bridget and Raymond Allchin, *Birth of Indian Civilization*, pp. 262-4. For iron, Dilip Chakrabarti in *Antiquity*, L (1976), pp. 119-22.
86. Brahmagiri and Maski, two sites of these inscriptions, are themselves prehistoric settlements.
87. For a somewhat different appraisal of the factors which caused this result, see R.S. Sharma, *Social Changes in Early Medieval India*, Delhi, 1969, p. 12.
88. It is, however, open to question whether the Brāhmaṇas were not preceded by the Jaina and Buddhist monks. But their social outlook in respect of *jātis* could not have been different from that of the Brāhmaṇas and they shared the same culture.
89. Burton Stein, *Peasant State and Society in Medieval South India*, Delhi, 1980, p. 71.
90. Ibid., pp. 70-1, 83. It would have been a strange alliance, where the Brāhmaṇas would not even concede a Vaiśya status to their allies.
91. *Introduction* . . . , p. 243.
92. The average yield became less (though compensated by somewhat improved methods of cultivation) as deforestation increased' (ibid., p. 228).
93. *Peasant State and Society* . . . , pp. 16ff. See p. 24 for the statement about agriculture technology. It is always dangerous to assume that a factor, just because it is unknown, must be a constant one.

94. Bridget and Raymond Allchin, *Birth of Indian Civilization,* p. 266.
95. E.H. Warmington, *The Commerce between the Roman Empire and India,* 2nd ed., Delhi, 1974, pp. 210-12.
96. Kosambi, *Introduction . . . ,* pp. 255-6.
97. The inscriptions are those of Rudradaman (AD 150) and Skandagupta (fifth century) on the same rock on which Aśokan rock edicts are inscribed (Girnar), See James Burgess, *Report on the Antiquities of Kathiawad and Kachh . . . ,* 1874-5, reprint, Varanasi, 1971, pp. 93-5, 128-38. R.N. Mehta gives a detailed report of his survey of the area with a persuasive reconstruction of the original works and the repairs. *Journal of the Oriental Institute,* XVIII, 1 and 2, 1968, pp. 20-38.
98. Burton Stein, *Peasant State and Society . . . ,* pp. 24-5.
99. *Introduction . . . ,* p. 281.
100. See Spate's description of the 'Madurai-Ramanathapuram Tank Country in O.H.K. Spate and A.T.A. Learmonth, *India and Pakistan,* London, 1967, pp. 775-8.
101. Lynn White, Jr. sees the first continuous rotary motion in the large *mola versatilis, Medieval Technology and Social Change,* New York, 1966, pp. 107-8; and Joseph Needham, *Science and Civilization in China,* IV, (2), Cambridge, 1995, pp. 187-90, dates its first appearance in both civilizations to the first half of second century BC.
102. John Marshall, *Taxila,* II, pp. 485-8. None of the specimens are large enough to have needed animal power. Marshall's reconstructions in vol. III, plate 140, are inaccurate in showing vertical crank-handles.
103. For references to threshing by circular treading of cattle see Lallanji Gopal, 'Technique of Agriculture in Early Medieval India (*c.* AD 700-1200)', *University of Allahabad Studies,* Ancient History Section, 1963-4, p. 56.
104. Cf. Needham, *Science and Civilization in China* IV (5), pp. 202-3, for a Hellenic 'analogue' of the Indian oil mill.
105. Cf. Irfan Habib in *IHR,* V (1-2), pp. 155-9.
106. *Agrarian System of Mughal India,* Bombay 1963, pp. 121-2.
107. They are found as an ostracised community at level with Chandalas in seventh and eighth century Sind; they are described as Śūdras in the tenth century; and as peasants and 'low Vaiśyas' in the seventeenth. See Irfan Habib, in *Essays in honour of Dr. Ganda Singh,* ed. Harbans Singh and N.G. Barrier, Patiala, 1976, pp. 92-103.
108. *IHR,* II (1), pp. 24-31; see the conclusions stated on p. 31.
109. *Manusmriti,* IX,44, tr. Buhler, p. 335. The *Milindapañho* ed. V. Trenckner, p. 219 (tr. T.W. Rhys Davids, II, p. 15) has a similar dictum: 'When a man clears away the jungle, he is called the owner of the land (*bhūmisamiko*).'
110. *Manusmriti,* IX, 52; tr. Buhler, p. 336.
111. Cf. R.S. Sharma, *Aspects of Political Ideas and Institutions in Ancient India,* Delhi, 1959, pp. 22-3.

112. Kosambi, *Introduction . . .*, pp. 300-1; R.S. Sharma, *Indian Feudalism, c. 300-1200,* Calcutta, 1965, p. 47.
113. I-tsing, *A Record of the Buddhist Religion* . . . tr. J. Takakusu, pp. 61-2. He says at one place (p. 61) that the monasteries took a sixth part of the produce, which was perhaps a theoretical amount only, after the proverbial sixth share of the king in the land's produce.
114. *A Record of the Buddhist Countries,* tr. Li Yung-hsi, Peking 1957, p. 35.
115. *Indian Feudalism,* pp. 53-7. B.N.S. Yadava would trace such subjection to Kusana times, 'Some aspects of the Changing Order in India during Saka-Kuṣāṇa Times', *Kusana Studies,* Allahabad, cited *IHR,* I (1), p. 19n.
116. This is assembled and cautiously presented in B.N.S. Yadava, *Society and Culture in Northern India in Twelfth Century*, Allahabad, 1973, pp. 163-73. Cf. also L. Gopal in *Journal of the Economic and Social History of the Orient,* VI. iii, 1963, pp. 297ff.
117. See G.K. Rai, *IHR,* III (i), 1976, pp. 16-42.
118. *Manusmriti,* VIII, 243, tr. Buhler, p. 297.
119. *Milindapañho,* ed. Trenckner, p. 360; tr. Rhys Davids, II, pp. 269-70.
120. *Kāmasūtra,* 5:5:5 and 6. I am indebted to S.R. Sharma for a literal rendering of this passage.
121. 'These small and extremely ancient Indian communities based on possession in common of the land . . .', (Karl Marx, *Capital,* I (1867), tr. S. Moore and E. Aveling, ed. Dona Torr, London, 1938, p. 350). Sir Henry Maine, *Village Communities in the East and West,* appeared first in 1871. His views were criticised by Baden-Powell, notably in *Indian Village Community,* London, 1896, mainly on the basis of Settlement Reports.
122. See Noboru Karashima, 'Allur and Isanamangalam, two South Indian villages of the Cola Times' *Proceedings of the first International Conference Seminar of Tamil Studies,* Kuala Lumpur, 1968, pp, 426-36. Karashima admits to presence of 'agricultural labourers, who are not members of the *ūr* (the village assembly)'.
123. *Milindapañho,* ed. V. Trenckner, p. 147; tr. Rhys Davids, I, pp. 208-9. 'Village headmen' may possibly be a better rendering of *gamāsāmiko.* In the last sentence, *gāmika* which Rhys Davids renders as 'peasantry' literally means 'villagers' here, almost certainly ordinary villagers.
124. A.S. Altekar, *State and Government in Ancient India,* 3rd edn., Delhi, 1958, p. 228. The terms occur in inscriptions of the Vākāṭakas, Pallavas and Gahāḍvālas. Eleventh century references to Brāhmaṇa *mahājans* in Karnataka are cited by Sister M. Liceria, A.C., in *IHR,* I (1), pp. 32-3. The Chola inscriptions have Peringurimakkal, 'the great men of the assembly' (Burton Stein, *Peasant State and Society* . . . , p. 145).
125. For the sabhās of the Brāhmaṇa villages in the Choḷa kingdom see Altekar, op. cit., pp. 231-5, and Burton Stein, *Peasants State and Society,* pp. 145ff. Kosambi in *Introduction* . . . , pp. 301-10, has some charming pages on the Brāhman village communities of Goa, a combination of

recorded information (traced to the fourth century) and his own personal recollections. See also his *Myth and Reality*, Bombay 1962, pp. 152-71; Baden-Powell, 'The Villages of Goa in the early Sixteenth Century', *JRAS*,1900, pp. 261-91, and Monserrate's description (1579), tr. Hosten, *JASB*, NS, XIII (1922), pp. 351-2, 365.

126. Kosambi, *Introduction* . . . , pp. 227, 253-4.
127. Ibid., p. 312.
128. Cf. B.N.S. Yadava, *Society and Culture* . . . , p. 267.
129. Cf. Karashima (*Proceedings of the First International Conference Seminar of Tamil Studies*, op. cit., p. 429, on the responsibility of the *ūr* (assembly in non-Brāhmaṇa villages) to pay tax (*irai*) on the village land.
130. Zia Barani, *Ta'rikh-i-Firuz-Shahi*, ed. Sayyid Ahmad Khan, W.N. Lees and Kabiruddin, Calcutta, 1860-2, p. 287.
131. U.N. Ghoshal, *Contributions to the History of the Hindu Revenue System*, 2nd edn., Calcutta, 1972, pp. 275-7, 280, 283-6, 299, 307, 319, etc. Cf., however, D.N. Jha, *Revenue System of Post-Maurya and Gupta Times*, Calcutta, 1967, pp. 53-6.
132. Cf. W.H. Moreland, *Agrarian System of Moslem India*, Cambridge, 1929, pp. 5-6.
133. U.N. Ghoshal, *Contributions* . . . , p. 71.
134. *Arthaśāstra*, II:15, tr. Shamasastry, Mysore, 1967, p. 99.
135. Translations of the passages in Diodorus Siculus and Strabo are in R.C. Majumdar (ed.), *Classical Accounts of India*, pp. 237, 264. There is some doubt as to whether Strabo means that the peasants paid or received one-fourth of the produce. Diodorus is apparently unambiguous here (*ibid.*, p. 287, n. 20); but see U.N. Ghoshal, *Contributions* . . . , pp. 224-9.
136. Cf. U.N. Ghoshal, p. 252; D. N. Jha, *Revenue System* . . . , pp. 43-5.
137. D.N. Jha in *Land Revenue in India—Historical Studies*, ed. R.S. Sharma, Delhi, 1971, p. 5.
138. D.N. Jha, *Revenue System* . . ., p. 43.
139. *Indian Feudalism*, p. 265. For these taxes see Lallanji Gopal, *Economic Life of Northern India*, 700-1200, Delhi, 1965, pp. 32-70.
140. *Subhasitaratnakosa* of Vidyakara, cited by Kosambi, *Introduction* . . . , p. 268, and Sharma, *Indian Feudalism*, p. 267.
141. Kosambi sets out his theory in *Introduction* . . . , pp. 274ff. in two chapters; the description of 'Indian Feudalism' as compared with European is given on pp. 326-8. Alienation of tax-rights by rulers led to 'Feudalism from above', while in 'feudalism from below' a class of 'landowners developed within the village, between the state and the peasantry, to wield armed power' over the population (ibid., p. 275). Sharma in his seminal work, *Indian Feudalism, c. AD 300-1200*, does not seem to consider the later process as contributing to feudalism. Sharma summarizes his conclusions on pp. 263-72.
142. Sharma's own date (*Indian Feudalism*, p. 283). See Ashton Coulborn's

perceptive remarks (in spite of his excessively narrow view of feudalism) on the role of Brāhmaṇas in *Comparative Studies in Society and History* (*CSSH*, X (3) 1968), pp. 357-9, esp. n. on p. 358).

143. R.S. Sharma, *IHR*, 1 (1), p. 5; B.N.S. Yadava, *IHR*, III (1), p. 44. The paucity of coins, as index of the decline, is also commented upon by L. Gopal, *Economic Life* . . . , pp. 215-21.

144. Cf. R.S. Sharma, *Indian Feudalism*, pp. 156-209; B.N.S. Yadava, *Society and Culture* . . . , pp. 136-63.

145. V.R.R. Dikshitar, *War in Ancient India*, Madras, 1944, pp. 165-6.

146. On the ineffectiveness of cavalry without saddle and stirrup see Sarva Daman Singh, *Ancient Indian Warfare* . . . , pp. 69-71. The arrival of the saddle in the West is dated first century AD, but its spread was slow (Lynn White, Jr., *Medieval Technology* . . . , pp. 7-8). A saddle is probably shown in a Khajuraho sculpture of the tenth century (Vidya Prakash, *Khajuraho*, Bombay, 1967, p. 38 and Plate 47). On the stirrup see Irfan Habib, 'Changes in Technology in Medieval India' *Studies in History* II (1), 1980, pp. 25-6.

147. *Chachnama*, ed. Umar Daudpota, Delhi, 1939, p. 169.

148. The historical implications of the emergence of the Rajput horseman are missing in most discussions of the period; but Coulborn, almost by chance, draws a linguistic parallel between the *rājaputra* and the 'knight' (*CSSH*, X(3), 1962, p. 369 n.).

149. On the emergence of the Rajputs see B.D. Chattopadhyaya, 'Origin of the Rajputs', *IHR*, III (1), pp. 59-82.

150. On the groups of villages, many of which survive as traditional territorial division under different Rajput clans, see Irfan Habib, 'Distribution of Landed Property in Pre-British India', *Enquiry*, N.S. II (3) (1965), p. 42, where other references will be found.

151. Barani, *Ta'rikh-i Firuz-Shahi*, pp. 287-8, 291.

152. I have tried to trace this transformation (thirteenth-fourteenth centuries) in *The Cambridge Economic History of India*, vol. I, ed. T. Raychaudhuri and I. Habib, Cambridge, 1982, pp. 54-60. The predominance of the Rajputs among the *zamindar* clans recorded against individual *parganas* in Akbar's Empire with numbers of retainers (horse and foot) (*Aiñ-i-Akbari: Account of the Twelve Subas*) is proof enough of the 'Indian-feudal' roots of that class.

153. *Manusmriti*, X, 34; tr. Buhler, p. 410.

154. R.S. Sharma, *Indian Feudalism*, p. 298. Cf. R.D. Banerji, *The Pālas of Bengal*, reprint, Varanasi, 1973, pp. 44-51.

155. H.C. Ray, *The Dynastic History of Northern India*, Calcutta, 1931, I, p. 364.

12

The Role of Peasants in the Early History of Tamiḷakam in South India

M.G.S. Narayanan

SOURCES AND STRATEGY

This paper is an attempt to present a historical analysis of the life and struggle of the peasantry in ancient Tamiḷakam in south India during the first millennium of the Christian era.

The chief source of detailed information about social life in this period is the corpus of the Śaṅgam works, mostly in the form of bardic songs orally transmitted for generations and collected in anthologies by the Śaṅgam academy towards the close of that age.[1] It has to be pointed out in the interest of proper assessment that the material culture of the period has been brought out by archaeological excavations which corroborated several statements in these works regarding the administrative centres of the chiefdoms and the harbour towns which attracted Roman settlement and trade.[2] Supplementary evidence is found in the Roman writings duly attested by the discovery of Roman coinage in different parts of south India.[3] Moreover, numerous megalithic remains including urn burials containing precious beads and iron tools, and hero stones of the type encountered in Śaṅgam works, have been discovered, opened and examined.[4] A few donative label inscriptions, mostly belonging to Jain centres and reflecting the condition of religion and culture, have been located in rock-cut caves.[5] All these have been discussed separately, and sometimes jointly in their historical context, so much so that it is possible now for us to review the progress of early Tamil society from the peasant's angle.

The period which follows immediately, characterized by the formation of State under the Pallavas, Cēras and Cholas as well as the emergence of a temple-centred economy and caste-oriented society culminated in the establishment of the Chola empire.[6] Though completely different on the surface, it now reveals the continuity with certain others in the growth of State power, and the enlargement of certain others like northern brāhmin influence in the courts and the countryside. Both of these may be traced back to the same practice of conferring land grants on political favourites—a practice which eventually led to the development of feudalism and the ultimate decline of the State.[7] It can be analysed with greater confidence in the light of clearer evidence. Therefore it helps us to place the earlier developments in historical perspective. However, it also points to an external factor influencing the growth of Tamil society, the waves of the great Aryan brāhmin migratory movement in search of cultivable land, which was also perhaps the greatest single movement in early Indian history concretely manifested in thousands of land-grant records all over India.[8] This phenomenon offers an explanation for many things in Indian history, though the causes, character and dimensions of the thing itself remain largely obscure. We find the evidence of its early impact in Śaṅgam Tamil society, and since this is the only non-Aryan society which left behind such a wealth of literary material from the remote past,[9] this may also be considered crucial to the understanding of the land-grant system in India as a whole. It is an acknowledged fact that Aryan brāhmin influence acting through the caste system and the institution of the temple, produced a near-monopoly of land power for the brāhmins and brāhmin-supported states in the great agricultural production centres, i.e. the fertile river valleys of India, thus promoting the uniformity of Indian culture by inducing the same type of changes in tribal or semi-tribal structures of society and their ideological superstructure. We do not intend to go into the details of post-Śaṅgam Tamil society but we take into account the studies of that later evidence made by ourselves and other scholars in formulating this interpretation of the struggle of the peasantry on the basis of earlier evidence.[10]

It is necessary to recognize at this stage that, in spite of detailed studies of ancient Tamiḻakam at the beginning of the Christian era, peasant life has not been subjected to scientific analysis and its vicissitudes have not been scrutinized properly.[11]

The peasant has been the underdog throughout early history and he has been subjugated and exploited because he has been the chief human agency for producing the items required for the maintenance of life. Ever since he emerged as a recognizable entity in ancient Tamiḻakam he was forcefully subordinated, first by the warlike *Maṛavar* groups from the less fertile regions in the neighbourhood, and then gradually by the immigrant landowning brāhmin groups in a more sophisticated manner as they acted with the connivance of the former groups without employing directly the instruments of violence. The peasant's voice has often been muffled, and his rights have been curtailed or completely removed. He did not occupy the centre of the stage where we find the fighting and ruling groups who lived in fortified capitals with the help of the surplus that the peasant produced. A little less visible were the courtiers, agents and recipients of land-grants with the supporting groups in handicrafts and trade. As these people have obscured the view of the peasant, the historian has to make a special effort to discover him and follow the course of his continuous and laborious struggle through life.

PEASANT SETTLEMENTS OF THE ŚAṄGAM AGE

Śaṅgam poetry conveys a vivid idea about five types of ecological-cultural regions, each with its own distinct occupational pattern and corresponding forms of worship, customs and manners, and even preference for moods and forms in literature.[12] Of these the *Marutam* regions were the fertile agricultural tracts along the fertile river valleys with prosperous villages known as *Ūr* inhabited by peasants called *Uḻavar, Veḷḷāḷar,* etc., in literature.[13] The term *Uḻavar* literally means ploughmen[14] and the term *Veḷḷāḷar* literally means masters of the soil indicating possession of land rather than work on other's land for wages.[15] They had their chiefs called *Kiḻāvar* or *Talaivar* who owned the village which was either gifted or patronized by a greater chief called *Vēndan* or *Araican*—this latter word is the Tamil form of *Rājan* in Sanskrit—in contemporary literature.[16] The *Kilāvar* were obliged to go to war in support of the *Vēndar.*[17] They shared the spoils of war in the form of booty and occasionally received the grant of villages as reward of distinguished military service.[18] The *Puṛam* songs give us the impression that the settlement of new agricultural villages, through the conversion of *kaḍu* and *nāḍu* under the patronage of the *Vēndar* went on continuously, though any attempt to quantify the same on the basis of bardic accounts would be quite arbitrary.[19]

A large number of poems mention the practice of the chief granting *Ūr* to the *panar* (traditional nomadic bards), *Brahmanar* (Vedic sacrificial priests) and the *Maṛavar* (tribal warlike bands).[20] The gifts are often made in the form of clothes, food, gold ornaments, elephants and chariots, but occasionally they take the shape of villages.[21] The gift of a village might be taken to mean the nomination of a person as the *Kiḷāvar* (chief) and the agent of the *Vēndar* (king) in that place. Thus it may be inferred that people drawn from different ethnic and professional groups were being transformed into landowning cultivators in course of time.[22] Even though the incidents and situations described by the poets may not be historical, or may be partly historical and partly imaginary, the authenticity of the practice cannot easily be questioned, since it is mentioned by several poets hailing from different places and celebrating a variety of themes. The present writer agrees that the very conventionalism of these traditional bards highlighted by Kailasapathy in his famous discussion of Tamil heroic poetry must be derived from, and based on, social reality at some stage. It must have a reference point somewhere, but as it is not located in earlier Sanskrit works it can only be attributed to the historical reality in contemporary Tamil society including society of a slightly older age.[24] Incidentally, this argument is applicable not only to grants but also to the entire social milieu in Śaṅgam literature.

The peasants in the village had their *Maṉṟam* or *Podūvil,* a common meeting ground under ancient banyan trees with a sacred spot or a shrine for ancestral gods or guardian deities.[25] This was frequented by the elders for consulting[26] the younger people for games or gambling[27] and the wandering bards and their womenfolk in search of a resting place.[28] The *Maṉṟam* was the social centre of the village and the target of invaders in the event of warfare.[29] The elders appear to have lost their authority and their function due to increasing helplessness in a period of constant warfare. The youngsters were forced to follow their chiefs into the field of battle. The traditional bards, who retained their primitive nomadic habits in anachronistic manner, lingered on as the representatives of a bygone age of egalitarian values and clannish loyalties.[30] They were getting progressively impoverished and sought the patronage of benevolent chiefs and kings who sometimes entertained them or dismissed them with presents or tried to settle them in agricultural villages.[31] As a result of all this, the *Mạṇṛam* was often deserted and neglected.[32]

In the *Marutam* agricultural tracts there is clear evidence of social stratification since the *Kilāvar* who were prosperous and powerful occupied a special status, and the other peasants who were their followers were obliged to follow them as ordinary warriors into the field of battle.[33] Besides these, there were *Adiyor* (slaves) and *Vinaiyor* (workers) also called *Kaḷamar* (field labourers) in the village.[34] Not much is known from the songs about the ordinary life of the ordinary peasants or other inhabitants, because literary conventions, obviously backed by notions of social prestige, prevented the poets from treating them as heroes and heroines.[35] This very distinction, formally stated by Tolkāppiyanar, shows that social stratification was well-established and deep-rooted in the sphere of culture. The high-low and rich-poor differences among the people are also built into the megalithic burial practice.[36]

It is evident from the general character as well as the specific references of the corpus of Śaṅgam works that the peasants were dominated and governed by the warlike *Maṛavar* from the relatively infertile hilly region. There was a constant flow of the *Maṛavar* groups endowed with fierce looks, cruel behaviour, supreme loyalty and death-defying courage, into the armies of the great clan chiefs and from there into the ranks of rich peasants, well-settled with agricultural land in the *Marutam* villages.[37] Even after this metamorphosis they continued to be at the beck and call of the *Vēndar*, to serve him in battle.[38] This curious connection between the occupations of the warrior and the peasant led, on the one hand, to the taming of the fierce *Maṛavar*, and on the other to the establishment of the hegemony of the ruling clans over the *Ūḷavar-Veḷḷāḷar* groups in the fertile regions of the river valleys in the Tamil part of south India. The power and prosperity of the *Mūvēndar* or *Mūvarasar*—the three great clan chiefs of the Chola, Cēra and Pāṇḍya—depended on the surplus of agricultural products in these river valleys. The strongholds of these three are found in the valleys of Kaveri, Periyar and Vaigai rivers, i.e. in the most fertile *Marutam* regions of the peninsula.[39] It was partly the surplus of peasant production in these areas, and partly the gains of the great inland trade between *Tamiḻakam* and the Deccan that made these three emerge as the masters of the land while the numerous chieftains of the hill-forts in Elimalai, Potiyilmalai, Kollimalai, Kutiramalai, Parambimalai, Venkatamalai, etc., in *Kuriñji* regions with scanty agricultural resources were gradually brought within their sphere of influence.[40] When the importance of the Roman trade increased in the first three centuries of the Christian era, the three great *Vēndar* or *Araśar* extended their power to the coastal areas, the Cēra to the West coast (Tondi and Muciri) and the Chola (Kaveri Poompattinam) to the East coast respectively.[41] Even then trade remained marginal and agricultural production by the peasants formed the decisive factor in social organization. Continuous wars maintained the flow of warlike groups into the *Marutam* region and the peasants were kept in bondage with the help of an elaborate war machine. The dynamics of this apparatus of war can be known from the numerous *Puṟam* songs which are devoted to warfare. They project the essential features of a cult of war in the ideological sphere.

CULT OF WAR AND MARTYRDOM

The elaboration and promotion of the cult of war is manifested in different ways in Śaṅgam literature. A picture of continuous warfare is presented by the poems composed by hundreds of poets and collected in anthologies of the *Akam* and *Puṟam* types.[42] The most celebrated attribute of the chief is his capacity for making war, defeating enemies, plundering territories and punishing recalcitrant subordinates.[43] Promotion of agriculture through the creation of irrigation facilities and patronage of the *Uḻavar-Veḷḷāḷar* group is, however, a royal attribute of secondary importance.[44] There would appear to be a rivalry between the two occupations, that of the warrior and that of the peasant, from the peasant from the *Kuṟiñji* and the *Marutam* respectively. While the greater number of poets are devoted to war and heroism, there are some among them who bestow praise on agricultural activity and peace. The cult of peace which is related to the outlook of the peasant is not so prominent as the cult of war, and this is a natural reflection of the power, wealth and status enjoyed by the two groups in the society of the period as the bards were the accredited spokesmen of that society and the keepers of their traditional values and conscience.[45] It is also interesting to note in this connection the frequent effort by the bards to draw a comparison between the action of the warrior in the battlefield and the peasant in the field of agriculture.[46]

The fierce cult of war is propagated through the celebration of the courage and valour of warriors, the voluntary sacrifice of their mothers and wives, and the rituals concerning the erection and worship of the hero stone.[47] The poets play endlessly on the warrior's hopes regarding the prospect of plunder,[48] the patron's gift of villages[49] and the pleasant sensations of the hero's paradise.[50] The pathetic side of it is demonstrated by the cynical indifference towards the sufferings of the peasant as a result of the constant warfare.

This is found in the case of the most frequent form of armed conflict known as *vetci* (cattle raid) and the sequel to it known as *karantai* (cattle recovery).[51] These events were misunderstood as marking the conventional opening gambit of war in the writings of the medieval commentators and the modern historians also when they followed the prescriptive formula of *Tolkāppiyam* and ignored the descriptive accounts found elsewhere.[52] The present writer has been able to show that *vetci* represented the typical form of martial combat in pastoral and agricultural villages, noticed by historians and anthropologists in all early societies including the Homeric society of the Greeks in the heroic age and the Aryan society of the Vedic age.[53] The cruel *Maṛavar* often feasted on the flesh of the cattle with heavy bouts of liquor (*kal*) and sometimes distributed the cattle among the needy followers.[54] The inhabitants of the victimized village could manage to recover the cattle if they organized a timely defense.[55] The heroes who fell in such engagements were deified and stone memorials were put up to them in the outskirts of the village.[56] There are some accounts of how temporary shrines were built by the villagers who cut and washed the stones with great ceremony, planted and decorated them with peacock feathers and offered worship there.[57] The spirits of the martyrs were propitiated with offerings and gradually they were transformed into the guardian deities of the village. Hundreds of these hero-stones of the early centuries of the Christian era, discovered in different parts of Tamiḷakam, testify to the vigour and continuity of this practice.[58] In recollecting the past one poet speaks of the times when there were only wild grains and nomadic tribes, and hero—stones were the only gods to be worshipped.[59] The 'conquest' of the fertile valleys by brāhmin landlords, brāhmin gods and brahmanical language constitutes an interesting chapter in the history of Tamiḷakam which can only be cited in passing without entering into the details here.

All these would go to prove the defenceless plight of the peasants and show how they were terrorized and subjugated by the armed bands from the barren lands around them, acting as agents of the chiefs of the fortified palace. The need for defending their cattle and their grain fields against marauding groups appear to have compelled the peasants to seek the protection of the powerful military chiefs, or at least to acquiesce in their claims of sovereignty and pay the tribute. This is how the foundations were laid for the emergence of a nebulous form of State. The process eventually led to the great bondage of the peasants as they had to support with their labour an expanding royal establishment with all its extravagance.

When regular wars were fought by the chiefs, they were not for conquest and annexation of territory, but only for plunder and revenge. A much advertised part of the expedition was the devastation of harvesting fields and the conversion of well-tended gardens into waste.[60] Setting fire to the peasant settlements and letting lose elephants into the field are often mentioned by the poets as acts of valour to be cherished with pride.[61]

Not only cattle and agricultural produce but also girls were carried away by force by the chiefs from the villages. When the warlike relatives resisted the demand for the girl, armed conflict followed. While romantic love in the paddy fields and groves has been depicted as the normal form of marital choice in hundreds of songs,[62] marriage by capture is also recognized by the theorists of this literature.[63] There is a group of songs in which the bards lament the miserable consequence of this practice.[64] They show how the attack of the chariot-riding chiefs with their elephants and horses, determined to go back with the girls only, ruined entire villages in due course.[65] This leads them to curse the beauty of the girls, but not the cruelty and callousness of the chiefs themselves.[66]

In spite of the harassment of armed bandits and the exploitation by the chiefs whose protection they sought for survival, the peasant villages enjoyed their life close to nature. There are references to vast fields where the workers were engaged in harvest and made merry with toddy served in mobile carts.[67] The womenfolk of the peasant families often joined their men in keeping their fields free from the attack of birds and beasts.[68] The happy portraits of these people singing and playing to pass time are found in plenty in this literature.[69] Sometimes the peasants kept vigil at night in the paddy and sugarcane fields to drive away the wild elephants by beating drums and maintaining a fire.[70] These occasions provided chances for love and romance.[71] There are also pictures of the lonely peasant woman spinning on the wheels at night on the verandah of her cottage in the dim light of the lamp when her husband was away serving the chief in the field of battle.[72] The noisy wild fowl near the village fence kept her company in solitude. While constant wars accompanied by plunder and massacre made the peasant's lot miserable, they had to face natural threats from droughts and wild animals too, and all these made their life a perpetual struggle. Still they tried to make it brighter by means of numerous festivals, games, music, dance and romance.[73]

The contradiction is caught and expressed beautifully in the corpus of Śaṅgam literature.

THE ADVENT OF THE BRĀHMINS IN COURT LIFE

The appearance of the brāhmin in the courts of the Tamil chieftains must be taken as a pointer to the future. The brāhmins are described as proficient in the four Vedas, as the performers of sacrifices, and as men of great piety and austerity well-versed in *Dharmaśāstra* literature.[74] There does not seem to have been any racial animosity between the Tamils or Dravidians and the incoming Aryan brāhmins who appeared in the courts of the chiefs like other supplicants and seekers of fortune.[75] It is quite significant that the brāhmins themselves are prepared to recognize the Tamil chiefs in the kṣatriya category of the *varṇa* order, bestow Aryan Vedic-Purāṇic ancestry on them by connecting them with the heroes of the *Mahābhārata*, and perform Vedic *yajñas* (sacrifices) in their names.[76] This implies the treatment of the Tamil chiefs on the same footing as the Aryan chiefs in practice.[77] These brāhmins competed with the *panas* in singing the praise of the chiefs, in legitimizing and glorifying their power, and they could do it with greater effect as they inherited the tradition of the *gāthā narasamsi* of the Vedic age.[78] Moreover, they were the products of a more advanced society of the Gangetic valley, more advanced in material as well as spiritual culture. They could impart lessons to their patrons from their knowledge of the *Arthaśāstra* and *Kāmasūtra*, *Jyotisha* and *Ayurvēda* and also bind the chiefs to a higher ethical code based on the *Dharmaśāstra* literature.[79] They claimed to be the new *panas* (bards) and assumed the role of the traditional *panas* in the courts, and rose to the position of confidants, messengers and councillors of the chiefs in due course.[80]

The advent of the cultured and capable brāhmins who brought new religion and new sciences into Tamiḷakam, as a rival to the *panas* had great significance at this particular juncture. It was a time when primitive tribal society with its communistic traditions had been giving way to stratified society built up on the surplus of agriculture. The Aryan Jainas and Buddhists had also entered society in Tamiḷakam, perhaps even earlier than the Vedic brāhmins, but they were not so effective.[81] The story of the brāhmin is the story of the honoured guest confiscating the household and its wealth and assuming the ownership of the establishment after enslaving the inmates. It is embodied in the beautiful myth of the Vāmana, an *avatār* of Viṣṇu in the guise of a brāhmin boy and begging for three feet of the earth from the Asūra king Mahābali, ultimately sending him into the nether world of *Pātāla*.[82] If the *pana* was member of a vanishing species, the relic of the old tribal society in Tamiḷakam, the brāhmin held the key to the future. The gift of land to the brāhmin is mentioned in some works,[83] probably belonging to the later part of the Śaṅgam age, and it is clear that several brāhmins had settled down in different parts of Tamiḷakam as indicated by the large number of Sanskritic terms, ideas and names.[84] These brāhmins apparently converted the chiefs to the Vedic religion—the old beliefs continued as part of it—and the new Aryan way of life of which a Tamilized version gradually came into existence.

The next phase of development is comparatively better documented in the form of hundreds of temples and temple inscriptions and a large corpus of *bhakti* literature, coins, artifacts and foreign notices to complete the picture. With the establishment of the brahmanized Pallava dynasty of Andhra origin at Kāñchi in the north-east corner of Tamiḷakam (*c.* AD 600) there were greater waves of immigration and settlement, the brāhmin section of which took the shape of *Agrahāras* which may be described as agrarian corporations of huge size.[85] Eventually they became temple-centred and propagated the ideology of *bhakti* which was congenial to the developing feudal social structure.[86] The present writer has shown in a study jointly undertaken with a research scholar how the Tamil *bhakti* movement, as different from the later medieval *bhakti* movement, was the ideological projection of the temple movement, which was in itself the offshoot of the *Agrahāra* movement to be traced back to the Pallava times.[87] The hindsight provided by this development enables us to see now the meaning of the brāhmin presence in the earlier Tamil courts of the Śaṅgam period in proper perspective. The foundations were laid during the close of the Śaṅgam period and a strong element of continuity is noticeable.[88] With the immigrant brāhmins, non-cultivating proprietors of the soil patronized by the rulers, establishing themselves in large fertile valleys, the old real producers, the rich and poor peasants of Tamiḷakam, were either pushed out or forced to accept a subordinate position acknowledging the brāhmin or the temple as the landlord and surrendering a part of their produce. This is illustrated by the *kuḍi ningi karayma* and the *kuḍi ninga karayma*, the first type evacuating the old peasants and the second permitting them to continue.[89] We do not know whether the process engendered much resistance from the local peasantry or witnessed a passive acceptance. Even if the peasants protested, there was little chance of their victory as they were scattered and unorganized and incapable of standing up to the organized military might of the new State and the social cohesion of the immigrants themselves.

In this connection the thesis of a brāhmin-peasant alliance put forward by the American scholar, Burton Stein, to explain the brāhmin ascendancy, is unsupported by evidence.[90] On the other hand the evidence of the Śaṅgam period indicated above suggest a brāhmin-chieftain alliance against the peasants which gave the proprietorship of great landed estates to the brāhmin immigrants and in return secured their support, blessings and court services for the chiefs who were trying to transform themselves into kings of the early medieval Gupta and post-Gupta period in every sense.[91]

This was part of the historical process of State formation in south India.[92] The present writer had suggested in an earlier paper discussing the evolution of Tamil society, a wedge hypothesis to explain the brāhmin ascendancy.[93] According to this the brāhmin courtiers who stepped into the role of the *panas* had succeeded in driving a wedge between the traditional Tamil chiefs in whose courts they lived and the traditional Tamil society of the tribal-pastoral-agrarian type.[94] The brāhmin priest was elevated to the position of the confidant, courtier and political adviser in the Tamil chief's palace. Many factors like the drying up of Roman trade, the migrations from brāhmin settlements and the cultural impact of Sanskrit education conspired to promote a new feudal social order and a new form of State.[95] The wedge hypothesis appears to be relevant in the context of the brāhmin-chieftain alliance and the consequent expansion and consolidation of brāhmin settlements which subjected the older peasantry to a new type of bondage.[96] The peasants were almost reduced to the status of serfs in many pockets though some of the luckier ones became tenants of the brāhmins and temples and occupied a middle station in life.[97]

FINDINGS AND THEIR PRESENT DAY RELEVANCE

To sum up the results of the survey, the peasants known as *Uḷavar* or *Veḷḷāḷar* were highly placed and respected in early Śaṅgam society which had already emerged from the primitive nomadic tribal stage and started producing agricultural surplus in the *Marutam* regions of Tamiḻakam where stratification also was clearly noticeable. The richer peasants who were chiefs and elders of their villages and even other peasants had to take up military functions for the sake of defence. The warriors from the *Maṛava* tribal groups in *Kuṛiñji* region also looked for good lands to settle down as peasants when they returned from the field of battle. Thus a close relationship and some rivalry existed between the two occupational groups in which membership was flexible.

The continuous wars and the growing cult of war invariably gave greater power to the warrior groups under the clan chiefs in due course. The peasantry which had to seek the protection of the chiefs against plunder of the fields, cattle raids and the capture of women by force tended to become integrated to the political system in which a rudimentary form of the State came into existence. In this period the peasant groups were clearly subjected to the warrior groups who established their dominance.

At this juncture the advent of the brāhmins as the courtiers and priests of the Tamil chiefs, in combination with a variety of other factors, led to the rise of the three clan chiefs of the interior, the Cēra, Chola and the Pāṇḍya, and the strengthening of the machinery of State. The growth of Roman trade in the early centuries of the Christian era might have played a part in this process, but it had no enduring impact on the predominantly agrarian social structure. The acceleration of stratification expressed itself through the brāhmin-chieftain alliance. It also led to the formation of a temple-centred and caste-oriented feudal social structure. The peasants lost their communal and family rights in land and were forced to accept the śūdra rank at the bottom of society. Some of them became tenants of brāhmins and temples while others were reduced to serfdom in due course. The latter were only slightly better off than the semi-nomadic outcaste groups of the wilder tribes who still exist on the fringes of civilized society in the same old food-gathering stage.[98]

This review and reinterpretation of the early phases of Tamil society from the peasant angle has a particular importance for the present and the future. A fierce animosity between the brāhmin landed aristocracy and the several non-brāhmin sections of the people has been recorded frequently in later medieval times.[99] This has been exploited and intensified by foreign missionary propaganda and literature.[100] The self-perception of society has been such that even today the conflicts of the past have been viewed in terms of Aryan-Dravidian dichotomy, i.e. in terms of racial, religious or linguistic differences.[101]The basic reality of the class combinations and class contradictions which resulted in the subjugation of the peasantry which formed the majority in society has been grievously overlooked.

The rediscovery of the real historical process of the alienation of land rights from the peasants, in its different stages from the remote past to the present, is an essential pre-requisite for the successful re-organization of the social system in south India.

NOTES

1. The corpus of Śaṅgam literature is classified as follows:

    (a). *Ettuttokai* (Eight anthologies)
    (b) *Pattuppāttu* (Ten poems)
    (c) *Patinenkilkkanakku* (Eighteen lesser accounts)
    (d) *Tolkkāppiyam* (A work on poetics)
    (e) *Cilappatikaram* and *Manimēkalai* (The twin epics)
    (f) *Takadur Yattirai* and *Paratam* (The two lost poems)

    The first collection is believed to contain the earliest compositions while the second, third and fourth (b, c, and d) are of a slightly later age. The twin epics could belong to the post-Śaṅgam period, though the plots are based on early tradition.

    The legend of the three Śaṅgams cannot be taken seriously. The conventional view that *Tolkkāppiyam,* the standard text on poetics, came first is unacceptable. The archaic language of Śaṅgam Tamil is obscure, like Vedic Sanskrit, and can be followed with the help of medieval commentaries only. Though their existence was known to the scholarly world throughout the past, the Śaṅgam texts were discovered and presented to the modern world in the beginning of the present century.

    For a discussion of chronology and other details, see N. Subrahmanian, Śaṅgam *Polity,* Bombay, 1966, Madurai, 1980; K.A.N. Sastri, *The Śaṅgam Age, Its Cults and Cultures*, Madras, 1973; K. Kailasapathy, *Tamil Heroic Poetry,* Oxford, 1968; S.V. Subramanian (ed.), *Historical Heritage of the Tamils*, Madras, 1983.
2. The most important excavations were those of Arikkamedu, Karur, Kaverippattinam, Kodumanal, Korkkai, Dadurai, Takadur, Urayur, etc. For a useful summary, see Clarence Maloney, 'Archaeology in South India: Accomplishments and Prospects' in Burton Stein (ed.), *Essays on South India,* Madras, 1975, New Delhi, 1976; K.V. Raman, 'Archaeological Investigations in the Recent Past' in B.K. Gururaja Rao, *A Decade of Archaeological Studies in South India*, Dharwad, 1978.

    For some important details, see R.E.M. Wheeler, 'Arikamedu—An Indo-Roman Trading Station on the East Coast of India', *Ancient India,* no. 2, July 1946, pp. 117-24; R. Nagaswamy, 'Excavations at Korkkai', *Damilica,* 1. Dec. 1970, pp. 50-4; R. Nagaswamy, 'Roman sites in Tamilnad: Recent Discoveries', *Madhu,* New Delhi, 1981, pp. 337-9; R. Champakalakshmi, 'Archaeology and Tamil Literary Tradition', *Puratattva,* no. 8, 1975-6, pp. 110-22; M.G.S. Narayanan, 'A Historian's View of the Archaeology of Tamilnadu and Kerala', in *Tamil Civilization,* vol. 5, nos. 1 and 2, Thanjavur, 1986.
3. For the Roman writings, see R.C. Majumdar, *Classical Accounts of India,* Calcutta, 2nd edn., 1922; K.A.N. Sastri, *Foreign Notices of South India,* Madras, 1939.

    For the Details of Roman trade, see E.H. Warmington, *The Commerce between the Roman Empire and India*, London, 2nd edn., 1974; R.E.M. Wheeler, *Rome Beyond the Imperial Frontier*, London, 1974. For the finds of Roman Coins, see P.L. Gupta, *Early Coins from Kerala*, Trivandrum, 1972; P. Srivastava, 'The Economic Significance of Roman Coins Found in India', *Journal of the Numismatic Society of India*, vol. XXVI, 1964, pp. 222-7; S.P. Kandaswamy, 'The Kongu and the Roman Coins', *Journal of the Numismatic Society of India*, vol. XLVI, 1984, pp. 39-44.

The important find spots of Roman Coins in Tamil Nadu are Pollachi (1800), Kalliyamputhur (1856), Karuwar (1878), Vellalur (1891), Coimbatore (1891), Yesvantpur (1891), and Pudukkottai (1891). Those in Kerala are Kottayam (1848), Eyyal (1945), Valluvalli in north Paravur (1984) and Puthenchira in Maala (1984).

4. For a detailed study of megaliths in this region, see Gururaja Rao, *The Megalithic Culture in South India*, Mysore, 1972; Leshnik, *The South Indian Megalith Burials: The Pandukal Complex*, Wiesbaden, 1974; B. Narasimhaiah, *Neolithic and Megalithic Culture in Tamilnadu*, New Delhi, 1980.

   For attempts to correlate the megalithic evidence with other evidence, see K.R. Srinivasan, 'The Megalithic Burials and Urn Fields of South India in the Light of Tamil Literature and Tradition', *Ancient India*, no. 2, July 1946, pp. 9-16; K.S. Ramachandran, 'Some Aspects of the Economy of the Indian Megalithic Builders', *Indian Historical Quarterly*, vol. XXXVII. R. Nagaswamy (ed.), *Seminar on Hero-stones*, Madras, 1974; P. Chinnian, 'Megalithic Monuments and Megalithic Culture in Tamilnadu', *Historical Heritage of the Tamils*, 1983.

5. A detailed study of the cave label inscriptions, is contained in T.V. Mahalingam, *Early South Indian Palaeography*, Madras, 1974.

   For the texts of inscriptions, see Iravatham Mahadevan, 'Corpus of Tamil Brahmi Inscriptions', in R. Nagaswamy (ed.), *Seminar on Inscriptions*, Madras, 1966, pp. 57-63 and *Tamil Brahmi Inscriptions*, Madras, 1970.

6. A standard survey of the history of the peninsula in this period may be found in K.A.N. Sastri, *A History of South India*, Madras, 1957.

7. For the general conceptual framework of social evolution in ancient India we follow the scheme of R.S. Sharma, *Indian Feudalism*, Calcutta,1965. The growth of feudal society traced chiefly through land grants by Sharma, following D.D. Kosambi, in the case of north India, is also applicable to south India.

8. While feudalism was a primary growth in the north, its institutional devices like land-grants, temples and the cultural baggage were imported from the Deccan to Tamiḷakam. For the early land-grants of the Deccan, see H.P. Ray, *Monastery and Guild: Commerce Under the Satavahanas*, New Delhi, 1986.

9. The presence of Aryan brāhmins, Jains and Buddhists and their cultural impact are clearly indicated in the earliest Tamil Śaṅgam works, pottery and inscriptions. See n 1 and 2.

For the spread of Aryan culture, see M.G.S. Narayanan, 'Vedic Purāṇic, Śastraic Element in Tamil Śaṅgam Society and Culture in *IHC Proceedings*, Aligarh, 1975. For a theoretical-historical materialist approach to ancient Tamil poetry, see Vanamanalai, 'Materialist Thought in Tamil Śaṅgam Literature', *Social Scientist*, September 1973. See also Siva Thamby, *Literary History in Tamil*, Thanjavur, 1986. For general histories of early Tamil, see S. Vaiyapuri Pillai, *A History of Tamil Language and Literature*, Madras, 1957; T.P. Meenakshi Sundaram, *A History of Tamil Literature*, Annamalai, 1962; C. Jesudasan and H. Jesudasan, *A History of Tamil Literature*, Calcutta, 1971.

10. See M.G.S. Narayanan, *Re-Interpretations in South Indian History*, Trivandrum, 1976; Burton Stein, *Peasant State and Society in Medieval South India*, Delhi, 1980; Noboru Karashima, *Indian History and Society*, Delhi, 1984. See also the review articles by R. Champakalakshmi, D.N. Jha and M.G.S. Narayanan in the following journals: *The Indian Economic and Social History Review*, vol. XVIII, nos. 3-4, 1984, pp. 411-26; *Social Science Probings*, June 1984; *Tamil Civilization*, vol. 3, no. 1, 1985.
11. Peasant life is incidentally described in the course of the study of society in the standard works but not viewed as the foundation of social life. See n 1. Awareness of problems relating to forces and relations of production and the role of classes in the appropriation of surplus has been conspicuous by its absence.
12. The conventional view of the concept of *aintinai* or five regions, a unique feature of the Śaṅgam literature, is outlined in *Tolkkāppiyam*, a work on poetics, placed by traditional Tamil Pundits at the beginning but by historians at the close of the Śaṅgam age. All the works are conscious of the differences which may be represented in a table:

Region	*Geography*	*Occupation*	*Cult*
Kuṛiñji	Hills/jungles	Food gathering & marginal agri.	Murugan/Seyon
Mullai	Forests/plains	Cattle tending & agri.	Vishnu/Mayon
Marutam	Fertile river valleys	Intensive agri.	Indra/Vendan
Neytal	Coastal area	Fishing/salt manf.	Varuna/Kadalon
Pālai	Dry lands deserts	Plunder/warfare	Durga/Koravai

For a recent discussion of Tinai concept, see K. Sivathamby, 'Early South Indian Society and Economy—The Tinai Concept', in *Social Scientist*, no. 29, Trivandrum, 1974.

13. N. Subrahmanian, *Śaṅgam Polity*, Bombay, 1960, Madurai, 1980, pp. 27-38.
14. The word *kaḷam* used in Tamil for the plough might have been derived

from *hala* in Sanskrit. The iron-tipped plough must have been used as iron is commonly found in the burials of the megalithic age.

15. The *Veḷḷāḷar* have been of two types according to the commentary of *Naccinarkkiniyar: Ulutu Unpavar* and *Uluvittu Unpavar*, i.e. those who are ploughmen and those who engaged ploughmen. See T.V. Kuppuswami, *Śaṅgam Chieftains and their Times*, Thanjavur, 1984, p.102. *Veḷḷāḷa* became a caste name for agriculturists at a later stage.
16. The term *Araica* is derived from *Rāja*. In the same way it is possible that the term *Vēnda* is derived from *Upēndra* in Sanskrit as the king was believed to have been the deputy of Indra in Sanskrit literature.
17. See *Puṟam*, nos. 312, 314, 318, 319, 320. These contain references to the *Taḷaivar* (chiefs) going to fight for the *Vēndar*. See also *Tolkkāppiyam*, 625, 626.
18. See *Puṟam*, nos. 7, 12, 297; *Patirruppattu*, 49, III *Patikam*, 43; *Akam*, no. 127; N. Subrahmanian, *Śaṅgam Polity*; pp. 173-5 and M.G.S. Narayanan, 'The Warrior Settlements of the Śaṅgam Age', in *IHC Proceedings*, Kurukshetra, 1982.
19. See *Puṟam*, no. 297 and others. What is described by Prof. N. Subrahmanian, as the distribution of tax-free lands must be viewed not as the grant of separate plots of lands but as the grants of the chiefship of villages. This is clear from the use of the term *ūr* meaning village.
20. For the gifts to *Panas*, see *Puṟam*, nos. 11, 12, 29, 69, 224 and 368 to 400. See also the collections like *Perumpanarruppadai* and *Cirupanar-ruppadai*. For the gifts to brāhmins, see *Puṟam*, nos. 12, 15, 21, 166, 224, 367, 377, etc. See also *Maduraikkāñci*, Ll. 200-4, 494-5 and *Patir-ruppattu*, 20, 70, 74. For the gifts to *Maravar*, see n. 18 and 19.
21. See the earlier note. The land gift to brāhmins mentioned in poetry finds corroboration in the Velvikkudi copper plates of the Pāṇḍyas. See K.A.N. Sastri, *The Pandyan Kingdom*, Madras, 1929, pp. 88-90.
22. The question of private property in agricultural land is crucial but elusive. Cultivation could have been chiefly communal in the sense that all the arable land in a village belonged to the villagers in common with the chief of the village acting as the leader and ruler of the village with the support of the elders meeting in the *Manram* or assembly of the village. In this context lands were common property in theory and individual property of the chief in practice.
23. This view of Kailasapathy is reflected throughout the work which applied the concept of the Heroic Age developed by Chadwick, Milman Parry and others to the corpus of Śaṅgam literature. See Kailasapathy, op. cit., Preface.
24. The organic relationship between Śaṅgam Poetry, Prakrit literary works like *Śattasāyi* of Haḷa and the megalithic culture of the Deccan and Tamilnad has been discussed by scholars. See George L. Hart, III, 'Some Related Conventions in Tamil and Indo-Aryan and their

Significance', *Journal of the American Oriental Society*, 94.2, 1974.

However, in spite of the influence of Prakrit and Sanskrit, it is clear that the Śaṅgam poetry reflected the conditions of Tamil society directly, along with its values and culture.

25. See N. Subrahmanian, *Śaṅgam Polity*, op. cit., pp. 118-20; *Pre-Pallavan Tamil Index*, pp. 609-10.
26. See *Maduraikkāñci*, 161; *Tirumurugarruppadai*, 226.
27. See *Malaippadukatam*, 492 and Naccinarkkiniyar's Commentary. See also *Puṟam*, no. 390.
28. See *Pattinappalai*, Ll. 246-89.
29. See M.G.S. Narayanan, 'The Mauryan Problem in Śaṅgam Works in Historical Perspective', *Journal of Indian History*, LIII. II. 1975.
30. See Kailasapathy, *Tamil Heroic Poetry*, op. cit., ch. III. 'Bards and Bardic Traditions', pp. 94-134. 'The bards and wise men of the early period were the custodians and perpetuators of antiquarian learning, genealogical lore, and other accounts of the past . . .', ibid., p. 2.
31. See *Tamil Heroic Poetry*, ch. III 'Bards and 'Bardic Traditions', pp. 96, 99, 115, 116, 159, 160, 164, etc. See also M.G.S. Narayanan, 'The Warrior Settlements of the Śaṅgam Age' in *IHC Proceedings*, Kurukṣhetra, 1982.
32. See *Puṟam*, nos. 52, 309, 375.
33. See *Puṟam*, nos. 289, 293; *Tolkkāppiyam*, 625, 626. Compare R.S. Sharma, *Material Culture and Social Formations in Ancient India*, New Delhi, 1983, p. 161 (Tribal militia and peasant militia).
34. See *Puṟam*, nos. 212, 387; *Kalittokai*, no. 88; *Tolkkāppiyam*, Porul, 25; see also K.A.N. Sastri, *The Śaṅgam Age*, p. 47.
35. *Tolkkāppiyam*, Porul, I-244.
36. Some burials are marked by big, strong and elaborate structures of laterite or granite. The inside of the chamber is furnished with rows of pots, iron implements like swords and bead ornaments. There are many hundreds of simple burials in pyriform urns called *nannangadi* without any of these features. See Gururaja Rao, *The Megalithic Culture of South India*.
37. See *Śaṅgam Polity*, pp. 133-5; T.V. Mahalingam, *Śaṅgam Chieftains and their Times*, pp. 36-7; *Tamil Heroic Poetry*, ch. VI. 'The World of Heroes', pp. 229-71.
38. See *Puṟam*, nos. 314, 318, 319, 320, 324, 326, 330, etc.
39. T.V. Kuppuswami, *Śaṅgam Chieftains and their Times*, pp. 30-4.
40. Ibid., pp. 41-62.
41. See Clarence Maloney, 'Archaeology in South India: Accomplishments and Prospects', in Burton Stein, *Essays on South India*, Delhi, 1978, pp. 12, 13, 19.
42. See *Puṟam*, nos. 18, 35, 68, 120, 289, etc.; *Tirukkurāi*, 104, 1031-6. See also *Akananuṟu*, *Naṟṟinai*, *Kuṟuntokai*, etc.
43. See *Tamil Heroic Poetry*, ch. VI. 'The World of Heroes', pp. 230-58.

Kailasapathy has listed (a) the desire for fame, (b) prowess in battle, (c) wrath, (d) lineage, and (e) wealth as the chief attributes of the warrior chiefs or aristocrats who are celebrated by the bards. He has given the necessary references from the Śaṅgam literature. See also Rajan Gurukkal, 'Early Iron Age Agriculture—The Problem of Agrarian Expansion', in B.D. Chattopadhyaya (ed.), *Essays in Ancient Indian Economy*, Delhi, 1987.

44. See *Śaṅgam Polity*, ch. IX, 'Economic Activities', Section 2, Agriculture, pp. 235-8. See also *Tirukkural*, ch. 104 on agriculture.
45. See *Tamil Heroic Poetry*, ch. III, 'Bards and Bardic Traditions', Section 3, Poets and Wise Men, pp. 121-4.
46. See *Puṛam*, nos. 35, 289, 369, etc. See also *Tolkkāppiyam*, Porul, 75.
47. See *Śaṅgam Polity*, ch. VI, 'Welfare and Military Organisation', pp. 126-86.
48. Ibid., pp. 152-3.
49. Ibid., pp. 153-4.
50. Ibid., pp. 135-6.
51. See *Śaṅgam Polity*, pp. 142-3, 162-3.
52. See *Tolkkāppiyam*, Porul, 59-63.
53. See M.G.S. Narayanan, 'Cattle Raiders of the Śaṅgam Age', *IHC Proceedings*, Bhubaneswar, 1977.
54. See *Puṛam*, nos. 257-8.
55. See *Puṛam*, nos. 259-61, 263, 269.
56. See *Puṛam*, nos. 260, 261, 263-5. See also *Tolkkāppiyam*, Porul, 63.
57. See *Puṛam*, nos. 221, 237, 260, 264-5, 306, 329.
58. See Gururaja Rao, *Megalithic Culture of South India*.
59. See Mankuti Kilar, *Puṛam*, no. 335.
60. See *Puṛam*, nos. 7, 15, 16, 23, 57, 345-51, 373, 393; *Patirruppattu*, 20; *Kalittokai*, 13; *Maduraikkāñci*, 126, 692.
61. Ibid. See also *Śaṅgam Polity*, p. 173.
62. See C.E. Ramachandran, *Akananuṛu in its Historical Setting*, Madras, 1974, ch. III, 'Social Conditions', pp. 60-8.
63. See *Tolkkāppiyam*, Porul, 89, 90.
64. See *Puṛam*, nos. 336-56.
65. Ibid. See nos. 339, 345-51, 354.
66. Ibid. See nos. 336, 339, 348-50.
67. See *Puṛam*, nos. 29, 42, 61, 68, 97, 166, 209, 212, 215, 321, 391, 395.
68. See *Kuṛinjippātu*, *Ainkuṛunuṛu*, 283, *Puṛam*, no. 29, *Akam*, nos. 28, 102, 126, 302, *Naṛṛinai* 27, *Kuṛuntokai*, 72, 142, 197. See also C. Balasubramanian, *The Status of Women in Tamilnadu during the Śaṅgam Age*, Madras, 1976, pp. 6, 8; K. Gnanambal, *Home Life among the Tamils*, Madras, 1947, pp. 19, 24, 34.
69. See *Puṛam*, nos. 84, 212, 372; *Akam*, nos. 141, 185; *Kalittokai*, 27.
70. See n 68.
71. The Śaṅgam poets have celebrated two stages of romance—*Karpu* (love)

and *Kalavu* (union) before marriage. Hundreds of songs in *Akananuru, Narrinai, Kurumtokai,* etc., have premarital romance as their theme. It is calculated that nearly 842 out of 882 love poems are on *Kalavu* type. See V.Sp. Manickam, *The Tamil Concept of Love,* Tirunelveli, 1962, p. 37; A.K. Ramanujam, *The Interior Land Scape,* London, 1967.

72. See *Puram,* no. 326.
73. See n 69.
74. See N. Subrahmanian, *Śaṅgam Polity,* pp. 102-3, III-3, K.A.N. Sastri, *The Śaṅgam Age,* pp. 43, 88-98; T.V. Kuppuswamy, *The Brahmanas and Brahmanism in Śaṅgam Literature,* Madurai, 1978.
75. Ibid.
76. Palai Gautamanar, patronized by Palyanai Cel Kelu Kuttuvan, performed ten sacrifices with the help of the wisest brāhmins. See *Patirruppattu,* III. 10, Patikam. Palyagasalai Mudukudumi Peruvaluti had several sacrificial halls as indicated by the title used as part of his name. He is said to have an equal number of battles fought and sacrifices performed. See *Puram,* no. 15. Rājasuyam Vetta Perunar Killi organized the *Rājasuya* as indicated by the title. Perum Ceral Irumporai, the Cēra king, conducted the *Putra-kameshti* sacrifice. See *Patirruppattu,* no. VII. 4. Karunkulalatan says that the Choḷa king Karikāla performed vedic sacrifices with elaborate rituals. See *Puram,* no. 224.
77. The Brāhmins were to conduct the Vedic sacrifices only for those who were authorized, i.e. for kṣatriyas of pure lineage. The Tamil kings were obviously elevated in caste by conferring on them genealogies which connected them with *purāṇic* dynasties of the solar and lunar race. The Pāṇḍyas were mentioned as descended for the moon and the Cholas from the sun. See *Śaṅgam Polity,* p. 44.
78. Kapila claims to be a brāhmin. See *Puram,* nos. 200, 201. He is also addressed as a brāhmin. See *Puram,* no. 126. He advises the king to appoint brāhmins as ministers. See *Patirruppattu,* VII, 2. Several names of brāhmin *gotras* appear among the poets of the age. For example, Kaundinya (Kauniyan), Gautama (Kautamanar), Kauśika (Kauśikanar), Bharadvāja (Parattayanar), etc.
79. The *Marayordeśam* (land of the Vedic people) was the model in discussing social institutions like marriage. See *Tolkkāppiyam,* Porul, 92.
80. See n 74.
81. The cave label inscriptions of the Śaṅgam period in Tamil Brahmi characters record several donations of rock beds and shelters to Jain monks who committed suicide by slow starvation. There is the famous legend of the southern migration of Chandragupta Maurya. Besides, the Jain and Ajivika philosophies are reflected in a few songs. The Buddhist missionaries had evidently penetrated to Tamiḷakam under Aśoka's influence. See M.G.S. Narayanan, 'The Mauryan Problem in Śaṅgam Works in Historical Perspective', *Journal of Indian History,*

Trivandrum, LIII.II. 1975. However, in spite of streaks of Jain and Buddhist ideas, the Śaṅgam works bear the heavy stamp of Brahmanical culture. See M.G.S. Narayanan, 'The Vedic-Puranic-Sastric Element in Tamil Śaṅgam Society and Culture' in *IHC Proceedings*, Aligarh, 1975.

82. The story of Vāmana as Trivikrama is a favourite motif in Pallava and Cāḷukya sculpture. Since the birthday of Vāmana in *Sravaṇa* is observed with great celebration at Tirupati, the Lord of Venkata hills was perhaps conceived as the Lord Vishnu in the incarnation of Trivikrama. It is from the north-eastern corner of Tamiḷakam which came to be occupied by the Pallavas at the close of the Śaṅgam period, that Aryan Brahmanical culture entered Tamiḷakam in a big way. See M.G.S. Narayanan and Kesavan Veluthat, 'The Bhakti Movement in South India', in D.N. Jha (ed.), *Feudal Formations in Early India*, New Delhi, 1987. This paper was originally published in *Indian Movements* by the Simla Institute, Simla, 1978.

83. See *Patiṟṟuppattu*, II. 10.

84. See n 74-80.

85. See C. Minakshi, *Administration and Social Life under the Pallavas*, 2nd ed. Madras, 1977; K.A.N. Sastri, *A History of South India*, Madras, 1966; M.G.S. Narayanan, *Re-Interpretations in South Indian History*, Trivandrum, 1975, 'Social and Economic Structure of South India', pp. 1-23.

86. The historical process of the brāhmin settlements, developing as agrarian corporations from the Pallava period onwards, deserves to be studied in detail. The relationship between the land-grant system, the brāhmin settlements, the south Indian temple, the *Bhakti* movement and the feudal order has to be analysed properly. In a series of studies culminating in a book, Prof. Burton Stein covered this theme also but certain doubtful theoretical assumptions regarding the peasant society on Chayanovian lines and a confused grasp of the contents of inscriptions have made the work undependable. See Burton Stein, *Peasant State and Society in Medieval South India*, Delhi, 1980. What he calls peasant state and society must be designated as feudal state and society in south India. Noboru Karashima has produced a more authentic and properly researched monograph in which the feudal character of Chola and post-Chola society is clearly outlined. See Noboru Karashima, *South Indian History and Society (Studies from Inscriptions, A.D. 850-1800)*, Delhi, 1985. See also M.G.S. Narayanan, 'Review Article: South Indian History and Society', in *Tamil Civilization*, vol. 3, no. 1, 1985, pp. 57-91.

87. See n 82. See also M.G.S. Narayanan, 'Devotional Movement in Ancient Tamiḷakam', in *Proceedings of the 31st International Congress of Human Sciences in Asia and North Africa*, Tokyo, 1984.

88. See n 74. The recent discovery (1979) of a *Brahmadēya* grant on a rock at Pulankurichi near Thanjavur, attributed to fourth-fifth centuries AD, would show that such land-grants and settlements had started

earlier than the seventh century when the Pāṇḍya revival started in the peninsula. The text has not been published. The present writer is thankful to Y. Subbarayalu and M.R. Raghava Varier for permission to use the text they prepared.

This is in line with the evidence of the Velvikkudi copperplate grant which refers to the donation of land to a brāhmin by Palyagasalai Mutukudumi Peruvaluti, the Pāṇḍyan ruler of the Śaṅgam age. According to this copper plate, the donated land was encroached upon by others during the *Kaḷabhra* period and re-allotted to the descendants of the original brāhmin family by Parāntaka Nedun Cadayan. See *Śaṅgam Polity*, p. 17.

89. See references under note 86. The important point here is that the *Kuḍikaḷ*, i.e. settlers who were obviously the Veḷḷāla peasants or cultivators were deprived of the ownership of land and transformed into tenants or sent out of the village.

Resistance on the part of the peasants is noticed in some cases. See Vanamamalai, 'Consolidation of Feudalism and Anti-feudal Struggles during Chola Imperialist rule', *Proceedings of the Second International Conference Seminar of Tamil Studies*, Madras,1968; Rajan Gurukkal, 'Non-Brahmana Resistance to the Expansion of Brahmadeyas: The Early Pandyan Experience', *IHC Proceedings*, Annamalai, 1984.

90. See Burton Stein, *Peasant State and Society*, ch. II. The factual and conceptual errors involved in Burton Stein's theory are clearly brought out in R. Champakalakshmi, 'Peasant', in *The Indian Economic and Social History Review*, vol. XVIII, nos. 3 and 4, 1983.

For a good criticism of the theory of Brahmin-Peasant alliance from the Marxist point of view, see D.N. Jha, 'Validity of the Brahmana-Peasant Alliance and the Segmentary State in Early Medieval South India', in *Social Science Probings*, June 1984, pp. 272-80.

91. The *Praśasti* or *Meykirti* portions of the inscriptions of the kings of south India in the post-Śaṅgam period clearly indicate their attempt to imitate the Hindu kings of north India. See Kesavan Veluthat, 'The Status of Monarch', *IHC Proceedings*, Kurukshetra, 1982.

92. This process has been discussed in some detail in the present writer's UGC National Lectures delivered at Delhi (JNU), Hyderabad and Madras in 1984. These lectures have not yet been published. R. Champakalakshmi presented a paper on State Formation in south India at Calicut University (1986) in which she traced the developments in Pallava-Chola periods with the help of inscriptions. This is also not published.

93. See M.G.S. Narayanan, 'The Cause of the Arrested Development of Tamil Tribal Groups in South India with Special Reference to Kerala', mimeographed paper presented at the Seminar on Tribal Development, Calicut, 1978.

94. While the kings were made to perform Vedic sacrifices and follow

Brahminical precepts, the local Tamil deities were identified with Sanskritic-Purāṇic deities, i.e. Vēndan with Indra, Mayon with Viṣṇu Murugan with Skanda, Korravai with Durga and Kadalon with Varuṇa. When the chiefs and their brahmin courtiers joined hands, the *panas* were gradually alienated. Political and cultural changes paralleled the developments in the sociōeconomic sphere of life. The replacement of the *Pana* bard by the brāhmin scholar in the Tamil court symbolised the change in the society and state.

95. See M.G.S. Narayanan, *Re-Interpretations,* op. cit., 'Social and Economic Structure of South India'.

96. The appearance of new brahmin landlords, the temporary strengthening of the State under the Chola empire and the progressive reduction of the status of the Veḷḷāla peasants are bought out with the help of inscriptions in N. Karashima, *South Indian History and Society*. These were the consequences of the brahmin-chieftain alliance in south India.

97. Ibid., ch. II. See also Elamkulam P.N. Kunhan Pillai, 'Kerala in the Grip of Chaturvarnya', in *Keralam Ancum Arun Noorrantukalil,* (Malayalam), Kottayam, 1960, and *Feudalism in Kerala* (Malayalam), Kottayam, 1964. The present writer is indebted to the inspiration and guidance of Elamkulam in the study of the early history of Kerala which formed an integral part of Tamiḷakam in ancient times.

98. The *Pulayar, Parayar, Cerumar,* etc., who are listed as scheduled castes and who were traditional agricultural workers having the status of agrestic slaves or serfs in medieval society must be the descendants of the early peasants who lost their lands. Those who could receive patronage from kings or brahmins were promoted but others were driven to the bottom when communal land was becoming private property. The caste system based on birth and marriage made self-improvement nearly impossible for such people by keeping their movement restricted to the village and forcing them to remain illiterate.

99. The district manuals and gazetteers compiled at the close of the nineteenth century and the beginning of the present century are full of such reports and accounts of criminal tribes. See also Edgar Thurston, *Castes and Tribes of South India,* Madras, 1910.

100. The work of foreign agencies like the London Mission Society, The Basel Mission Society, etc., engaged in conversion to Christianity often undertaken with the open or tacit support of the British imperial power, encouraged caste conflicts. The Dravidian theory, interpreting Tamil society in racial and communal terms, owes much to the writings of Bishop Caldwell, G.U. Pope, etc. There was an element of genuine protest, released by a modern education and way of life, but it was often channelized into communal hatred and cultural chauvinism through the Dravidian separatist movement which took roots among the people.

101. Historiography of south India has been vitiated by Aryan or Dravidian

bias, brāhmin or anti-brahmin bias and Sanskrit or Tamil bias in addition to regional pride. This has confused foreign students and researchers also. It is only recently that materialistic interpretations based chiefly on economic factors and class analysis has been slowly clearing the debris to reconstruct history as objectively as possible. This new trend is fostered by writers like Vanamalalai, Kailasapathy, Champakalakshmi, Karashima, Sivathamby, D.N. Jha, Y. Subbarayalu, Shánmugham, Kesvan Veluthat, Rajan Gurukkal *et al.* in the field of Tamil history in ancient and medieval times. See R. Champakalakshmi, 'Historiography of South India: New Directions', Presidential Address, South Indian History Congress, Madras, 1986, Historiography Section.

13

From the Ancient Labour Tax to the Feudal Corvee: A Marxist Approach to the Study of *Viṣṭi*

Marlene Njammasch

In Ancient Oriental societies the state demanded general taxes in kind and cash from the ordinary producers of the material wealth, especially from the peasant proprietors in the rural areas as well as from the urban population. This duty of paying taxes to the state included labour.[1] In many ancient societies a great number of people had to render labour services that were absolutely necessary for the subsistence of the states.

Public labour was used for the construction and the maintenance of irrigation systems, for roadworks, fortifications and other works required for the state. Work was done likewise for purposes of prestige and it should be mentioned in this connection that in the earlier period of the oriental history at least a part of the surplus produce was utilized for the parasitic consumption of the ruling classes (for instance the erection of the Egyptian pyramids).

This labour required by the state in early societies cannot be referred to as forced labour in the strict sense of the term but it was by no means a voluntary decision of an individual to work for the state. According to our opinion the demand for labour might be seen as a remnant of the former society. In the earlier stages of history, in primitive society as well as in the early days of class society, the productive forces and the relations of production developed very slowly and on a low level. At this early stage of civilization man could not control nature very well. For the reproduction of a given community and its economy at that time the state had to keep the material resources as well as a large potential of manpower under state control.[2] To a certain degree these economic and social conditions still existed in the more developed stages of the ancient oriental societies.

In the early tribal stage or even in the post-tribal stage the head of the tribe/clan or community, known as the chief or the king, received contribution in labour from the people for the upkeep of certain communal facilities. Mutual aid in labour rendered by one family to the other was a common practice in kin-based societies. But when the kin-based communities came to be divided into classes labour contributions came to be used mainly for the benefit of the ruling classes, for the ruler projected his image as the well-wisher of the community as a whole.

In the period of the ancient class society in India the demand for labour was called *viṣṭi*. In *KA* II, 5, 24[3] which identifies the sources of revenue in a systematic manner, *viṣṭi* or labour tax as a source of public revenue of the state is not included in the paragraph dealing with the state revenues (*āyaśarīram*) but can be found among the public expenditures (*vyayaśarīram*). *Viṣṭi* is mentioned in connection with the expenses for the royal sector of economy and the army. Therefore there is some evidence that *viṣṭi* or labour service was required but paid for,[4] probably in kind as it is suggested by *Gaut.* X, 24-35[5] and recorded by *KA* V, 3.

In *KA* II, 35, 54 and 55 Kauṭilya instructs the head-collector of the empire to register all the villages in the state and to classify them:

—those which were exempt from taxes (*pārihārika*),

—those which had to supply the royal troops (*āyudhīya*),

—those which were obliged to pay taxes in grain (*dhānya*), in cattle (*paśu*), cash (*hiraṇya*), raw material (*kupya*), labour (*viṣṭi*) and additional taxes (*pratikara*).

Obviously it was not the village as a corporate unit that had to render the services mentioned above. Every household (or family) in the village was responsible for paying the various types of contributions. Kauṭilya prescribes the following order for the head-collector of taxes: he has to make inquiries about the exact number of peasants, herdsmen, traders, artisans, hired workers and slaves living in every village. On the basis of the results obtained the head-collector of taxes was bound to assess the amount of taxes and the type of duties in kind, cash and labour to be derived from every household, *KA* II, 35, 54 and 55. According to Kauṭilya's view the independent peasantry living in the villages had to perform *viṣṭi*, especially for the state.[6] While the taxes in kind generally amounting to 1/6 up to 1/4 of the crop yields were collected mainly from all people dealing with agriculture and cattle breeding, the taxes in cash were demanded from all citizens of the state. Some regulations connected with this kind of taxes can be found in Kauṭilya too. The *viṣṭi* was derived from the peasants only, as Kauṭilya tells us. But none of the ancient Indian sources—neither legal nor literary—gives the amount of labour involved in *viṣṭi*. This seems to be strange; perhaps the amount had been customary for ages in India and did not need to be recorded. In the Hittite society for example the amount of labour required by the state was laid down according to rules.[7]

Probably *viṣṭi* was mainly imposed on the village people, as Kauṭilya maintains. Lawgivers such as *Gaut.* X, 31-4 and *Manu* VII, 138[8] refer to special duties of the artisans, workers in arts and Śūdras earning their living by working as hired labourers. According to these lawgivers such persons were to work one day a month for the king, in the royal workshops for example. Strabo XV, 1, 46[9] refers to the class of artisans and traders and states that most of them not only had to pay various dues but also to perform fixed duties for the king.

In the *KA* we are informed of the state's use of the labour mainly from its rural population:

II, 15, 63—royal granaries,

II, 7, 2—royal workshops,

X, 1, 9; 4, 17—*viṣṭi* for the army—clearing of the encampments, the roads and the irrigation works, transport of arms and food supply for the troops as well as carrying away the wounded from the battle-fields.[10] We have no evidence even in these cases how much time it took an ordinary peasant to perform *viṣṭi* for the army. It can only be supposed that *viṣṭi* or labour service had to be rendered during a military campaign. Taking into consideration the legal regulations for labour requirement of other ancient oriental societies we may assume that the *viṣṭi* to which the free peasantry was subjected had its fixed limits in the ancient Indian society too. The state could not be interested in burdening the rural population up to such an extent that the cultivation of the soil would be neglected and taxation would become counterproductive.

As a rule *viṣṭi* was imposed by the state on those occasions, when most of the agricultural work had been done, as is recorded in many other ancient sources of the ancient Near East.[11] Special duties for the army demanded in war time might have been exceptions. The development of property relations, particularly the rise of private ownership in the soil and the expansion of private property relations over a civilized area wider than ever before (to the western and southern parts of India), led gradually to a change in the nature of *viṣṭi*. Rudradāman, the ruler of the dynasty of the western Kṣatrapas in the middle of the second century AD, boasted of the fact that the repair of the dam at the lake Sudarśaṇa was carried out by him 'without burdening the people in the towns and the villages of the Empire with taxes, forced labour and other dues'—*āpiḍayitvā karaviṣṭipraṇayakriyābhiḥ paurajānapadaṁ janam.*[12] Perhaps there was a slow process leading to changes in the content of the old *viṣṭi*. The ancient form of *viṣṭi* which all the immediate producers were obliged to perform was gradually replaced by the work of an intermediary class of hired labourers. The reason for this development might be seen in the growing social mobility of the immediate producers and a sharp process of differentiation in property relations,[13] i.e. a gradual increase in the lower class strata of society and their impoverishment. This process led to the rise of a class of producers deprived of their private property and compelled them to earn their living by all kinds of paid work, so that they functioned as a class of ancient 'wage workers'. This is clearly indicated in the ancient law-books, the Smṛtis. A considerable part of the *karmakaras* were generally hired workers, but not always independent.[14] The development of feudal relations within the framework of the ancient class society (seen in connection with the decline and decay of this first class society in the world in the second half of the first millennium AD) appears to have caused changes regarding the use of labour for the state. India underwent a transition from ancient to medieval times, as can be inferred from the inscriptions of the early Vākāṭakas (third to fifth century AD) and the Traikūṭakas (second half of the fifth century AD). The epigraphic records refer to the exemption from *viṣṭi* for the villagers living in the donated areas. The majority of inscriptions record the donation of revenue-free villages, handed over to Brāhmaṇas, temples and monasteries of various religious sects and makes them exempt from the payment of *viṣṭi* to the state. In *CII*, III, 56[15] the Vākāṭaka Mahārāja Pravarasena II, in the eighteenth year of his reign granted the village Brahmapūraka to the Brāhmaṇa Devaśarman including the following privileges:

(i) *ā-candr-āditya-kāliyaḥ* = as long as the moon and the sun exist, i.e. lasting for ever as a perpetual grant,

(ii) *putra-pautr-ānugāmi* = for the sons, grandsons and the generations to come, i.e. in succession for all descendants,

(iii) *a-bhaṭa-cchātrā-prāveśyaḥ* = not to be entered by soldiers and royal officials, i.e. with partial freedom from the royal administration. Some Indologists assume that *chātra* may be equated with the term *cāṭa* as expressed in the formula *ā-cāṭa-bhaṭa-prāveśyaḥ*. D.C. Sircar translates the term *chātra* literally as 'one bearing an umbrella', or 'the king's umbrella-bearer'. He considers it probably identical with the *cāṭa* or the leader of a group of *bhaṭas* (*pāiks* or *piādas*) as in *ā-cāṭa-bhaṭa-prāveśyaḥ*; a peon of the law-court.[16] King Pravarasena II Vākāṭaka donated the village (*CII*, III, 56) with the above-mentioned privileges and the additional formula '*sarva-viṣṭi-parihāra-parihṛtah*', (the village is given) with immunity from all kinds of labour requirement and obligations (to be paid to the state or to be made for the state), see also *EI*, 22, 17.[17] Donations of larger or smaller pieces of cultivated lands were made on the same conditions. In *EI*, 3, 35 in his twenty-third regnal year, Pravarasena II transferred 25 *bhūmis*[18] of land in the village of Darbhamalaka to the Brāhmaṇa Yakṣārya and he gave another 60 *bhūmis* of land in the village Karmakāra to a second Brāhmaṇa named Kāliśarman with all the privileges and immunities usually mentioned in the case of donated villages along with its inhabitants to a given donee. The two pieces of land were donated with the exemption from all types of *viṣṭi* or forced labour (*sarva-viṣṭi-parihāra-parihṛtau*).[19] The formula includes exemption from labour duties for the state but it is not said whether these labour performances could be used by the donee.

In Traikūṭaka inscriptions, e.g. *EI*, 6, 29; 11, 21; 12, 7 the land was handed over along with the formula *sarva-ditya-viṣṭi-parihinaḥ,* without all *viṣṭi* and *ditya.* According to D.C. Sircar *ditya* is 'a name of a tax . . . ; probably the same as *dātti,* i.e. a gift or occasional present to be offered to the landlord; . . . *ditya* is probably derived from Prakrit *dijja* = Sanskrit *deya,* "to be given", "an object that has been given away" in the sense of "customary presents".'[20]

Ditya might be taken as 'gifts', 'irregular presents' to the king or his officials of the state bureaucracy on the occasion of special events, i.e. the birth of a crown prince or the provisioning of royal troops passing through a village as well as those made to inspecting officers on tour.[21] The formula *sarva-ditya-viṣṭi-parihīnaḥ* might mean that all (irregular) presents and *viṣṭi* were to be omitted.

However, it is remarkable, that the inscriptions do not contain formulas expressing complete immunity from the operation of the state administration. Only the formula *a-cāṭa-bhaṭa-prāveśya,* i.e. (the village) is not to be entered by soldiers and royal officials, can be found in the inscriptions of the Traikūṭakas and Kalacuris dealing with donations of land and whole village territories. Administrative immunity on a larger scale is indicated by the term *sarva-rāja-kiyānām = ahasta-prakṣepanīya,* i.e. not even to be touched with the hands by all kinds of the king's agents. This expression is well-known to later inscriptions, but it is not mentioned in the Traikūṭaka records. Such a concession confirms the entire immunity of the land property donated by the king from all the supervisory acts of the state officials not only in an administrative but also in a broad legal sense. The Traikūṭaka and the Kalacuri inscriptions while granting partial immunity to the village from the royal administration also exempt it from *viṣṭi* and occasional presents to the king and royal officials. Apart from this, the Traikūṭaka inscriptions show no evidence that *viṣṭi* and *ditya* were now transferred to the donee. Moreover, the donated areas might have continued to be at least partially under royal control.

In the case of the Vākāṭaka dominions by far not all the inscriptions recording land-grants include the exemption from *viṣṭi* for the state, although they cover the same immunities and privileges as the *viṣṭi*-free endowments, e.g. *EI,* 15, 4; 19, 44. For a transitional phase in the fifth century AD we may assume that donations of land and villages recorded in copper-plate inscriptions were only exempt from *viṣṭi* required by the state. But it seems that the right to exact labour or the *viṣṭi* was not transferred to the donee.

A further development regarding the *viṣṭi* is indicated in the inscriptions of the Maitraka dynasty of Gujarāt. The early Maitraka inscriptions of the fifth and of the first half of the sixth centuries neither mention the term *viṣṭi* nor *udraṅga* (the ground-rent). It is not before the middle of the sixth century that the term *udraṅga* appears in the inscriptions of Dhruvasena I; *viṣṭi* is mentioned in the records of Guhasena for the first time. The inscriptions preceding those of Dhruvasena I contain no formulas indicating the exemption of the donated areas from the *viṣṭi* for the state.

An early inscription of Dhruvasena I, dating from AD 526/27, contains a formula similar to that found in the Traikūṭaka and Kalacuri inscriptions. According to *EI*, 3, 46, the king donated 8 *khaṇḍa*[22] (or 300 *pādāvarta*)[23] of land in the village Hariyanaka in the district (*āharaṇī*) Hastavapra[24] to a Brāhmaṇa named Dhammila living in the same village (*iva vāstavya*).

The donation consisted of two pieces of land, 4 *khaṇḍa* each, in the western border area and in the eastern border area of the village, respectively. In addition to this the Brāhmaṇa received a double cistern (*yamalavāpi*)[25] with an area of 40 *pādāvarta* and another cistern with an area of 20 *pādāvarta* in the north-western border district of the said village. The land and the cisterns were handed over by means of a charter expressing the eternity of the donation and confirming the right of inheritance. The grant was made as a *brahmadeya* and according to the rule of *bhūmicchidra*, which meant that one first brought the high land under cultivation held it as his property. In this land charter, the formula which seems to be connected with the exemption from state labour reads as follows: *dānakara-viṭṭollakakara-viśuddham*. D.C. Sircar explains *dāna* as 'the so-called voluntary gifts of subjects'[26] and *viṭṭolakara* 'as the contribution in forced labour'.[27] E. Hultzsch compared in *EI*, 3, 46, p. 323 *viṭṭollaka* with the Telugu term *veṭṭi* and the Kanarese term *biṭṭi* and pointed out that 'the designation of the lowest village servant, *Veṭṭivāḍu* in Telugu and *Veṭṭiyāṇ* in Tamil, is derived from this word'.[28] D.C. Sircar equals *biṭṭi* and *veṭṭi* with the Sanskrit word *viṣṭi*.[29] Therefore the formula could be translated 'free from the gift tax and the labour tax'. In this special case

Brāhmaṇa Dhammila and the inhabitants of the donated village could have been exempt from duties such as giving presents on particular occasions (maybe, the birth of a prince, etc.) and they could have enjoyed the right not to be burdened with labour requirement by the state.

The Maitraka inscriptions dating from the middle of the sixth century AD (beginning with Dhruvasena's records) do no longer record the exemption from *viṣṭi* for the state but indicate its transfer to the donee who was granted by the king a certain piece of land, a village territory or whole rural areas, including a number of villages, for instance *IA*, 5,1876,[30] p. 206 fol.; *EI*, 11,5; 21; 30; *CII*, III, 38; *IA*, 8, 1879, p. 301 fol.; 7/1878, p. 68 fol.; 6, 1877, p. 9 fol. (sixth century AD); Disalkar I, 1, No. 6; 7;[31] 8; 17; *EI*, 21, 18; *IA*, 9, 1800, p. 237 fol.; *EI*, 11, 17 (seventh century AD). The whole formula reads '*s-otpadyamāna-viṣṭi-kaḥ* and refers to the labour requirement of the state as it may arise in the land or the village. What was demanded by the state earlier was now transferred to the donees. The beneficiaries of these donations were Brāhmaṇas, Buddhist, Jinist and Hindu temples and monasteries, now enjoying the right to claim *viṣṭi* from the inhabitants of the village granted to them.

The term denoting the labour requirement for the benefit of the state and inherited from the ancient class society of India continued to be used in the early phase of feudalism in northern India. Considering the form of the *viṣṭi* existing in the fifth and sixth centuries AD in the western and northern parts of India we might possibly say that it changed only marginally. *Viṣṭi* continued to be used for such purposes as were well-known in the ancient class society—repairs of irrigation systems, roads, construction and repairs of village temples, etc. But apart from this the *viṣṭi* was handed over by the state to the feudal lords who established themselves as a class during those two centuries. When the state transferred landed property it also bestowed the right to *viṣṭi* upon the donees.

The donation of landed property to corporate bodies (temples, monasteries) and particularly to private persons must have caused considerable modifications regarding the character of the ancient labour requirement. The former 'labour tax' given to the state instead of or in addition to the revenues in kind and cash was privatized. The ancient right of the king to have the right of disposal over the manpower resources within the borders of his kingdom, a sovereign right of a ruler in any ancient oriental society, was transformed into individual relations of exploitation.

With the rise of feudal relations, particularly with the development of feudal private property, *viṣṭi* or labour tax changed into corvée or labour rent, a form of the feudal ground-rent, a process taking place in those two centuries of transition. *Viṣṭi* handed over to the feudal clerical and secular assignees is never specified in inscriptions. A similar phenomenon can be observed with regard to the revenues in kind the amount of which is not mentioned in the epigraphic records. With the development of feudal relations the *viṣṭi* together with the right of the ancient ruler to collect revenues in kind and cash from his subjects passed into the hands of the class of feudal landholders, who formed a class of intermediaries between the crown and the ordinary peasants. The donation of real landed property to the feudal lords modified the character of the ancient revenue system in India. Seen in connection with its transfer to individual persons or corporative bodies such as temples and monasteries another form of the feudal ground-rent emerged, the produce rent.[32] In the early phase of Indian feudalism the amount of the ground-rent seems to have been the ancient 'one-sixth' or 'one-fourth' of the crop yields, as recorded by the Chinese accounts of early medieval times. The formula *s-otpadyamāna-viṣṭikaḥ* means that *viṣṭi* or labour service could be demanded by the donee from his subjects whenever he needed it. The performance of *viṣṭi* was not limited in the early feudal society just as it was not limited in the ancient society; however according to some lawgivers labour services could be demanded only from the artisans.[33]

Viṣṭi as it might arise was demanded by the landlord (a corporate body or an individual) from the inhabitants of the granted villages or larger plots of land. This process was intimately connected with the transformation of the ancient labour tax into the feudal corvée or labour rent. Since the *viṣṭi* was not defined in inscriptional records its unlimited use cannot be ruled out in the feudal set-up. Land grants including the *viṣṭi* given to Brāhmaṇas, temples and monasteries were not a widespread phenomenon until the second half of the sixth century AD. Perhaps we can recognise two phases in the development of the corvée or labour rent. In the first phase (the second half of the fifth century and the first half of the sixth century) the inhabitants of the granted land were exempt from the kind of *viṣṭi* demanded formerly by the state. In the second phase the ruler explicitly delegated the right to levy *viṣṭi* to the donee who was consequently authorized to demand *viṣṭi* from his direct subjects whenever he needed it. His right was apparently limited only by the rules of normal *viṣṭi* practice when he tried to make excessive use of the labour duties of his peasants. The granting of land in the second phase (from the second half of the sixth century onwards) was fully immune from the royal administration *ā-cāṭa-bhaṭa-prāveśya; samasta-rājakiyānām = a-hasta-prakṣepaniya*. One could thus conclude that the granted land was exempt from *viṣṭi* claimed by the state.

Moreover, the ruler presented *viṣṭi* 'as it might arise' for eternity (*a-candr-ārk-ārṇava-kṣiti-sarit-parvata-samakālina*), i.e. as long as the moon, the sun, the seas, the earth, the rivers and mountains exist. The king enabled the donee and all his descendants to come to enjoy the granted land on a hereditary basis (*putra-pautrānvaya-kramopabhogya*).

Just as *viṣṭi* was neither limited nor specified in the first phase, so was it in the second. This might be explained by the existence of customary laws. R.S. Sharma poses the question whether *viṣṭi* in the early Middle Ages had to be done on the fields of the donees, i.e. the landlords, or whether *viṣṭi* meant public work as practised in the ancient Indian society.[34] But this question seems to concern the physical nature of *viṣṭi* rather than its character. The existence of feudal manors of a kind similar to the European 'Fronhofsystem' cannot easily be proved in early medieval times in India. There is some evidence that such manors might have existed in the kingdom of the Maitrakas of Gujarat (*EI*, 11, 2; 5; 21, 30; *CII* III, 38; Disalkar, 1, 1, 7, etc.), but manors of this type were by no means typical of the development of feudalism in India.

Some evidence for the existence of forced labour can already be found in the *Kāmasūtra* of Vātsyāyana.[35] In V.5.5. of this text a village headman demanded *viṣṭi* from the wives of peasants in the form of working in his granary, in his house and in his fields and of spinning and weaving for him and his family. Later inscriptions of the eighth and ninth centuries AD inform us that the village headmen known as *grāmika, grāmakūṭa, grāmādhipati,* etc., were frequently minor feudal lords running their own estates. In the early stage of feudalism in Sri Lanka villages with all the inhabitants were granted by the rulers to Buddhist monasteries. The peasants and artisans of the donated villages paid the ground-rent to the monasteries (*vihāras*). As a rule, the ground-rent took the form of a produce rent but labour rent was not unknown. Some inhabitants of the villages (*vārika*, workers) were obliged to work three days a year in the monastic estate. They had to do all kinds of agricultural work, to repair and to erect monastic buildings but they were paid for their duties.[36]

North Indian inscriptions, while stating the purpose of the land-grants to the Buddhist monasteries, indicate the kind of obligations the inhabitants of the granted villages had to fulfil. They had to provide the monks (*bhikṣu*) and nuns (*bhikṣūṇi*) with clothes (*āvara, cādana*), food (*grāsa, āsana*), beds (*śayana*), medicine (*bhaiṣajya*) and alms (*piṇḍapāta*).[37] In addition to this they were obliged to provide the monastery with lamps (*dīpa*) for the cult, oil (*taila*), flowers (*puṣpa*) and fragrances (*gandha*). The inhabitants of the village attached to the monasteries had to carry out repairs on the monastic buildings which is conveyed by the passage *khaṇḍa-sphuṭita-viśirna pratisaṁṣkāraṇa*, i.e. repair of the broken, cracked and faulty parts, *IA* 6, 1877, 12ff. Part of these duties was incorporated in the produce rent consisting not only of the agricultural produce but also of the products manufactured by peasant families at home to provide the monks and nuns with the necessary clothings. Many of the duties mentioned above are corvée of the type existing in the West European Middle Ages. The right to *viṣṭi* of this kind was granted particularly in Gujarat and Maharashtra.[38]

In the early Middle Ages in India the labour rent was referred to as *viṣṭi*, the term used for the ancient labour duties demanded by the state from its subjects. This picture obviously became far more complex due to the circumstance that the feudal labour rent existed along with the obligation to perform work for the state in the early Middle Ages in India. In Kalacuri inscriptions (for instance *EI*, 6, 29; 12, 7) dating back to the seventh century AD villages were offered with the ground-rent (*udraṅga*), feudal taxes (*uparikara*), with all additional duties, with proprietary rights to land (*bhūmicchidranyāya*), with partial immunities from royal administration (*a-cāṭa-bhaṭa-prāveśyaḥ*) with formulas expressing the eternity of the donation and the right to inheritance of the granted land. The formula *s-otpadyamāna-viṣṭikaḥ* was however not included in the inscriptions of the Kalacuris, but a different fixed expression is mentioned instead, namely, *sarva-ditya-viṣṭi-prātibhedika-parihīna* free from special taxes on relevant occasions (*ditya*), from *viṣṭi* and *prātibhedikā*. *Prātibhedikā* is a term difficult to translate. D.C. Sircar offers two interpretations. According to him the term is 'supposed to be related to *umbara-bheda*' and means a special levy on defaulters in the payment of taxes.[39] He further equates *prātibhedikā* also with *prātivedhanika*, 'punching-fee collected from merchants at the time of the inspection of weights and measures, as indicated by the *Arthaśāstra*'.[40]

Seen in connection with the whole formula as referred to above *prātibhedikā* could have been the performance of a certain duty for the benefit of the state from which the inhabitants of the granted villages were now exempt. Similar to the Traikūṭaka inscriptions of the fifth century AD the Kalacuri inscriptions dating from the beginning of the seventh century AD do not mention whether the *viṣṭi*, *ditya* and *prātibhedikā* had to be performed for the donee or not. If donated villages could still be exempt from *viṣṭi* in the seventh century AD then this may indicate the continuing existence of the ancient Indian form of *viṣṭi* in the early feudal phase.

Viṣṭi of this kind was not transformed into the feudal labour rent, since it did not touch upon the question of landownership. *Viṣṭi* demanded by the state was a remnant of the former social formation maintained by the new ruling class (the king and his feudal officials) for economic reasons. It continued due to the fact that royal ownership over a considerable part of the land in the kingdom was not abolished during the downfall of the former society and the dawn of the new feudal relations.

Similar to conditions in ancient oriental society in the early phase of feudalism, *viṣṭi* represented the sovereign right of the ruler to exact labour. The king was legally authorized to claim this right for the benefit of the state or to grant it otherwise. In the early phase of feudalism *viṣṭi* was transformed into labour rent only as a consequence of the transfer of royal proprietary rights on the land to secular and religious donees. The Chinese Buddhist pilgrim Xuan Zang seems to confirm the assertion that the ancient form of *viṣṭi* demanded by the state continued to exist in the early Middle Ages. He wrote in his *Si-Yu-Ki*: 'When the public works require it, labour is exacted but paid for. The payment is in strict proportion to the work done'.[41] Here we may see the reason for the continuous existence of the ancient form of *viṣṭi* from the earliest times to the Middle Ages. Xuan Zang remarks that this phenomenon was based on the peculiar economic structure of the Indian as well as many other Asiatic societies which always required that the central power held the command over a broad manpower potential to a certain degree.[42] This command over the manpower should not only be seen in connection with the maintenance of the irrigation systems. Public works were required in many fields, as has been shown in this paper earlier.

Nevertheless the ancient form of *viṣṭi* gradually changed its character qualitatively as well as quantitatively in the early Middle Ages. Xuan Zang informs us further that seen on the whole the population was not obliged to do forced labour for the state. Only those who cultivated state lands had to perform duties, the Chinese pilgrim noted, but they were not subject to a strong exploitation rate. 'In this way, the taxes on the people are light, and the personal service required of them is moderate.'[43]

In ancient Indian society an important task of the bureaucratic state authorities was the registration of all households in the kingdom in order to determine the tax yield in kind, cash and labour performance of the primary producers (*KA* II, 35, 54 and 55). But the Chinese pilgrim Fa-hien observed quite different conditions towards the end of the fourth and the beginning of the fifth century AD in Madhyadeśa: 'The people are numerous and happy; they have not to register their households, or attend to any magistrates and their rules.'[44] In the seventh century AD Xuan Zang wrote likewise that the households were not registered by the state.[45] From about the fifth century AD onwards more and more households formerly under the direct control of the state and taxed by it must have dropped out of being subjects to state power and seem to have come under the rule of the emerging class of religious and secular feudal lords, i.e. private individuals or corporate bodies. A good many land-grant inscriptions dating from at least the fifth century AD apparently confirm this view. More and more land with the peasants as well as large territories including one or even more villages fell under the rule of the Brāhmaṇas and religious institutions of different sects and schools.

Since in most cases the right to demand *viṣṭi* was granted together with the land and the cultivators the ancient form of *viṣṭi* was transformed into the labour rent to be exacted by private individuals to whom proprietary land rights were transferred by the state. Even in the case where usufructuary rights on the soil were given 'lasting for ever' (as long as the moon and the sun, etc., exist), a process must have been set off which led to substantial changes in the character of the old *viṣṭi.*

As a rule the donee was authorized to demand *viṣṭi* from the peasants and artisans of the smaller or larger territories that were granted. In this way the state was deprived of its rights to demand work from the inhabitants of the donated land.

In comparison to Western Europe, the types of the feudal ground-rent, the labour-rent, produce-rent and cash-rent originated in India from different sources. Feudal ownership of land arose mainly out of the nature of the ancient state and royal ownership of land in India. The taxes levied by the state from the immediate producers in ancient Indian class society changed into the produce rent due to a process of privatization resulting from the transfer of proprietary land rights to the donees.

Similarly the labour services which had formerly to be rendered for the benefit of the state developed into labour rent. The taxes in cash to be paid to the state became feudal dues in cash to be given to the feudal landlord.[46] The exploitation of the small private landowners or the process of their being deprived of the soil[47] apparently took place in the last stage of ancient Indian society on a larger scale while in Western Europe this process emerged in the early feudal period, for instance in the Merovingian kingdom, which is indicated by the statement of Friedrich Engels.[48]

It appears that the process of alienation of the free peasants from their soil must have developed from Gupta times onwards. The economic and social position of the peasant class seem to have been considerably undermined and worsened when the class of feudal landlords emerged. This is clearly demonstrated by the existence of an enormous number of land-grant inscriptions almost over all parts of India.

The principal form of the ground-rent in the early stage of feudalism in India was not the lowest form, the labour-rent, but the produce-rent, *bhāgabhogakara.* The significance of this lies in the fact that the produce-rent preempts a higher stage of feudal economy than the labour-rent. I would like to suggest that the reason for this phenomenon could be seen in a relatively great continuity in the transition from ancient Indian class society to feudalism as well as in the likewise relatively high level of the productive forces in that transition phase of the fifth to the eighth centuries AD.[49]

To complete the outline of the further development of feudal relations in India we should add that the produce-rent remained the dominant form of the feudal ground-rent for centuries. The produce-rent did not change sufficiently into money-rent in the period of developed feudalism (thirteenth to sixteenth centuries AD) because the increase in the productive forces and the development of towns and bourgeois powers was limited in the tenth to twelfth centuries AD, due to a number of reasons which cannot be dealt with here. But the development of private feudal ownership seems to have played an important role in this process. However, around the tenth century AD the terms *viṣṭi*, *udraṅga* and at least *uparikara* gradually became rare in inscriptions and finally disappeared from them in western and central India, which had played an important, progressive role in the origin of feudal relations in the country. This suggests that the donees or intermediaries in land were no longer authorized to collect *viṣṭi* or labour-rent from the peasants in central and western zones around the tenth century and later.

NOTES

1. Cf. G.A. Melikisvili, 'Nekotorve aspekty voprosa o social no ekonomiceskom stroe drevnich bliznevostoeynch obscesty' *Vestnik drevnei istorii*, Moscow, 132 (1975) 2, p. 31; I.M. Diakonov, 'Problemy economiki, O strukture obscestva Bliznego Vostoka do serediny II tys. do n.e.', ibid., 106 (1968) 4, p. 27; *Geschichte der Alten Welt. Chrestomathie*, hrsg, von W.W. Struve, ed. 1 *Der Alte Orient*. Berlin 1959, pp. 57ff. Dekret A aus Koptos.
2. Cf. Karl Marx, *Das Kapital. Kritik der politischen Okonomio*, Bd. 1, Marx, Engels, Werke, ed., 23, Berlin, 1977, pp. 353f.: *Weltgtschichte bis zur Herausbildung des Feudalismus*, hrsg. von einem Autorenkollektiv unter der Leitung von I. Sellnow, Berlin, 1977, pp. 142, 158 (Babylonia), 171 (Hittite Empire), 179 (Crete), 196, 207 (Egypt).
3. The *Kauṭilya Arthaśāstra*, pt. 1. A Critical edition with a Glossary by R.P. Kangle, Bombay, 1960.
4. Cf. E. Bruckner, 'Offontlicher Haushalt, staatliche Wirtschafts-planung und Finanzkontrolle im Kauṭilyā-Arthaśāstra', *Journal of the Economic and Social History of the Orient* 23 (1980) III, p. 309.
5. *Śrī-Gautama-Dharma-Śāstram, The Institutes of Gautama*, ed. A.F. Stenzler, London, 1876.

6. Cf. E. Ritschl-M. Schetelich, *Studien zum Kauṭilya Arthaśāstra,* Berlin, 1976, pp. 285f. R.S. Sharma, *Indian Feudalism: c. 300-1200 A.D.*, Calcutta, 1965, pp. 50f.
7. Cf. E.A. Menabde, *Chettskoe cbscestvo. Ekonomika, sobstvennost', zemlya i nasledovanie,* Tbilisi 1965, pp. 113, 120.
8. *Mānava-Dharma-Śastra, The Code of Manu,* ed. J. Jolly, London, 1887.
9. *Strabonis Geograpica,* hrsg, von A. Meineke, Ed. 8, Leipzig, 1877.
10. Cf. E. Ritschl-M. Schetelich, op. cit., p. 286.
11. Cf. *Weltgeschichte bis zur Herausbildung des Feudalismus,* p. 200.
12. 'Junāgaṛh Rock Inscription of Rudradāman I (Śaka) year 72 (150 A.D.)', *Select Inscriptions, Bearing on Indian History and Civilization,* vol. 1. From the Sixth Century AD, ed. D.C. Sircar, Calcutta 1965, pp. 175ff., n 67.
13. Cf. M. Njammasch, 'Probleme der Stadtentwicklung und der Stadt-Land-Bozie-hung in Indian vom 1. bis zum 5. Jahrhundert u. Z.' *Klio* 63 (1981) 1, Berlin, pp. 116ff; cf. A.M. Samezvancec, 'Ob *evoljucii drevneindiskoi teorii sobstvennosti', Uzlovnye problemy istorii Indii, Sbornik statej,* Moscow 1981, pp. 118ff.
14. Cf. E.M. Medvedev, 'Karmakara i bhṛtaka. K. *probleme formirovanija nizśich kast,' Kasty v Indii, sbornik statej,* Moscow 1965, pp. 137ff.; *Nārada Smṛti, The Institutes of Nārada,* ed. J. Jolly, Calcutta 1885 (= Bibliotheca Indica, work 102), V, 3-5; 22; cf. R.S. Sharma, *Śūdras in Ancient India: A Social History of the Lower Order down to circa A.D.* 600, Delhi, 1980, pp. 248ff.
15. *Corpus Inscriptionum Indicarum,* vol. III: *Inscriptions of the Early Gupta Kings and Their Successors,* ed. J. Fleet, Calcutta, 1888, rev. Varanasi, 1963.
16. D.C. Sircar, *Indian Epigraphical Glossary,* Delhi, 1966, p. 73 (fol. D.C. Sircar, *IEG*).
17. *Epigraphia Indica,* vol. 1, Calcutta, 1888-92ff.
18. D.C. Sircar, *IEG,* p. 58, 'a particular land measure sometimes also called *bhū* and regarded as equal to four *bhūmāsakas*'.
19. Cf. *CII,* III. 55.
20. D.C. Sircar, *IEG,* p. 98.
21. Cf. D.C. Sircar, *Indian Epigraphy,* Delhi-Varanasi-Patna, 1965, pp. 390ff.
22. *Khaṇḍa* or *khaṇḍi,* land measure, cf. D.C. Sircar, *IEG,* p. 155.
23. Pādāvarta, land measure of the Maitraka inscriptions, cf. D.C. Sircar, *Indian Epigraphy,* pp. 418f. 1 *pādācarta* = 100 square feet; the exact size of this land measure is still controversial; cf. R.N. Saletore, *Early Indian Economic History,* Bombay, 1973, p. 509.
24. P. Gupta, *Geography in Ancient Indian Inscriptions* (*up to AD 650*), New Delhi, 1973, p. 20, Hastavaprāhāra 'region around Hathab in Gogho tāluq of Bhavnagar district'.
25. D.C. Sircar, *IEG,* p. 384, *yamala* 'two' more likely 'double'.
26. Ibid., p. 78.
27. Ibid, p. 380.

28. 'Ganeśgad Plates of Dhruvasena I (Gupta) Samvat 207', ed. E. Hultzsch, *Epigraphia Indica,* vol. 3, no. 46, p. 323.
29. Cf. D.C. Sircar, *IEG,* pp. 411, 426.
30. *The Indian Antiquary. A Journal of Oriental Research,* Bombay-London, 1872ff.
31. D.B. Disalkar, 'Some Unpublished Copper-plates of the Rulers of Valabhi', *Journal of the Bombay Branch of the Royal Asiatic Society,* New Series, ed. by V.S. Sukhthankar, vol. I, pt. 1, London-Bombay, 1925, pp. 15ff.
32. Cf. Karl Marx, *Das Kapital,* ed. 8, in Marx/Engels, *Werke,* ed. 25, Berlin, 1974, pp. 802ff.
33. *Gaut.* X, 24-35; *KA* V, 3; *Manu* VII, 138, *Strabon* XV, 1. 46.
34. Cf. R.S. Sharma, *Feudalism,* p. 122.
35. *Kāmasūtra of Vātsyāyana with the Commentary Jayamaṅgala of Yaśodhara,* ed. by G.D. Sastri, Benares, 1929.
36. Cf. E.S. Semēka, *Istorija buddizma na Cejlone Saṅgha v drevnosti iv srednie veka,* Moscow, 1969, p. 73.
37. Piṇḍa-pāṭa acc. to D. C. Sircar, *IEG,* p. 251 'food [for the Buddhist monks]'.
38. Cf. R.S. Sharma, *Feudalism,* p. 122.
39. D.C. Sircar, *IEG,* p. 258.
40. Ibid., p. 261.
41. *Si-Yu-Ki, Buddhist Records of the Western World,* transl. from the Chinese of Hiuen-Tsang (AD 629), by S. Beal, London, 1906, vol. 1, p. 87; even in the later Middle Ages public works were demanded by the state from its subjects, compare I.P. Vogel, *Antiquities of Chambā State,* pt. 1, *Inscriptions of the Pre-Muhammadan Period,* Calcutta, 1911 (Archaeological Survey of India, New Imperial Series, vol. 30), p. 132, fn. 2. The meaning of Persian *begār* (i.e. *kār-i be'gār)* is 'unpaid labour'. In the title-deeds of the Muhammadan period we find the tautologic expression *biṭh-begār* or *beṭh-begār,* the first member of the compound being derived from Skr. *viṣṭi* 'forced labour'.
42. Cf. Karl Marx, *Das Kapital,* Bd. 1, p. 353.
43. *Sī-Yū-Ki* I, p. 57.
44. *A Record of Buddhistic Kingdoms, Being an Account by the Chinese Monk Fuhien of His Travels in India and Ceylon,* (*c. AD 399-414*), transl. by J. Legge, Oxford 1886 (rpt Leiden, 1965), p. 42; cf. R.S. Sharma, *Feudalism,* p. 9.
45. *Si-Yu-Ki* I, p. 87.
46. Cf. M. Njammasch, *Untersuchung zur Genesis des Feudalismus in Indien,* Berlin, 1984, pp. 121ff.
47. Cf. E. Müller-Mertens, 'Skizze zur weiteren Verstandigung über das feudale Produktionsverhāltnis', *Ethnographisch-Archaologische Zeitschrift* 13 (1972) 4, p. 568 'the exploitation of the small private landowners or their deprivation of the soil, respectively'.

48. Friedrich Engels, 'Ehe als frei franken Hintersassen irgend jemandes werden konnten, mussten sie ihr bei der Landnahme erhaltenes Allod auf.irgendeine Weise verlaren, musste sich eine Klasse landloser freier franken gebildethaben.' 'Die Frãnkische Zeit', Marx Engels, *Werke,* Bd. 19, Berlin, 1973, p. 480.
49. Cf. M. Njammasch, op. cit., pp. 81ff.

14

Landholding and Peasantry in the Brahmaputra Valley *c.* fifth-thirteenth Centuries AD

Nayanjot Lahiri

INTRODUCTION

The basic historical sources of this period in the Brahmaputra valley are thirty-two inscriptions, twenty of which record royal grants of land to the brāhmaṇas (Table 1). The text of these grants is largely taken up by the genealogies of the donor and the donee in verse, the reconstruction of the agrarian economy being dependent on the relatively smaller prose section which contains the description of the donated land and the rights granted with it. The settlements mentioned in the inscriptions reflect only the riparian, rice-cultivating tract along the Brahmaputra and its tributary valleys. The hills which fringe this tract virtually on all sides are of no significance as far as the physiography of the inscriptional settlements is concerned. Secondly, these inscriptions are spread all along the east-west ends of the Brahmaputra in Assam and lend no credence to the assumption that 'during the 5th-12th centuries, the land-grants, by and large, represented islands of private domains in a sea of communally held tribal lands of shifting cultivators'.[1]

THE POSITION OF THE BRĀHMAṆAS IN THE SYSTEM OF LANDHOLDING

The grants record for the donees, i.e. the brāhmaṇas, both fiscal and administrative-judicial privileges. The element of the fiscal privilege is underlined by a grant of the seventh century by

TABLE 1

Inscription and Date	*Findspot (District)*	*The Details of Donated Land*
Nagajari rock inscription - 5th cent.	Sibsagar	Incomplete
Dubi plates - 7th cent.	Kamrup	Incomplete
Nidhanpur plates - 7th cent.	Sylhet	Land to support 208 Brahmins
Hayunthal plates - 7th cent.	Mikir hills	Incomplete
Tezpur plates - 9th cent.	Darrang	One village
Parbatiya plates - 9th cent.	Darrang	One village
Uttarabarbil plates - 9th cent.	Mikir hills	Land yielding 2000 units of paddy
Ulubari plates - 9th cent.	Darrang	same
Nowgong plates - 9th cent.	Nowgong	Land yielding 4000 units of paddy
Bargaon plates - AD 1035	Darrang	Land yielding 2000 units of paddy
Suwalkuchi plates - AD 1036	Kamrup	Land yielding 3000 units of paddy
Coratbari plates - early 11th cent.	Nowgong	Land yielding 4000 units of paddy
Gauhati plates - AD 1058	Kamrup	same
Guwakuchi plates - AD 1071	Kamrup	Land yielding 2000 units of paddy
Gachtal plates - AD 1080	Nowgong	Land yielding 8000 units of paddy
Subhankarapataka plates - 12 cent.	Unknown	Land yielding 6000 units of paddy
Pushpabhadra plates - 12 cent.	Kamrup	Land yielding 10000 units of paddy.
Khonamukh plates - 12 cent.	Nowgong	Land yielding 6000 units of paddy.
Kamauli plates - AD 1142	Varanasi	Two villages
Assam plates - AD 1185	Darrang	Seven villages

Note: The basic source of these inscriptions is M.M. Sharma (ed.), *Inscriptions of Ancient Assam*, Gauhati, 1977.

Bhāskaravarman of the Varman dynasty. This grant confirms the exemption of revenue on the donated land which had been granted to the same donee by the king Bhūtivarman of the same dynasty, but which had become liable to revenue because of the loss of the charter.[2] Moreover, from the ninth century onwards, a number of administrative functions and judicial powers also devolved on the donees, a trend which continued till the twelfth century. The Ulubari plates of Balavarman III are fairly illustrative of this point.

. . . this plot of land consisting of homestead land, paddy fields, dry lands, ponds, grounds and mounds standing as it is up to its own boundaries is (by virtue of this grant rendered) out of bounds to all the trouble-makers like the *rājni*, the *rājaputra*, the *rānaka*, the favourite of the king, the old female guard of the harem, the collectors of the *Hastibandha* tax and the *Naukābandha* tax, the officers in charge of the recovery of stolen property, the policeman, the inflictor of punishment, and the collector of tenants' taxes and duties and the (royal) umbrella bearer.[3]

It can easily be surmised that the combination of these fiscal and administrative-judicial privileges with the traditional socio-religious privilege enjoyed by the brāhmaṇas because of their position in the caste-hierarchy imparted to this class a nodal position in the contemporary system of landholding.

THE NATURE OF THE LAND TENURE

The basic point is that the donated land was in settled village areas where agriculture had long been practised and where the peasant cultivators were obviously supposed to give to the donees what they were originally supposed to give to the king. This is apparently in contrast to the situation reflected in the early medieval inscriptions of such areas in Rajasthan, Gujarat and Maharashtra, which, as has been argued,[4] gave the brāhmaṇa donees absolute control of land tenure, including the expulsion of peasant tenants from donated plots of land. The inscriptions of this period in the Brahmaputra valley were not in waste lands which were colonised by the brāhmaṇas but in the valley proper where all the granted land was clearly settled and contributing revenue to the state. The description of the donated property which was made up of 'land, along with the homesteads, paddy fields, dry lands, ponds, grazing grounds, refuse land, etc.',[5] is evocative of an existing rural settlement. The peasants who were occupying and cultivating the land, surrendered that part of their produce to the brāhmaṇas which earlier had accrued to the king. It is worth mentioning in this context that the language of the inscriptions is interspersed with a number of Khasi, Bodo and other non-Sanskritic tribal word formations which are indicative of the substratum in that region.[6] It is possible that the Brahmaputra valley was settled by these tribal people just as the forest and waste land were colonised and reclaimed by tribals in the Mishmi hills and the Karbi Anglong district in the modern period. In the cutting of trees and the raising of crops the role of the controlling authority was nil, a fact recognized in the provisions that the colonisers were allowed to raise crops for one or two years without rent. Later on, when rent was levied the original cultivators seem to have enjoyed a permanency of tenure.[7] The model we suggest is that these cultivators were already paying taxes to the king for access to the land and its resources. These taxes were transferred to the donee without affecting the rights of the resident peasantry in a significant way. The insecurity of tenure and landlessness could hardly be a feature of pre-modern Assam. A report written in the beginning of the twentieth century is a pointer in this direction:

> The great obstacle to the extension of cultivation is the absence of a labouring class. In the Surma valley, Kamrup and Goalpara agricultural labourers are extremely scarce, and in central and upper Assam they are practically non-existent. The climate of the country in the rains is not calculated to stimulate the inhabitants to prolonged physical exertion, and ryots, who are compelled to plough, plant and reap with their own hands, are not likely to cultivate more land than is absolutely necessary to their maintenance.[8]

We do not consider it likely that the situation in our period was qualitatively different.

THE RANKS OF THE PEASANTRY

In addition to the brāhmaṇas and apparently tribals, the ranks of the peasantry in the Brahmaputra valley of this period included certain castes which are generally considered lowly. The *Kaivarttas*, traditionally associated with boating and fishing, appear to be an important such group. The *Abanchi Kaivarttas,* having Abancha as the occupant, enjoyed the land to the west of the donated land of *Guheśvara-Digdola Vrddhagrāma* in the twelfth century AD.[9] The *Kaivarttas* also controlled large *bils* or ponds as, for instance, the *Svalpadyuti Kaivarttas* who had rights over *Bhogadīrghikā.*[10] In the Puspabhadra plates of Dharmapāla a boatsman (*nokka*) is mentioned as occupying land.[11] Similarly, in the Suwalkuchi plates the boundaries of the lands of a large number of boatsmen are mentioned.[12] The Puspabhadra plates may also refer to a plot of land owned by a potter.[13] The land of the *Orāngi Tantras* who were weavers is referred to in the Subhankarapataka plates of Dharmapāla.[14]

It is likely that the boatsmen, weavers and potters were peasant cultivators since the demand for their professional services was not adequate enough to support full-time production. In this context the nature of artisanal production in Assam has to be understood. On the basis of our knowledge of Ahom Assam and the nineteenth century ethnographic literature on Assam we may say that the economic organization of society in this region has always been relatively simple with no specialization of function in handicrafts which in other parts of India was confined to special castes under the *jajmani* system. The Gazetteer of North-East India is worth quoting in detail.

> The economic organization of the Province is of a very simple character and the great majority of the population are supported by agriculture. In the hills and the Assam valley there is very little subdivision of function: the ordinary cultivator builds and repairs his own house, makes his own agricultural implements, has his own clothes woven at home and in fact supplies all his own simple wants.[15]

Even in the nineteenth century a large number of occupational castes had taken to agriculture for subsistence. The *Patias,* mostly found in Nowgong district, who theoretically were matmakers, abandoned their traditional occupation and took to agriculture. Similarly, the *Jugis* who traditionally were weavers by profession took to cultivation. This process may be related to the general availability of cultivable waste land in Assam as late as the beginning of the twentieth century. The following are the figures of total area of Kamrup district provided by the Assistant Surveyor General, Calcutta, in 1902-3:[16]

	Sq. miles
Area of the district	3,858
Settled area	2,102
Area of reserved forests	149
Area of waste land	2,697

Kamrup, incidentally, was one of the most populous districts of Assam. This may partly explain why an occupationally specialised society did not emerge strongly in the Brahmaputra valley in our period.

The inclusion of occupational castes in the ranks of the peasantry is also related to the general insignificance of trade. The references to urban centres, which are very meagre, are only to the political centres, the general appearance of which must have resembled that of the Ahom capital Garhgaon invaded by the Mughal general Mir Jumlah in March 1662. According to the report of Shihabuddin Talish who chronicled the Mughal invasion the inhabitants of Garhgaon were in the habit of storing one year's supply of food of all kinds, since there was no practice of grain trading. Also, there were no eatables available in the daily bazaar of Garhgaon; only betel leaves and areca nuts were on sale. The city with its mud-walled citadel at the centre appeared to the invaders as a mere aggregation of irregularly laidout villages.[17] The structurally unprepossessing character of the urban centres together with the absence of empirical references to market centre underlines the insignificance of the demand for non-agricultural production.

THE NATURE OF PEASANT PRODUCTION

The basic social unit of production was the family. Land was cultivated largely through family labour. The Assam plates of Vallabhadeva which explicitly mention that the land was given to the donee along with five assistants and their sons and wives, suggests the importance of familial labour.[18] Peasant households, incidentally, were scattered over a wide area. A study of the operative clauses of the inscriptions reveals that rice was grown on broad plains, dotted over with clumps of bamboo and fruit trees in which were located the houses of the cultivators. A village in the sense of a compact block of houses set in the midst of fields was almost entirely absent. The peasant household was geared mainly to production for the basic consumption needs of the family plus the enforced dues to the brāhmaṇa landholders. Basically the whole situation must have been centred around the cultivation of rice which, if the inscriptional references to *bunds* for holding water either in the fields or in a wider area (*Ksetraālis* and *Vrihadālis*) are any indication,[19] must have been aided by some sort of an irrigational system. According to William Robinson in 1851 the Kachari population of Assam in that period contributed effectively to the maintenance of such an irrigation system.[20] The work of N.K. Shyamachaudhuri of the Anthropological Survey of India on the system of indigenous irrigation through fieldwork in three multi-ethnic villages, two in Darrang and one in Goalpara, is also instructive on this point.[21] Large unused areas around these villages had been made cultivable through the excavation of canals and other methods, solely on the initiative of the cultivators. In these three villages only the Kachari people were found to be associated with this distinguishing activity, a fact also mentioned by S. Endle in his monograph on the Kachari.[22] As the most important branch of the Bodo group the Kacharis extend from Sadiya to Dhubri in the Brahmaputra valley. That a considerable Kachari population peopled the Brahmaputra valley in our period can be postulated through a linguistic study of the inscriptions. The epigraphs, though inscribed in Sanskrit, are interspersed with not merely Prakrit words but also words of specifically non-Sanskritic origin. In an interesting study of the place and personal names in certain Assamese inscriptions B. Kakati showed the occurrence of a number of words of Bodo origin in these inscriptions.[23] Bodo is the language spoken by the plains Kacharis. These words include the following: *dijjinā* from Bodo *dija* (*o*) which means 'to melt'[24]; *hangsibā*[25] from Bodo *haing* which means 'relation' and *sibā* [26] which means a river, *gu* which is a grasshopper and *ma* which indicates biggishness; *nandi*[27] from Bodo *nandu* which means a hut in a cultivated field and so on and so forth.

The data are awfully meagre but it is worth recording that from the fifth to the ninth centuries only thirteen village settlements are mentioned in our inscriptions. From the thirteenth century onwards approximately fifty village settlements find mention.[28] Similarly, whereas the boundaries of the donated plots in earlier inscriptions are mostly natural, by the twelfth century the signs of human habitations are much more significant.[29] On this basis it should be possible to postulate a significant amount of increase in population and agricultural production through the centuries in our chosen period.

THE ISSUE OF INTERACTION

The peasantry of pre-Ahom Assam was multi-ethnic in character. The dominant impression is of a number of tribal groups such as the Mikirs, Khasis, Kukis and Kacharis having taken to cultivation on a permanent basis at some point in the past before the creation of a dominant class of brāhmaṇa landholders. At the same time there is an irresistible correlation between the peasant economy and the principles involved in the caste structure in Assam. There is no group of tribesmen in this region which has not involved itself in the caste structure in some form or the other after the adoption of wet rice cultivation. In the process of detribalisation and their inclusion in the traditional Hindu fold the brāhmaṇas were extremely significant. Detribalization involved, among other things, a renunciation of tribal forms of worship and the acceptance of traditional Hindu gods and goddesses. At a later stage, in the sixteenth century, proselytization by a Vaiṣṇavite apostle Śaṅkaradeva took place through the medium of *nāma-samkīrtana* which involved collective chanting and direct homage to the deity. The followers of Śaṅkaradeva paid little attention to caste, were willing to accept a Śūdra as their head priest and were allowed to eat the flesh of domesticated animals. The beginning of *nāma-samkīrtana* is to be found in the eighth century *Śaṅkara-Nārāyana* image inscription.[30] The Deopani Viṣṇu image inscription dated in the ninth century mentions that the twice-born classes, along with the śūdras and women can worship Viṣṇu. This inscription also contains a reference to *Bhaktas* which implies that the cult of Bhakti was gaining ground as early as ninth century.[31]

That the village settlements of our inscriptions bore names of Sanskritic origin is also significant in this context: *Mahādevapātaka, Kāśīpātaka* and *Chokkapātaka*, among others.[32] There was also a Prakritization of various Sanskrit terms[33] and the inclusion of a number of Khasi, Bodo and other tribal word formations as well. The formation of this mixed language system is inexplicable without postulating close contacts between the dominant class and the peasantry. It is interesting to note that although the Ahoms ruled over Assam subsequently for a considerable length of time, only a few words of Tai origin are to be found in the Assamese language, with Sanskrit contributing the major share to the stock of Assamese vocabulary. The pre-Ahom inscriptions are important inasmuch as they provide us with the earliest evidence of the existence of a class of people of an Indo-Aryan speech system at the village level.

Throughout this period the caste system was loosely organized, not expressing in any way the division of labour and specialization of function traditionally subsumed under it. In a large number of cases, referred to earlier, occupational castes and others such as the *Kaivarttas* who, in other regions of India, were considered impure are included in the ranks of peasantry. Also, in one of the inscriptions, not the only one of its kind, the donee while being the son of a brāhmaṇa well-versed in scriptures, was a charioteer by profession.[34] Hereditary occupational association within the framework of the caste system seems to have been insignificant in this period.

SUMMARY

In the world of the Brahmaputra valley inscriptions between the fifth and the twelfth/thirteenth centuries AD the brāhmaṇas, traditionally at the apex of the caste hierarchy, had their position as the dominant landholding class buttressed by certain fiscal and administrative-judicial privileges that went along with the donations of land they received from the contemporary kings. However, in contrast to certain other areas of India, such as Rajasthan, Gujarat and Maharashtra where the donated plots of land were supposedly in waste areas, giving the donee brāhmaṇas absolute land tenure rights, the rights of the already existing peasantry in the donated plots of land in the Brahmaputra valley were unlikely to have been impaired because these plots of land were in already settled regions and not in areas to be reclaimed. The reclamation of land went on in the hilly fringe of the Brahmaputra valley as late as the nineteenth century, and the peasants, originally tribals, enjoyed a permanency of tenure in the land they reclaimed. The Brahmaputra valley was reclaimed before the period of our inscriptions, and this means that the brāhmaṇas got only the rent which the resident peasantry used to give earlier to the king. The ranks of the peasantry also included such occupational groups as boatsmen, potters and weavers, suggesting on the whole, a picture of occupational mobility which could be found even in the early twentieth century Assam, mainly because of the general availability of cultivable waste land and the insignificance of trade conducive to the growth of occupational groups. The peasant production was geared to wet rice cultivation which had an irrigational system, perhaps honed by the Kachari element of the population of our period, to fall back upon. The Kachari participation in this irrigation system can be surmised both from the occurrence of the related language words in the inscriptions and the general ethnographic literature on pre-modern irrigation in the Brahmaputra valley. The interaction between the brāhmaṇas and the general range of peasantry which undoubtedly had a significant tribal element ushered in what would be called the process of Sanskritization of the grassroots village level in the Brahmaputra valley.

The data on the systems of landholding and the general character of the peasantry are not much in the inscriptions of our period, constituting, in fact, its basic historical source, but viewed in the light of the relevant ethnographic evidence in the context of pre-modern Assam, even this limited amount of data can offer a coherent picture, howsoever brief.

NOTES

1. A. Guha, 'Pre-Ahom roots and the mediaeval state in Assam', *Social Scientist,* 12 (1984), p. 75.
2. M.M. Sharma (ed.), *Inscriptions of Ancient Assam* (hereafter cited as *IAA*), Gauhati, 1977, no. 6, lines 49ff.
3. *IAA,* Appendix no. 5, lines 33-8.
4. R.S. Sharma, *Indian Feudalism,* Delhi, 1980 (2nd edn.), p. 97.
5. *IAA,* no. 12, lines 33ff.
6. B. Kakati, 'Place and personal names in the early land grants of Assam', *A Cultural History of Assam* (ed. B. Barua), Nowgong, 1951, pp. 202-3.
7. M.C. Goswami, 'Peasants and non-peasants in northeast India and their new dimension', *Social Anthropology of Peasantry* (ed. J.P. Mencher), Bombay, 1983, p. 271.
8. B.C. Allen *et al.,* *Gazetteer of Bengal and N.E. India,* Delhi, 1979 (rpt.), pp. 66-7.
9. *IAA,* no 20, line 51.

10. *IAA*, no. 15, line 47.
11. Ibid.
12. *IAA*, no. 14, lines 58ff.
13. *IAA*, no. 20, line 50.
14. *IAA*, no. 19, line 49.
15. B.C. Allen *et al.*, op. cit., p. 81.
16. C.S. Mullan, *Assam District Gazetteer, Kamrup*, p. 138.
17. A. Guha, 'The Ahom political system: an enquiry into the state formation process in mediaeval Assam (1228-1714)', *Social Scientist*, 11 (1983), p. 6.
18. *IAA*, no. 22.
19. *IAA*, nos. 16, 18, 26, etc.
20. W. Robinson, *A Descriptive Account of Assam*, Delhi, 1979 (rpt.), p. 221.
21. N.K. Shyamachaudhari, 'Indigenous irrigation in Assam: An eco-cultural trait', *Professor Surya Kumar Bhuyan Commemoration Volume* (eds. N. Neog and H.K. Barpujari), Gauhati 1966, pp. 295ff.
22. S. Endle, *The Kacharis*, London 1911, pp. 12-13.
23. B. Kakati, op. cit.
24. Ibid.
25. Ibid.
26. Ibid.
27. Ibid.
28. Nayanjot Lahiri, 'The pre-Ahom roots of mediaeval Assam', *Social Scientist*, 12 (1984), p. 65.
29. Ibid., p. 66.
30. *IAA*, Appendix.
31. Ibid.
32. *IAA*, nos. 13, 15 and 18.
33. B. Kakati, op. cit.
34. *IAA*, no. 19, verse 20.

15

The Socio-Economic Milieu of the Kerala Temple: A Functional Analysis *c.* AD 800-1200

Rajan Gurukkal

The period from the eighth to the twelfth century AD, the earliest documented phase in the history of Kerala, saw the emergence and decline of the Makotai Kingdom, the only royal line which ever ruled practically the whole land of modern Kerala. The period also witnessed the proliferation and consolidation of temple-nucleated brāhmin settlements throughout the fertile areas of Kerala.[1] Three major characteristics distinguish this period from the history of the preceding centuries:

(*a*) The establishment of kingship based upon the *Cakravartin* model as exemplified by the early medieval monarchs in India;[2]
(*b*) the consolidation of the temple-centred rural brāhmin settlements as relatively autonomous agrarian units of contemporary society and polity; and
(*c*) the formation of a new society consequent on the institutional socio-economic functions of the temple.

Brāhmins emerged as the chief landed beneficiaries during the pre-Makotai period (before the ninth century AD). The Cera rulers of the Śaṅgam period had richly endowed the Brāhmaṇas with land and gold.[3] The existence of a number of Brahmanical settlements in this period is borne out by several references. Cellūr (Perumcellūr of *Keralōlpatti*), one of the traditional thirty-two brāhmin settlements of Kerala, is referred to in the *Akanānūru*, an early Tamil work.[4]

It appears that the traditional thirty-two settlements were established much before the emergence of a centralized monarchy in Kerala. Unlike elsewhere in India, the brāhmin settlement of Kerala does not have original royal charters mentioning the origin of the settlement. The earliest known record of Kerala belongs to the ninth century AD and it speaks of a subsidiary settlement (*upagrāma*) of Tiruvalla, one of the traditional settlements.[5] It seems that before the emergence of the Makotai kingdom all Kerala was controlled by brāhmin corporations (This is indicated in the *Kēralōlpatti* which, though a comparatively late composition, draws its theme from an old oral tradition). The political predicament of brāhmin-controlled pre-Makotai Kerala, aggravated by disunity and centrifugal tendencies must have constrained the brāhmins to have a common authority which would favour and protect their own interests. The Makotai kingdom thus owes its origin to the pre-Makotai brāhmin corporate rule of Kerala. The consecrated status of Makotai kingship and high sounding ritual titles of the *cakravartin* model, as testified by the very first record of Kerala, indicate a brahmanized consecrated monarchy.[6] During the three centuries under review the institution of kingship went through two developmental phases: an initial phase which witnessed a brāhmin-ruler concord for the firm establishment of the socio-economic interests of the former and the consecrated status and political power of the latter; and a phase of local autonomy which witnessed the anti-royal assertions of the brāhmins and the consequent decline of the centralized consecrated monarchy in Kerala.

During the initial phase of brāhmin-ruler interdependence a large number of temples sprang up throughout the length and breadth of Kerala. Incidentally, none of them was as massive as the temples of Tamilnadu. This might be because most of these temples were built by the brāhmin corporations themselves and were not royal foundation. However the temples were richly endowed by the rulers and landed aristocracy of the time which accounts for the growth of the temple during this period. The present paper will examine the functional details of the temple, so as to understand the socio-economic infrastructure of the time.

Temples possessing considerable wealth, surrounded by brāhmin settlements, scattered through early medieval south India, played a pivotal socio-economic role. Each temple was the nucleus of a brāhmin settlement and the dominant brāhmin caste was the custodian of the temple as well as the proprietor of the village (*Ūr*). The brāhmins held almost all the agrarian tracts of the settlement as individual landholdings (*brahmasvam*) and, collectively, temple property (*dēvasvam*). The brāhmin elders of the settlement had an oligarchic caste-council called the *sabhā*, which administered the village (*Ūr*).[7] The members of the *sabhā* were referred to by various names such as *ūrāṭar* (proprietor of the *Ūr*), *Sabhaiyār* (member to the *sabhā*), *nāṭṭār* (the villager), etc. Often their numerical strength was also indicated by a prefix to the term *nāṭṭār*. For instance, the members of the *Tirūvāṟṟuvāy sabhā* were called *Tirūvāṟṟuvāy patineṭṭunāṭṭār*, the eighteen residents of Tiruvāṟṟuvāy.[8] Similarly the *sabhaiyār* of Nedumpuram Tali and Pudikkode were also called *patineṭṭunāṭṭār*.[9] The implication is that the respective villages were administered by eighteen residents. The term *nāṭṭār* is used in Tamil records apparently to denote non-brāhmin villagers, members of the *Veḷḷan vagai* villages.[10] But in Kerala it is clear that the term indicated only brāhmin residents.[11] The numerical term *patineṭṭu* being traditional, it has sometimes been suggested that it does not refer to any particular number. However, as a peculiar feature we find in the records of Kerala other numerical terms also used as epithets for the brāhmin residents of the settlement. The residents of Kumāranallūr brāhmin settlement were called *paināṟumar*, 'the sixteen', and those of *Avaṭṭipputtūr* as *irupa tteḷuvar*, 'the twenty-seven'.[12] From the reference to numerical strength it is inferred that all the brāhmin families were represented in the council by their elders. The council was a corporate body whose session required always the full quorum of all the members and all decisions taken by it were unanimous as indicated by the term *avirōtattāl* (without opposition).[13] But it can be inferred from the records that disagreements did occur in the council, which were moderated by the local ruler or the chief of his militia.[14] The term *tirukkaikkīlu* (under the royal hand) used in the records indicates the involvement of the royal force in the decision-making session of the *sabhā*. Here the operation of the represented royal force of the local ruler is a mechanism which works from above to bring about unity among the brāhmin oligarchs, the absence of which would affect the power of the monarchy. This helps one to visualize the probable political predicament, in pre-Makotai days, of the brāhmin oligarchy without a co-ordinating royal force, and also reveals the expediency of founding Makotai rule by brāhmins.

It is notable that the brāhmin assembly of the Tamil region described by scholars of south Indian polity differs from that of Kerala in its structure and character. Nilakanta Sastri and T.V. Mahalingam have interpreted *sabhā* as the general assembly of the village.[15] In the Tamil region it is identified as a caste-council of the brāhmins and a corporate body. In Kerala the executive work of administration of the temple affairs was discharged by a sub-committee of the caste-corporation, called *paraṭi* (*parishad*).[16] The exact constitution of this committee is not known. A twelfth-century record from Kiḷimānūr states that from among the ten *Ūrāḷar* of the settlement two were to be entrusted with the duty of managing the temple affairs for each year, and this was to go on by rotation for generations according to primogeniture.[17] All the important decisions with regard to the temple affairs were taken by the joint council of the *paraṭai, sabhā* and *poduvāl* (temple secretary). In certain cases the chief of the local militia is referred to as the royal representative in the sessions passing resolutions. Usually the local military force is mentioned in the records by referring to its numerical strength such as *āyiravar*, (the thousand), *eḷūnūṟṟūvar* (the seven hundred), *aññūrruvar* (the five hundred), *munnūrruvar* (the three hundred) and *arunnūṟṟuvar* (the six hundred). Reference to local militia by their numerical strength seems to be peculiar to Kerala. *Niḷal* and *Kāval* are the other two terms used generally to indicate the local militia. It appears that it constituted the companions of honour of the local chieftain.[18] As far as the temple was concerned these were the security forces which protected the temple property and successfully assisted the execution of endowments.[19] The temple paid *rakshābhōga* (tax for protection) to the local chieftain for the protection rendered by his security units. It is indicated in a record that if the force failed to carry out its responsibilities the local ruler would forfeit the *rakshābhōga*.[20] The socio-political strength and assertive nature of the brāhmin oligarchy are clear in such cases. The brāhmins acquired economic and social dominance and consequently political powers through their control over the economic functions of the temple. The temple was the institutional manifestation of their superior religious merit, and ritual status in the society. It supplied the required ideology for the legitimization and perpetuation of the consequent socio-economic order. The concentration of economic, social and political powers in the brāhmin caste council made it coterminus with the temple centred settlement.[21] Within the temple-centred rural society existed a code of law agreed upon by the temple corporation. This is called the *Kaccam.*[22] Usually a certain established *kaccam* was followed by most of the corporations. The most commonly quoted precedent in the records of Kerala is the Mūḷikkaḷam *kaccam,* i.e. the precedents set up by the corporation of Mūḷikkaḷam, one of the most prominent settlements of the time.[23] Other codes of laws like Śaṅkaramangalattu *kaccam,* Kadamkāṭṭu *kaccam* and Tavaranūr *kaccam* are also quoted in the inscriptions of the time.[24] These codes contain certain punitive clauses prescribing stringent measures against the erring members of the brāhmin councils. Punishments were so severe that an individual brāhmin acting on his own without the community's sanction was charged with the sin of cohabiting with his own mother, or of patricide, or both, or of killing his teacher, which were some of the worst sins.[25] The accused was to be socially and politically ostracized and his property confiscated. This was evidently to check disruptive tendencies among the brāhmins which would have destroyed internal stability and information control, the essential factors of their economic supremacy.[26] Internal discord could have affected the autonomy of the brāhmins by inviting too much royal interference. Thus the secret of the severity of the punitive clauses lies in the eagerness to maintain a cohesive and corporate character which made them the dominant class.

The *kaccam* imposes a lot of restrictions on the brāhmins of the settlement by forbidding them from obstructing the tenants, or collecting gold from them for paying back loans taken from the temple, holding tenancy individually, receiving bribes in connection with the appointment of temple functionaries like the officiating priests or professors of *Mahābhārata,* and so on.[27] One record of the Trikkākkara temple forbids the royal authority giving loans to the temple priests and he who accepted loans in defiance of the *kaccam* was to be expelled from service.[28] All these restrictions were to safeguard the common economic interests of the corporation against centrifugal forces. Control through the institution of *kaccam* is a peculiarity of Kerala and the term does not occur in Tamil records in a similar capacity.

We have some evidence for the temple-centred para-military organization of the brāhmins. The *śāla* was the school of martial arts and scriptures, where brāhmin youth, the *cāttirar* (caṭṭas—chatra), were trained.[29] The role of the *śāla* as a para-military training centre is clear from certain references in inscriptions, such as the prohibition of the *cattiras* from entering the temple with their weapons, or fighting each other.[30] It appears that *śālas* were constituted by the temple corporation to ensure its security by organizing their men into an armed defence group. However, it is clear that not all temple corporations established such para-military schools because many of them sought armed protection from the local royal militia and paid *rakshābhōga* for it. Interestingly we do not find the local militia interfering in the affairs of those big temple corporations which had *śālas*. Certain Chola records mention military officers belonging to Kerala serving under the Cholas, and some of them might well have been war captives from the *śālas*.[31]

The chief resource-base of society was agricultural produce. Since the temple was the chief landowner, it acquired a central place in the realm of the agrarian economy. In the light of available records it can be said that large agrarian tracts were acquired by the brāhmins in the form of royal endowments and private donations to the temple.[32] The centralization of agrarian activities under the institutional supervision of the temple resulted in the establishment of an elaborate agrarian order and an unprecedented expansion of agriculture. With its resources the temple could easily have organized society for various activities for higher production. But unlike some of the major south Indian temples, the temple of Kerala did not engage in large-scale irrigation works or land improvement schemes.[33] One possible reason for this might be the natural hydraulic facilities in the agrarian tracts of Kerala. It appears that minor irrigation works and small-scale reclamation were carried out by the tenants as part of their tenancy obligation. The temple gained a great deal of control over society through agrarian management, by integrating the landed intermediaries, tenants, sub-tenants and the tillers into a system of production and distribution based on ties and obligations from the base to the top. By making the temple the nucleus of such an integrated society, the corporate brāhmin oligarchy was establishing controls over people at various social levels. The kings were drawn to the temple as chief patrons for the legitimization of their power, and the landed aristocracy for socio-political ascendancy. Some of the landed nobles were obligated to the temple as the recipients of loans of gold. All individual brāhmins were tied to the temple through their ritual or other obligations. A large group was made dependent on the temple as functionaries and tenants. The numerous artisans and craftsmen settled on temple-land were at the disposal of the temple corporation. At the base was the bulk of tillers who worked on the temple land.

There were various types of land rights such as complete proprietorship (*aṭṭippēru*), revenue-cum-tenancy rights (*kīḻīṭu*), and temporary endowments.[34] These lands were further distributed by the temple among the members of the corporation, who in their turn distributed it to tenants, and the tenants to sub-tenants. The land right transferred were rights of ownership from the holder to the temple, the right to cultivate from the temple to its tenants and the right of occupation from the tenants to artisans and craftsmen[35]

The endowments that reached the temple were divided among the members of the *sabhā*, by whom various trusts (*gaṇam*) were constituted to look after the respective rituals.[36] They leased out land to tenants who were made responsible for providing the requirements of the specified rituals or ceremonies for the maintenance of which the endowments were made. This shows how the tenancy dues could provide a definite and regular resource-base for the perpetuation of the rituals and ceremonies in the temple. In case of default the dues were doubled and in extreme cases the tenants had to forfeit their tenancy. The tenancy rights seem to have been hereditary. In certain cases the lands were leased out to tenants nominated by the donors and in certain other cases it was stated that the land leased out to one individual should not be given to another. In certain cases the records indicate injunctions prohibiting the donor or his nominees from being the tenants of the donated land.[37] It is specifically mentioned in certain records that the brāhmins should not hold tenancy individually.[38] Inscriptions referring to the division of land endowment among the members of the trust (*gaṇa*) have sometimes been subjected to the interpretation that in the initial stages brāhmins themselves constituted part of the temple tenants.[39] But this is not the impression that one gets from the records.

Actually the members of the trusts were made trustees of the land endowed to the temple with responsibilities of maintaining the respective ritual or ceremony out of the accruing revenue. Here the trustees were virtually enjoying proprietary rights and not the right of tenancy.

Through the redistribution of land and land rights, the temple established a peculiar land system in which the proprietorship (*ūrāṅmai*) was with the temple corporation, the tenancy rights (*kārāṅmai*) with the non-brāhmins (chiefly Nairs), and the occupation rights (*kuṭimai*) with the artisans and craftsmen (*kuṭi*).

Large sums of gold which flowed into the temple treasury in the form of gifts from kings, nobles and merchants constituted a major source of wealth for the temple.[40] A considerable sum of gold reached the temple coffers as fines.[41] Land provided an effective form of investment for the temple's huge stock of gold. There are instances of purchase of land by the temple in exchange for gold.[42] Gold was also lent out at interest by the temple and loan recipients had to pledge their land to the temple. In certain cases the loan was not to be returned at all and the interest was in the form of oil or paddy meant for a specific ritual or ceremony.[43] It is mentioned in certain records that when the gold was returned to the temple it was to be invested in land.[44] Generally the local rulers, landed nobles and brāhmins received gold-loans from the temple. There is even an instance of a dancing girl being given a loan by the temple of Tiruvalla.[45] The practice of local rulers taking loans from the temple and perhaps also using them for issuing loans to temple servants appears to have led to a prohibitory order at Trikkākkara, against lending gold. The reference is to Kannan Puraiyan, the ruler of Kālkkarainātu, who borrowed gold from the Trikkākkara temple, and apparently used it for giving loans to temple-servants.[46] A prohibitory order was issued by the temple corporation in AD 958, reiterating an earlier resolution probably of AD 950.[47] The repetition of the order by a fresh resolution obviously indicates the violation of an earlier order. In spite of the prohibitory order the practice seems to have continued. References to gold loans from the same temples are found in other records.

Gold-lending brought the temple more and more agrarian control and land rights. Loans were given generally to the landed group alone and invariably the borrower of gold had to mortgage a portion of land. Most of the loans were taken by the landed brāhmins themselves, who invested it in land. It is implied in certain records that at times the brāhmin lords tried to raise gold from their tenants for paying back the loan.[48] Here the raising of gold from tenants by the brāhmins to repay their own loans is banned not to protect tenants in any way but to protect the economic interests of the temple corporation.

Through the gold-lending and land accumulating processes the temple was performing once again the economic function of resource redistribution, both of gold and land. The gold accumulated in the temple in the form of endowments or fines was redistributed by the temple corporation in three ways:

(*a*) by using gold as a medium of exchange to buy new lands;
(*b*) by lending it out at interest for procuring more and more tenancy rights and thereby increasing its agrarian resource control; and
(*c*) by occasionally giving gold as wages or rewards to temple servants.

Certain records refer to a stable gold-paddy exchange ratio established by the temple through its transactions.[49] Throughout the period under review the ratio appears to have remained constant and formed a strong basis for the stabilization of inter-commodity exchange ratios. The lengthy plates of Tiruvalla give a detailed list of inter-commodity exchange ratios.[50]

The prevalence of regular inter-commodity exchange rates and the non-fluctuating gold-paddy ratio seems to indicate the absence of monetization in the economic transactions of the temple. The different units of gold with specific heat, weight and fineness covered the purpose of money in the high-level transactions of the temple.[51] The coins mentioned in the records of the period are the Arab Dinār (*tīnāram*) and the Tamil *Paḷamkāsū* which seem to have circulated among the merchant guilds.[52] In spite of the prevalence of the monetized transaction system of the trade guilds and the royal issues of coinage by the Pallavas and Cholas, rural transactions in south India remained chiefly non-monetized.[53] In the case of Kerala this was particularly true. There is no reference to the state issue of coinage in Kerala during this period.[54] The dearth of coins and the stabilized inter-commodity exchange system became prominent in the temple-centred rural society because there was widespread service tenure and localization of production without exchange-profit motives. References to the settlement of various artisans and craftsmen or professional castes in the temple-centred village show that the brāhmin settlements aimed at self-sufficiency. Once they were settled in the temple-land they ceased to be free wage earners and became bondsmen to the temple and the village. In the total assemblage of all these economic factors we see a social organization based on economic ties of mutual dependence between the lowlier groups and the higher. It is interesting that contemporary religion provided an ideological basis for existing social relations by inculcating the cult of self-surrender through *bhakti*.[55] The main aspect of the religion of the period was *bhakti* and the Kerala temple had very effective institutional devices for disseminating the ideology into the rural areas. A large number of *bhaṭṭas* or professors recited and explained *Mahābhārata* stories. Large-scale *kūttu* (dance-drama) by the *cākkaimār* was another system by which the Purāṇic stories were enacted before the people. Festivals and ceremonies of the Kerala temples were capable of creating a spirit of *bhakti* in the society. The Tamil *bhakti* movement of *ālvārs* and *nāyanārs* which laid the foundation of a new religious sensibility persisted in Kerala with more vigour through the religious functions of the temple. The temple popularized the ideology of spiritual oneness among a people with glaring material inequalities through the illusion that all are equal before the eyes of God. It made the people believe that the secret of *mōksha* rested only in sincerity and loyalty, thus sanctifying the allegiance that passed from the lowest groups in the hierarchy to the top of the contemporary agrarian order.

The social aspects of this integration seem to have taken a unique pattern in Kerala, although it was within the order of a caste society. The large number of temple functionaries recruited for the various services of the temple constituted endogamous caste groups, a unique feature of the temple-centred society in Kerala. The brāhmin and non-brāhmin functionaries of the Kerala temple seem to have built up separate hierarchies within themselves. The internal functional variations of the brāhmin caste created two separate hierarchies: one of ritual status and the other of material status often the ritually highest for example, the *tantrikaḷ* who were the *āgamic* instructors of the temple, practising endogamy within the closed group. The hierarchy of ritual status within the brāhmin caste was headed by the *tantrikal* and others in the hierarchical order were the *śāntiaṭikaḷ* (officiating priests), *ṅambi* (ritual assistants), *paṭṭakaḷ* (*bhaṭṭas*) and *cāttirar* as the highest. Although the priest of the temple had a very high ritual status, his material benefits were very low when compared to those of the brāhmins who performed managerial roles in the temple.

The large number of non-brāhmin functional associates who constituted the larger temple community are also of interest. The *poduvāḷ* was the general secretary of the temple who acted as the official appointed by and functioning on behalf of the brāhmin corporation. The *madhyasta* of the Tamil inscriptions may be regarded as parallel to the *poduvāḷ*. There were the *akappoduvāl*, secretary to internal affairs of the temple such as daily rituals and ceremonies, and the *purappoduvāḷ*, secretary of external affairs such as temple revenue and endowments. The *vāriyār* was a member of the temporarily constituted functional supervisional committee of *vāriyāms* such as the *kaḷanivāriyām* (field supervising committee), the *ērivāriyām* (irrigation tanks supervising committee) and the *tōṭṭavāriyām* (garden supervising committee). The *chakkaimar* were actors and the *naññaimār* the temple courtesans, both groups constituting the artist functionaries of the temple, among whom were also dance-instructors called *naṭṭuvanār*, musicians called *kāndarppikar* and drummers called *koṭṭikaḷ*. Apart from these there were gate-keepers, sweepers and other manual servants. The internal inequality among those non-brāhmin functionaries was also twofold: the inequality of ritual and material status. It appears that differences in the material status of the temple servants were determined by their private holdings of land and not by the rewards from the temple. There do not appear to have existed any marked disparities in the remunerations of the temple functionaries.

All services in the temple, because of its consecrated character, carried relatively high socio-ritual status. Naturally those who were not associated with the temple became inferior to the temple caste called the *antāraḷajāti*. The assimilation of temple functionaries into the *Varṇa-jāti* complex with caste and social status differential between the brāhmins and Nairs may be considered a peculiarity of Kerala. Once the temple functionaries began to serve the temple as workers of hereditary specialization and were hence labelled by different professional names, these turned into castes names. The present writer has noted these two stages in the process of the evolution of endogamous caste groups among the temple functionaries. Land rights were the basis of this. The system of service tenure promoted and intensified the hereditary specialization of profession. This led to the emergence of profession-labelled groups such as the *poduvāḷ vāriyar,* and *cākkaimār.* These profession-labelled endogamous groups were accommodated into the *varṇa-jāti* system. There appears to be no comparable and clear-cut constitution of caste groups on a professional basis in Tamil Nadu.

The origin of the Nair community as a dominant factor in the socio-political realm of the medieval period must be attributed to the temple. It appears that they constituted the majority of the temple-tenants. It was from this class that the *sāmanta* chieftains emerged. It seems that military recruitment was mainly made from among this community. This class of intermediary tenants, enjoying the privileges of nobility and owing allegiance only to the brāhmins, succeeded in asserting themselves in the temple society through the institutional agency of the temple, although they had no direct relations with temple ritual or other functions.

The large number of artisans and craftsmen were also fitted into the *varṇa/jāti* by the institutional force of the temple. The temple settled them on its land to make their services available. This service bond with the temple created status variations among the personnel according to the relationship with the temple.

The base of the social order was constituted by the *pulayar* (the tillers and soil workers) who were apparently tied down to the land, and hence gifted and sold with it. They constituted the untouchables of the time.

To sum up, the temple through its kaleidoscopic dimensions of social relations accomplished a unique socio-economic nexus effecting a structural transformation in the society that it served. Kerala stands as a separate cultural entity detached from the Tamils because of the transforming influence of her temple-culture. Her social transformation and family organization which differ from that of Tamils became crystallized during this period. Above all the genesis of the Malayalam language was centred in the new society that emerged around the temple during this period.

NOTES

1. The problem has been considered in detail by M.G.S. Narayanan in his unpublished Doctoral Dissertation, 'Political and Social Conditions of Kerala under the Kulasekhara Empire, *c.* AD 800-1124', Kerala University, 1972. Also Kesavan Veluthat, *Brahman Settlements in Kerala, Historical Studies,* Calicut University, 1978.
2. The earliest of such consecrated monarchical epithets in south India appear in the Pallava inscriptions. See Burton Stein, 'The Segmentary State in South Indian History', in R.G. Fox (ed.), *Realm and Region in Traditional India,* New Delhi, 1977, pp. 21-6. The epithet 'Sri rājarājādhirāja paramesvara bhattāraka rājaśekhara tēvar', used in the Valappaḷḷy copper plate of the ninth century AD (the earliest known epigraph of Keraḷa), is suggestive of the *cakravartin* concept of Kingship in the case of Kerala. See Rajan Gurukkal, Socio-economic Role of the Kerala Temple, *c.* AD 800-1200, unpublished M.Phil. Dissertation, Jawaharlal Nehru University, 1977, ch. II: 'The Changing Socio-religious Order'.
3. N. Subrahmanian, *Sangam Polity,* Madras, 1966, p. 324.
4. Cellur is one of the thirty-two traditional brāhmin settlements; Kesavan Veluthat, op. cit., ch. 2.
5. M.G.S. Narayanan, 'Index to the Cera Inscriptions', unpublished companion volume to his Doctoral Dissertation, op. cit. For uniformity of reference the present writer has followed his Index. For the Valappaḷḷy record see Index no. A.I.
6. Index no. A.I.
7. M.G.S. Narayanan, 'Political and Social Conditions of Kerala under the Kulasekhara Empire', chapter entitled 'Local Bodies'. Also Kesavan Veluthat, 'Community Organisation and Village Administration in the Brahman Settlements of Kerala in the later Cera Period, *c.* AD 800-1200', *Indian History Congress,* Jadavpur, 1974.
8. Index no. A.I.
9. Index Nos. A. 27, L1. 2-3, L1. 2-4; 9, L1. 2-4; 70, L1. 1-3, 21.
10. The Valappaḷḷy copper plate of Rajasekhara refers to Tiruvatruuia patineṭṭunaṭṭar (the eighteen residents of Tiruvaṟṟuvai settlement) and Valappaḷḷy *ūrār* regulating the affairs of the temple. Another record of the same temple ascribed to the seventeenth year (AD 861) of King Sthanuravi refers to Tiruvaṟṟuvai *sabhai* and *aṭikaḷmār* (priests of the temple) regulating the temple affairs. *Patineṭṭunāṭṭār* mentioned in the former record are obviously the members of *Tiruvāṟṟuvāi sabha. Sabhāi* being the caste council of a brāhmin village the term *nāttār* used for its members only indicates brāhmins themselves but not the representatives of the non-brāhmin settlements as pointed out by Y. Subbarayalu in the case of Chola country. See his *Political Geography of the Chola Country,* Madras, 1973, pp. 30, 90.
11. See n 10.

12. Index Nos. C. 43, L1. 2-3, and A. 10 L1. 2-4.
13. M.G.S. Narayanan, *Index . . . passim.*
14. '. . . *pullūr kumaran kumarāticcanāna neḍumpuṛanāṭṭu paṭaināyaruḷḷirunnu tevakāriyamum veñṭum kuravara paraññotukkikkoṭuttu* . . .' Index no. A. 70 L1. 2-4.
15. See *Coḷas,* Madras, 1975, pp. 494-503 and *South Indian Polity,* Madras, 1967, p. 353.
16. Kesavan Veluthat, *Brahman Settlements in Kerala,* pp. 55ff.
17. Ibid., p. 56.
18. *niḷal* and *kāval* are two terms used in the inscriptions to denote the local militia. See M.G.S. Narayanan, *Reinterpretations in South Indian History,* Trivandrum, 1977, pp. 99-112.
19. Rajan Gurukkal, op. cit., see ch. IV, 'Economic Functions'.
20. Index no. A. 36. L1. 26-7.
21. Rajan Gurukkal, op. cit., ch. V, 'Social Functions'.
22. Kesavan, Veluthat, *Brahman Settlements in Kerala,* p. 58.
23. Some seventeen temples from one end of Kerala to the other have records referring to *Mūḷikkaḷam Kaccam.* Rajan Gurukkal, op. cit., p. 39. Details of the *kaccam* are given in *Rama Varma Research Institute Bulletin,* vol. IX. p. 134. Also Iḷamkulam Kunhan Pillai, *Janmi Sampradāyam kēralathil,* Kottayam, 1959, pp. 28-38 and M.G.S. Narayanan, 'Kullasekhara Empire . . .', pp. 332-5.
24. Sankaramangalathu *kaccam* is mentioned in the Tiruvalla plates. Index no. A. 80. For Kadamkāṭṭu *kaccam* see Āvaṭṭipputtur inscription of king Kotaravi's twentieth year (AD 903). Index no. A. 10. L. 18. Tavaranur *kaccam,* see *South Indian Inscriptions,* vol. V, no. 772, p. 334; no. 775, p. 335; no. 783, p. 338.
25. Index Nos. A.I. L1. 3-4; 3. LI. 10-12; 80. LI. 28-30; c. 36, L1. 7-11. Most of the punitive clauses refer to *pancamahāpatakas.* M.G.S. Narayanan, 'Socio-economic Implications of the concept of *Mahāpātaka* in the Feudal Society of South India,' *Indian History Congress,* Calicut, 1976.
26. Erving Goffman has discussed the significance of information control in increasing group integrity while dealing with the nature of sub-stratum communication structure of the present day society. See his *Presentation of Self in Everyday Life,* Harmondsworth, 1972, pp. 77ff.
27. Index no. A. 42, L. 2.
28. Index no. B.9.
29. Rajan Gurukkal, op. cit., pp.103-4.
30. M.G.S. Narayanan, 'Kantalur Salai: New Light on Nature of Aryan Expansion to South India', *Indian History Congress,* Jabalpur, 1970. For an examination of the meaning of the terms *caṭṭas* and *bhaṭṭas* figuring in the inscriptions of northern India from Gupta times, in the light of new interpretations, Kesavan Veluthat, 'The *Caṭṭas* and *Bhaṭṭas*: A new interpretation', *Indian History Congress,* Aligarh, 1975.
31. Ibid.

32. Rajan Gurukkal, op. cit., ch. IV, 'Economic Functions'.
33. The irrigation works carried out by the temples of south India have been discussed by Burton Stein, in 'The State, the Temple and Agricultural Development: A Study in Medieval South India', *Economic Weekly*, Annual Number, February 1961, vol. XIII, pp. 179-88. Also 'The Economic Function of a Medieval South Indian Temple', *Journal of Asian Studies*, vol. 27, 1960, pp. 163ff.
34. This has been considered in detail in the M.Phil dissertation of the present writer, in ch. IV, 'Economic Functions'.
35. Redistribution refers to the centralized collection of goods or rights over goods and their subsequent reallocation. Karl Polanyi,'The Economy as Instituted Process', in K. Polanyi *et al.* (eds.), *Trade and Market in the Early Empires*, Glencoe, 1959, pp. 243-70. It was Burton Stein (op. cit.) who tested the hypothesis of temple-centred resource-redistribution in the context of medieval south Indian temples. A study of resource redistribution in the Tanjore temple has been made by George W. Spencer, 'Temple Money-lending and Livestock Redistribution in Early Tanjore', *Indian Economic and Social History Review*, vol. V, no. 3, September 1968, pp. 277-92. Richards S. Kennedy has made a brief analysis of similar processes during the Sangam Age, through the chieftain's distribution of war fruits. 'King in Early South India: Chieftain and Emperor', *Indian Historical Review*, vol. III, July 1976, p. 3. Temple centred redistribution has been discussed by A. Appadurai and C.A. Breckenridge, 'The South Indian Hindu Temple: Authority, Honour and Redistribution', *Contributions to Indian Sociology*: New Series, December 1976.
36. M.G.S. Narayanan, op. cit., p. 332.
37. Index no. A. 25. Ll. 4-5 '. . . *ippūmi nāduvāḷ umavaraḷāka avaṛkaḷakku cārnavaralāka pāṭṭamāḷapperār* . . .'.
38. Index no. A. 10 Ll. 12-6., 42. L.5 and c. 17.
39. M.G.S. Narayanan, *Kulasekhara Empire* . . . , p. 332.
40. Rajan Gurukkal, op. cit., ch. IV, 'Economic Functions'.
41. Ibid.
42. Ibid.
43. Ibid.
44. Ibid.
45. The amount of gold borrowed by her is not mentioned in the record. But it is stated that she was to pay 90 *para* of paddy, as interest. Since other records would have us believe that the rate of interest was 5 per cent, i.e. seventy *kalañcu* and five *kāṇam.*
46. Index no. A. 42.
47. Index nos. B. 9 and 7 respectively.
48. It is stated in certain records that the amount of gold borrowed from the temple was not to be raised from the tenants. Index nos. A. 80. Ll. 334-5 and 19. Ll. 3-5.

49. Index no. A. 80.
50. *Kānam* and *kalañcu* are the two units of gold frequently mentioned in the records. '*Cūṭumuriyum varuvitu,*' a phrase generally used in south Indian inscriptions, refers to the prescribed heat, weight and fineness. Index no. B. 20 L. 6. no. 218 of 1911.
51. Index nos. A.1.L1. 3., 9-10, no. 136 of 1908. no. A. 30 L. 2. The weight of the *paḷamkāśu* is mentioned as three *kalañcu* in Chola record no. 176 of 1915. This is confirmed by a Kerala record, Index no. A. 28, L. 1.
52. B.D. Chattopadhyay, *Coins and Currency System in Early South India: c. AD 259-1300,* pp. 303-4. Also in D.N. Jha, 'Temples as Landed Magnates in Early Medieval South India, *c.* AD 700-1300', *Indian Society: Historical Probings,* New Delhi, 1977, 2nd edn., p. 207.
53. See P.L. Gupta, *Early Coins of Kerala,* Trivandrum, 1966, *passim.* Also M.G.S. Narayanan, Kulasekhara Empire. . . , op. cit.
54. For the interpretations of the socio-economic implications of the *bhakti* movement see D.D. Kosambi, *Myth and Reality: Studies in the Formation of Indian Culture,* Bombay, 1962.
55. George W. Spencer, 'Religious Networks and Royal Influence in Eleventh Century South India,' *Journal of Economic and Social History of the Orient,* vol. XII, p. 1, January 1969, pp. 42-56; R.S. Sharma, 'Problem of Transition from Ancient to Medieval in Indian History', *Indian Historical Review,* vol. 1, March 1974, pp. 1-9; Champakalakshmi, 'The Bhakti Movement and Religious Persecution in Tamil Nadu', *Indian History Congress,* Calicut, 1976, and M.G.S. Narayanan and Kesavan Veluthat, 'The Bhakti Movement in South India' (unpublished research paper), Calicut University, 1977.

16

Agriculture under the Kākatīyas of Warangal

Y. Gopal Reddy

The Kākatīyas realized the need for the improvement of economic resources of the empire and paid much attention to agriculture, for it was the primary source of revenue. This policy was pursued in three directions, viz., (1) construction of a large network of tanks, (2) reclamation of deserted villages and lands, and (3) formation of new villages and granting them as *agrahāras* to brāhmins.

The construction of a tank was regarded as an act of charity resulting in the acquisition of great religious merit. It was regarded as one of the seven meritorious acts—*saptasantanas,* the remaining six being the procreation of a son, the composition of a poem, the hoarding of a treasure, the planting of a grove, the marriage of a girl to a brāhmin, and the construction of a temple.[1]

The sporadic allusions to the construction of tanks and dykes that are scattered in inscriptions and literary compositions and the numerous remains of the old irrigational works that are distributed in the Telangana region of Andhrapradesh bear testimony to the care with which such facilities were provided by the Kākatīya kings. The Motupalli pillar inscription of Gaṇapatidēva records that Prola I excavated a tank known as *Kesarī-taṭakam* which was like 'a representative of the ocean and the collection of all waters that were originally created'.[2] Beta II laid out a garden and a tank named Śivapura in the city of Hanamkoṇḍa.[3] He is also said to have undertaken the building of two tanks namely *Setti-kereya* and *Kesarī-samudra* and to have performed in that connection the ceremony of *Varuṇa-pratishtā* or the installation of Varuṇa—

the presiding deity of waters.[4] An undated record from Kazipeta mentions that Prola II founded a tank known as *Sarī-samudra.*[5] Tradition ascribes the excavation of another tank, viz., *Kama-samudra* to him.[6] The Hanamkoṇḍa inscription of Śaka 1084 states that Rudradēva, having destroyed the forest and fort of king Cōḍōdaya, constructed a big tank.[7] The *Pratāpā-caritra*[8] mentions that Gaṇapatidēva founded many tanks at Nellore, Gaṅgapuram, Ellore, Ganapapuram, Ekasilapuri, etc. The same authority credits Rudramadevī and Pratāparudradēva with the construction of many tanks.[9]

The nobles and officials, like their overlords, also took interest in the construction of tanks. Thus the Koṇḍiparti epigraph, dated Śaka 1125, records that the general Caunda of the Maalyāla family constructed an extensive tank which blew away the pride of all oceans and named it as *Caunda-samudra.*[10] The same inscription describes the tank thus: 'Which tank eternally creating on the bank a line of big moon-dishes in the form of the balls of foam rising by the action of high waves, put down the universally spreading fame of the milk-ocean, originally from the birth of a single moon as a result of the churning-rod of the revolving *Manthara*'. Another epigraph dated Śaka 1162 states that 'the earth had been shattered to pieces by the construction of ponds, wells and big tanks' by Maalyāla Kata.[11] Malla of the Viriyala family founded a tank in the village of Gumuduru.[12] The Bothpur inscription refers to the construction of a tank by Guṇḍa.[13] It is recorded in the Kaṭukuru inscription that Viriyala Śura built a tank in the village of Ayyanavolu.[14] Cente Rami Nāyaka constructed two tanks at Betura.[15] The Canarese inscription at Hanamkoṇḍa, dated C.V.E. 42, mentions that Beta, excavated a tank at Hanamkoṇḍa.[16] The Karimnagar inscription of Śaka 1092 states that Gaṅgādhara, the minister of Rudradēva, constructed a tank.[17] *Mahāpradhāni* Goderaya Gaṅgidēvayamgaru is said to have constructed a tank at Ravuḷakolanu.[18] The Tripurantakam inscription notes that Ambadeva of the Kāyastha family constructed two tanks in the village of Peḍapulaceruvu.[19] The Sōmavaram inscription, dated AD 1213 records that Recherla Beti Reddi established two tanks.[20] Aṇṇaya of the Induḷūri family is said to have constructed many tanks along the banks of the Krishna and Godavari rivers respectively.[21]

The Hanamkoṇḍa *Niroshtya-kāvya* inscription states: 'In the country (i.e. Andhradeśa) are hundreds of tanks and thousands of rivulets, and they indeed appear to be the ocean and his consorts respectively.'[22]

A large number of tanks, with suffixes, *samudra, ceruvu* or *teruvu* and *kere* or *kereya* are referred to in the inscriptions. *Samudra* may be a tank having large dimensions and supplying water for some thousands of acres. *Ceruvu* may be a village tank whereas *Kereya* may be Kannaḍa equivalent for a village tank. Some of them are as follows:

Samudras

Keśari-samudra[23]
Prola-samudra[24]
Udaya-samudra[25]
Cōḍa-samudra[26]
Eraka-samudra[27]
Bas-samudra[28]
Po-samudra[29]
Lakuma-samudra[30]
Gaṇapa-samudra[31]
Malla-samudra[32]
Kama-samudra[33]
Caunda-samudra[34]
Nama-samudra[35]
Anugū-samudra[36]
Viśvanātha-samudra[37]
Sabbi-samudra[38]
Lakṣmi-samudra[39]
Kuppa-samudra[40]
Rāma-samudra[41]

Ceruvus or teruvus

Mamdarāju-ceruvu[42]
Cimtala-ceruvu[43]
Gudla-ceruvu[44]
Ḅikkimalya-ceruvu[45]
Kamtidevī-ceruvu[46]
Taiḷapadeva-ceruvu[47]
Nandigāma-ceṛuvu[48]
Penugamchiprolu-ceruvu[49]
Kamarāju-ceruvu[50]
Yanamaḍaḷa-ceruvu[51]
Liṅgagiri-ceruvu[52]
Samiseṭṭi-ceruvu[53]
Kalyake-ceruvu[54]
Gaṅgaciya-ceruvu[55]
Erram-ceruvu[56]
Jiluguballī-ceruvu[57]
Koḷikuḍla-ceruvu[58]
Uppalapati-ceruvu[59]
Dubala-ceruvu[60]
Miriyala-ceruvu[61]

Kereya

The Hanamkoṇḍa inscription of Betesa mentions a tank known as *Seṭṭi-kereya.*[62]

It is evident from the above discussion that the *ceruvus* or *teruvus* or *kereyas* were named after the persons who excavated them or the villages where they were located. It would be of absorbing interest to mention in this connection that some of the irrigational works founded by the Kākatīyas are in existence and irrigating some thousands of acres in the Telengana region of Andhrapradesh even now. Gulam Yazdani observes: 'Warangal, the metropolis of this dynasty (Kākatīya) abounds in magnificent tanks, and the titanic dykes and sluice gates of Pakhal, Lakhmavaram and Ramappa lakes are object lessons even to the modern engineer.'[63] The following details will clearly show how pivotal a part the above-mentioned tanks are playing in the twentieth century irrigational works of Andhrapradesh.

Pakhal Lake

It is situated about 32 miles east of Warangal and 9 miles away from Necconda Railway Station, and 7 miles north-east of Narasampet, the taluka headquarters. The lake lies in the basins of the Krishna and the Manair rivers. King of the Geographical Survey of India, writing on the lake observes: 'It is a splendid sheet of water lying back in two arms on either side of a good big hill east-south-east of the bund, while from there are long bays reaching up behind low ridges of out-cropping Vindhyas. On every side there is far stretching jungle. Even below the bund for miles there is the thickest and densest jungle, only broken here and there by a few patches of rice cultivation.'[64]

The combined drainage area of the lake is 80 sq. miles of which 40 sq. miles are intercepted. The annual rainfall in the basin is 40 in. and the yield from the catchment amounts to 2987 Mc. Ft. The capacity of the tank is 2452 Mc. Ft, capable of irrigating about 17258 acres. The present cultivation under this lake is 9,037 acres. The huge dam composed of laterite pebbles and red-earth is one mile long with forty artificial channels, the earthen dam having a top width of 30 to 50 ft. The lake is not known to have dried up and there are crocodiles in it.[65] According to a pillar inscription which is standing in the centre of the bund, it was constructed during the time of Gaṇapatidēva *mahārāja*.[66]

Rāmappā Lake

It is situated at a distance of 44 miles north-east of Warangal and 12 miles from Mulug, the headquarters of the same taluka. This magnificent lake is formed by a ring of hills on three sides with a colossal bund only on one side—on north—an excellent testimony to the care and skill of Kākatīyas in irrigation works of a high order. The epigraphic evidence shows that it was also founded during the reign of Gaṇapatidēva.[67]

Ghanpur Tank

It is situated nearly 6 miles away from the Rāmappā lake. Tradition attributes the credit of constructing this tank to Gaṇapatīdēva.[68]

Besides the earlier-mentioned lakes and tanks there are many other tanks which are in a very good state. The Udaya-*samudram* (near Panugal in the Nalgonda district), Eraka-*samudram* (near Yarakavaram), Malla-*samudram* (near Matedu in the Khammamett district), and the Bayyaram-*ceruvu* (near Bayyaram in the same district)[69] stand prominent.

The maintenance of irrigation works was at least as important as the construction of new ones. Their maintenance involved the repair of damaged tanks and the removal of slit to prevent the tank or other irrigation work from being closed up. Generally the state, the village community and the private individuals appear to have taken keen interest in these matters. Thus the residents of Pottapi-*nāḍu* in AD 1272-3 met in the *maṇḍapa* and decided to raise one *māḍa* from every village in the district to construct an embankment on the side of the river Ceyyeru and prevent possible damage from the fields to the temple.[70] Another inscription registers the assignment of 5 *kuntas* of land, under the tank at Gandrasiṅgampalle, and a levy (?) of 1 *kunca* for every *aḍḍa* of grain for the maintenance of a tank by Damana Liṅgappamgaru.[71] A similar endowment is recorded in another inscription found at Nellore.

Closely connected with the tanks and lakes is the excavation of *Kaḷuvas* (canals) and *tumus* (sluices). The Kulpak inscription of AD 1279 records the construction of a canal by name *Vaṁśavardhana kaluva* in Kollipaka.[73] Another inscription refers to the construction of a canal by Malyāla Guṇda.[74] The Nelakoṇḍapalli inscription records that Oḍayana Cōḍa-*mahārāja* of Kandur constructed a sluice.[75] Ambadeva-*mahārāja* is said to have excavated two canals namely Rayasahasramalla-*kaluva* and Gaṇḍapendaru-*kaluva* at Lembaka and Tadḷapaka respectively.[76] The Amarābād inscription also records the construction of a canal.[77]

The canals were dug to bring water from the rivers and to fill the tanks situated in the vicinity. Of this class may be mentioned the Museti-*kaluva,* Antaragaṅga-*kaluva,* Krishṇavēni-*kaluva,* etc.[78] They were also dug to carry water from the tanks to water the fields. The *anakaluva* and the *kaṭṭuṅgommu-kaluva* may be temporary embankments of earth and stones, called *anas* and *kaṭṭuṅgommus.*[79] Sub-soil water, from springs and *uṭa-kaluvas* or canals dug deep into the earth, was also used to fill the tanks in certain areas.[80] In this connection it may be of interest to mention some of the canals that are referred to in the inscriptions of the period under our study. They are as follows:

Kucineni-kaluva[81]	*Lomtalim-kaluva*[82]
Ravipuli-kaluva[83]	*Kalamareddī-kaluva*[84]
Bommakani-kaluva[85]	*Reddi-kaluva*[86]
Tumu-kaluva[87]	*Aḷugu-kaluva*[88]
Uttamagaṇḍa-kaluva[89]	*Dadla-kaluva*[90]
Utum-kaluva[91]	*Cimtala-kaluva*[92]
Tamti-kaluva[93]	*Vramta-kaluva*[94]
Maddi-maddu-kaluva[95]	*Raddi-yedam-bhappiṇa-kaluva*[96]

Construction of wells and irrigation with the help of well-water were known in the Kākatīya period. The Guḍuru inscription refers to the construction of a well by a Malla.[97] Another inscription, dated Śaka 1162, records the construction of a well by Malyāla Kata.[98] Under well-water irrigation the water-bailing mechanism, *etam,* was used to lift water from wells, either by the use of bullock-power or man-power, to supply water to the fields situated nearby. The Hanamkoṇḍa inscription refers to the use of *etam.*[99] The Dosapaḍu inscription, dated AD 1254, records the gift of a water-lifting pulley, *ratnam,* together with two bullocks.[100]

Reclamation, from the economic point of view, may be considered as supplying a means of coping with the pressure of population. It was followed in two ways: (1) clearance of waste or land covered with jungle and bringing it under cultivation for the first time or of the land under cultivation but later deserted, and (2) foundation of new villages. Traditions and archaeological evidence show that both these types of land reclamation were used in the period under study.

The local tradition preserved in the *Kaifiyats* of several villages throws some light in this connection. It is said that Pratāparudradēva in his campaign against Ambadēva, reached Koccerlakoṭa in the north of Nellore district and ordered his officers to cut down the forests which then covered the neighbouring country.[101] The country to the west of the Śrīśaila mountain corresponding to a large portion of the present Nandikotkur taluka of the Kurnool district was also at that time covered by dense woods which were cleared at the instance of the king.[102] The Hanamkoṇḍa inscription of Śaka 1084,[103] and the Tripurāntakam inscription of Śaka[104] 1174-5, refer to the clearance of forests and the construction of tanks.

In granting *agrahāras* and founding new villages the motive might have been acquisition of religious merit for the donor, but there is no doubt that they fulfilled a real economic purpose, for a new settlement invariably meant increase of cultivated area by the conversion of the forest tracts or cultivable waste-land into fields. Gaṅgādhara is said to have established an *agrahāra* town.[105] An inscription dated AD 1214, records the establishment of a village named Gaṇapatipura.[106] The Gaṇapeśvaram inscription of the time of Gaṇapatidēva states that Rudradēva destroyed many towns of his enemies and established many quarters named after the destroyed, in the city of Warangal, and peopled them with their respective inhabitants, while in the devastated towns he built celebrated temples of Rudreśvara and settled fresh inhabitants.[107] The *Pratāpacaritra* states that Gaṇapatidēva established a village known as Gaṇapapuram.[108] According to a local tradition, Irugappa-Keti-Nāyaka built the village of Dupulapaḍu which may be identified with the modern Dupaḍu in the Nellore region.[109] Several new villages are said to have been established in the country to the west of Śrīśaila mountain by Pratāparudradēva and placed incharge of a Kāyastha chief, Śrī Siṅgala-rāja, who had migrated with his wife Śri Naguladevī from Kalyān in the north.[110] Videmu Kommaya, to whom Pratāparudradēva had granted the territory in the neighbourhood of Kurnool as *nāyaṁkāra*, felled trees and established Nagaluti near Damegatla and several other new villages in that region.[111] Donation of waste lands, i.e. cultivable waste may also be treated under reclamation of land. In this case the presumption is that the donee after receiving the gift of waste-land had to clear off the forest or bushes if there be any and make it fit for cultivation. The produce thus obtained from that land may be enjoyed by the donee at his will. References to the granting of waste-land, though rare, are not unknown to the inscriptions of our period. A record from the Nellore district mentions a grant of 1000 *kuntas* of dry-waste-land to a priest.[112] Another inscription, dated Śaka 1130, refers to the donation of 10 *marturus* of waste-land by certain Eṛakasani.[113]

But the information regarding the concessions that were granted by the state to bring such forests, deserts and waste lands under cultivation is scanty in the extreme. When jungle lands had to be brought under plough, the jungle had to be cleared, stumps had to be excavated and water canals had to be provided. The inducements offered by the state in this connection were granting taxes and exemption from taxation. More often, a graduated scale of assessment was adopted to encourage the ryots to bring land under tillage. In some cases when lands were neglected wilfully, the imposition of tax itself was calculated to induce the cultivators to keep the lands under cultivation.[114]

We have seen above the various irrigation works that were established, and land reclamation measures adopted for the improvement of agriculture by the Kākatīya kings. Now we may proceed to analyse the material available as regards the agricultural and horticultural products of the time. But an account of agricultural products should begin with land.

Arable land may be divided broadly into three kinds, viz., *nir-nela* (wet-land), *veḷi-poḷamu* (dry-land) and *tomta-poḷamu* (garden-land).[115] The wet-land was the most valuable one, as it is now, from the economic point of view, for different varieties of paddy were cultivated on it due to the abundance of water facilities. This was not the case with dry-land. But the dry-land may be converted into wet-land by having a channel cut to irrigate it for growing paddy. The garden-lands were generally located within the village and mainly produced horticultural products.

Coming now to details, we may note that fields had a variety of names, and they afford interesting sidelights on the practice of tillage. The fields were named after the nature of the soil, its adaptability to particular crop, ownership, and after the name of villages, etc. Some of them are given as follows:

1. *Krishna-kṣetra*[116]—Black-soil, suited for cotton.
2. *Pamdura-kṣetra*[117]—Yellowish-white soil, may be suited for paddy if water is available.
3. *Uppu-bhūmi*[118] or Cavuṭa-bhūmi[119]—Salty soil
4. *Celuka-bhūmi*[120]—Fallow land.
5. *Uḍupa-bhūmi*[121]—Land actually under crop.
6. *Garuvu-bhūmi*[122]—Land which contained a crop or newly sown.
7. *Kotta-nela*[123]—Land newly brought under cultivation.
8. *Meṭṭu-nela*[124]—Rocky soil
9. *Regadi-nela* or *Regadu*[125]—Suited for rice.
10. *Vari-nela* or *Śālī-kṣetra*[126]—Suited for rice.
11. *Jonna-nela* or *Jonnā-bhūmi*[127]—Suited for maize.
12. *Navula-bhūmi*[128]—Suited for Sesamum.
13. *Dukkībaḍḍa-polamu*[129]—Ploughed land.
14. *Raca-polamu*[130]—Crown-land.
15. *Damana-Boyunī-cenu*[131]—Land of Damanna-Boya.
16. *Daḍi-polanācenu*[132]—Land of Dadipolana.
17. *Mamgalagiri-polamu*[133]—Land belonging to the village of Mamgalagiri.
18. *Lamjepaṭi-polamu*[134]—Land belonging to the village of Lamjapaḍu.
19. *Nandigāma-polamu*[135]—Land belonging to the village of Nandigama.
20. *Veḷagapumḍi-polamu*[136]—Land belonging to the village of Veḷagapumdi.
21. *Penumbaḍiya-polamu*[137]—Land belonging to the village of Penumbadiya.
22. *Mirtivada-polamu*[138]—Land belonging to the village of Mirtivada.
23. *Poganuri-cenu*[139]—Land belonging to the village of Poganuru.

The other varieties of land that are referred to in the epigraphs are *Gṛha-kṣētra*[140] (land suitable for the building of houses), *Vramta-cenu,*[141] *Kamci-polamu*[142] (pasture land?), *Gosagi-cenu,*[143] *Telkula-cenu,*[144] *Divya-cenu*[145] (temple land), *Jitalā-cenu*[146] (land assigned for pay),

Uttarapu-polamu[147] (land situated on the north), *Budama-cenu,*[148] *Patimimidi-cenu,*[149] *Bodavari-kumtā-padumata Tampuri peḍḍi ceta konna cenu*[150] (land purchased by Tampuri peddi and situated to the west of *Bodavari-kunta*), etc.

Regarding the size of the fields we have not much evidence. The inscriptions generally refer to plots of land in terms of *maruturus, nivartanas, khaṇḍugas,* etc., which would indicate the existence of fragmentation of holdings. The occurence of the terms *accukaṭṭu*[151] and *aḍapagaṭṭu*[152] also indicate the use of balks of unploughed turf marking off the various small strips into which the wet-land was divided for purposes of proper irrigation.

Inscription give us valuable information regarding agricultural and horticultural products of the time. Paddy was the staple crop as is even now. Referring to the rice fields in the village of Gaṇapatipura, the Gaṇapeśvaram inscription of Śaka 1135 makes the following observations: 'Where (in that village) shines a large sea-like excellent tank, whose water (was) clear and sweet, the paddy crops bent by big weight of the ripe corn, drank (this water by their roots, which were) surrounded by channels and appeared to have bent their heads as if to drink again with their mouths also.'[153] Another inscription records,

> There is the great Andhradesa full of rice (fields) of golden hue, resembling the dales of the garden mountain (i.e.) Meru with jems. There the rice fields, containing waving waters inside, resemble the shores of the sea with dark tinged verdant. . . . The entire country (seems to be) covered by a blue raiment because of the spreading of the sheaf of crops in the fields.[154]

Another inscription records that the lands in the village of Pillaḷamarri were very rich in yielding paddy, pulses and other things.[155] The *Bhīmeśvara-purāṇa* says that the Godavari delta region was famous for yielding *prasaṅgu* type of rice.[156]

Indigo, maize (Indian corn), wheat, sesamum (*Sesamum indicum*), green-lintels, mustard (*Saladora persica*), castor (*Recinus communis*) colam, etc., are the other agricultural products mentioned in the inscriptions.[167] Among the garden crops, arecanut (*Areca catechu*), betel (*Piper betle*), tamarind (*Tamarindus indica*), mangoes (*Mangifera indica*), palmyra (*Borassus flabellifer*), citron and sugar-cane figure prominently.[158] The root products like tarmeric, ginger (*Zingiber officianle*), Kanda (*Typhonium orixense*), *Pemdalam* (*Dioscorea alata*), *Cema* (*Colocasia antiquorum*), *Mullamgi* (*Raphanus sativus*), etc., and vegetables like *Potla-kakara* (*Trichosanthes coluorina*), *Gummadi* (*Cucurbita pepo*), *Vamga* (*Solanum Melongena*), *Baccali* (*Ceropegiga tuberosa*), *Nurulli* (*Allium cepa*), *Cirugadā-dumpa*, etc., are also referred to in the inscriptions and literature.[159]

The epigraphical evidence gives us some valuable information regarding the system of cultivation that was in vogue during our period. Rotation of crops, double and single, was known. According to the former system, there was one harvest in the month of *Kārttika* in winter and another in the month of *Vaiśākha* in the summer. Under the single crop system there was only one harvest in either of these months. It is recorded that Recherḷa Nami Reddi gave some lands of God Nameśvara for cultivation during both the seasons.[160] Paddy fields with plenty of crops in *Kārttika* and *Vaiśākha* are referred to in an inscription dated Śaka 1209.

It is evident from what has been stated above that the Kākatīya kings and their *sāmantas* and *mahāsāmantas* paid very keen interest and attention to improving the agricultural potentialities of the empire by excavating tanks, wells and canals, establishing *agrahāra* villages and bringing under plough the cultivable waste-lands.

NOTES

1. The Gaṇapeśvaram inscription of Gaṇapatidēva *mahārāja* describes the *saptasantanas* in the following way:

   Sampaditair yathavat sukakrti nidhivana vivāha ṣuragehaih
   Satatakair vah saptabhir etaih samtanavan bhavati EI, III, pp. 88ff.

   The Karimnagar inscription of Gaṅgādhara, minister of Rudradeva, (Śaka, 1092) also alludes to the *saptasantanas*:

   Tana pemcina santanamum = dāna nalillunu vanamunum
   Jeruvunu guditunu jana vinutamul = aina septasamtanambulu HAS, no. 13, p. 173, verse. 32.
   Cf. *Sutulu totalu nallumdlu krutulu nidhulu namara saramambulunu taṭakamulu nanaga dharaṇi celuvamdu saptasamtanamuluna badasi Gannaya Rudra nripalavarudu*
   Śivayogasaramu, *Subhash*, vol. 1, pt. 1, Oct. 1927, p. 35.
2. *EI*, XII, pp. 188ff. But curiously enough the Ekāmranātha inscription credits Prola II, the grandson of Prola I, with this achievement *IA*, XXI, pp. 197ff.
3. *HAS*, no. 13, p. 29.
4. Ibid., p. 24; *AR*, 31 of 1957-8; Cf. *EHD*, p. 678.

5. *Kākatīyā-samcika,* App. Incs. no. 5.
6. *Siddheśvara-caritra,* p. 92.
7. *HAS,* no. 13, p. 12, verse. 27.
8. *Pratāpā-caritra,* pp. 31ff.
9. Ibid., pp. 40-8.
10. *Yah prottumgā-taramga-samagati-bhavad-dimdira-pimdā-cchalat = tire tara tar emudū-mamdalā-mayim malam sadorvadayam bhramyan = mamdara - mamtha-mamthanavasad = ek - emdu -sambhutijam - ksir-abdher = adharikaroti paritah kirt* (t) *im jagad-vyapinim.* Ibid., p. 39, verse 25.
11. Ibid., p. 49, verse 23.
12. Ibid., p. 81.
13. Ibid., pp. 152ff.
14. *HAS,* no. 18, Km. 4.
15. *SII,* X, no. 312.
16. *EI,* IX, pp. 256ff.
17. *HAS,* no. 13, pp. 169ff.
18. *AR,* 3 of 1939-40.
19. *SII,* X, no. 475.
20. *HAS,* no. 13, pp. 134ff.
21. *Śivayogasaramu, Subhashi,* p. 33.
22. *EI,* XXXVI, p. 217, verse 21.
23. *HAS,* no. p. 24.
24. Ibid., p. 70.
25. Ibid., p. 102.
26. Ibid., p. 109; *EI,* III, p. 91.
27. Ibid., p. 113.
28. Ibid, p. 114.
29. *HAS,* no. 18, Km. 12-13.
30. *SII,* X, no. 375.
31. *HAS,* no. 13, p. 39.
32. Ibid., pp. 69, 91, 93.
33. Ibid., p. 71.
34. Ibid., pp. 91-113.
35. Ibid., p. 165.
36. Ibid., p. 113.
37. Ibid., p. 134.
38. Ibid., p. 133.
39. Ibid., p. 141-50.
40. Ibid., p. 159.
41. *SII,* X, no. 134.
42. *HAS,* no. 13, p. 71.
43. Ibid., p. 76.
44. Ibid., p. 122.
45. Ibid., p. 136.
46. *AR,* 132 of 1954-5.

47. *HAS*, no. 18, Km. 10-17.
48. *SII*, X, p. 142.
49. Ibid., p. 143.
50. Ibid., p. 174.
51. Ibid., no. 501.
52. *HAS*, no. 13, p. 72.
53. Ibid., p. 109.
54. Ibid., p. 122.
55. Ibid., p. 176.
56. *AR*, 132 of 1954-5.
57. *HAS*, no. 18, Mn. 9.
58. *SII*, X, p. 143.
59. Ibid., p. 215.
60. Ibid., p. 220.
61. Ibid., p. 226.
62. *HAS*, no. 13, p. 24.
63. *Memoirs of the Archaeological Survey of India*, no. 6, p. 1.
64. Bilgrame and Willmott, *Historical and Descriptive Sketches of His Highness The Nizams Dominions*, II, pp. 706ff.
65. *JAHRS*, VI, p. 239.
66. *HAS*, no. 4.
67. Ibid., no. 3.
   Particulars of the lake:
   Year of restoration—AD 1919.
   Water spread—9,00 sq. miles
   Length of the bund—2,000 ft.
   Height of the bund—56 ft.
   Depth of the water above the silt—35 ft.
   Proposed irrigation : (1) Abi—3484 acres.
   (2) Tabi—871 acres.
   Channels: (1) Voger channel—5 miles 4 furlongs—1521 acres.
   (2) Veerla channel—2 miles 5 furlongs—986 acres.
   (3) Berugu channel—2 miles 7 furlongs—346 acres.
   (4) Somi channel—5 miles 4 furlongs—1011 acres.
68. *Particulars of the tank*:
   Year of restoration—AD 1909.
   Type of the bund—Earthen.
   Length of the bund—7,000 ft.
   Height of the bund—48 ft.
   Proposed irrigation: (1) Abi—3094 acres.
   (2) Tabi—439 acres.
   Channels: (1) Solipet channel—4 miles 3 furlongs—1050 acres.
   (2) Burrakayal channel—4 miles 2 furlongs—350 acres.
   (3) Kota channel—3 miles 3 furlongs —1089 acres.
   (4) Pydi channel—1 mile 5 furlongs—405 acres.

69. For details of the Bayyaram tank see: *Epigraphia Andhrica*, vol. I, p. 71, n 1.
70. *AR*, 404 of 1911.
71. Ibid., 286 of 1949-50.
72. *NDI*, II, p. 628.
73. *HAS*, no. 13, pp. 82ff.
74. Ibid., pp. 152ff.
75. *HAS*, no. 18, Km.15.
76. *SII*, X, no. 448.
77. *HAS*, no. 18, Mn. 6.
78. SII, X, no. 207.
79. Ibid., *EHD*, p. 682.
80. *EHD*, p. 682.
81. *HAS*, no. 13, p. 70.
82. Ibid., p. 71.
83. Ibid., p. 96.
84. Ibid., no. 18, Km. 10.
85. *HAS*, no. 13, p. 133.
86. Ibid., p. 162.
87. Ibid., p. 18, Km. 10.
88. Ibid., no. 13, p. 71.
89. Ibid., p. 105.
90. Ibid., p. 162.
91. Ibid., no. 18, Km. 10.
92. Ibid., Km. 9.
93. Ibid., Km. 5.
94. Ibid.
95. *SII*, X, no. 207.
96. Ibid., p. 211.
97. *HAS*, no. 13, p. 81.
98. Ibid., p. 49, v. 23.
99. Ibid., p. 24.
100. Ibid., no. 18, Ng. 3.
101. *EHD*, p. 681.
102. Ibid.
103. *HAS*, no. 13, p. 18, verse 27.
104. *SII*, X, no. 340.
105. *AR*, 28 of 1957-8.
106. *HAS*, no. 13, p. 71.
107. *EI*, III, pp. 82ff.
108. *Pratāpacaritra*, p. 34.
109. *EHD*, p. 681.
110. Ibid.
111. Ibid.
112. *NDI*, II, p. 628.

113. *HAS*, no. 13, p. 133.
114. A. Appadorai, *Economic Condition in Southern India, (AD 1000-1500)* Madras, 1936, pp. 192ff.
115. *HAS*, no. 18, Mn. 5-8.
116. Ibid., Mn. 24.
117. Ibid.
118. *SII*, IV, no. 1243.
119. Ibid., X, no. 482; *HAS*, no. 18, Km. 10.
120. *SII*, V, no. 80.
121. *JAHRS*, IV, p. 21.
122. *SII*, V, no. 80.
123. Ibid., IV, no. 1234.
124. *JAHC*, IV, p. 21.
125. *SII*, X, nos. 482, 488, 503.
126. *SII*, IV, no. 1243.
127. Ibid., V, no. 82.
128. Ibid., IV, no. 1243.
129. *HAS*, no. 18, Km. 6.
130. Ibid., no. 13, p. 89.
131. *SII*, X, no. 451.
132. Ibid.
133. Ibid., no. 459.
134. Ibid., no. 10.
135. Ibid., no. 420.
136. Ibid., p. 207.
137. Ibid.
138. Ibid., no. 451.
139. Ibid., no. 408.
140. Ibid., no. 435.
141. *HAS*, no. 18, Km. 10.
142. *SII*, X, no. 477.
143. *HAS*, no. 18, Km. 5.
144. Ibid., Mn. 5.
145. *SII*, X, no. 451.
146. Ibid.
147. Ibid., no. 275.
148. Ibid., no. 510.
149. Ibid., no. 420.
150. Ibid.
151. *HAS*, no. 18, Km. 6.
152. Ibid., no. 13. p. 201.
153. Ibid., p. 77, verse. 16.
154. *EI*, XXXVI, verses, 1, 2, 10; pp. 215-17.
155. *HAS*, no. 13, p. 132, verse, 36.
156. Asvasa, II, verse, 54.

157. *HAS.* no. 13, pp. 13 and 132.
158. Ibid., no. 18. Wg 18 and *SII,* X, Nos. 295. 142, 468; *EI,* XIX, p. 163, verse 16.
159. *HAS,* no. 13, p. 61: *Bhūmeśvarapurāṇa,* II, verse, 56.
160. Ibid., p. 113.

17

Landed Magnates as State Agents: The Gāvuḍas under the Hoyśāḷas in Karnataka

Kesavan Veluthat

The present paper reports the results of a preliminary enquiry into certain aspects of the socio-political organization in early medieval Karnataka, taking up a few inscriptions of the Hoyaśāḷas as a case study. It underlines the need for taking a fresh look at the inscriptional material from Karnataka, placing the information within the context of the pattern of socio-political evolution in early Medieval South India, and explaining it within the perspective of historical development in the Indian subcontinent in a general way. In spite of the greater success of conceptual exercises in other parts of India, historiography in Karnataka has largely remained at the same conventional level. The theoretical refinement that has been brought to bear upon historical understanding in other parts of south India has not affected it to any considerable extent; nor has any advanced tools of research been developed or made use of in this part of the country. The present study is only in the form of suggesting the need for a reorientation in the historical writing of ancient and early medieval Karnataka. For the purpose of this study we have taken up references to the *gāvuḍas* or *gāvuṇḍas* or *gāuḍas* figuring in Kannaḍa inscriptions, with special reference to the period of the Hoyśāḷas.

The *gāvuḍas* are met with in inscriptions dealing with affairs of a locality such as regulating the services in a temple, transacting landed property at the village level, construction and upkeep of irrigation works, assessment and collection or remission of taxes, etc. Epigraphists and historians, ever since these inscriptions were deciphered and subjected to historical study, have taken *gāvuḍa* to mean 'a village headman'.[1] He is identified always as 'an officer' of the state, functioning at the village level. He was the 'Chief executive' of the village assembly.[2] However, there is some lack of clarity as to whether he was exclusively an officer of the 'central' government placed at the village level or whether he was an officer recruited and maintained by the villages themselves, where very vital and autonomous bodies looked after the 'administration'. It is also not clear in these writings as to what exactly the source of his authority was.

The problem becomes slightly more complex when we find more than one such 'headman' in the same village, the number going up to as many as 106 in one record.[3] Those figuring in fewer numbers have been sought to be explained away in the following ways:

(*a*) This was probably due to the necessity of accommodating the claims of the numerous branches of the original family. Usually, however, claims were adjusted by allotting the office to each branch by rotation.[4]

(*b*) Sometimes a number of hamlets were knit together into a single unit for administrative convenience, which was placed under a chief headman with headmen of the various hamlets of the group under him.[5]

(*c*) In a big town, they appear to have represented different parts of it. Thus in Liṅga (Lingusugur in Raichur district), there were separate headmen for its eastern and western parts.[6] In fact, historians have even gone to the extent of describing two of them, stated to be hailing from two separate streets or *keris* as headmen of those streets.[7]

II

Unfortunately, these references to the *gāvuḍas* have not been examined within the context of their occurrence in the records; much less have the records themselves been placed in the geographical/ecological and chronological contexts of their provenance. We do not claim to have undertaken any such systematic examination either; but this is one way in which greater clarity can be achieved in interpreting inscriptional terms. Such limited enquiry as we have made, however, suggests an unmistakable connection between the *gāvuḍas* and agriculture. It is from records, mostly pertaining to transactions of land that we learn about them; they are almost exclusively holders of land known as *gāvuḍagoḍuge;*[8] and in inscriptions dealing with other sections such as the pastoral groups and artisanal and trading communities they are not generally met with. In fact, G.S. Dikshit has suggested that the expression is used also to mean 'farmers',[9] although he does not recognize, let alone reconcile, the contradiction involved in his positions.

The *gāvuḍas* are otherwise referred to as *ūrodeya.*[10] In a Sanskrit inscription, there is the exact translation of this term.[11] In speaking about a certain Āditya, the record says that he was the lord (*Iśvara*) of the village of Catagrāma. The expressions *oḍeya* in Kannada and *iśvara* in Sanskrit indicate ownership, possession, etc., thereby suggesting that the *ūroḍeya* or *grāmeśvara* was the 'owner' or 'possessor' of the village. But when we come across too many 'owners' or 'possessors' in the same village, even this meaning would not to be apt to describe the significance of the term and its implications. Moreover, absolute 'ownership' or proprietorship of whole villages by an individual would raise other problems for the nature of economy and society, disturbing the nature of our understanding of the history of India in this period.

In this connection, information available from the neighbouring region of the Tamil country, in the very period of our own study, comes in very useful as it illumines the dark areas and provides very clear insights. Such expressions as *ūr-uḍaiyān, ūr-kiḻāvan,* etc., figure in the inscriptions from the Tamil country in the period from the ninth-tenth century onwards. *Ūr-uḍaiyan* literally means, like *ūroḍeya* in Kannaḍa, the 'owner' or 'possessor' of a village and *ūr-kiḻāvan,* the village elder, which can be translated into Sanskrit as *grāmā-vṛddhạ,* the Prakrit form of which is *gāvuḍa.* It is possible, therefore, to derive *gāvuḍa* in Kannaḍa inscriptions from Sanskrit *grāma-vṛddhạ,* although what has been suggested by earlier historians is derivation from *grāmakūṭa* on the basis of comparison with Marathi records.[12] *Grāmavṛddhas* are frequently met with in Sanskrit records, literary and epigraphical.[13]

The comparability between the *ūroḍeya gāvuḍa* and the *ūr-uḍaiyan ūr-kiḻāvan* does not depend upon the derivation of a word which can be looked upon as dubious. It goes further to the similarity of their nature and functions in the two situations. Both of them figure as landowners; both of them are found prominently in connection with transactions related to landed property and other agricultural activities; both had a significant role in the matter of the assessment and collection of revenue in the locality. In fact, a closer comparative study of the two situations would clarify several of the obscure aspects on either side.

III

The information from the Tamil side is far richer and more systematic for the fabulously larger number of records from there and the rigorous computational analysis they have been subjected to. In a computerised concordance of personal names in the Chola inscriptions, which takes up 9590 names, about twenty per cent of the population represented there bore names which had a segment indicating possession of a place or a village, expressions such as *uḍaiyan, kiḷān, kiḷāvan*, etc., were preceded by the name of the village signifying possession.[14] Since there are more than one person who 'possesses' the same village, it has been shown that the expression should be taken to mean one who possessed some land in the village.[15] It cannot have been used to mean simply a resident of the village, for not all residents of the village bore such a segment in their names. A large number of instances support the inference that wherever such expressions indicating possession of a village occurs, it meant possession of land in a village.[16] To take just one case, a Kudumiyanmalai inscription of AD 1232 records the sale of land by the *ūr* of Visalur, where the new owner was permitted to enjoy all privileges due to the holder of the title *kiḷāvan*.[17] That the *uḍaiyān* title indicated landownership is proposed further by the fact that, of the 119 cases where names of the members of different *ur* assemblies are known, more than 60 per cent bore a title indicating possession;[18] even in the case of the remaining 40 per cent it is suggested that the *uḍaiyān* or related title is left out in order to avoid repetition when two or more *uḍaiyān* of the same village are mentioned in quick succession. That the assembly of *ūr* consisted of the chief landholders of the village is a fact accepted on all hands. The computational analysis of names with the *uḍaiyān* title has shown a tendency for this title to increase steadily as Chola rule progresses in the Cholamaṇḍalam region.[19] This has been explained as pointing to a steady increase in the number of landowners, suggesting the deeper entrenchment of the idea of private property in land outside the brāhmin settlements and also a greater utilisation of land, a pattern which is brought out by independent evidence.

A similar title indicating ownership of land is *veḷān* which also points to the caste status of the bearer of the title. Closely related to this title was the significant title of *mūventaveḷān*. Another one of equal or slightly higher status was the pseudo-chiefly title or *araiyan*. The Chola records show clearly that it was from among the holders of such titles indicating possession of land that functionaries of the state, known as 'bureaucracy' to an earlier generation of historians, were drawn.[20] The graded hierarchy among the landowners, going up along the scale of the *ūḍaiyān-veḷān-mūventaveḷān-araiyan* title holders in that order, is relevant for the offices also. For, the higher positions were held by those who were higher in this hierarchy. In fact, a couple of records state in so many words that petty officials could not take the titles of *veḷān* and *araiyan*.[21] When thus the close connection between these titles on the one side and state offices on the other is recognized, the fact of the landed magnates being identified and made use of by the state as its agents comes out with clarity.

There is no reason why the pattern was different in Karnataka. Nine representatives from five villages in Mysore Taluk, all of them *gāvuḍas*, are stated to have met as the *Nāḍu* (*bandhu-samartha-nagaḍi*)[22] which clearly reminds us of five different *ūrs* meeting as the *nāḍu* of Vada = chiravayil = *nāḍu* as recorded in a Kiranur inscription from the former Pudukottah State. In a similar way, wherever information on the functionaries is available, we see that many of them sported titles such as *gāvuḍa*, *alva*, etc., exactly in the same way as their counterparts in the neighbouring Tamil country did. The process of the identification of such a magnate, holding the title of *ūroḍeya* or *grāmeśvara*, by the Hoyśāḷa ruler and his being enlisted as a functionary of the state is clearly brought out in a recently published copper plate inscription.[23] The presence of a number of *gāvuḍas* in the agrarian villages, as members of the *ūr* assembly also would suggest the similarity of the pattern on either side. Dikshit has identified the functions of the village magistrate and the head of the village militia as among those of the *gāvuḍa* with the help of inscriptions.[24] In an agrarian society characterized by peasant communities of a relatively autonomous character, it is only natural that these functions should be arrogated by the more prominent landed magnates. This could be appreciated better if one looks at the process of socio-economic evolution which led to the formation of state in this part of the country.

The present essay, by no means exhaustive or complete, stresses the need for placing the evidence from the epigraphical material from Karnataka concerning ostensibly political institutions within their socio-economic context. A comparative study with similar situations elsewhere in south India can be of great value. Such exercises can go a long way in exposing the mechanism and implications of the formation of the state in different parts of the country under dissimilar provocations.

NOTES

1. Among the pioneers of Kannada epigraphy J.F. Fleet, R.C. Temple and B.L. Rice had suggested this translation in the pages of *Indian Antiquary and Epigraphia Carnatica*. Later epigraphists and historians have largely followed them without any questioning. In the case of the Hoyśāḷas the first full-length monograph on them by William Coelho, *The Hoyasalvamsa*, Bombay, 1950 is a conventional dynastic history which has practically nothing to say about the *gāvuḍas*. J.D.M. Derrett, *The Hoysalas: A Medieval Indian Royal Family*, Oxford, 1957 is very idealistic in dealing with administration. He consigns the *gāvuḍa* to the lowest rung of an administrative hierarchy, p. 187.
2. G.S. Dikshit, *Local Self-Government in Medieval Karnataka*, Dharwar, 1964, p. 64.
3. This is recognized earlier. Dikshit, op. cit., p. 63, n 42-3.
4. A.S. Altekar, *State and Government in Ancient India*, rev. edn, Delhi, 1972, p. 226, n 6; idem. *The Rashtrakutas and their Times*, Poona, 1936, pp. 189-90.
5. *JBBRAS*, vol. 10, p. 270 quoted in Dikshit, op. cit., p. 64, n 45.
6. P.B. Desai (ed.), *A Corpus of Inscriptions in the Kannada Districts of Hyderabad State*, Hyderabad, 1958, no. 16, ll. 53-62.
7. Dikshit, op. cit., p. 64. For the text of the inscription, *SII*, vol. II, i, no. 50.
8. Dikshit, op. cit., p. 64.
9. Ibid., p. 6.
10. Cf. *EI*, vol. 19, p. 236. See also Dikshit, op. cit., p. 62.
11. Anekannambadi Plates of Hoyaśāḷa Vīra Sōmeśvaradeva in M.S. Nagaraja Rao and K.V. Ramesh, eds., *Copper Plate Inscriptions from Karnataka—*

Recent Discoveries, Mysore, 1985, p. 94. 11. 90-101.

12. Altekar, *State and Government*, op. cit., p. 226.
13. *Arthaśāstra*, Bk. III, ch. 12 quoted in ibid., 229, n 6; Kalidāsa's *Raghuvaṁśa* I. refers to grāmavṛddhas which is but one example of the numerous other references in the romantic literature.
14. Noboru Karashima. Y. Subbarayalu and Toru Matsui, *A Concordance of the Names in the Cōḷa Inscriptions*, Madurai, 1978 under Title groups TA 020 021 022. Also Appendix III, pp. xiv-xvii. For an analysis Kesavan Veluthat, 'The Power Structure of Monarchy in South India: *c.* AD 700-1300.' Unpublished Ph.D. Thesis, University of Calicut, 1987, pp. 127-8.
15. Karashima *et al.*, op. cit., p. xvi.
16. Ibid., Y. Subbarayalu, 'The State in Medieval South India'. Unpublished Ph.D. Thesis, Madurai Kamaraj University, 1976, pp. 115-18.
17. *Inscriptions of the Pudukotta State* (Pudukotta, 1929), no. 301.
18. Karashima *et al.*, p. 118.
19. Karashima *et al.*, op. cit., Appendix III, pp. xiv-xvii.
20. Veluthat, op. cit., pp. 139-51.
21. *Annual Reports of Epigraphy*, 1918, nos. 429 and 538.
22. *EC* (New Series), vol. V, Mysore, 1988 passim.
23. Nagaraja Rao and Ramesh, loc. cit.
24. Dikshit, op. cit., pp. 64-5.

18

Immobility and Subjection of Indian Peasantry in Early Medieval Complex

B.N.S. Yadava

The restrictions on the mobility of peasants and other humble folk and their subjection under the conditions characterized by closed, local economy, and the emergence of landed intermediaries and a hierarchy of ruling landed aristocracy are well known ingredients of feudalism[1] as a wider concept. On this point a wide range of epigraphic evidence together with the Chinese accounts and some contemporary texts pertaining to the Indian context have recently been examined by R.S. Sharma.[2] The practice of transferring all the cultivators of a village has been traced by him to the sixth century AD in the backward areas of Orissa and the neighbouring regions of central India.[3] In the eleventh and twelfth centuries some inscriptions not only from these regions but also from Assam, Bengal (Sena grants), Bihar, Bundelkhand (Candella grants), Rajasthan, Maharashtra and the hill state of Camba mention, individually or collectively, peasants and in some cases artisans and even merchants and village attendants along with the lands or villages donated by rulers to religious institutions and brāhmaṇas.[4] We also notice some secular grants of this nature.[5]

The inscriptions are not explicit about the curbs on the movement of peasants, artisans, etc., and their subjection. This has led some scholars to conclude that 'to give a village is really the same as to give a village along with the villagers which means that the king's rent paying subjects in the villages should henceforth pay taxes to the donee'.[6] It has been argued that the mention of peasants, artisans, etc., in connection with the gift of a village indicates neither any constraint on their movement nor their state of dependence and that this only shows that some of them were slaves and others enjoyed state land or common village land as village attendants or followed occupations the revenues from which were a state monopoly.[7]

The Purāṇa, Dharmaśāstra and other classes of contemporary literature clarify and supplement the information obtained from the epigraphs. The *Skanda Purāṇa*, which may be attributed to the period from about the eighth-ninth centuries AD, to the thirteenth provides interesting sidelights. It gives a long description of a legendary grant[8] of a number of villages along with 36,000 vaiśyas as well as śūdras four times that number made in times of yore by king Rāma to 18,000 brāhmaṇas after the performance of certain religious rites. The vaiśyas and śūdras were evidently intended to serve the donees,[9] who later divided the villages amongst themselves. Rāma enjoined the people so transferred to obey the commands of the donees and to serve them devotedly.[10] He further declared that a śūdra serving them with humility would become prosperous and attain heaven and one deflecting from this course of conduct would fall a prey to poverty.[11] The Yavanas, Mlecchas, Paityas or Rākṣasas creating any kind of obstruction to the donees were threatened with getting burnt to ashes.[12] The story further runs that in the Kali age the descendants of the donees were deprived of their estates by king Kumārapāla, a follower of Jainism, who is said to have been the lord of Brahmāvarta.[13] The brāhmaṇas made a complaint against Kumārapāla to king Āma,[14] the father-in-law and probably also the overlord of Kumārapāla, who resided at Kānyakubja, but they could not succeed in getting back their villages with his help. At last some of them went to Setubandha Rameshvara to seek the assistance of Hanumat. While explaining their distress to this god, they claimed the right not only to the villages donated to their ancestors by Rāma, but also to the people[15]—vaiśyas and śūdras whose ancestors had been transferred along with the donated villages. With the help of Hanumat they succeeded in prevailing upon the king to grant them a number of villages along with the śūdras known as *aḍhabija* who were attached to them for rendering service.[16] The śūdras who served the *dvijas* with devotion and refrained from Jainism are here regarded as *uttama*.[17] As against this, those śūdras and also *vipras* who violated the instruction were, as the expression *pratibandhena yojitāḥ*[18] suggests, tied down to the set-up emerging as a result of the village grant. The ideal course of conduct prescribed for the śūdras and vaiśyas was to render services and pay dues[19] to the grantees and not to leave or transfer allegiance from them.[20]

Social consciousness can hardly be regarded as completely divorced from social being and as such this story may reflect the actual conditions prevailing in many estates held by the priestly beneficiaries. Clearly the śūdras as also the vaiśyas who were transferred[21] and attached to the donees were not slaves; nor were all of them village attendants. The relation of dependence involving lifelong services and payment of dues to the donees appears to have been thought of as continuing from generation to generation. Further, although in seeking to impose restrictions on mobility religious sanction was invoked, the expression *pratibandhena yojitāḥ* suggests resort to some forcible methods in this respect.

There is ample evidence to conclude that the śūdras were largely peasants during the period *c.* AD 600-1200,[22] although some sections practised industrial arts and crafts as well as other vocations. It has been held[23] that the transformation of śūdras who were mainly slaves and hired labourers in the earlier age into peasants was a significant phenomenon from the point of view of the emergence of feudalism in India. The tendency of levelling the vaiśyas down to the status of the śūdras, traces of which may be found in the earlier age, had acquired considerable proportions during this period.[24]

Medhātithi (ninth century) reiterates the theory of the general dependence of the śūdras on members of the higher *varṇas* and as a corollary lays emphasis on the confinement of the śūdras to the locality of their masters. This naturally envisages restrictions on their migration, which could only strengthen the hands of the landed intermediaries and ruling chiefs in keeping peasants and other working folk under subjection. Thus commenting on a verse of the *Manusmṛti* he states:[25]

> Inasmuch as the service of the twice-born constitutes the duty of the śūdra, it follows as a matter of course that the latter should reside in their locality and continue to obtain his living by serving the twice-born on whom he is dependant. In case the śūdra has a large family or becomes unfit for service, to acquire wealth he may go and live in any other country except where the Mlecchas are in a majority.

However, Medhātithi elsewhere recognizes the right of a śūdra possessed of wealth to freedom from dependence on the men of higher *varṇas.*[26]

The bondage of the śudras may be seen in a religious ideology which acquired considerable force during the early medieval period. In spite of the fact that they were allowed to endow tanks, wells, feeding houses, orchards, etc. (*pūrtadharma*)[27] and to acquire merit, Medhātithi[28] denied them the right to liberation, the reward of the fourth *āśrama,* on the ground that they could function only as householders (*gṛhastha*) and acquire merit by serving the twice-born and procreating offspring. In the eleventh century Alberuni noticed such an attitude not only towards the śūdras but also towards the vaiśyas,[29] though he referred to others who did not subscribe to this view.[30] In fact, such a disability was not contemplated in the realm of higher philosophy.

The Jains used to attack the caste system, but according to the *Yaśastilaka* (tenth century) of Somadeva Sūri the orthodox section among them had developed the notion that the śūdras were not entitled to religious initiation.[31] The denial of the right to spiritual liberation to the śūdra may be regarded as a reflection of his earthly subjection. However, by the eleventh and twelfth centuries there had come into prominence a number of religious orders of the *tāntrikas* and others which recognized the śūdra's right to liberation.

We get some idea of the condition of peasants and other working people in the estates and territories of chiefs and rulers. A verse from the *Nāradasmṛti*[32] quoted with approval in the *Rājadharma-kāṇḍa* of Lakṣmidhara (twelfth century), conceives of the subjects depending for their means of livelihood on the ruler as having been purchased by him with the power of his *tapas* or austerities and enjoins them to be subservient to his command. Here the political unit is thought of as a community of dependants functioning under constraints. The explanation[33] of the term *vārtā* as agriculture, cattle-rearing, etc., by Lakṣmīdhara and the omission of trade which formed its essential element in the ancient texts in this context suggests the predominance of the agrarian set-up.

In the *Bauddhadohā* (*Caryāpada* 12) *citta* immersed in ignorance, which is the source of bondage, is called *ṭhakkura,*[34] well-known title of the ruling landed aristocracy from the tenth century onwards. In the *Upamitibhavaprapañcakathā* (beginning of the tenth century) too, in which the feudal hierarchy is clearly reflected, the bondage of *saṃsāra* is compared with the estate of a chief or ruler. Some verses of this text suggest that the miserable people living in the principality of a ruler were dependant upon him for their means of subsistence and only death could take them out of the closed set-up and liberate them from servitude.[35] In spite of an element of exaggeration in the allegory, the reality cannot be missed.

The subjection of the peasants is implied in a verse of the *Bṛhannāradiya Purāṇa* (ninth century), which refers to men attached to the plough (*baddhahālaiḥ*)[36] for carrying on cultivation and speaks of the decline of agriculture in the Kali age. A model document for *bhūmisaṃsthā* in the *Lekhapaddhati*[37] is also significant in this context. A form of charter (*guṇapatra*) to be granted by a *rāṇa* to the inhabitants of the villages of a region, it asks the peasants (*kuṭumbikas*) living in the huts to cultivate the fields recorded in the registers against their names (*nibandhabhūmi*), to suffer some penalty if they keep any part uncultivated and to render dues and services according to local customs,[38] including the payment of part of the produce to local officials, village artisans,[39] etc. It provides for the supply of seeds of rice, wheat, barley, *ciṇā* and *lāṭa* from the barnyard or the threshing floor, the procurement of the other seeds being the responsibility of the peasants. The peasants are required to carry two-thirds of the grain to the chief's granary as his share and allowed to have the remaining one-third and the grass for themselves. A peasant found stealing grain is to be warned once, but if he persists he is to be deprived of his share of the produce and, finally, to be turned out of the village. Complaints of peasants are to be entertained not individually, but only when four of them go together with the *guṇapatra*. The fields, grain, cattle and other property of a peasant who leaves the village and moves away elsewhere are to be taken over by the chief or ruler.[40]

The exploited and dependant peasantry here represents a type of sharecroppers,[41] who were entitled to only one-third of the produce. All this may be taken to have been a local practice in western India and Rajasthan, for the text reflects the conditions of these regions. But the practice of sharecropping becoming widely prevalent during this period is clear from many pieces of evidence and, above all, from the fact thatthe *ārdhika* (sharecropper) is mentioned for the first time as a separate mixed caste in the *Parāśarasmṛti*[42] (*c.* AD 600-900).

The form of document under consideration has been assigned a late date (Saṃvat 1407) in the text,[43] but it represents an earlier tradition. The evidence of *Lekhapaddhati* may be put alongside that which we find in the *Ādi Purāṇa* of Jinasena (ninth century), which also reflects the condition of the same region. The *Ādi Purāṇa* asks the ruler to protect and give subsistence to his subjects like a *gopālaka* to his cattle.[44] It is recommended that just as a herdsman grazes his cows in a rich pasture and then milks them for his own purpose, the ruler should also carry on cultivation in the *bhaktagrāmas* through the *karmāntikas* by providing them with seeds and by making other efforts.[45] The assignment of land is of course implied here. He is advised to do the same through the *kṛṣivalas* in other regions throughout his principality and to take a just part of the produce from all of them.[46] The ruler therefore is prominently represented as a landlord cultivator. The peasants, especially those in the *bhaktagrāmas*, appear as sharecroppers or temporary tenants in a state of dependence on the ruler as well as the land. Apparently, the whole account shows an attempt to give an ideological polish to the institution of peasant subjection. A similar practice with dependant tenure may be found in the lands held by the Buddhist monasteries, which provided the peasants with the fields and bulls and usually received one-sixth of the produce.[47] However, there is no evidence to show that the peasants were under acute servitude.

Mention may also be made of an inscription (AD 1173) from south India which shows how restrictions were sought to be imposed on the movements of the humble folk in the local units of a more or less closed economy. The record runs:

> Those who engage themselves in these services beyond the village will be considered to have transgressed the law, to have committed fault against the great assembly and to have ruined the village.[48]

The relative isolation of villages may always be found to have been a characteristic of the Indian socio-economic set-up. But during this period, owing to feudal tendencies, localism backed by somewhat closed economy became so much accentuated that there developed a set of special local observances and obligations which differed from village to village. The late Purāṇic passages in the *Bṛhannāradiya*, the *Devībhāgavata* and the *Skanda* recommend the observance of *grāmācāra*,[49] *grāmadharma*[50] or *sthānācāra*[51] in addition to *deśadharma* and *jātidharma*. The feudal aristocracy was actively connected with the accentuation of localism and regionalism.[52] The villages, however, cannot be said to have been completely isolated units. In religion and some other matters such as marriage they entered into relations and contacts with the outside world.

The attitude of the princes and chiefs towards peasants and their anxiety to maintain the local agrarian economy are also expressed at one place in the *Yuktikalpataru* of Bhoja (eleventh century). The text stresses the necessity of protecting or rather preserving the *kṛṣivalas* (peasants) in every village on the ground that agriculture, the source of all wealth, depends upon their labour.[53] This kind of attitude must have reinforced restrictions on the movement of the peasants and their subjection. The rulers of the period began to grant to the temples, monasteries, individual brāhmaṇas and also to their officers and vassals not only the revenues of villages carrying with them authority only in a subsidiary capacity over the inhabitants thereof, but also estates with specified authority over their residents such as peasants, artisans, etc., in the village grants. Even with the grants of the former type the power of the beneficiaries over the people could have increased, especially with waning of the central authority. But this did not necessarily lead to the subjection of the people in all cases. The chances for it were greater in those regions whose economy was backward.

With the emergence of a hierarchically organized ruling aristocracy and the weak functioning of exchange economy, especially in the agrarian set-up characterized by localism, the magnitude of forced labour naturally grew in volume during the post-Gupta period.[54] We get ample evidence of heavy taxation and oppression in the estates of the chiefs and village lords and in the principalities of kings. Extra-legal and arbitrary exactions were legalized in some regions.

The estates of the chiefs, officers, military men, and even of the brāhmaṇas and religious institutions may be regarded as only roughly corresponding to the estates of the vassals of European feudalism, known as manors, which, as pointed out by Marc Bloch, were first and foremost communities of 'dependants who were by turns protected, commanded and oppressed by their lords to whom many of them were bound by hereditary links'.[55] But the classical manorial system being a 'type of economic, social and administrative organization based on land tenure' and 'well adapted to an age of economic decentralization and barter economy'[56] was different in many respects from its Indian counterpart. The intensity and scope of subjection and dependence of the peasants in the Indian context were much less than the servitude of the peasantry in Western feudalism, which overburdened the peasants with service on the lord's farm and payment of various dues, and rendered them dependant on the lord as well as on the land.[57]

The *Bṛhannāradiya Purāṇa*[58] shows that under acute distress caused by famines and burdensome taxes the people migrated *en masse* to regions rich in wheat and barley. A verse in the *Subhāṣitaratnakośa* of Vidyākara (twelfth century) also indicates that the people oppressed by the *bhogapati* (landlord or feudal chief) left the village.[59] Furthermore, the social function of wages had not become so insignificant in India as in the Western manorial system.[60] It may also be noted that with the wide hold of the Dharmaśāstra literature in this age[61] the regulating principles of *dharma* contained therein may have worked as a unifying force of considerable importance against localism, which is the chief mark of feudalism, more or less like the public law in England,[62] with the result that justice and social usages including property laws could not have been largely feudalized. The complex mass of feudal laws, in spite of the fact that there were some similar practices, could not be systematized and consolidated in India as in some parts of medieval Europe.

The Indian economy had not changed to such an extent as to bring about all the conditions which are noticed in classical Western feudalism. For general resemblance we are perhaps to look not so much to the manorial system of the first feudal era, that is, the age of classical feudalism, as to that of the later feudal age which appears there in the twelfth century and which was characterized by a decline in the size of the *démesné*, reduction of compulsory labour service, the lord's abandonment of the personal exploitation of the estate, the transformation of peasants into producers, heavily taxed but economically autonomous, and, above all, the comparative relaxation of the bond of human domination.[63]

It has been pointed out that the śūdras in servitude may at times have resorted to violence. Attention has been drawn in this connection to the armed revolts[64] of the Kaivartas in Bengal in the time of Mahipāla and Rāmapāla. But we do not come across many instances of this type, and the situation in India does not appear to have been similar to that in medieval Europe. The hold of traditionalism, the particular type of religious and social ideology making men acquiesce in the existing set-up and the division of society, especially the proliferation of the śūdras into numerous caste groups,[65] tended to minimize the possibility of organized armed revolts. However, some pieces of evidence do suggest refractoriness on the part of the śūdras. The *Skanda Purāṇa* makes a sweeping remark[66] to this effect and speaks of the violation of the charters under which the villages were held by the beneficiaries. A story in the *Kathāsaritsāgara*[67] also indicates that oppression and maladministration could lead to the holders of estates being thrown out of their possessions. But it is not known whether this could happen as a result of the resumption of the village grants under such circumstances or because of popular revolts and uprisings.

The literary, epigraphic and numismatic data indicate some progress in trade and commerce and greater use of money particularly in western India in the eleventh and twelfth centuries.[68] The methods of agriculture and the crops mentioned in literature and inscriptions of the age betoken a developed stage of agrarian economy. These economic developments may naturally have contributed to the loosening of restrictions on the mobility of peasants and artisans. But on the other hand traditionalism as manifested in the caste system and the self-sufficient village economy emphasized localism together with social and geographical immobility.[69] Any change of considerable magnitude was therefore ruled out. In any case we notice regional variations depending on the predominance of one or the other of the two factors.

In the *Laṭakamelaka*, which reflects the conditions obtaining in the kingdom of the Gāhaḍavālas in the twelfth century, the village chief Saṅgrāmavisara is depicted as being very particular about making money by all possible means. This kind of attitude was obviously favourable to the disuse of labour service and the abolition of restrictions on the mobility of the humble village folk. The *Rājataraṅgiṇi* bears witness to the circulation of money in Kashmir where forced labour was sometimes commuted into payment in cash.[70] Interestingly enough, the term *viṣṭi* (meaning forced labour) is conspicuous by its absence in some inscriptions (eleventh-twelfth centuries) of the Cāhamānas, the Chālukyas, the Paramāras, the Gāhaḍavālas and the Candellas. This, however, does not necessarily imply the total abolition of forced labour, especially in view of the fact that the term is mentioned in some contemporary literary works.[71]

We have some evidence of the feudalistic set-up adapting itself to the developing economy.[72] Some Cāhamāna grants[73] (twelfth century) specifically refer to the transfer of landless peasants to a god, which signify the continuing dependence of peasants and restriction on their mobility in spite of the increasing use of coins in Rajasthan. As a matter of fact such conditions continued to exist in some regions there down to the British period.[74]

But on the whole during the Sultanate period the classical Indian feudal system appears to have declined. The economic forces had already begun to inhibit it in western India in the eleventh and twelfth centuries, though its decline was caused mainly by the change in the character and composition of the ruling aristocracy with the break-up of the old ruling hierarchy and the wider circulation of coins coinciding with the regular practice of payment to the peasants in cash,[75] which was bound to contribute to the growth of economic mobility. Large-scale trade between the town and the country is also said to have developed in the fourteenth century.[76] All these factors may have tended to loosen the restrictions on peasantry.

NOTES

1. For a discussion of the various standard definitions and the essential elements of feudalism see J.W. Hall, *Comparative Studies in Society and History*, v, no. 1 (1963), pp. 16ff.
2. *Indian Feudalism: c. AD 300-1200* (Calcutta University, 1965).
3. Ibid., p. 55. The trend of peasant subjection had, however, started a few centuries earlier, 'Some Aspects of the Changing Order in India During the Śakā-Kuṣāṇa Age', *Kuṣāṇa Studies* (Department of Ancient History, Culture and Archaeology, Allahabad University, 1968).
4. R.S. Sharma, op. cit., pp. 231ff.
5. For example, the Candella inscription of the time of Kirtivarman refers to the grant of a village along with the people of Jajuka of the Vāstavya family, *EI*, xxx, no. 17.
6. D.C. Sircar, ed., *Land System and Feudalism in Ancient India* (Calcutta University, 1966), p. 61.

7. Ibid., pp. 61f.
8. *teṣāṃ śuśrūśaṇārthāya vaiśyānrāmo nyavedayat saṭtriṃśacca ṣahasrāṇi śūdrāṃstebhyaścaturguṇān*, *Skanda Purāṇa* (*Brahmakhaṇḍa*), 3.3.35. 44ff.
9. The donees claimed lordship or proprietary rights (*svāmyam*) over the villages which they lost when they were dispossessed of them (*labdhaśāsanakā viprā luptasvāmyā aharniśam*, ibid., 3.2.36.47).
10. *viprājnā nollaṃghaniyā sevaniyā prayatnataḥ*, ibid., 3.2.35.56.
11. Ibid., 3.2.35.57f.
12. Ibid., 3.2.35.58.
13. Ibid., 3.2.36.59, 183.
14. Āma has been identified as king Āmarāja, son of king Yaśovarman of Kanauj, who flourished in the eighth century AD, D.C. Sircar, *Bhāratīya Vidyā*, Bombay, vi (1945), 237-40; viii (1947), 102f; *Studies in the Society and Administration of Ancient and Medieval India*, i (Calcutta 1967), 153f.
15. The descendants of the vaiśyas and śūdras, originally transferred by Rāma, are enumerated in detail.
16. *Skanda Purāṇa*, 3.2.38.48.
17. Ibid., 3.2.38.60. Apparently by becoming the followers of Jainism and other heretical religions the śūdras became somewhat refractory.
18. *ye ca pākhaṇḍaniratā rāmaśāsanalopakāḥ sarve viprāstathā śūdra pratibandhena yojitāḥ*, ibid., 3.2.38.61.
19. The persons attached to the donees are called *vṛttidāḥ* and *sevāsu tatparāḥ*.
20. Ibid., 3.2.40.59-60.
21. The term dattāḥ, pradattāḥ, nirūpitāḥ, etc., are used for the transfer of the vaiśyas and śūdras in the literary texts, but in inscriptions we generally find the prefix sa used with the names of the groups of people mentioned along with the donated lands or villages.
22. For cultivation (kṛsi) as the duty of the śūdras see *Laghu Āśvalāyana*, 22.5; *Vṛddha Hārita*, 7.181: *Narasiṃha Purāṇa*, 58.11 (also quoted in the *Gṛhasthakāṇḍa of Lakṣmidhara*, p. 273); *Bṛhaddharma Purāṇa*, Bibliotheca Indica edn., p. 189, v. 8. Cf. *Mahāpurāṇa* of Jinasena,17.164. Not only Hsūan Tsang (*On Yuan Chwang's Travels in India*, 1st Indian edn., Delhi, 1961, p. 169), but also Ibn Khurdadbeh (Elliot and Dowson, *History of India as told by Its own Historians*, i, London, 1866, 16f) and al-Idrisi (Ibid., p. 76) attest the practice.
23. R.S. Sharma, op. cit., p. 63.
24. E.C. Sachau (ed. and tr.), *Alberuni's India*, i (London, 1910), 101.
25. *śudrasya dvijātiśuśrūṣāyā vihitatvātāddeśanivāse sarvadā prāpte tatrājāvato deśāntaranivāso'bhyanujñāyate. Yadā bahukuṭumbatayā śuśrūṣāśaktyā vā'yaṃ dvijātimāśritaḥ sa enaṃ bibhṛyāt. tadā deśāntare sambhavati dhanārjane nivaset. tatrāpi na mlecchabhūyiṣṭhe* . . . . Medhātithi's Comm. on *Manu*, ii. 24.
26. *yadi śūdra vidyamānadhanaḥ svātantryeṇa jīved brāhmaṇādyanapāśrito na jātu duṣyet*, G.N. Jha (ed.), *Medhātithi on Manu*, p. 231.
27. *Agni Purāṇa*, 209.2.

28. On *Manu*, vi. 97; Kane, *History of Dharmaśāstra*, ii, pt. i (Poona, 1941), 163. In this context we find the expression *mokṣam tvarjayittvā*. The idea that the service of the higher class cannot bear the fruit of liberation for śūdra is found in the *Śānti Parva* (63. 12-4) also.
29. Sachau, op. cit., p. 104.
30. Ibid.
31. *Yaśastilaka* (Nirnaya Sagar Press, Bombay, 1916), viii, Section 43; cf. K.K. Handiqui, *Yaśastilaka and Indian Culture* (Sholapur, 1949), p. 331.
32. *tapaḥ kritāḥ prajā rājñaḥ prabhurāsām tathānṛpah, tasmāttadvacasi stheyaṃ vārtā tadāśrayā, Rājadharmākāṇḍa*, p. 5: also K. Sambasiva Sastri (ed.), *Nāradīya-Manusṃhtā*, 18.23. In another verse of the *Nāradasmṛti* the relation between the king and his subjects is equated with that between husband and wife. The old idea that the king is a servant receiving one-sixth part of the produce as his salary (*vetana*) is also repeated at one place in the text.
33. *vārtā kṛṣipaśupālyādivṛttiḥ, Rājadharmakāṇḍa*, op. cit.
34. *thakkuramavidyācittam*, Nagendranatha Upadhyaya, *Tāntrika Bauddha Sadhanā aur Sāhitya* (in Hindi) (Nagari Pracarini Sabha, Kasi, Saṃvat 2015), p. 324.
35. *Upamitibhavaprapañcakathā*, pp. 647-8.
36. *saritīre baddhahālairvapayiṣyanti cauṣadhiḥ, alpaṃ alpaṃ phalaṇ teṣāṃ bhaviṣyanti kalau yuge, Brlhannāradīya Purāṇa*, 38.43. Hazra's translation of the term *baddhahāla* as 'men with set ploughs' (*Studies in the Upapurāṇas*, I, Calcutta, 1958, p. 332) does not appear to be convincing. For this rendering of the term I am indebted to my friend and colleague, Dr. S.N. Roy of the Department of Ancient History, Culture and Archaeology, Allahabad University.
37. *Gaekwad Oriental Series*, Baroda, 1925, xix, 18f.
38. Ibid., p. 19.
39. We find the mention of five artisans (*pañcakāruka*) who may be the carpenter, the ironsmith, the potter, the barber and the washerman (ibid., p. 108).
40. *anyatra praṇaśyagatakuṭumbikasya kṣetrakhalakadhaura-prabhṛti sarvaṃ rājakule svādhīnaṃ kartavyam*, ibid., p. 19. To threaten a fugitive with confiscation was one of the methods adopted by the lords in feudal Europe to prevent the migration of their subjects. They tried to retain their peasants, for under the condition of closed agrarian economy it was useless to have an estate without labour to work it. But owing to the fragmentation of authority and the abundance of virgin soil, especially in certain regions of France, it was difficult to prevent desertions. Marc Bloch, *Feudal Society*, I (London, 1965), p. 263.
41. The term *kuṭumbika* here appears to mean the sharecropper. The same meaning of the word *kuṭumbī* is found in the commentary of Medhātithi on *Manu*, iv. 253.

42. *vaiśyakanyāsmudbhūtaḥ brāhmaṇena tu saṃskṛtah, sa kyārddhika iti jñeyo bhojyo viprairna saṃśayah, Prāyaścittakāṇḍa*, xi, 25. It is well known that *ardhasīrīs* or *ārdhikas* generally belonged to the śūdra caste, but the way in which their origin has been explained suggests that the vaiśyas had also been largely reduced to the status of sharecroppers.
43. *Lekhapaddhati*, p. 18.
44. 42, 139ff.
45. Ibid., 42, 174-6.
46. Ibid., 42, 177.
47. Takakusu, *Record of the Buddhistic Religion as Practised in India and the Malay Archipelago by Ī-tsing* (Oxford, 1896), p. 65.
48. Cited in A. Appadorai, *Economic Conditions of South India (AD 1000-1500)*, i (Madras, 1936), p. 273.
49. *Bṛhannāradiya Purāṇa*, 22.11.
50. Devībhāgavata cited in Hazra, *Studies in Upapurāṇas*, II (Calcutta, 1963), 325.
51. *Skanda Purāṇa* (*Brahmakhaṇḍa*) 3.2.40.65. See also *Smṛticandrikā* (twelfth century), section on *Deśadharma*.
52. In the *Lekhapaddhati* (p. 51) we find a form of document called *śilapatra* being issued by the ruler to settle the disputes among the Rājaputra village chiefs regarding particular fields and families of village inhabitants (*kṣetraikasya viṣaye kuṭumbaviṣaye paruspuraṃ sañjātavairau*) and to impress upon them that they should remain contented with their own fiefs (*grāsa*). But villages were not always coterminous with the holdings of the chiefs.
53. *rājñopāyena saṃraksya-grāme grāme kṛṣivalāḥ tebhyaḥ kṛṣistataścārthā arthebhyah sarvasampadaḥ* (*Yuktikalpataru*, Calcutta, 1917, p. 6). A system of clientele oscillating between protection and oppression led to the constitution of serfdom in Western Europe (Marc Bloch, op. cit., p. 265).
54. *EI*, xxx, no. 30; *Yaśastilaka*, 3.172.
55. Op. cit., p. 279.
56. *Encyclopaedia of Social Sciences*, x, 97.
57. According to Marc Bloch, 'the manor in itself has no claim to a place among the institutions which we call feudal', though it acquired great prominence in Western feudalism, op. cit., 279. The classical form of manorialism and serfdom typical of Western Europe could not emerge in China or Japan under feudal conditions (Wu-Ta-K'un, *Past and Present*, no. 1, 1952, 192: J.W. Hall, *Comparative Studies in Society and History*, v. no. 1, 1963, 35). Full serfdom with attachment to the soil developed in Russia much later when it had become a closed country (Owen Lattimore, *Past and Present*, no.12, 55). On the basis of a survey of the twelfth century it has been remarked that real serfs, *servi* or *nativi*, were in a small minority in England (R.H. Hilton, *Past and Present*, no. 31, 1965, 11).

58. 38.87.
59. 35.28, D.D. Kosambi and V.V. Gokhale (ed.), Harvard Oriental Series, xlii (Harvard, 1957). However, some families, in spite of the miserable state to which they were reduced, continued to stay there under the deep-rooted belief that it was their ancestral land, ibid.
60. See the author's article in D.C. Sircar (ed.), *Land System and Feudalism in Ancient India* (Calcutta, 1966), pp. 93-4.
61. *grāmācārastathā grāhyaḥ smṛtimārgāvirodhataḥ*, *Bṛhannāradīya Purāṇa*, 22.11. According to Derrett the Śāstra was preaching cultural and jurisprudential harmony, if not homogeneity : the Śāstra was on the whole 'recommendatory or at most directory, rather than mandatory' (*Journal of the Economic and Social History of the Orient*, vii, 1964, 117, 119).
62. Maitland, *The Constitutional History of England*, p. 164.
63. Cf. Marc Bloch, op. cit., pp. 253f.
64. A.N. Bose, *Social and Rural Economy of Northern India*, II (Calcutta, 1945), 486; R.S. Sharma, op. cit., pp. 156, 268.
65. *Skanda Purāṇa* (3.2.39.290) refers to the śūdras as *jātibandhena pīḍitāḥ*.
66. Ibid., 1.2.40.227.
67. Tawney (tr.), ii, 59.
68. Cf. R.S. Sharma, op. cit., ch. VI; Lallanji Gopal, op. cit., chs. VI-IX.
69. The hold of traditionalism had obviously minimized the need to take recourse to positive means of imposing restriction on the mobility of the people.
70. v. 172ff; vii. 1088. The term *rūḍhabhāroḍi* occurs in the *Rājataraṅgiṇi* for forced labour employed in carrying loads.
71. Lakṣmidhara's *Kṛtyakalpataru, Rājadharmakāṇḍa*, p. 94.
72. A phenomenon of a somewhat similar nature is noticed in the seventeenth-century Russia where serf economy 'began to adapt itself to the developing markets' (A.M. Pankratova, ed., *A History of the USSR*, pt. i); Moscow, 1947, 201).
73. *EI*, xxxiii, vi (April 1960), 245-6.
74. Even in later times the class of cultivators known as *basai*, though not destitute of property or civil rights, resided in their master's estate (Tod, *Annals and Antiquities of Rajasthan*, ed., W. Crooke, I, 206). The degraded cultivator called *hali* (ploughman) was also compelled by the need for defence against external violence to surrender the land he owned to the protector and then to labour on it for subsistence (ibid.).
75. Moreland, *The Agrarian System of Moslem India* (Cambridge, 1929), p. 204.
76. Irfan Habib, 'The Social Distribution of Landed Property in pre-British India', *Enquiry*, New Series, ii, no. 3 (1965), 46, 52.

19

Problems of Peasant Protest in Early Medieval India

R.S. Sharma

The early medieval socio-economic formation was marked by a grossly unequal distribution of land rights and also of the agricultural produce. A large number of landlords were not directly engaged in cultivation but lived on rent, mainly in kind, collected from the cultivators. They also exploited the labour of the peasants for various purposes, including construction and transport. Since trade and handicrafts were languishing and metal money was not much in use in day-to-day transactions, it was difficult for the peasants to go to the market to seek relief.

How did the socio-economic formation characterized by an unequal distribution of land arise? We can identify three processes. The practice of assignment of land revenues or of plots of land for religious purposes was the most important of these. Although epigraphic records indicating such grants for administrative or other services are not so common, land assignments were undoubtedly made for services other than religious. The second process related to the transformation of the village headman and other functionaries into landed magnates. Thirdly, in certain cases, specified imposts levied from the peasants were earmarked for the maintenance of fiscal and administrative officers. In course of time, these officers seem to have acquired permanent control not only over these imposts but also over the land which was the source of such income.

What led to the wide prevalence of the practice of assignment of land and revenues? In all probability it was the outcome of bitter social conflicts, though we can make only very general statements. The earliest passages which refer to the *kali* age in the Purāṇas date to the last quarter of the third and the first quarter of the fourth centuries. A good part of their descriptions of the *kali* age becomes conventional in later times. But the passages, when they occur first, cannot be dismissed as figments of imagination. They show that peasants were oppressed with taxation, and the vaiśyas and the śūdras refused to perform the functions ascribed to them.[1] Such things happened earlier also. Examples of popular revolts against oppressive rulers appear in the Buddhist birth stories called the *jātakas*, which belong to 500-200 BC. According to B.C. Sen, 'whenever a story is told of a popular victory over royal absolutism or acts disapproved by the people, it is shown to be the result of an amalgamation of the Brāhmaṇas, the Kṣatriyas and the Vaiśyas. The voice exercised by these communities was made effective by the joint use of physical force'.[2] But the king was supposed to represent the kṣatriyas, and it seems that in several cases the brāhmaṇas led the revolt. In one instance, both town and country folk joined in the revolt, and the king was beaten to death along with his priest.[3]

We can better appreciate the significance of the *kali* phenomenon if we bear in mind the nature of the socio-economic formation which seems to have been upset by it. In spite of the presence of some rich landowners in the Buddhist birth stories, in ancient times we do not find unequal distribution of the chief means of production, i.e. land, on any large scale. We however find unequal distribution of agricultural products as well as the forcible use of the labour power of the śūdras for the cultivation of land and other purposes. A good portion of the produce of the land went as taxes to the rulers who were called kṣatriyas. Another portion went to the brāhmaṇas and other religious elements in the form of gifts. For supplying labour to the three higher *varṇas* including the vaiśya peasants and merchants, the śūdras were considered to be the common source. But really śūdra labour seems to have been utilized more by landowning village communities or individuals comprising the kṣatriyas and brāhmaṇas, who were exempted from taxes. This kind of social formation, in which the vaiśyas were the principal taxpayers and the śūdras supplied the main source of labour, was certainly riven with contradictions. Many instances of deviation from this norm could be cited. But by and large until Gupta times this kind of production relations existed in its essentials.

The social conflicts indicated by the passages describing the *kali* age leave no doubt that the rulers found it difficult to collect taxes; apparently the brāhmaṇas together with various types of renouncers could not receive gifts. Thus the *kali* social disorders affected those who exercised authority but did not produce directly for themselves. In order to put down the disorders effective use of force or violence was recommended. *Daṇḍa* was glorified in a manner in which it was never done before. From the fourth century onwards payment for services through grants of land revenues became a significant factor in a good part of the country. Although the texts do not clearly connect the widespread practice of land-grants with the preceding social crisis, the former seems to have followed from the latter. From the fourth and fifth centuries onwards land-grants on a large scale served to solve the problem of tax collection and its disbursement to non-producing classes engaged in military, administrative and religious services. Much remains to be done about the area, period and the dynastic kingdoms or personalitics involved in the resurrection of the machinery of surplus collection in a new garb. However as early as the fourth and fifth centuries some of the kings who claim to have restored *dharma* also issued land-grants for religious purposes. The social formation that emerged out of the widespread practice of land-grants was dominated by the landlords. The royal charter which gave lands tended to deprive a large number of peasants of communal rights which they enjoyed in respect of pasture grounds, pathways, fisheries, forests, orchards, etc. The new assignees had the right to enjoy these communal resources at the cost of the village or the tribal community. The assignees were given the right to collect not only the fixed taxes which hitherto went to the king but were also empowered to levy fresh taxes. The list of land taxes in early medieval charters gets longer and longer. On the one hand it presupposes agrarian expansion and increase in productivity. On the other it shows that the burden of taxes was becoming heavier and heavier in the areas directly governed by the State but more so in the benefices granted by it. The charters worsened the production relations. There could be conflict between one beneficiary and the other, between the king and his vassals, and above all between the landlords and the peasants.

These conflicts could assume various forms. One important

form was litigation to which obviously only the beneficiaries and advanced sections of the peasantry could resort. The landed beneficiaries and some other landed elements who may have acquired land by force or custom may have been involved in lawsuits. Apparently it was the need of settling land disputes in favour of the grantees that a new provision was inserted and emphasized in the *Dharmaśāstras* or the law-books. According to it, the claim based on royal charter would override the claims based on custom, agreement and religion. In other words, a *rājśāsana* would prevail over *dharma, vyavahāra* and *carita.* This particular provision first appears in verse form in the *Arthaśāstra* of Kauṭilya, which is mostly written in prose; the provision therefore may have been inserted in it at a later stage. It occurs from the fifth to the tenth century in the law-books of Nārada, Bṛhaspati and Kātyāyana, and also in the *Agni Purāṇa.* It is obvious that the claim to land made by the peasant or any other party on the basis of custom, contract or even religion was not sustainable in the face of the charter-based claim of the beneficiary.[4]

In addition to litigation, peasants protested in various other ways. They took advantage of royal visits to complain to the king. When Harṣa's army was passing through the countryside, a large number of rural folk came out to welcome him, but at the same time they complained to him against the oppressions of the *bhogpatis* who had been given the right to enjoyment of revenues from the villages. Self-immolation, particularly in south India, was another form of protest. People registered protests by killing themselves in public. A dancing girl threw herself from the temple tower to fight for the right of her relations to till the land assigned to her for her maintenance. More importantly a brāhmaṇa immolated himself to establish the right of the temple guards and servants who also died for the same thing.[5] Many Jainas believed that they would attain salvation by subjecting themselves to physical hardships leading to the end of their lives. Perhaps these religious methods of ending life for the sake of salvation adopted by the Jainas were repeat performances of the actual methods adopted by the peasants to articulate their protests against the exploitation of feudal landlords in south India. It seems that self-immolation prevalent in south India till recent times such as one on the occasion of the death of M.G. Ramachandran is a survival of the practice of protest against unbearable conditions of life.

Several instances of violent conflict between the landlords, who were brāhmaṇas, and the peasants in the eleventh-thirteenth centuries in Karnataka and Andhra Pradesh have been cited. The peasants launched armed attacks on brāhmaṇa landlords, and the landlords burnt a whole village and the standing crops, and carried on war against peasant villages.[6]

Many commemorative stones were raised in south India in order to record the acts of bravery performed by those who laid down their lives in defence of the brāhmaṇa's land or those who died in violence unleashed by the landed religious elements or others. Such stones are called *vīragaḷa* or *vīrakaḷa* (hero stones) and are found not only in Karnataka but also in many other parts of southern India. An inscribed hero stone from Hasan district in Karnataka shows that in 1212 the Chief of Hanche fell fighting against the people of Kerehalli for a pond, for which a stone was raised in his memory.[7] In the eleventh-fourteenth centuries many inscriptions in Karnataka mention not only the endowment, construction and maintenance of tanks but also speak of battles for their possession. All this was natural since the tank formed the chief means of irrigation. The case referred to above suggests that the peasantry in the whole village was pitted against the chief who wanted a larger share of water for himself. It would be worthwhile to map such 'hero stone' inscriptions areawise and periodwise and to work out their implications from the point of view of rural conflicts.

Numerous instances of peasant protest occur in the Chola and other inscriptions found in Tamil Nadu and the neighbouring areas. I have consulted the summaries of these inscriptions published in the *Annual Reports of South Indian Epigraphy* (*ARE*). Even these summaries give a fair indication of the strong reaction of the peasants to the oppression of the landlords and occasionally of the royal agents during the first half of the thirteenth century under the Chola king Rājarāja III. We find that his vassals benefited from the discomfiture of the Chola monarch at the hands of the Pāṇḍyas. The Pāṇḍya invasions were followed by troubles and agitation (*kṣobham*) marked by insecurity and damage to property. Temples were deserted, images removed and, what is more significant, land records and title deeds destroyed. All this happened in the heart of the Chola kingdom in Tanjore district.[8] Records and title deeds may have been destroyed by vassals and rival beneficiaries, but the temple tenants and other peasants who suffered from oppressive taxes would be none the less interested in doing so. In such cases sometimes the temple managers took the side of those who were engaged in the service of the temple. An inscription from Shrirangam in the ninth year of Maravarman Sundara Pāṇḍya who came to the throne in 1216 shows that the temple managers colluded with the *Oṭṭar* to the detriment of the income of the temple. Venkataramayya takes the word *Oṭṭar* as *Offiya* (people of Orissa) and postulates a Kaliṅga invasion as far as Shrirangam around about 1224.

But according to Venkatasubba Ayyar the term *Oṭṭar* must be taken to mean 'those who have undertaken to do a thing or given an agreement to the temple'. The people of Orissa are referred to as *Oḍḍiyar* in Tamil inscriptions and not as *Oṭṭar*.[9] Ayyar's interpretation of *Oṭṭar* apparently refers to the servicing sections which included artisanal groups and agricultural labourers who were given land for their maintenance. These also might include *devadāna-kammi,* i.e. serfs attached to temple lands. It seems that the managers of Shrirangam temple took up the cause of the servicing sections and rose against the temple head; their action reduced the income of the temple and upset its normal routine. Eventually the managers were expelled by the Pāṇḍya king Maravarman Sundara. Lasting for two years, evidently it was a major protest of the temple artisans and land labourers who were led by its managers.

Records full of cases of turmoil, social disorder and anti-State activities are found towards the end of the reign of Rājarāja III. On account of such cases there are many instances of confiscations and public sale of property. A record of the twenty-third year of Rājarāja from Tanjore district gives details which can be considered typical of several others of its kind.[10] According to it two temple priests who were called *Śiva-brāhmaṇas* were punished by the congregation of *Śaiva* worshippers called *maheśvaras* who were joined in this act by the village assembly (*ūr*) consisting of the non-brāhmaṇas. The temple priests were punished for *rāja-droham* and *śiva-droham,* i.e. treason against the king as well as Śiva. The accused had handed over to a concubine the jewels of the goddess, misappropriated the temple funds placed in their charge, refused to pay dues on the lands held by them and had misbehaved in other ways. They ignored royal commands and ducked the king's messengers. They had committed indescribable sins through the Kannadigas and are said to have collected 50,000 *kāśus*. For all this they were expelled from the temple and ostracized, and the property, movable and immovable including servants, was confiscated by the State.[11] This record shows non-brāhmaṇa *Śaivas* to be enthusiastic supporters of the temple grant system which was being violated by some brāhmaṇa priests serving in the temple of Śiva.

In the nineteenth year of the reign of Rājarāja III a document registered the renewal of the title deeds through the village assemblies to all the residents who enjoyed lands in the several hamlets of the village up to the eighteenth year of the king. This renewal was effected by two functionaries with the surname of *Piḷḷai*, whose names suggest that they held high positions in the State. This action had to be undertaken because old registers and documents had been lost in the disturbed state of the country in the fifth, eleventh and sixteenth year of the reign of the king. All this relates to the temple of Saṅkhanārāyaṇeśvara which was located in Tanjore district.[12]

What has been stated above shows that the reign of Rājarāja III was punctuated with rural revolts, especially in the first quarter of his rule even in the heart of the Chola kingdom. In every case the records relating to land were lost, suggesting that the peasants were not prepared to accept the religious beneficiaries. In the case of Sankhanārāyaṇeśvara, eventually the village assembly comprising the assignees had to renew the titles of those who enjoyed lands in various hamlets of the villages.

A similar case of protest is found in the twenty-third year of Rājarāja's reign. The record states that at the time of a famine a person called Andaranda in combination with others opened the coffers of the temple, mutilated the image of the deity and mismanaged the temple lands. For all this, according to the decision of the judges and other residents of the village, his lands as well as those of his associates were confiscated. All this happened in the district of Tanjore.[13] This cryptic account leaves many things untold. It is not clear in what ways the leader and his supporters mismanaged temple lands; obviously they settled lands with agriculturists or remitted rent on account of the ravages of the famine. Apparently because of this 'mismanagement' the income or advantages from the temple lands were directed to the tillers in times of famine. Eventually the leader and his supporters were punished with the deprivation of their lands.

We have also a case of *rāja-drohins,* i.e. traitors, being punished, but it is not clear whether they acted against the local landlords like the *Śiva-brāhmaṇas* and their followers; certainly they had acted against the king. This anti-king conspiracy was put down through the ethnic device of divide and rule. According to record,[14] Kulōttunga Chola III, when encamped in the Pāṇḍya country, called one of the chiefs and ordered him to accept the chiefship of a village in the Toṇḍaimaṇḍalam. The Pāṇḍya chief accepted the offer and coming to the village he punished the traitors to the king (*rājadrohin).* One of the reasons for asking a native of the Pāṇḍya country to rule over a village of Toṇḍai was evidently the disturbance caused by the traitors whom the new chief must have eventually expelled from the village.[15]

I am sure that many more instances of rural tension and violence can be collected. Though none of these cases clearly indicates the revolt of organized peasant groups against the State or the landlords, yet the destruction of land records and titles, which were usually based on charters granted to the temples and the brāhmaṇas, is of special significance. The peasants would certainly take advantage of the rivalry between the various types of beneficiaries, religious and non-religious, and also of the rivalry between beneficiaries and the State. Since the peasants themselves were not enlightened enough, they were invariably led by such priests as were either enlightened or disgruntled.

We have a few instances, particularly of tribal peasants, rising in open revolt against the landed powers. Around the sixth century in south India, we have the famous case of the revolt of *Kaḷabhras,* who seemed to have been a tribal people. Nilakanta Sastri, who refers to this revolt in several of his writings,[16] has never a single good word for the *Kaḷabhras.* They are considered the scourge of humanity and the enemy of civilization. The *Kaḷabhra* chiefs are called evil kings, and they are charged with the resumption of *brahmadeya* lands enjoyed by the beneficiaries. The Pāṇḍya inscriptions of the eighth and ninth centuries speak of the loss of such lands in the wake of the *Kaḷabhra* aggression and also of the encroachment of the śūdras on a donated village.[17] The period for which the *Kaḷabhras* dominated the scene in Tamilnadu, especially at the cost of the Cholas, is called a dark age. Although their rule lasted only for 75 years or so, they upset the existing social and political relationships. The Pāṇḍyas brought to an end the so-called dark period inaugurated by the *Kaḷabhras*.

In eastern India we may refer to the revolt of the *Kaivartas*. They were both fishermen and cultivators. As a tribe the *Kaivartas* were absorbed in brahmanical society as a low mixed caste. According to Manu (X.34), the *Kaivarta* was a boatman. But in east Bengal most of them seem to have been peasants, and as such were identical with the *Mahīsyas*, who were considered to be the offspring of a kṣatriya father and vaiśya mother.[18] Some *Kaivarta* chiefs were given land as service tenures by the Pāla rulers. These lands were resumed by Mahīpāla I around the end of the tenth century,[19] and the *Kaivartas* were oppressed with taxes. Eventually they revolted against Mahīpāla II and wiped out the Pāla authority for a considerable period of time.[20] Hitherto the *Kaivarta* revolt has been seen either as a popular upsurge against tyranny[21] or as a civil disturbance against an established and legitimate authority upsetting law and order;[22] the first view is intended to justify democratic rule and the second to support the *status quo* and discourage revolts under all circumstances. In the process the peasant dimension of the *Kaivarta* problem has been overlooked.[23]

There is need for analysing the character of the few revolts that are known to us. It appears that so far we have no examples of revolt in settled and clearly caste-divided areas. Both the *Kaḷabhras* and the *Kaivartas* were tribal peasants least infected with caste ideology or brahmanization. The *Kaivartas* were a fierce tribe. In their revolt against the Pālas they did not possess any chariots.[24] On the other hand they rode buffaloes and fought with bows and arrows.[25] It is significant that the buffalo appears as the *vāhana* or conveyance of Lord Yama who is the God of Death. The fact that the buffalo was also associated with the *Kaivartas* shows them to be as fierce as Yama. At any rate it is clear that the *Kaivartas* retained their tribal identity under the leadership of Bhīma. We find repeated references to the slaughter of the kinsmen of Bhīma in the *Rāmacarita* of Sandhyākara Nandi.[26] Although Rāmapāla is depicted as one who never caused any injury to his kinsmen, he put down the *Kaivartas* not with the support of his kinsmen but a large number of vassals called *sāmantas*, of whom fourteen are specifically mentioned in the text.[27] Many of these vassals were tribal chiefs ruling over forest tracts.[28] It therefore appears that the protracted struggle between Rāmapāla on the one hand and the *Kaivartas* on the other caused a dent in the supra-tribal solidarity, with the result that the *Kaivartas* were left alone to fend for themselves. Hence the problem of the extent of the kin-based solidarity in these revolts has to be examined.

In analysing the nature of these revolts one has also to locate the role of religion in mobilizing peasants against their oppressors. Clearly the *Kaḷabhras* were anti-brahmanical, and they are called Buddhists. Reference to the *Kaḷabhra Kula* is found in the writings of a Buddhist monk[29] of about the seventh century or so. Similarly the *Kaivartas* were Saivites, and they were pitted against the Pālas who were very much pro-Buddhists. Although Nārāyaṇapāla granted land to the *Paśupatas* and erected temples for them[30] in the tenth century, in later centuries Buddhism and Saivism were locked in opposition in eastern India. The iconography of eastern India shows aggressive Buddhist gods. Trailokya Vijaya from Orissa (tenth century) is a Buddhist deity trampling Saivite divinities under-foot. Similarly a tenth century pantheon from Nālandā shows the dominance of the Buddhist deity Aparājita over Śaivite and other deities.[31] This religious conflict cannot be isolated from the social situation in which the Buddhist monasteries enjoyed huge landed properties at the cost of both the brāhmaṇa beneficiaries and the ordinary peasants following Hindu religion. Bhīma, the *Kaivarta* chief, was a devotee of Śiva and Bhavāni,[32] and his community may have been Śaivite. It is significant that when Rāmapāla gained victory over the *Kaivartas* he constructed a large number of Śiva temples in the newly founded capital Rāmavati in order to pacify the people,[33] who were obviously *Kaivartas*.

The situation was different in south India where the Śaivites and the Vaiṣṇavites persecuted the Jainas and the Buddhists. The competing claims for grant of lands may have been an important cause; the Jainas were granted lands for the *vasadis* and the Buddhists for *vihāras*. In the long run such antagonisms ended in reconciliation. Since references to these revolts are not found in non-religious or secular idiom, it is all the more necessary that their social dimensions be examined.

Sometimes those discontented brāhmaṇas who were not fortunate enough to receive grants also led revolts against landed brāhmaṇas by mobilizing the peasants. It is significant that in the *Jātaka* stories revolts are led by brāhmaṇas with the backing of the common masses. They result in the replacement of the tyrannical king by another ruler who promises to govern according to the norms set by religion and society.

It is not easy to identify the aims and objects of the peasant revolts and the issues involved in them. Mostly the issues were of immediate concern to those who revolted. The *Kaivartas* apparently wanted the lands that had been resumed from them by Mahīpāla I and transferred to the Buddhists. They also sought relief from oppressive taxes imposed on them by the Pālas. The brief period for which they supplanted the Pāla rule did not bring about any transformation in social and political relationships; only the place of the Pāla ruler was taken by the *Kaivarta* chiefs, Dibyoka and his son Bhīma.

The revolt seems to have raised the ritual status of the *Kaivarta* community. Formerly a brāhmaṇa could not accept the food of a *Kaivarta*, who was called an *antyaja* (literally last-born but really untouchable). But later the myth of his origin from the union of a kṣatriya father and vaiśya mother was popularized,[34] and he was considered a *sat śūdra* who could perform certain ceremonies and whose food could be accepted. It is stated in a text of the sixteenth century attributed to Vallālasena (twelfth century) that he raised the social status of the *Kaivartas* and prescribed menial or domestic service as their livelihood. Maheśa, the headman of the *Kaivartas*, was honoured with the rank and title of *mahāmaṇḍalika*.[35] Sridharasvāmi (*c.* AD 1400) in his comment on a verse from the *Bhāgavata Purāṇa* also shows that the *Kaivartas* gained in status.[36]

The *Kaḷabhras* who supplanted the power of the three Tamil kingdoms for a short spell in the deep south do not seem to have left much trace of the nature of their rule. They seized the lands granted to the brāhmaṇas, and were probably more egalitarian.The *Kaivartas* also may have been inspired by the egalitarian spirit. But neither of them can be credited with any vision for recasting social relationships or production relations through revolts.

Whether peasant protests and revolts undermined the existing socio-economic formation needs investigation. The possibility of their linkage with the revival of trade and handicrafts from the eleventh century onwards in many parts of the country has been suggested but not explored.[37] We also cannot state whether these revolts were spontaneous or organized. These questions cannot be answered for lack of sufficient sources and adequate research.

One thing is, however, clear that by the twelfth century or so the enormity and ferocity of the various types of evils and oppressions associated with land-grants had been sufficiently publicized and realized. This seems to be particularly true of south India where we find some preemptive protests. In one instance, during the twelfth century a whole village refused to be converted into a religious/educational grant called *agrahāra*.[38] This open opposition to being placed at the mercy of landed beneficiaries may have encouraged other villagers to act similarly.

In spite of instances of peasant protests assuming varied forms in early medieval times, by and large the peasants lived in a state of reconciliation and resignation with the situation imposed on them as a result of the rise of landlords and the erosion of their communal rights. This state of affairs can be explained in different ways.

In certain parts of the country, particularly in backward areas, serfs were tied to the land-granted to the beneficiaries, but serfdom was not a general feature of Indian feudalism. Wherever the serfs worked on the land, they existed in small numbers. The lack of numbers weakened their position and division into castes hampered organization. This difficulty was further compounded by wide spatial distribution. But in one case in Karnataka the bonded labourers attacked a brāhmaṇa benefice, and the warrior who fought in its defence claims to have killed many of these labourers (*besa-vagal*) in the fight.[39]

Perhaps the corporate unity of the village community mostly kept the peasants at bay. If the landlord and the peasants belonged to the same village the common belongingness would be used to keep them under the same umbrella. If they belonged to the same kin and caste, the illusion of corporate unity would be stronger. At least for four centuries or so from the sixth century onwards this belongingness was strengthened by the blending of agriculture and handicrafts based on the jajmani system, a phenomenon which has been debated repeatedly under the title of the Asiatic mode. The initial stage of agrarian expansion meant the multiplication of numerous self-sufficient villages and provided a congenial climate for 'corporate' life.

Equally important seems to have been the ideological and ritualistic factor. Land seizures do not seem to have been infrequent. The donors constantly feared that the land-granted by them could be either seized by their successors or resumed by the existing peasants who had been in possession of it for a long time. In order to forestall such possibilities all kinds of curses were heaped on those who would dare violate the provisions of the land charters granted to the beneficiaries. It was repeatedly stated at the end of the land charters that those who violate them live in hell for 60,000 years and those who observe them live in heaven for the same period. It will be interesting to find out how hell and heaven were deliberately visualised to indoctrinate the mass of the peasants and other people in the norms of feudal patriarchal society. One of the main reasons why the illusion of hell and heaven was developed very much in early medieval times seems to have been to protect the landed property of the brāhmaṇas and others against encroachment by their equally entrenched rivals and also by the mass of the peasantry.

Connected with the concept of hell and heaven was the *Vedānta* theory of *Karma*. The *Karma* theory emphasized the point that if people performed the duties assigned to their stations by their birth, they could look forward to social promotion in the existing social framework in the next birth. The theory of *punarjanma* or rebirth therefore was preached to the peasant masses and others through numerous religious stories which were recited as *kathās*. Hence the belief that there was no escape from the consequences of birth and heredity was ingrained in the minds of the people in ancient times but more strongly in early medieval times when social classes became more and more unequal.

Further, the *varṇa* theory handed over from ancient times was refurbished in a new manner. One of its greatest proponents was Kṛṣṇa who taught in the *Bhāgavad Gītā* that people should carry out the functions assigned to them by their respective *varṇas*. As time went on, the teachings of the *Gītā* received more publicity and increasingly came to be regarded sacred. However complications were created by the rise of many landed groups or powerful families who would not fit in the fourfold traditional system. In order to absorb them and contain social discontent, new provisions were made in the Dharmaśāstras. If some powerful indigenous tribal families or foreign tribes managed to capture power, they came to be recognized and legitimized as kṣatriyas. This theory was put forward clearly around AD 400 by Sabarasvāmi who wrote a commentary on Jaimini's *Mimamsa Sūtra*. Now the theory prevailed that any *rāja* could be recognized as a kṣatriya, i.e. *kṣatriyo rāja ucyate.*

Similarly when land-grants helped annex numerous tribals to the brāhmaṇical system, the new peasants came to be considered śūdras. In a way the śūdras who served mainly as domestic servants, slaves, artisans, and agricultural labourers in ancient times were now called peasants in some texts, and more so in foreign accounts. The number of *saṁskāras,* i.e. domestic ceremonies, was increased, and those which were not associated with Vedic *mantras* could be performed by the śūdras. Obviously many brāhmaṇa priests officiated in these ceremonies although their status may have been low in society. But those śūdra peasants who could afford to perform these *saṁskāras* would certainly have a feeling of social promotion and of closeness to the highest *varṇa.*

It would therefore appear that attempts were made to give ritualistic recognition to the social changes that were taking place in production relations. The rituals served to satisfy the vanity and psychological aspirations of the śūdra peasants and to make them resign to the new situation in which they had been deprived of their egalitarian tribal rights.

What distinguished the early medieval period was the proliferation of the caste system; particularly the śūdra peasant castes proved to be numerous. Based on regions, clans and tribes, they were arranged in some ritualistic gradation. The theory of the origin of these śūdra castes was known as the theory of mixed castes, which attributed the origins of numerous peasant castes to the union of the existing castes in the reverse order, i.e. in the *pratiloma* order. This theory was conceived in such a manner that almost every mixed caste was either inferior or superior to the other caste.[40] Thus although the peasants were exploited more or less in the same manner, they were the victims of endless division caused by the castes based on ritualistic distinctions of inferiority or superiority. The element of ritualism tended to distort the reality of exploitation to which the peasants were subjected. Therefore the solidarity of the peasants against the landlords could not be achieved easily.

The two important religious movements that influenced the thinking of the peasant masses in early medieval times were tantrism and *bhakti.* Tantrism emphasized the worship of the mother goddess, many of whose names sound non-Sanskritic. Its rituals and ordination were open to both men and women without any distinction. Though tantrism affected Śaivism, Vaiṣṇavism, Jainism and Buddhism, it really originated as a result of land-grants to brāhmaṇas and others in the outlying areas inhabited by tribal and non-brahmanical people. The superimposition of a class of beneficiaries substantially took away the rights of the tribals to land and communal resources, but their egalitarian ritualistic rights were recognized in a tantric garb. Even the brahmanized peasant castes who did not enjoy such rights under the *varṇa* system could perform tantric ceremonies.[41] Tantrism enjoyed a large following, particularly in the backward tribal areas. With the accommodation of the mother goddess in the Hindu set-up and her elevation to a very high status in it, the exponents of the *tantra* system obviously succeeded in reconciling the tribals to the hardships resulting from the land-grants. The initial appeal of the *tantra* to the tribals may have petered out in the long run when the tantric hierarchy was modelled on the feudal hierarchy, and when war and sex, with which the landlords were obsessed, were given prominence in the *tantra* system.

But a more powerful factor that helped to contain and channelize the discontent of the peasant masses was the medium of *bhakti*. Originating in a new incarnation in south India around the seventh century it affected Vaiṣṇavism as well as Śaivism. The *bhakti* movement in the early medieval period was inspired by the feudal social set-up. But when it crystallized it seems to have acquired an autonomous character. The peasant devotees offered the same allegiance to their landlord as they offered to their god. They seem to have sincerely believed in the 'invisible realities' resulting from the blessings of the all-powerful and ever-compassionate god. The idea of complete surrender to the god was developed further in late medieval times. The god was conceived as father, mother, kinsman, companion, wealth and learning. His constant imaginary company was considered a great solace for those who experienced exploitation and hardships arising out of the increasing burden of taxation[42] in medieval times.

Various other methods were used to keep the peasants and the landlords together. Special mention may be made of *vratas* or religious vows including festivities which were prescribed for all sections of society, high and low. More importantly, *tīrthas* and temples, which diluted distinctions between landlords and peasants, became a common feature. There is no way to compute the number of rituals that were actually performed by various princes, chiefs, landed magnates and temples in the early medieval period. But rituals were considered necessary for legitimizing quick changes in authority and social status. This partly accounts for the provision of a large number of *vratas* in medieval texts. A ritual was an occasion not only for making gifts to the priests but also for holding sumptuous feasts and distributing *prasāda* by the temple and other authorities. This meant sharing of common food both by the landlords and the peasants and artisans attached to them. In a way rituals offered opportunities for 'redistribution' in medieval times. Thus the process of integration and reconciliation was promoted through different devices in which arousing hopes for the next world and rituals of legitimacy and 'redistribution' played an important part.

The measures mentioned above were communicated to the people through the written or the spoken word. The written word may have been confined to few literates, but the spoken word through the citation of the Purāṇa stories reached even women and śūdras. The ideological and ritualistic propaganda was backed by the medium of art. Social and religious ideals were articulated in representations of gods and goddesses in numerous pieces of sculpture in stone and bronze. Their number in early medieval times is so large that one encounters them in almost all the settled parts of the country.

NOTES

1. For details see R.S. Sharma, 'The Kali Age: A Period of Social Crisis', in S.N. Mukharjee (ed.), *India: History and Thought (Essays in Honour of A.L. Basham)*, Calcutta, 1982.
2. B.C. Sen, *Studies in the Buddhist Jatakas*, Calcutta, 1974, pp. 77-97.
3. *Jātaka* no. 432, in *Jātaka*, III, 305-6, tr. E.B. Cowell from Pali.
4. The problem had been discussed in detail in R.S. Sharma, '*Rājaśāsana*', *Proceedings of the Indian History Congress*, Calicut Session, 1976.
5. N. Vananalai, 'Consolidation of Feudalism and Anti-feudal Struggles during Chola Imperial Rule', *Proceedings of the Second International Conference Seminar of Tamil Studies*, III (Madras, 1968) 242-3 quoted in D.N. Jha (ed.), *Feudal Social Formations in Early India*, Delhi, 1987, pp. 21-2.
6. R.N. Nandi, 'Growth of Rural Economy in Early Feudal India', Presidential Address, Ancient India Section, Indian History Congress,

45th Session, Annamalai University, Annamalainagar, 1984, pp. 64-7.

7. *Epigraphia Carnatica*,V, Hasan Taluq, Inser. no. 42 (Eng. tr.).
8. *ARE*, no. 141 of 1926 (yr 16-1); 213 of 1925 (yr 19); 309 of 1927 (n.d.).
9. V. Venkatasubba Ayyar, *Epigraphia Indica*, XXVII (1947-8), p. 193, fn. 4.
10. *ARE*, no. 279 of 1927; *ARE*, 1927, pt. II, para 13.
11. *ARE*, 1927, pt. II, para 30.
12. *ARE*, no. 213 of 1925, p. 86.
13. *ARE*, no. 225 of 1927.
14. *ARE*, for 1913, para 39.
15. Ibid.
16. K.A. Nilakanta Sastri, *History of India, Part I—Ancient India*, Madras, 1950, pp. 147-8; *A History of South India*, OUP,1958, pp. 138-9.
17. Rajan Gurukkal, 'Non-Brahmana Resistance to the Expansion of Brahmadeyas: The Early Pandya Experience, *Proceedings of the Indian History Congress*, 45th Session, Annamalai University, Annamalainagar, 1984, pp. 161-3.
18. R.C. Majumdar, *History of Ancient Bengal*, Calcutta, 1971, pp. 437-8.
19. *Epigraphia Indica*, XXIX, 5.
20. Chapter II of the *Ramacarita of Sandhyakaranandin*, ed. H.P. Sastri and seviced by R.C. Basak,Calcutta, 1969 (hereafter *RC*), deals with this revolt.
21. This seems to be the view of Jadunath Sarkar, R.P. Chanda and U.N. Ghoshal, Majumdar, op. cit., p. 187, fn. 197.
22. This is the view of R.C. Majumdar, op. cit., p. 197.
23. R.S. Sharma, *Indian Feudalism, c. AD 300-1200* (2nd edn.), Delhi, 1980, pp. 127, 220.
24. *RC*, II 40. At one place, however, the commentary speaks of the elephants, houses and buffaloes of Bhima (II. 33).
25. *RC*, II, 42.
26. Ibid., II, 48-9.
27. The names mentioned in the text are amplified and associated with various regions in the country which seem to have belonged to the twelfth century. See commentary to *Ramacarita*, II. 5-6.
28. Ibid. The term *Samart-ātavika-sāmanta-cakra* is significant.
29. K.A. Nilakanta Sastri, *History of India, Part I, Ancient India*, p. 148.
30. *RC*, Introd., p. 23.
31. These pantheons are housed in Patna Museum.
32. *RC*, II, 26.
33. Ibid., III, 41.
34. R.C. Majumdar, op. cit., pp. 437-8.
35. Extracts from the *Vallalacarita* (compiled in the sixteenth century) quoted in Majumdar, op. cit., p. 252.
36. *Bhāgavata Purāṇa*, ed. J.L. Sastri, Delhi, 1983. XII. 325; also see Introduction, p. 7.
37. On this point see Nandi, op. cit.

38. Ibid.
39. *Epigraphia Carnatica,* VIII, Sorat, nos. 252 and 253 quoted in ibid., p. 26.
40. S.J. Tambiah, 'From Varna to Caste through Mixed Unions', Goody (ed.), *The Character of Kinship*, p. 207.
41. R.S. Sharma, 'Material Milieu of Tantrism', R.S. Sharma and V. Jha, ed., *Indian Society: Historical Probings.* In Memory of D.D. Kosambi, Delhi, 1974.
42. This point has been discussed in my *Indian Feudalism.*

Bibliography

SECTION I: RURAL SETTLEMENTS

Acharya, S.K., 'Rural Settlements in South Kosala', *The Journal of Orissan History*, XIII-XIV, 1995, pp. 48-53.

Agrawal, D.P. and B.M. Pande (eds), *Ecology and Archaeology of Western India*, Delhi, 1977.

Agrawal, D.P. and D. K. Chakrabarti (eds), *Essays in Indian Protohistory*, Delhi, 1979.

Agrawal, D.P., *The Archaeology of India*, London, 1982.

Allchin, B. and F. Raymond, *The Rise of Civilization in India and Pakistan*, Indian reprint, New Delhi, 1983.

Allchin, F.R. *The Archaeology of Early Historic South Asia, The Emergence of Cities and States*, Cambridge, 1995.

Anand, Snehlata, 'Brahmanical Settlements in Gujarat and Rajasthan', unpublished Ph.D. Thesis, Delhi University, 1985.

Bhattacharyya, P.K., *Historical Geography of Madhya Pradesh from Early Records*, Delhi, 1977.

Champakalakshmi, R., 'The Study of Settlement Patterns in the Cōḷa Period: Some Perspectives', *Man and Environment*, XIV, no. 1, 1989, pp. 91-101.

Chattopadhyay, A., 'Some Aspects of the Village in Ancient Bengal: Size and Periphery', *PIHC*, Aligarh Session, 1994, pp. 108-114.

Chattopadhyaya, B.D., *A Survey of Historical Geography of Ancient India*, Calcutta, 1984.

———, *Aspects of Rural Settlements and Rural Society in Early Medieval India*, Calcutta, 1990.

Choudhary, A.K., *Early Medieval Village in North-Eastern India (A.D. 600-1200)*, Calcutta, 1971.

Datta, Swati, *Migrant Brāhmaṇas in Northern India: Their Settlement and General Impact c. A.D. 475-1030*, Delhi, 1989.

Deglurkar, G.B., 'Institution of *Agrahara* in Maharashtra', *PIHC*, Waltair Session, 1979, pp. 195-202.

Deo, S.B., *Megalithic Problems of the Deccan*, Cambridge, 1984.

Dikshit, K.N. (ed.), *Archaeological Perspective of India Since Independence, B.B. Lal Felicitation Volume*, New Delhi, 1984.

Dutt, Brahma, 'Settlements of the PGW in Haryana', Unpublished Ph.D. Thesis, Kurukshetra University, 1980.

Ghosh, A. (ed.), *An Encyclopaedia of Indian Archaeology*, Delhi, 1989.

Gururaja Rao, B.K., *Megalithic Culture in South India*, Mysore, 1972.

Kohli, Deputy, 'Material Culture of Northern India during the NBPW Phase', Ph.D. Thesis, University of Delhi, 1984.

Lal, Makkhan, *Settlement History and Rise of Civilization in the Ganga-Yamuna Doab*, Delhi, 1984.

———, 'The Development and Dispersal of Agricultural Settlements in the Ganga-Yamuna Doab (2nd and Ist Millennium B.C.)', *PIHC*, Goa Session, 1987, pp. 730-40,

Lal, S.N., 'An Aspect of Rural landscape in the Rashtrakuta Kingdom', *PIHC*, Mysore Session, 1993, pp. 89-100.

Leela Shanthakumari, *History of the Agraharas in Karnataka, 400-1300*, Madras, 1986.

Mahajan, Malti, *A Cultural History of Maharashtra and Goa: From Place Names Inscriptions*, Delhi, 1989.

Mangalam, S.J., *Historical Geography and Toponomy of Andhra Pradesh*, New Delhi, 1986.

Morrison, B.M., *Political Centres and Cultural Regions in Early Bengal*, Tuscon, 1970.

Mukherjee, A.B., 'Rural Settlements in the Jatakas', *Geographical Review of India*, XXXI, no. 2, 1969, pp. 17-32.

Mulay, Sumati, *Historical Geography and Cultural Ethnography of the Deccan*, Poona, 1972.

Murty, M.L.K., 'Pre-Iron Age Agricultural Settlements in South India: An Ecological Perspective', *Man and Environment*, XIV, no. 1, 1989.

Narayanan, M.G.S., 'The Warrior Settlements of the Sangam Age', *PIHC*, Kurukshetra Session, 1982, pp. 102-9.

Niyogi, Puspa, *Brahmanic Settlements in Different Sub-Divisions of Ancient Bengal*, Calcutta, 1967.

Prasad, B. Rajendra, 'Early Historic Andhra Desa - A Perspective', Presidential Address, section I, *Proceedings of the Andhra Pradesh History Congress*, XVIII, pp. 8-12.

Ratnagar, Shereen, 'Archaeological Perspectives on Early Indian Societies', in R. Thapar (ed.), *Recent Perspectives of Early Indian History*, Bombay, 1995, pp. 1-52.

Ray, A., *Villages, Towns and Secular Buildings in Ancient India*, Calcutta, 1964.

Ray, H.P., *Monastery and Guild: Commerce Under the Satavahanas,* New Delhi, 1986.

———, 'Early Historical Settlement in the Deccan: An Ecological Perspective', *Man and Environment,* XIV, no. 1, 1989, pp. 103-8.

Raychaudhuri, H.C., 'Geography of the Deccan', in G. Yazdani (ed.), *Early History of the Deccan,* Oxford, 1960.

Roy, T.N., *The Ganges Civilization,* Delhi, 1983.

Sankalia, H.D., *Studies in the Historical and Cultural Geography and Ethnography of Gujarat: Places and Peoples in the Inscriptions of Gujarat (300 B.C.-1300 A.D.),* Poona, 1949.

Shrimali, K.M. 'Pattern of Settlements under the Vakatakas', *PIHC,* Burdwan Session, 1983, pp. 101-12.

———, *Agrarian Structure in Central India and the Northern Deccan - A Study in Vākāṭaka Inscriptions,* New Delhi, 1987.

Singh, K. K., 'Changing Landscape of Rural Settlements in Early Medieval India', a review article, *Social Scientist,* nos. 242-3, 1993, pp. 79-88.

Srivastava, K.M., *Community Movements in Protohistoric India,* Delhi, 1979.

Subbarao, B., *The Personality of India,* second edn, Baroda, 1958.

Suresh, B., 'Historical and Cultural Geography and Ethnology of South India with Special Reference to Cola Inscriptions', unpublished Ph.D. Thesis, Deccan College, Pune, 1965.

Tripathi, V., *The Painted Grey Ware: An Iron Age Culture of Northern India,* Delhi, 1976.

Varma, Supriya, 'Changing Settlement Patterns in Kathiawar', in *Studies in History,* VI, no. 2, 1990, pp. 137-61.

Veluthat, Kesavan, *Brāhmaṇ Settlements in Kerala: Historical Studies,* Calicut, 1978.

SECTION II: THE CONCEPT OF VILLAGE COMMUNITY AND GENERAL PROBLEM OF OWNERSHIP OF LAND

Adhya, G.L., *Early Indian Economics (Studies in the Economic Life of Northern and Western India, c. 200 B.C.- 300 A.D.),* Bombay, 1966.

Altekar, A.S., *A History of Village Communities in Western India,* Bombay, 1927.

Appadorai, A., *Economic Conditions in Southern India, 1000-1500 A.D.,* 2 vols, Madras, 1936.

Asopa, J.N., *Feudalism in North India (700-1200 A.D.),* University of Rajasthan, Jaipur, n.d.

Baden-Powell, B.H., *The Origin and Growth of Village Communities in India,* London, 1899.

Bandyopadhyaya, N.C., *Economic Life and Progress in Ancient India,* 1945, reprint, Allahabad, 1980.

Banerjee, Diptendra, 'Marx and the "Original" Form of Indian Village

Community', in Diptendra Banerjee (ed.), *Marxian Theory and the Third World*, New Delhi, 1985, pp. 133-71.

Bhattacharya, S.C., 'Land, Soil, Rainfall, Irrigation - Some Aspects of the Backdrop of Agrarian Life in the *Arthaśāstra* of Kauṭilya', *IESHR*, XV, no. 2, 1978, pp. 211-19.

Bongard-Levin, G.M., *Mauryan India*, New Delhi, 1985.

———, 'Some Problems of the Social Structure of Ancient India' in Bongard-Levin's *A Complex Study of Ancient India: A Multi-Disciplinary Approach*, Delhi, 1986, pp. 107-48.

Bose, A.N., *Social and Rural Economy of Northern India c.600 B.C. - A. D. 200*, 2 vols., Calcutta, 1942-5.

Breman, Jan, *The Shattered Image: Construction and Deconstruction of the Village in Colonial Asia*, Centre for Asian Studies, Amsterdam, 1988.

Chaudhary, R.K., 'Some Historical Aspects of Feudalism in Ancient India Down to the 14th Century A.D., Based Mainly on the Epigraphic Sources', *Journal of Indian History*, 37, pt. 3, pp. 385-406; 38, pt 1, pp. 193-203.

Cohn, Bernard S., 'African Models and Indian Histories', in R.G. Fox (ed.), *Realm and Region in Traditional India*, New Delhi, 1977, pp. 90-113.

Darian, S.G., 'The Economic History of the Ganges to the end of the Gupta Times', *JESHO*, XIII, 1970, pp. 67-87.

Das, S.K., *The Economic History of Ancient India*, Calcutta, 1929.

Datta, B.N., *Studies in Indian Social Polity*, Calcutta, 1944.

Derrett, J.D.M., 'Kuṭṭa, a Class of Land Tenure in South India', *BSOAS*, XXI, 1958.

———, 'An Indian Contribution to the Study of Property', *BSOAS*, XVIII, 1955, pp. 475-98.

———, 'Bhū-bharaṇa, Bhū-pālana and Bhū-bhojana: An Indian Conundrum', *BSOAS*, XXII, 1959, pp. 108-23.

Dharma Kumar, 'Private Property in Asia? The Case of Medieval South India', *Comparative Studies in Society and History*, 27, no. 2, April 1985, pp. 35-61.

Dikshit, G.S., *Local Self-Government in Medieval Karnataka*, Dharwar, 1964.

Dumont, Louis, 'The 'Village Community' From Munro to Maine', *Contributions to Indian Sociology*, 1967, pp. 67-89.

Dutta, Saroj, *Land System in Northern India, c. A.D. 400-700*, Delhi, 1995.

Fick., R., *The Social Organization in North-East India in Buddha's Time*, English tr., Calcutta, 1920

Gadgil, V.A., 'The Village in Sanskrit Literature', *Journal of the Bombay Branch of the Royal Asiatic Society*, 1927.

Ganguly, D.K., 'Different Categories of Brahmin Donees', *PIHC*, Bombay Session, 1980, pp. 184-94.

Ghoshal, U.N., *Contributions to the History of the Hindu Revenue System*, Calcutta, 1929.

———, *The Agrarian System in Ancient India*, Calcutta, 1930.

———, *The Beginnings of Indian Historiography and Other Essays*, Calcutta, 1944.

Gopal, K. K., Feudal Composition of Army in Early Medieval India', *JAHRS*, XXVIII, 1962-63, pts 3-4, pp. 30-49.

———, 'The Assemblies of Sāmantas in Early Medieval India', *JIH*, XLII, 1964, pt 1, pp. 241-50.

Gopal, L., 'On Some Problems of Feudalism in Ancient India', *ABORI*, XLVI, 1963.

———, 'Quasi-Manorial Rights in Ancient India', *JESHO*, VI, pt 3, 1963, pp. 296-308.

———, 'Sāmaṇta: Its Varying Significance in Ancient India', *Journal of the Royal Asiatic Society of Great Britain and Ireland*, 1963, pp. 21-37.

———, *Economic Life of Northern India (c. A.D. 700-1200)*, Banaras, 1965.

Gunawardana, R.A.L.H., 'The Analysis of Pre-Colonial Social Formations in Asia in the Writings of Karl Marx', *IHR*, II, no. 2, 1976, pp. 365-88.

Gupta, K.M., *The Land System in South India Between A.D. 800- A.D. 1200*, Lahore, 1933.

Gurukkal, Rajan, 'Medieval Landrights: Structure and Pattern of Distribution', *PIHC*, Hyderabad Session, 1978, pp. 279-84.

Habib, Irfan, The Social Distribution of Landed Property in Pre British India (A Historical Survey)' in R.S. Sharma and V.N. Jha (eds), *Indian Society: Historical Probings*, 2nd edn, New Delhi, 1977, pp. 264-316.

———, 'Classifying Pre-Colonial India', *Journal of Peasant Studies*, XII, nos 2-3, 1985, pp. 44-53.

Heitzman, J. and Raja Gopal, 'Temple Landholding and Village Geography in the Chola Period: Reconstruction through Inscriptions', *Tamil Civilization* (Journal of the Tamil University), III, nos 2-3, 1985.

Inden, Ronald, *Imagining India*, Oxford, 1990.

Jayadevan, P., 'Land Rights of A Kingdom Based on Inscriptions', *PIHC*, Srinagar Session, 1986, pp. 187-91.

Jayaswal, K.P., *Hindu Polity*, 1920, 3rd edn, Bangalore, 1955.

Karashima, N., 'The Village Communities in Chola Times; Myth or Reality', *JESI*, VIII, 1981, pp. 85-96.

———, 'The Prevalence of Private Landholding in the Lower Kaveri Valley in the Late Cola Period and its Historical Implications', in N. Karashima (ed.) *Socio-Cultural Change in Villages in Tiruchirapalli District, Tamilnadu, India*, pt 1, Tokyo, 1983, pp. 71-90.

Kosambi, D.D., *An Introduction to the Study of Indian History*, reprint, Bombay, 1990.

———, *The Culture and Civilization of Ancient India in Historical Outline*, sixth impression, New Delhi, 1981.

Krishnamurty, V., 'Temple Endowments in Medieval Andhra', *JAHRS*, XXVI, 1960-61.

Leshnik, L.S. and G. Sontheimer, *Pastoralists and Nomads in South Asia*, Wiesbaden, 1974.

Liceria, Sister M., 'Emergence of Brahmanas as Landed Intermediaries in Karnataka (*c.* A.D. 1000-1300)', *IHR*, I, no. I, 1974, pp. 28-35.

Maine, H.S., *Village Communities in the East and West*, London, 1871.

Maity, S.K., *Economic Life of Northern India in the Gupta Period (cir. A.D. 300-550)*, Calcutta, 1957.

Majumdar, R.C., *Corporate Life in Ancient India*, Calcutta, 1922.

Mazumdar, B.P., *Socio-Economic History of Northern India (A.D. 1030-1194)*, Calcutta, 1960.

———, 'Epigraphic Records on Migrant Brahmanas in North India (A.D. 1030-1225)', *IHR*, V, nos 1-2, 1978-79, pp. 64-86.

Morris, Morris D. and Burton Stein, 'The Economic History of India: A Bibliographic Essay', *Journal of Economic History*, XXI, 1961, pp. 179-207.

Mukherjee, Radhakamal, 'Origin of Indian Village System', *Indian Inheritance*, II, Bombay, 1956, pp. 15-24.

Mukherjee, S.N., 'The Idea of the Village Community and the British Administrators', *Enquiry*, New Series, III, no. 3, 1971.

Mukhia, Harbans, 'Was There Feudalism in Indian History?', Presidential Address, Medieval India Section, *PIHC*, Waltair Session, 1979, pp. 229-80.

———, 'Marx on Pre-Colonial India - An Evaluation', in Diptendra Banerjee (ed.), *Marxian Theory and the Third World*, New Delhi, 1985, pp. 173-84.

Narayanan, M.G.S. and Kesavan Veluthat, 'The Traditional Land System in Kerala: Problems of Change and Perspective', paper presented to the Logan Centenary Seminar on 'Land Reforms in Kerala', Calicut, 1981.

Nath, Pran, *A Study in the Economic Condition of Ancient India*, 1929, reprint, Allahabad, 1980.

Nath, Vijay, *Dana: Gift System in Ancient India (c. 600 B.C. - c. A.D. 300)*, Delhi, 1987.

Niyogi, Puspa, *Contributions to the Economic History of Northern India (from the 10th to the 12th century A.D.)*, Calcutta, 1962.

O'Leary, Brendan, *The Asiatic Mode of Production: Oriental Despotism, Historical Materialism and Indian History*, Oxford, 1989.

Parasher, Aloka, 'Writing on Villages and Peasants in Early India: Problems in Historiography' in V.K. Thakur and A. Aounshuman (eds), *Peasants in Indian History*, I, Patna, 1996, pp. 66-91.

Prakash, Buddha, 'The Genesis and Character of Landed Aristocracy in Ancient India', *JESHO*, IX, 1971, pp. 196-220.

Prakash, Om, *Early Indian Landgrants and State Economy*, Allahabad, 1988.

Randhawa, M.S., *A History of Agriculture in India*, vol. 1, New Delhi, 1980.

Rhys Davids, T.W., *Buddhist India*, London, 1905.
Sammadar, J. N., *Economic Conditions of Ancient India*, Calcutta, 1922.
Sastri, K.A.N., *Studies in Cola History and Administration*, Madras, 1932.
———, *The Colas*, 2nd edn, Madras, 1955, 1975.
Sharma, R.S., *Indian Feudalism (c. 300-1200)*, 1965, 2nd edn, Delhi, 1980.
———, 'How Feudal was Indian Feudalism?' *Social Scientist*, no. 129, Feb. 1984, pp. 16-41
———, 'From Gopati to Bhūpati : Changing Position of the King', *Studies in History*, II, no. 2, 1980, pp. 1-10.
———, *Light on Early Indian Society and Economy*, Bombay, 1966.
———, 'Problems of Social Formations in Early India', General Presidential Address, *PIHC*, Aligarh Session, 1975, pp. 1-14.
———, *Perspectives in Social and Economic History of Early India*, Delhi, 1983.
———, *Material Culture and Social Formations in Ancient India*, Delhi, 1983.
Sharma, R.S. and D.N. Jha, 'Economic History of India upto A.D. 1200: Trends and Prospects', *JESHO*, XVII, pt 1, 1974, pp. 48-80.
Sircar, D.C. (ed.), *Land System and Feudalism in Ancient India*, Calcutta, 1966.
———, *Landlordism and Tenancy in Ancient and Medieval India as Revealed by Epigraphic Records*, Lucknow, 1969.
———, 'Kraya-Sasana and Kara-Sasana', in D.C. Sircar's *Studies in the Political and Administrative Systems in Ancient and Medieval India*, Delhi, 1974, pp. 66-75.
Srinivas, M.N., 'The Indian Village: Myth and Reality', in M. N. Srinivas, *The Dominant Caste and Other Essays*, Delhi, 1987, pp. 20-59.
Thapar, Romila, *The Past and Prejudice*, New Delhi, 1975.
———, *From Lineage to State (Social Formations in the Mid-First Millennium B.C. in the Ganga Valley)*, New Delhi, 1984.
Venkateswarlu, M., 'Land Grants in Medieval Andhra' *JAHRS*, XX, 1949.
Yadava, B.N.S., 'Secular Landgrants of the Post-Gupta Period and Some Aspects of the Growth of Feudal Complex in Northern India', in D.C. Sircar (ed.), *Land System and Feudalism in Ancient India*, Calcutta, 1966, pp. 72-94.
Yamazaki, T. Toshio, 'Some Aspects of Land-Sale Inscriptions in Fifth and Sixth Century Bengal', *Acta Asiatica*, 43, Japanese Studies in Ancient and Medieval Indian History, Tokyo, 1982, pp. 17-36.

SECTION III: AGRARIAN CHANGE, STRUCTURE OF RURAL SOCIETY AND RURAL UNREST

Appadorai, Arjun, 'Right and Left Hand Subcastes in South India', *IESHR*, XI, pts 2-3, 1974.
Aquique, Md., *Economic History of Mithila (c. 600 B.C. -1097 A.D.)*, New Delhi, 1974.
Bajpai, Ranjana, *Society in India in the Seventh Century A.D.*, New Delhi, 1992.

Banaji, Jairus, 'The Peasantry in the Feudal Mode of Production: Towards an Economic Model', *Journal of Peasant Studies,* III, no. 3, 1976.

Beck, Brendra, E.F., *Peasant Society in Konku,* Vancouver, 1972.

Behera, S.K., 'Evolution of the Structure of Polity in Orissa *c.* A.D. 350-1100', Unpublished Ph.D. Thesis, Jawaharlal Nehru University, 1996.

Bhattacharya, S.C., *Some Aspects of Indian Society (From c. 2nd Century B.C. to c. 4th Century A.D.),* Calcutta, 1978.

Bhattacharjee, J.B., 'Land Grants, Land Management and the Nature of Social Formation in Ancient Srihatta', in J.B. Bhattacharjee's *Social and Polity Formations in Pre-Colonial North-East India,* New Delhi, 1991, pp. 18-40.

Bloch, Marc, *Feudal Society,* 2 vols, translated from the French by L.A. Manyon, London, 1965.

Byres, T.J. and Harbans Mukhia, (eds), *Feudalism and Non-European Societies,* Special Issue, *Journal of Peasant Studies,* XII, nos 2-3, 1985.

Chakrabarti, D.K., 'Beginning of Iron and Social Change in India', *Indian Studies: Past and Present,* XIV, no. 4, 1972-3, pp. 329-38.

———, *The Early Use of Iron in India,* Delhi, 1992.

——— and N. Lahiri, 'The Iron Age in India: The Beginning and Consequences', *Puratattva,* 24, 1993-4, pp. 12-32.

Chakravarti, Ranabir, 'Early Historical India: A Study in its Material Milieu (*c.* 600 B.C. - 300 A.D.)', in D.P. Chattopadhyaya (ed.), *History of Science and Technology in Ancient India,* Calcutta, 1991, pp. 305-50.

———, '*Kuṭumbikas* of Early India' in V.K. Thakur and A. Aounshuman (eds), *Peasants in Indian History,* vol. I, Patna, 1996, pp. 179-98.

Chakravarti, Uma, 'Of Dasas and Karmakaras: Servile Labour in Ancient India', in U. Pattnaik and M. Dingwaney (eds), *Chains of Servitude: Bondage and Slavery in India,* New Delhi, 1985, pp. 35-75.

———, *The Social Dimensions of Early Buddhism,* Delhi, 1987.

———, 'In Search of the Peasant in Early India: Was the *Gahapati* a Peasant Producer?', in V.K. Thakur and A. Aounshuman (eds), *Peasants in Indian History,* vol. I, Patna, 1996, pp. 150-78.

Champakalakshmi, R., 'Peasant State and Society in Medieval South India', A review article, *IESHR,* XVIII, nos 3-4, 1981, pp. 411-26.

———, 'The Agrarian Order in Early Tamil Nadu: Problems and Perspectives', Paper presented at the Seminar on 'The Agrarian Order in South India', University of Mangalore, 1989 (forthcoming).

———, 'State and Economy: South India Circa A.D. 400-1300', in Romila Thapar (ed.), *Recent Perspectives of Early Indian History,* Bombay, 1995, pp. 266-308.

Chanana, Devraj, *Slavery in Ancient India,* English trans., Delhi, 1960.

Chattopadhyaya, B.D., 'Transition to the Early Historical Phase in the Deccan: A Note', in B.M. Pande and B.D. Chattopadhyaya (eds),

Archaeology and History (Essays in Memory of Sri A. Ghosh), vol. II, Delhi, 1987, pp. 727-32.
——— (ed.), *Essays in Ancient Indian Economic History*, Delhi, 1987.
———, 'Historiography, History and Religious Centres: Early Medieval North India, *c.* A.D. 700-1200', in Vishakha N. Desai *et al.* (eds), *Gods, Guardians and Lovers, North Indian Temple Sculptures c. 700-1200*, Ahmedabad, 1993, pp. 34-46.
———, *The Making of Early Medieval India*, Delhi, 1994.
———, 'State and Economy in North India: Fourth Century to Twelfth Century', in R. Thapar (ed.), *Recent Perspectives of Early Indian History*, Bombay, 1995, pp. 309-46.
———, 'Geographical Perspectives, Culture Change and Linkages: Some Reflections on Early Punjab', Presidential Address, Ancient Section, Punjab Historical Conference, Patiala Session, 1995 (forthcoming).
Chaudhary, R.K., '*Vishṭi* (Forced Labour) in Ancient India', *IHQ*, XXXVIII, pp. 77-92.
———, 'Peasants in Ancient India', *Journal of the Bihar Research Society*, LIX, pts 1-4, pp. 9-20.
———, 'Theory of Commendation and Subinfeudation in Ancient India', *PIHC*, Bhagalpur Session, 1968, pp. 115-20.
Das, D.R., *Economic History of the Deccan*, Delhi, 1969.
Dhar, M.K., Political Instability in Early Medieval Kashmir', *PIHC*, Srinagar Session, 1986, pp. 113-21.
Duby, George, *The Early Growth of European Economy*, London, 1974.
———, *The Chivalrous Society*, London, 1977.
Elizabeth, V.S., 'Hero-Stones in the Rashtrakuta Period: Their Implications for Society and Polity', *PIHC*, Gorakhpur Session, 1989, pp. 828-33.
Erdosy, George, *Urbanization in Early Historic India*, BAR International Series 430, Oxford, 1988.
Finley, M.I., *The Ancient Economy*, London, 1973.
Fussman, G., 'Central and Provincial Administration in Ancient India: The Problem of the Mauryan Empire', *IHR*, XIV, nos 1-2, 1987-88, pp. 43-72.
Gopal, L., 'Techniques of Agriculture in Early Medieval India (*c.* 700-1200 A.D.)', *University of Allahabad Studies*, 1963-64, pp. 1-37.
———, *Aspects of History of Agriculture in Ancient India*, Varanasi, 1980.
Guha, Amalendu, 'Pre-Ahom Roots and the Medieval State in Assam: A Reply', *Social Scientist*, no. 133, June 1984, pp. 70-7.
———, *Medieval and Early Colonial Assam: Society, Polity, Economy*, Calcutta, 1991.
Gupta, Chitrarekha, 'The Writers' Class of Ancient India - A Case Study in Social Mobility', *IESHR*, xx, no. 2, 1983, pp. 191-204.
———, '*Khila-Ksetras* in Early Bengal Inscriptions', in G. Bhattacharya and

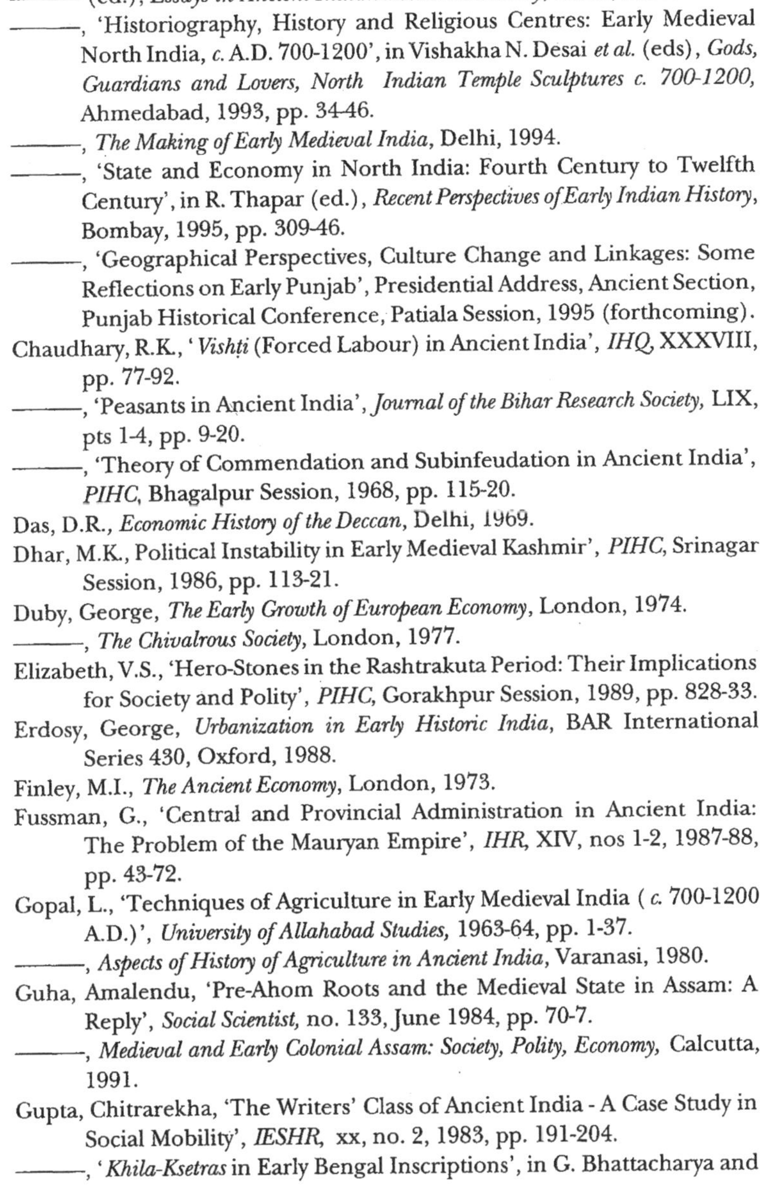

D. Mitra (eds), *Nalnikanta Bhattasali Satavarsiki Volume*, Calcutta, 1989, pp. 271-83.

———, 'Evolution of Agrarian Society in Kamarupa in Early Medieval Period', *IHR*, XIX, nos 1-2, 1992-3, pp. 1-20.

Gupta, Dipankar, 'From *Varṇa* to *Jati*: The Indian Caste System from the Asiatic to the Feudal Mode of Production', in K.L. Sharma (ed.), *Social Inequality in India*, Jaipur, 1995, pp. 159-91.

Gurukkal, Rajan, 'Non-Brahmana Resistance to the Expansion of the Brahmadeyas: The Early Pandya Experience', *PIHC*, Annamalainagar Session, 1984, pp. 161-3.

———, 'The Agrarian System and Socio-Political Organization Under the Early Pāṇḍyas A.D. 600-1000', Unpublished Ph.D. Thesis, Jawaharlal Nehru University, New Delhi, 1984.

———, 'Aspects of Warrior Power in Localised Agriculture: The Case of Pandya Region During the Early Medieval Period', *PIHC*, Srinagar Session, 1986, pp. 192-8.

———, 'Forms of Production and Forces of Change in Ancient Tamil Society', *Studies in History*, V, no. 2, 1989.

———, *Kerala Temples and Early Medieval Agrarian System*, Sukapuram, 1992.

———, 'Towards the Voice of Dissent: Trajectory of Ideological Transformation in Early South India', *Social Scientist*, nos 236-7, Jan.-Feb. 1993, pp. 2-22.

Habib, Irfan, 'Caste in Indian History', in Irfan Habib's *Caste and Money in Indian History*, Department of History, Bombay University, Bombay, 1987, pp. 1-19.

Hilton, Rodney, *Bondmen Made Free: Medieval Peasant Movements and the English Rising of 1381*, London, 1973.

Jain, P.C., *Labour in Ancient India*, Delhi, 1971.

Jain, V.K., *Trade and Traders in Western India (A.D. 1000-1300)*, New Delhi, 1990.

———, 'Dynamics of Hydraulic Activity in Mauryan and Post-Mauryan Times', *PIHC*, New Delhi Session, 1992, pp. 162-169.

Jaiswal, Suvira, 'Caste in the Socio-Economic Framework of Early India', Presidential Address, Ancient India Section, *PIHC*, Bhubaneswar Session, 1977, pp. 23-48.

———, 'Studies in Early Indian Social History: Trends and Possibilities', *IHR*, VI, nos 1-2, 1979-80, pp. 1-63.

———, 'Changes in the Status and Concept of the Śūdra Varṇa in Early Middle Ages', *PIHC*, Bombay Session, 1980, pp. 112-21.

———, 'Varṇa Ideology and Social Change', *Social Scientist*, XIX, nos 3-4, 1991, pp. 41-8.

———, 'The Changing Concept of *Grihapati*', *PIHC*, Warangal Session, 1993 pp. 87-96.

Jamwal, Suman, 'Land System in Early Kashmir', *PIHC*, Aligarh Session, 1994, pp. 83-87.

Jha, D.N., *Revenue System in Post-Maurya and Gupta Times*, Calcutta, 1967.

———, 'Temples as Landed Magnates in Early Medieval South India (*c.* A.D. 700-1300)', in R.S. Sharma and V.N. Jha (eds), *Indian Society: Historical Probings*, second edn, New Delhi, 1977, pp. 202-16.

———, 'Early Indian Feudalism: A Historiographical Critique', Presidential Address, *PIHC*, Waltair session, 1979, pp. 15-45.

———, 'Validity of the Brahmana-Peasant Alliance and the Segmentary State in Early Medieval India', *Social Science Probings*, I, no. 2, 1984, pp. 270-96.

———, (ed.), *Feudal Social Formation in Early India*, Delhi, 1987.

———, *Economy and Society in Early India: Issues and Paradigms*, Delhi, 1993.

———, (ed.) *Society and Ideology in India (Essays in Honour of Professor R.S. Sharma)*, Delhi, 1996.

Jha, V.M., 'Settlement, Society and Polity in Early Medieval Rural India', *Social Science Probings*, XI-XII, 1996, pp. 35-65.

——— '*Varṇasaṁkara* in the Dharma Sūtras: Theory and Practice', *JESHO*, 1970, pp. 273-88.

———, 'Stages in the History of Untouchables', *IHR*, II, no. 1, 1975, pp. 14-31.

———, 'Agricultural Labour and Village Artisans in Early North Indian History (up to *c.* 500 B.C.)', *Social Science Probings*, I, no. 4, 1984, pp. 543-62.

———, 'Caṇḍāla and the Origin of Untouchability', *IHR*, XIII, nos 1-2, 1986-7, pp. 1-36.

———, 'Social Stratification in Ancient India: Some Reflections', Presidential Address, Ancient India Section, *PIHC*, Calcutta Session, 1990, pp. 23-43.

Karashima, N., 'Allur and Isanamangalam', *IESHR*, II, 1965, pp. 150-62.

———, 'Land Revenue Assessment in Cola Times as seen in the Inscriptions of the Thanjavur and Gangaigondacholapuram Temples', in N. Karashima (ed.), *Socio-Cultural Change in Villages in Tiruchirapalli District Tamilnadu, India*, pt 1, Tokyo, 1983, pp. 53-70.

———, *South Indian History and Society (Studies from Inscriptions A.D. 850-1800)*, New Delhi, 1984.

Karashima, N. and B. Sitaraman, 'Revenue Terms in Chola Inscriptions' *Journal of Asian and African Studies*, Tokyo, V, 1972, pp. 87-117.

———, Y. Subbarayalu and Toru Matsui, *A Concordance of the Names in the Chola Inscriptions*, 3 vols, Madurai, 1978.

———, Y. Subbarayalu and P. Shanmugam, 'The Pandyan Revenue Terms in the Inscriptions of the Tiruchirapalli District and the Former Pudukkottai State', in Karashima (ed.), *Socio-Cultural Change in Villages in Tiruchirapalli District, Tamilnadu, India*, pt 1, Tokyo, 1983, pp. 91-122.

Kher, N.N., *Agrarian and Fiscal Economy in the Mauryan and Post-Mauryan Age (c. 324 B.C. -320 A.D.)*, Delhi, 1973.

Kosambi, D.D., 'Origins of Feudalism in Kashmir', *JBBRAS, (Sardhaśatābdi Commemoration Volume, 1804-1954)*, 1956, pp. 108-20.

———, *Myth and Reality*, Bombay, 1962.

Kulke, H. 'Kshatriyization and Social Change: A Study in Orissa Setting', in S.D. Pillai (ed.), *Aspects of Changing India: Studies in Honour of Professor G.S. Ghurye*, Bombay, 1976, pp. 398-409.

———, 'Early State Formation and Royal Legitimation in Late Ancient Orissa', in M.N. Das (ed.), *Sidelights on History and Culture of Orissa*, Cuttack, 1977, pp. 104-14.

———, 'Fragmentation and Segmentation versus Integration: Reflections on the Concept of Indian Feudalism and the Segmentary State in Indian History', *Studies in History*, IV, no. 2, 1982, pp. 237-63.

———, 'The Early and Imperial Kingdom: A Procedural Model of the State in Early Medieval India', Idem (ed), *The State in India 1000-1700*, Delhi, 1995.

Kumari, M. Krishna, *History of Medieval Andhradesa*, Delhi, 1989.

Kuppuswamy, G.R., *Economic Conditions in Karnataka, A.D. 973-A.D. 1336*, Dharwar, 1975.

Lahiri, Nayanjot, 'The Pre-Ahom Roots of Medieval Assam', *Social Scientist*, no. 133, June 1984, pp. 60-9.

———, *Pre-Ahom Assam (Studies in the Inscriptions of Assam between the 5th and the 13th Centuries A.D.)*, Delhi, 1991.

Lal, Makkhan, 'Iron Tools, Forest Clearance and Urbanization in the Gangetic Plains', *Man and Environment*, X, 1986, pp. 83-90.

Mazumdar, B.P., 'Role of the Ḍāmaras in Medieval Kashmir', *PIHC*, Patna Session, 1946. Reproduced in K.M. Shrimali (ed.), *Essays in Indian Art, Religion and Society*, Delhi, 1987, pp. 27-36.

———, 'Land Revenue in Early Medieval North India (*c.* 600-1200)', in R.S. Sharma (ed.), *Land Revenue in India -Historical Studies*, Delhi, 1971, pp. 20-32.

Mencher, J.P., 'Kerala and Madras: A Comparative Study of Ecology and Social Structure', *Ethnology*, V, no. 2, Pennsylvania, April 1966, pp. 136-71.

Minakshi, C., *Administration and Social Life Under the Pallavas*, 1938, revised edn, Madras, 1977.

Momin, M., 'Polity and Society of Assam (*c.* A.D. 600-1200)', Unpublished Ph.D. Thesis, Jawaharlal Nehru University, 1987.

Murty, M.L.K., 'Environment, Royal Policy and Social Formation in the Eastern Ghats South India, A.D. 1000-1500', Presidential Address, Section, V, *PIHC*, Warangal Session, 1992-3, pp. 615-31.

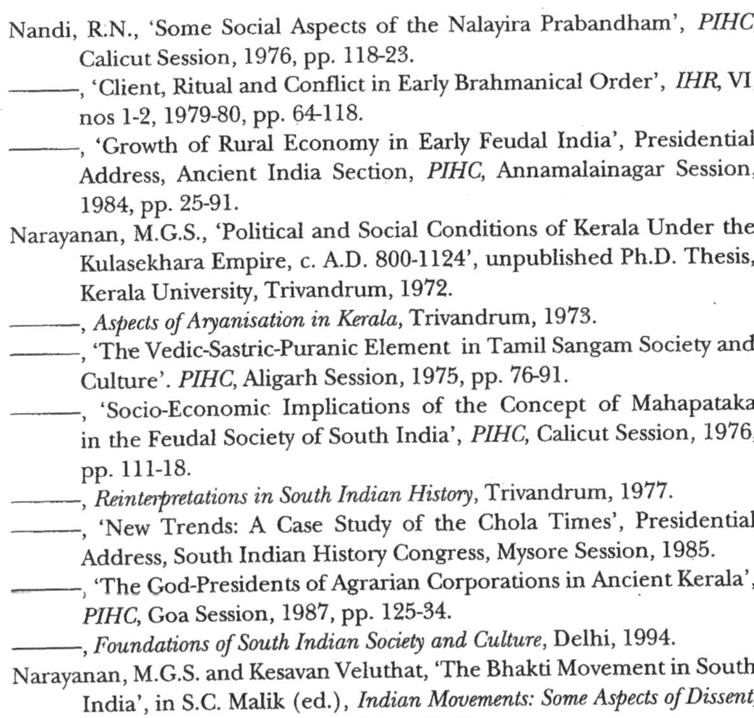

Nandi, R.N., 'Some Social Aspects of the Nalayira Prabandham', *PIHC*, Calicut Session, 1976, pp. 118-23.

———, 'Client, Ritual and Conflict in Early Brahmanical Order', *IHR*, VI, nos 1-2, 1979-80, pp. 64-118.

———, 'Growth of Rural Economy in Early Feudal India', Presidential Address, Ancient India Section, *PIHC*, Annamalainagar Session, 1984, pp. 25-91.

Narayanan, M.G.S., 'Political and Social Conditions of Kerala Under the Kulasekhara Empire, c. A.D. 800-1124', unpublished Ph.D. Thesis, Kerala University, Trivandrum, 1972.

———, *Aspects of Aryanisation in Kerala*, Trivandrum, 1973.

———, 'The Vedic-Sastric-Puranic Element in Tamil Sangam Society and Culture'. *PIHC*, Aligarh Session, 1975, pp. 76-91.

———, 'Socio-Economic Implications of the Concept of Mahapataka in the Feudal Society of South India', *PIHC*, Calicut Session, 1976, pp. 111-18.

———, *Reinterpretations in South Indian History*, Trivandrum, 1977.

———, 'New Trends: A Case Study of the Chola Times', Presidential Address, South Indian History Congress, Mysore Session, 1985.

———, 'The God-Presidents of Agrarian Corporations in Ancient Kerala', *PIHC*, Goa Session, 1987, pp. 125-34.

———, *Foundations of South Indian Society and Culture*, Delhi, 1994.

Narayanan, M.G.S. and Kesavan Veluthat, 'The Bhakti Movement in South India', in S.C. Malik (ed.), *Indian Movements: Some Aspects of Dissent, Protest and Reform*, Simla, 1978, p. 33-66.

Nath, Vijay, 'Tirthas and Acculturation: An Anthropological Study', *Social Science Probings*, X, nos 1-4, 1993, pp. 28-54.

Njammasch, Marlene, 'Social Structure of the Village in Kathiawar in the 6th-7th Centuries A.D.', *Social Science Probings*, IX, nos 1-4, 1992, pp. 1-7.

———, 'Feudal Structures in the Village of Madasara (Kathiawar) in A.D. 675', in V.K. Thakur and A. Aounshuman (eds), *Peasants in Indian History*, vol. 1, Patna, 1996, pp. 269-82.

Panda, Shishir K., *Medieval Orissa: A Socio-Economic Study*, New Delhi, 1991.

Pandeya, B.K., *Temple Economy Under the Cōḷas*, New Delhi, 1984.

Paranjape, Binda, 'Agrarian Structure in Konkan as Reflected through the Silahara Inscriptions', in V.K. Thakur and A. Aounshuman (eds) *Peasants in Indian History*, I, Patna, 1996, pp. 223-9.

Parasher, Aloka (ed.), *Social and Economic History of Early Deccan—Some Interpretations*, New Delhi, 1993.

Rai, G.K., 'Forced Labour in Ancient and Early Medieval India', *IHR*, III, 1976, no. 1, pp. 16-42.

———, *Involuntary Labour in Ancient India*, Allahabad, 1981.

Rai, Jaimal, *The Rural-Urban Economy and Social Change in Ancient India (600 B.C. to 600 A.D.)*, Varanasi, 1974.

Rajukumar, M.D., 'Struggles for Rights during Later Chola Period', *Social Scientist*, II, 1974, pp. 29-35.

Reddy, P. Bhaskar, 'Temple as a Promoter of Agriculture: A Study of Land Grants of Simhachalam', *Journal of the Epigraphical Society of India*, XX, 1994, pp. 57-60.

Reddy, P.K.M., 'Agriculture in Ancient Andhra, *Proceedings of the Andhra Pradesh History Congress*, XVIII, pp. 16-19.

Rösener, Werner, *The Peasantry of Europe*, Translated by Thomas M. Barker, Cornwall, 1994.

Sah, A.P., *Life in Medieval Orissa (A.D. 600-1200)*, Varanasi, 1976.

Sahi, M.D.N., 'Agricultural Production During Early Iron Age in Northern India,' *PIHC*, Kurukshetra Session, 1982, pp. 95-101.

Sahu, B.P., 'The Brahmanical Model Viewed as an Instrument of Socio-Cultural Change - An Autopsy', *PIHC*, Amritsar Session, 1985, pp. 180-9.

———, 'Ancient Orissa: The Dynamics of Internal Transformation of the Tribal Society', *PIHC*, Annamalainagar Session, 1984. Reproduced in K.M. Shrimali (ed.), *Essays in Indian Art, Religion and Society*, Delhi, 1987, pp. 169-80.

———, 'Patterns of Animal use in Ancient India', *PIHC*, Goa Session, 1987, pp. 66-75.

———, 'Early Medieval Orissa: Recent Historiographic Trends', *PIHC*, Dharwad Session, 1988, pp. 159-67.

———, 'Aspects of Rural Economy in Early Medieval Orissa', *Social Scientist*, nos 236-37, Jan.-Feb., 1993, pp. 48-68.

———, 'The Past as a Mirror of the Present: The Case of Oriya Society', *Social Science Probings*, IX, nos 1-4, 1992, pp. 8-23.

———, 'Agrarian Changes and the Peasantry in Early Medieval Orissa (*c.* A.D. 400-1100)', in V.K. Thakur and A. Aounshuman (eds.) *Peasants in Indian History*, I, Patna, 1996, pp. 283-311.

———, 'Power and the Politics of Patronage: Political and Social Processes in Early Orissa', *Economic and Political Weekly* (forthcoming).

Sampath, M.D., 'Agricultural Guild', in D.C. Bhattacharya and Devendra Handa (eds), *Prāci-Prabhā: Perspectives in Indology (Essays in Honour of Professor B.N. Mukherjee)*, New Delhi, 1989, pp. 67-74.

Saran, K.M., *Labour in Ancient India*, Bombay, 1957.

Seneviratne, S., 'Kalinga and Andhra: The Process of Secondary State Formation in Early India', *IHR*, VII, nos 1-2, 1980-81, pp. 54-69.

———, 'Pre-State Societies to State Societies: Transformations in the Political Ecology of South India with Special Reference to Tamil Nadu', Seminar Paper on 'State-Formation in Pre-Colonial South India, JNU, New Delhi, March 1989 (forthcoming).

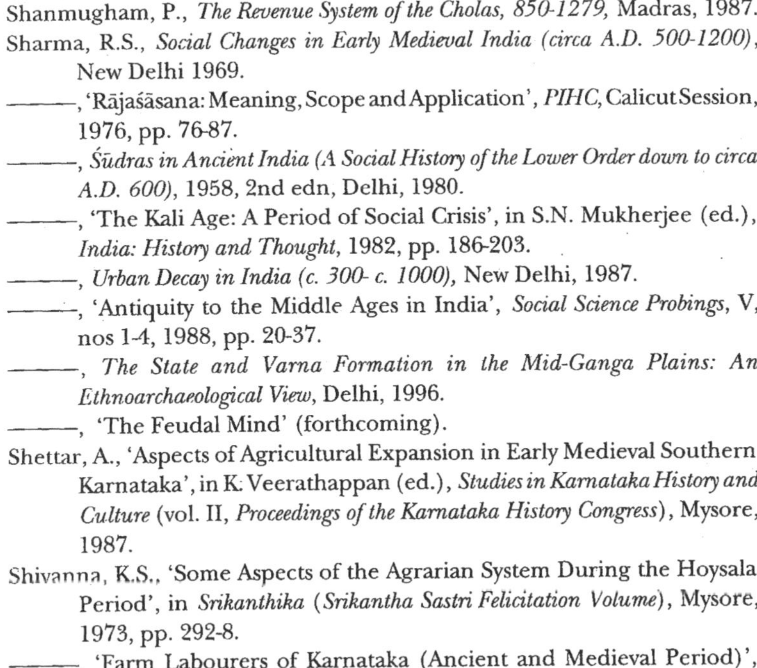

Shanmugham, P., *The Revenue System of the Cholas, 850-1279,* Madras, 1987.

Sharma, R.S., *Social Changes in Early Medieval India (circa A.D. 500-1200)*, New Delhi 1969.

———, 'Rājaśāsana: Meaning, Scope and Application', *PIHC,* Calicut Session, 1976, pp. 76-87.

———, *Śūdras in Ancient India (A Social History of the Lower Order down to circa A.D. 600)*, 1958, 2nd edn, Delhi, 1980.

———, 'The Kali Age: A Period of Social Crisis', in S.N. Mukherjee (ed.), *India: History and Thought,* 1982, pp. 186-203.

———, *Urban Decay in India (c. 300- c. 1000),* New Delhi, 1987.

———, 'Antiquity to the Middle Ages in India', *Social Science Probings,* V, nos 1-4, 1988, pp. 20-37.

———, *The State and Varna Formation in the Mid-Ganga Plains: An Ethnoarchaeological View,* Delhi, 1996.

———, 'The Feudal Mind' (forthcoming).

Shettar, A., 'Aspects of Agricultural Expansion in Early Medieval Southern Karnataka', in K. Veerathappan (ed.), *Studies in Karnataka History and Culture* (vol. II, *Proceedings of the Karnataka History Congress*), Mysore, 1987.

Shivanna, K.S., 'Some Aspects of the Agrarian System During the Hoysala Period', in *Srikanthika* (*Srikantha Sastri Felicitation Volume*), Mysore, 1973, pp. 292-8.

———, 'Farm Labourers of Karnataka (Ancient and Medieval Period)', *PIHC,* Hyderabad Session, 1978, pp. 142-46.

Shivanna, K.S. and G.R. Rangaswamiah, 'Agriculture During the Ganga Period', in *Srikanthika* (*Srikantha Sastri Felicitation Volume*), Mysore, 1973, pp. 299-303.

Shrimali, K.M., *History of Pañcāla,* vol. I, Delhi, 1983.

———, 'Land Relations in Central India, *circa* A.D. 350-*circa* A.D. 450' (mimeographed).

Singh, K. Amarendra, 'Some Aspects of Agrarian History Under the Vakatakas', *PIHC,* Amritsar Session, 1985, pp. 159-69.

Singh, K.S., 'A Study in State-Formation Among Tribal Communities', in R.S. Sharma and V.N. Jha (eds), *Indian Society: Historical Probings,* second edn., New Delhi, 1977, pp. 317-36.

———, 'Varna, Jati and Jana: An Anthropo-Historical Perspective', Paper Presented at the Symposium on 'Tribe and Caste in Indian History', *PIHC,* Burdwan Session, 1983, pp. 731-44.

Singh, Upinder, *Kings, Brahmanas and Temples in Orissa (300-1147 C.E.),* Delhi, 1994.

Singh, Y.B., 'Hālika-Kara : Crystallization of a Practice into a Tax', *PIHC,* Kurukshetra Session, 1982, pp. 130-3.

———, 'System of Land Grants in Early Medieval Kashmir, *PIHC,* New Delhi Session, 1991-2, pp. 115-20.

Sinha, Nandini, 'Rural Society and State Formation in Early Medieval South-Western Rajasthan', *PIHC*, Aligarh Session, 1994, pp. 123-31.

———, 'State and the Tribe: A Study of the Bhils in the Historic Setting of Southern Rajasthan', *Social Science Probings*, X, nos 1-4, 1993, pp. 55-67.

Sinha, Surajit, 'State Formation and Rajput Myth in Tribal Central India', *Man in India*, 42, no. 1, 1962, pp. 35-80.

——— (ed), *Tribal Polities and State Systems in Pre-Colonial Eastern and North Eastern India*, Calcutta, 1987.

Sivathamby, K., 'Early South Indian Society and Economy: The Tinai Concept', *Social Scientist*, no. 29, Dec. 1974, pp. 20-37.

Sontheimer, Guenther D., 'The Vana and the Ksetra: The Tribal Background of Some Famous Cults', in G.C. Tripathi and H. Kulke (eds), *Eschmann Memorial Lectures*, I, Bhubaneswar, 1987, pp. 117-64.

Spencer, George W., 'Temple Money-Lending and Livestock Redistribution in Early Tanjore', *IESHR*, V, no. 3, 1968, pp. 277-93.

Stein, B., 'Integration of the Agrarian System of South India', in R.E. Frykenberg (ed.), *Land Control and Social Structure in Indian History*, Madison, 1969, pp. 175-216.

———, 'The State and Agrarian Order in Medieval South India: A Historiographical Critique', in B. Stein (ed.), *Essays on South India*, New Delhi, 1976, pp. 64-92.

———, *Peasant State and Society in Medieval South India*, New Delhi, 1980.

———, 'Politics, Peasants and the Deconstruction of Feudalism in Medieval India', *Journal of Peasant Studies*, XII, nos 2-3, 1985, p. 54-86.

Subbarayalu, Y., *Political Geography of the Chola Country*, Madras, 1973.

———, 'Classification of Land and Assessment of Land Tax in Early Medieval Tamil Nadu from 950 to 1300', *PIHC*, Bhubaneswar Session, 1977, pp. 341-6.

———, 'The Plāce of Ūr in the Economic and Social History of Early Tamilnadu, A.D. 750-1350', in A.V.N. Murthy and B.K. Gururaja Rao (eds), *Rangavalli: Recent Researches of Indology*, Delhi, 1983, pp. 171-7.

———, 'The Peasantry of Tiruchirapalli District from the 13th to the 17th centuries', in N. Karashima (ed.), *Socio-Cultural Change in Villages in Tiruchirapalli District, Tamilnadu, India*, pt 1, Tokyo, 1983, pp 123-31.

———, 'The Cola State and the Agrarian Order - Some Clarifications', Paper presented at the Seminar on 'State-Formation in Pre-Colonial South India', Centre for Historical Studies, JNU, New Delhi, March 1989 (forthcoming).

———, 'The Nāṭṭār in South Karnataka in the Eleventh to Fourteenth Centuries', in H.V. Sreenivasamurthy *et al.* (eds), *Essays on Indian History and Culture* (*Felicitation Volume in Honour of Professor B. Sheik Ali*), New Delhi, 1990, pp. 101-7.

Sundaram, K., *Studies in Economic and Social Conditions of Medieval Andhra A.D. 1000-1600,* Madras, 1968.

Syed, A.J. (ed.), *D.D. Kosambi on History and Society: Problems of Interpretation,* University of Bombay, 1985.

Thakur, V.K., 'Beginnings of Feudalism in Bengal', *Social Scientist,* nos 66-7, 1978, pp. 68-82.

———, *Historiography of Indian Feudalism: Towards a Model of Early Medieval Indian Economy,* Patna, 1989.

———, 'The Peasant in Early India: Problems of Identification and Differentiation', in V.K. Thakur and A. Aounshuman (eds), *Peasants in Indian History (Essays in Memory of Professor R.K. Chaudhary),* vol. I, Patna, 1996, pp. 123-49.

Thapar, R., *Ancient Indian Social History - Some Interpretations,* 1978, reprint, New Delhi, 1987.

———, *The Mauryas Revisited,* New Delhi, 1987.

———, *Clan, Caste and Origin Myths in Early India,* New Delhi, 1992.

———, *Interpreting Early India,* Delhi, 1993.

———, (ed.), *Recent Perspectives of Early Indian History,* Bombay, 1995.

Tirumalai, R., 'Land Reclamation of Flood-Damaged and Sand-cast Lands: A Study in Prices, Rentals and Wages in Later Chola Times (from A.D. 1070 to A.D. 1210) - Based on Srirangam Inscriptions', *Journal of the Epigraphical Society of India,* 11, 1984, pp. 65-87.

———, *Land Grants and Agrarian Reactions in Cōḷa and Pāṇḍya Times,* Madras, 1987.

Vaidehi, A.V.K., *Social and Economic Conditions of Eastern Deccan 1000-1250 A.D.,* Secundrabad, 1970.

Vajpeyi, Raghavendra, 'Socio-Economic Tensions in Bhojakaṭa Rājya of Vākāṭaka Kingdom in the time of Pravarasena II', *PIHC,* Annamalainagar Session, 1984, pp. 139-47.

Vanamalai, N. 'Consolidation of Feudalism and Anti-Feudal Struggles during Chola Imperialist Rule', *Proceedings of the Second International Conference Seminar of Tamil Studies,* Madras, 1968, II, Madras 1970, pp. 239-43.

Veluthat, Kesavan, 'The Temple-Base of the Bhakti Movement in South India', *PIHC,* Waltair Session, 1979, pp. 185-94.

———, 'Labour Rent and Produce Rent: Reflections on the Revenue System Under the Cholas (A.D. 850-1279)', *PIHC,* Dharwad Session, 1988, pp. 138-44.

———, 'The Nature of Agrarian Corporations in South Canara Under the Āḷupas and Hoyśāḷas', *PIHC,* New Delhi, Session, 1991-2, pp. 108-14.

———, *The Political Structure of Early Medieval South India,* Delhi, 1993.

———, 'The Structure of Land-rights and Social Stratification in Early Medieval South India', in V.K. Thakur and A. Aounshuman (eds),

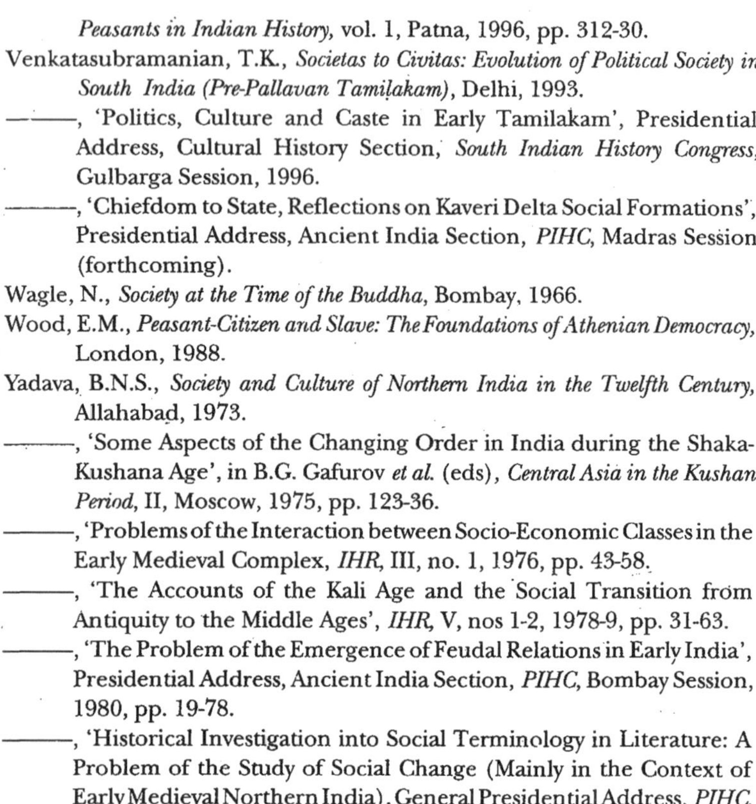

Peasants in Indian History, vol. 1, Patna, 1996, pp. 312-30.

Venkatasubramanian, T.K., *Societas to Civitas: Evolution of Political Society in South India (Pre-Pallavan Tamiḷakam)*, Delhi, 1993.

———, 'Politics, Culture and Caste in Early Tamilakam', Presidential Address, Cultural History Section, *South Indian History Congress*, Gulbarga Session, 1996.

———, 'Chiefdom to State, Reflections on Kaveri Delta Social Formations', Presidential Address, Ancient India Section, *PIHC*, Madras Session (forthcoming).

Wagle, N., *Society at the Time of the Buddha*, Bombay, 1966.

Wood, E.M., *Peasant-Citizen and Slave: The Foundations of Athenian Democracy*, London, 1988.

Yadava, B.N.S., *Society and Culture of Northern India in the Twelfth Century*, Allahabad, 1973.

———, 'Some Aspects of the Changing Order in India during the Shaka-Kushana Age', in B.G. Gafurov *et al.* (eds), *Central Asia in the Kushan Period*, II, Moscow, 1975, pp. 123-36.

———, 'Problems of the Interaction between Socio-Economic Classes in the Early Medieval Complex, *IHR*, III, no. 1, 1976, pp. 43-58.

———, 'The Accounts of the Kali Age and the Social Transition from Antiquity to the Middle Ages', *IHR*, V, nos 1-2, 1978-9, pp. 31-63.

———, 'The Problem of the Emergence of Feudal Relations in Early India', Presidential Address, Ancient India Section, *PIHC*, Bombay Session, 1980, pp. 19-78.

———, 'Historical Investigation into Social Terminology in Literature: A Problem of the Study of Social Change (Mainly in the Context of Early Medieval Northern India), General Presidential Address, *PIHC*, Warangal Session, 1993, pp. 1-35.

Contributors

SIBESH BHATTACHARYA is Professor in the Department of Ancient Indian History, Culture and Archaeology, Allahabad University, Allahabad.

R.N. MISHRA is Professor in the Department of Ancient Indian History and Culture, Jivaji University, Gwalior.

K.V. RAMAN is Professor in the Department of Ancient Indian History, Culture and Archaeology, Madras University, Madras.

P. SHANMUGAM is Professor in the Department of Ancient Indian History, Culture and Archaeology, Madras University, Madras.

LALLANJI GOPAL is retired Professor of the Department of Ancient Indian History and Culture, Banaras Hindu University, Varanasi.

K.K. GOPAL is a Professor in the Department of Ancient Indian History and Culture, Banaras Hindu University, Varanasi.

B.P. MAZUMDAR was a Profesor in the Department of History, Patna University, Patna.

Y. SUBBARAYALU is Professor in the Department of Epigraphy, Tamil University, Thanjavur.

G.R. KUPPUSWAMY is a Professor in the Department of History and Archaeology, Karnataka University, Dharwar.

T.V. MAHALINGAM was Professor in the Department of Ancient Indian History, Culture and Archaeology, Madras University, Madras.

GUYLA WOJTILLA is research staff member Library of the Hungarian Academy of Sciences, Budapest.

IRFAN HABIB is Professor at the Centre of Advanced Study in History, Aligarh Muslim University, Aligarh.

MARLENE NJAMMASCH is a Professor at the Institute of South Asian Studies, Humboldt University Berlin, Germany.

M.G.S. NARAYANAN is a retired Professor of the Department of History, Calicut University, Calicut, Kerala.

Y. GOPAL REDDY was Lecturer in History, Government College, Anantapur, Andhra Pardesh.

NAYANJOT LAHIRI is a Reader in the Department of History, University of Delhi, Delhi.

RAJAN GURUKKAL is Director of the Inter-Disciplinary School in Social Sciences, Mahatma Gandhi University, Kotayam, Kerala.

KESAVAN VELUTHAT is Reader in the Department of History, Mangalore University Mangalagangotri, Mangalore, Karnataka.

B.N.S. YADAVA is a retired Professor of the Department of Ancient Indian History, Culture and Archaeology, Allahabad University, Allahabad.

R.S. SHARMA is a retired Professor of the Department of History, University of Delhi, Delhi.